Educational Psychology
Second Edition

Kelvin Seifert and Rosemary Sutton

Copyright © 2009 Kelvin Seifert

For any questions about this text, please email: drexel@uga.edu

Editor-In-Chief: Kelvin Seifert

Associate Editor: Marisa Drexel

Editorial Assistant: Jackie Sharman

Proofreader: Rachel Pugliese

The Global Text Project is funded by the Jacobs Foundation, Zurich, Switzerland

About the authors and reviewer

Author, Kelvin Seifert

Kelvin Seifert is professor of educational psychology at the University of Manitoba, Winnipeg, Canada. He earned a BA from Swarthmore College in 1967 and a PhD from the University of Michigan in 1973, in a combined program from the School of Education and the Department of Psychology. His research interests include the personal identity development of teachers, the impact of peers in opre-service teacher education, and the development of effective strategies of blended learning. He is the author of four university textbooks (with Houghton Mifflin, in traditional print format) about educational psychology, child and adolescent development, and lifespan human development. He is also the editor of the online *Canadian Journal of Educational Administration and Policy*. Recent publications include "Student cohorts: Support groups or intellectual communities?" (*Teachers College Record*) and "Learning about peers: A missed opportunity for educational psychology" (*The Clearinghouse*). His professional service includes serving as chair of the Department of Educational Administration, Foundations, and Psychology at the University of Manitoba, and serving as president of the American Educational Research Association Special Interest Group on Teaching Educational Psychology. During his career of 35 years, he has taught introductory educational psychology over 75 times.

Author, Rosemary Sutton

After four years of teaching high school mathematics in New Zealand, Dr Rosemary Sutton attended graduate school and earned her MS in Educational Psychology from the University of Illinois and her PhD from Pennsylvania State University in Human Development. She joined the Cleveland State University faculty in Cleveland, Ohio in 1983 and since that time has taught pre-service and in service undergraduates and graduate students educational psychology and educational technology. She has received several University awards for her teaching and has conducted numerous workshops for teachers in North East Ohio.

Dr Sutton has published a variety research articles on teacher development as well as equity issues in mathematics, technology, and assessment. Her recent research interests have focused in two areas: teaching educational psychology and teachers' emotions. Recent publications can be found in Social Psychology of Education, Educational Psychology Review, Journal of Teacher Education, and an edited volume, Emotions and Education.

Since 2004, Dr Sutton has been working as an Administrator, first as the Director of Assessment for the University. This position involved coordinating the student learning assessment for all graduate, undergraduate, and student support programs. In August 2007, Dr Sutton was appointed Vice Provost for Undergraduate Studies and is now responsible for overseeing offices and functions from academic and student service areas in order to create a campus culture that coordinates student services with the academic mission of the University.

Reviewer, Sandra Deemer

Sandra Deemer is professor of educational foundations at Millersville University, in Millersville, PA. She is also the editor of the online journal called "Teaching Educational Psychology," and has contributed to the development of the Special Interest Group on Teaching Educational Psychology (TEP SIG) sponsored by the American Educational Research Association. She teaches courses in educational psychology and educational research; her research interests focus on how motivational theory can be used to create learning-focused classrooms.

Table of Contents

Preface

Dr. Kelvin Seifert: Why I wanted this book to be part of the Global Textbook Project

I have taught educational psychology to future teachers for nearly 35 years, during which I used one or another of the major commercial textbooks written for this subject. In general I found all of the books well-written and thorough. But I also found problems:

(1) Though they differed in details, the major textbooks were surprisingly similar in overall coverage. This fact, coupled with their large overall size, made it hard to tailor any of the books to the particular interests or needs of individuals or groups of students. Too often, buying a textbook was like having to buy a huge Sunday newspaper when all you really want is to read one of its sections. In a similar way, commercial educational psychology textbooks usually told you *more* than you ever needed or wanted to know about the subject. As a format, the textbook did not allow for individualization.

Dr. Kelvin Seifert

(2) Educational psychology textbooks were always expensive, and over the years their costs rose faster than inflation, especially in the United States, where most of the books have been produced. Currently every major text about educational psychology sells for more than USD 100. At best this cost is a stress on students' budgets. At worst it puts educational psychology textbooks beyond the reach of many. The problem of the cost is even more obvious when put in worldwide perspective; in some countries the cost of one textbook is roughly equivalent to the average annual income of its citizens.

(3) In the competition to sell copies of educational psychology textbooks, authors and publishers have gradually added features that raise the cost of books without evidence of adding educational value. Educational psychology publishers in particular have increased the number of illustrations and photographs, switched to full-color editions, increased the complexity and number of study guides and ancillary publications, and created proprietary websites usable fully only by adopters of their particular books. These features have sometimes been attractive. My teaching experience suggests, however, that they also distract students from learning key ideas about educational psychology about as often as they help students to learn.

By publishing this textbook online with the Global Textbook Project, I have taken a step toward resolving these problems. Instructors and students can access as much or as little of the textbook as they really need and find useful. The cost of their doing is minimal. Pedagogical features are available, but are kept to a minimum and rendered in formats that can be accessed freely and easily by anyone connected to the Internet. In the future, revisions to the book will be relatively easy and prompt to make. These, I believe, are desirable outcomes for everyone!   --**Kelvin Seifert**

1. The changing teaching profession and you

A teacher named Ashley reflects: She looked around the classroom, enjoying a blessed moment of quiet after the students left at the end of the day. "Ashley, the teacher, that's me", she said proudly to the empty room. "But why am I doing this?" she asked herself quietly—and realized she wasn't always sure of the answer. But then she remembered one reason: she was teaching for Nadia, who sat at the table to the left, always smiled so well and always (well, usually) tried hard. And another reason: she was teaching for Lincoln, tired old Lincoln, who needed her help more than he realized. She remembered twenty other reasons—twenty other students. And one last reason: she was also teaching for herself, challenging herself to see if she really could keep up with twenty-two young people at once, and really accomplish something worthwhile with them. She was teaching so she could keep growing as a person, keep connecting with others, keep learning new ideas. That's why she was teaching.

The joys of teaching

Why be a teacher? The short answer is easy:

- to witness the diversity of growth in young people, and their joy in learning

- to encourage lifelong learning—both for yourself and for others

- to experience the challenge of devising and doing interesting, exciting activities for the young

There is, of course, more than this to be said about the value of teaching. Consider, for instance, the "young people" referred to above. In one class they could be six years old; in another they could be sixteen, or even older. They could be rich, poor, or somewhere in between. They could come from any ethnic background. Their first language could be English, or something else. There are all sorts of possibilities. But whoever the particular students are, they will have potential as human beings: talents and personal qualities—possibly not yet realized—that can contribute to society, whether as leaders, experts, or supporters of others. A teacher's job—in fact a teacher's *privilege*—is to help particular "young people" to realize their potential.

Another teacher reflects: Nathan paused for a deep breath before speaking to me. "It's not like I expected it to be," he said. "I've got five kids who speak English as a second language. I didn't expect that. I've got two, maybe three, with reading disabilities, and one of them has a part-time aide. I've had to learn more about using computers than I ever expected—they're a lot of curriculum materials online now, and the computers help the kids that need more practice or who finish activities early. I'm doing more screening and testing of kids than I expected, and it all takes time away from teaching.

"But it's not all surprises. I expected to be able to 'light a fire' under kids about learning to read. And that has actually happened, at least sometimes with some children!"

As a teacher, you will be able to do this by laying groundwork for *lifelong learning*. You will not teach any one student forever, of course, but you will often work with them long enough to convey a crucial message: that there is much in life to learn—more in fact than any one teacher or school can provide in a lifetime. The knowledge may be about science, math, or learning to read; the skills may be sports, music, or art—anything. Whatever you teach, its immensity can be a source of curiosity, wonder and excitement. It can be a reason to be optimistic about life in general and about your students in particular. Learning, when properly understood, is never-ending, even though it often focuses on short-term, immediate concerns. As a teacher, you will have an advantage not shared by every member of society, namely the excuse not only to teach valuable knowledge and skills, but to point students *beyond* what they will be able to learn from you. As an old limerick put it (before the days of gender-balanced language), "The world is full of such a plenty of things, I'm sure we should all be as happy as kings."

Jennifer Fuller, a third teacher reflects: "OK", suddenly getting businesslike in her tone. "Here's my typical day teaching tenth grade: I get up at 6:30, have a quick breakfast, get to school by 7:45 if the traffic's not bad. Then I check my email—usually there's a little stuff from the principal or some other administrator, maybe one or two from parents concerned because their child is doing poorly in one of my classes, maybe one or two from students—"I'm going to be sick today, Ms Fuller!"—that sort of thing. Now it's 8:15 and I have two hours before my first class—this term I teach only biology, and I only teach periods 2, 3, and 5. Maybe I have marking to do before class, or maybe I have to get a lab demonstration ready. Or maybe we all have to troupe down to the library for a staff meeting (groan...). Whatever I don't finish in the morning, I have to finish after school. But that's also when I meet with the Ecology Club (I'm the faculty advisor), so I might have to finish stuff in the evening. I try not to do it then, but a lot of times I have to. But I always quit by 9:00—that's always when I watch TV for an hour, or just "vegetate" with a book."

Whatever you teach, you will be able to feel the satisfaction of designing and orchestrating complex activities that communicate new ideas and skills effectively. The challenge is attractive to many teachers, because that is where they exercise judgment and "artistry" the most freely and frequently. Your students will depend on your skill at planning and managing, though sometimes without realizing how much they do so. Teachers will need you to know how to explain ideas clearly, to present new materials in a sensible sequence and at an appropriate pace, to point out connections between their new learning and their prior experiences. Although these skills really take a lifetime to master, they can be practiced successfully even by beginning teachers, and they do improve steadily with continued teaching over time. Right from the start, though, skill at design and communication of curriculum is one of the major "perks" of the job.

The very complexity of classroom life virtually guarantees that teaching never needs to get boring. Something *new and exciting* is bound to occur just when you least expect it. A student shows an insight that you never expected to see—or fails to show one that you were sure he had. An activity goes better than expected—or worse, or merely differently. You understand for the first time why a particular student behaves as she does, and begin thinking of how to respond to the student's behavior more helpfully in the future. After teaching a particular learning objective several times, you realize that you understand it differently than the first time you taught it. And so on. The job never stays the same; it evolves continually. As long as you keep teaching, you will have a job with novelty.

Are there also challenges to teaching?

Here, too, the simple answer is "yes". Every joy of teaching has a possible frustration related to it. You may wish to make a positive difference in students' lives, but you may also have trouble reaching individuals. A student seems not to learn much, or to be unmotivated, or unfriendly, or whatever. And some teaching problems can be subtle: when you call attention to the wonderful immensity of an area of knowledge, you might accidentally *discourage* a student by implying that the student can never learn "enough". The complexity of designing and implementing instruction can sometimes seem overwhelming, instead of satisfying. Unexpected events in your classroom can become chaos rather than an attractive novelty. To paraphrase a popular self-help book, sometimes "bad things happen to good teachers" (Kushner, 1983). But as in the rest of life, the "bad things" of teaching do *not* negate the value of the good. If anything, the undesired events make the good, desired ones even more satisfying, and render the work of teaching all the more valuable. As you will see throughout this book, there are resources for maximizing the good, the valuable, and the satisfying. You can bring these resources to your work, along with your growing professional knowledge and a healthy dose of common sense. In this sense you will not need to "go it alone" in learning to teach well. You *will,* however, be personally responsible for becoming and remaining the best teacher that you can possibly be; the only person who can make that happen will be *you.* Many of the resources for making this happen are described in this book in the chapters ahead.

Teaching is different from in the past

In the past decade or two teaching has changed significantly, so much in fact that schools may not be what some of us remember from our own childhood. Changes have affected both the opportunities and the challenges of teaching, as well as the attitudes, knowledge, and skills needed to prepare for a teaching career. The changes have influenced much of the content of this book.

To see what we mean, look briefly at four new trends in education, at how they have changed what teachers do, and at how you will therefore need to prepare to teach:

- **increased diversity**: there are more differences among students than there used to be. Diversity has made teaching more fulfilling as a career, but also made more challenging in certain respects.

- *** increased instructional technology**: classrooms, schools, and students use computers more often today than in the past for research, writing, communicating, and keeping records. Technology has created new ways for students to learn (for example, this textbook would not be possible without Internet technology!). It has also altered how teachers can teach most effectively, and even raised issues about what constitutes "true" teaching and learning.

- **greater accountability in education**: both the public and educators themselves pay more attention than in the past to how to assess (or provide evidence for) learning and good quality teaching. The attention has increased the importance of education to the public (a good thing) and improved education for some students. But it has also created new constraints on what teachers teach and what students learn.

- **increased professionalism of teachers**: Now more than ever, teachers are able to assess the quality of their own work as well as that of colleagues, and to take steps to improve it when necessary. Professionalism improves teaching, but by creating higher standards of practice it also creates greater worries about whether particular teachers and schools are "good enough".

How do these changes show up in the daily life of classrooms? The answer depends partly on where you teach; circumstances differ among schools, cities, and even whole societies. Some clues about the effects of the trends on classroom life can be found, however, by considering one particular case—the changes happening in North America.

New trend #1: diversity in students

Students have, of course, always been diverse. Whether in the past or in the present day, students learn at unique paces, show unique personalities, and learn in their own ways. In recent decades, though, the forms and extent of diversity have increased. Now more than ever, teachers are likely to serve students from diverse language backgrounds, to serve more individuals with special educational needs, and to teach students either younger and older than in the past.

Language diversity

Take the case of language diversity. In the United States, about 40 million people, or 14 per cent of the population are Hispanic. About 20 per cent of these speak primarily Spanish, and approximately another 50 per cent speak only limited English (United States Census Bureau, 2005). The educators responsible for the children in this group need to accommodate instruction to these students somehow. Part of the solution, of course, is to arrange specialized second-language teachers and classes. But adjustment must also happen in "regular" classrooms of various grade levels and subjects. Classroom teachers must learn to communicate with students whose English language background is limited, at the same time that the students themselves are learning to use English more fluently (Pitt, 2005). Since relatively few teachers are Hispanic or speak fluent Spanish, the adjustments can sometimes be a challenge. Teachers must plan lessons and tasks that students actually understand. At the same time teachers must also keep track of the major learning goals of the curriculum. In Chapter 4 ("Student Diversity") and Chapter 10 ("Planning Instruction"), some strategies for doing so are described. As you gain experience teaching, you will no doubt find additional strategies and resources (Gebhard, 2006), especially if second-language learners become an important part of your classes.

Diversity of special educational needs

Another factor making classroom increasingly diverse has been the inclusion of students with disabilities into classrooms with non-disabled peers. In the United States the trend began in the 1970s, but accelerated with the passage of the Individuals with Disabilities Education Act in 1975, and again when the Act was amended in 2004 (United States Government Printing Office, 2005). In Canada similar legislation was passed in individual provinces during the same general time period. The laws guarantee free, appropriate education for children with disabilities of any kind—whether the impairment is physical, cognitive, emotional, or behavioral. The laws also recognize that such students need special supports in order to learn or function effectively in a classroom with non-disabled peers, so they provide for special services (for example, teaching assistants) and procedures for making individualized educational plans for students with disabilities.

As a result of these changes, most American and Canadian teachers are likely to have at least a few students with special educational needs, even if they are not trained as special education teachers or have had no prior personal experience with people with disabilities. Classroom teachers are also likely to work as part of a professional team focused on helping these students to learn as well as possible and to participate in the life of the school. The trend toward inclusion is definitely new compared to circumstances just a generation or two ago. It raises new challenges about planning instruction (such as how is a teacher to find time to plan for individuals?), and philosophical questions about the very nature of education (such as what in the curriculum is truly important to learn?). These questions will come up again in Chapter 5, where we discuss teaching students with special educational needs.

Lifelong learning

The diversity of modern classrooms is not limited to language or disabilities. Another recent change has been the broadening simply of the age range of individuals who count as "students". In many nations of the world, half or most of all three- and four-year-olds attend some form of educational program, either part-time preschool or full-time child care (National Institute for Early Education Research, 2006). In North America some public school divisions have moved toward including nursery or preschool programs as a newer "grade level" preceding kindergarten. Others have expanded the hours of kindergarten (itself considered a "new" program early in the 20th century) to span a full-day program.

The obvious differences in maturity between preschoolers and older children lead most teachers of the very young to use flexible, open-ended plans and teaching strategies, and to develop more personal or family-like relationships with their young "students" than typical with older students (Bredekamp & Copple, 1997). Just as important, though, are the educational and philosophical issues that early childhood education has brought to public attention. Some educational critics ask whether preschool and day care programs risk becoming *in*appropriate substitutes for families. Other educators suggest, in contrast, that teachers of older students can learn from the flexibility and open-ended approach common in early childhood education. For teachers of any grade level, it is a debate that cannot be avoided completely or permanently. In this book, it reappears in Chapter 3, where I discuss students' development—their major long-term, changes in skills, knowledge, and attitudes.

The other end of the age spectrum has also expanded. Many individuals take courses well into adulthood even if they do not attend formal university or college. *Adult education,* as it is sometimes called, often takes place in workplaces, but it often also happens in public high schools or at local community colleges or universities. Some adult students may be completing high school credentials that they missed earlier in their lives, but often the students have other purposes that are even more focused, such as learning a trade-related skill. The teachers of adult students have to adjust their instructional strategies and relationships with students so as to challenge and respect their special strengths and constraints as adults (Bash, 2005). The students' maturity often means that they have had life experiences that enhance and motivate their learning. But it may also mean that they have significant personal responsibilities—such as parenting or a full-time job—which compete for study time, and that make them impatient with teaching that is irrelevant to their personal goals or needs. These advantages and constraints also occur to a lesser extent among "regular" high school students. Even secondary school teachers must ask, how they can make sure that instruction does not waste students' time, and how they can make it truly efficient, effective, and valuable. Elsewhere in this book (especially in Chapters 9 through 11, about assessment and instruction), we discuss these questions from a number of perspectives.

New trend #2: using technology to support learning

For most teachers, "technology" means using computers and the Internet as resources for teaching and learning. These tools have greatly increased the amount and range of information available to students, even if their benefits have sometimes been exaggerated in media reports (Cuban, 2001). With the Internet, it is now relatively easy to access up-to-date information on practically any subject imaginable, often with pictures, video clips, and audio to accompany them. It would seem not only that the Internet and its associated technologies have the potential to transform traditional school-based learning, but also that they have in fact begun to do so.

For a variety of reasons, however, technology has not always been integrated into teachers' practices very thoroughly (Haertel & Means, 2003). One reason is practical: in many societies and regions, classrooms contain only one or two computers at most, and many schools have at best only limited access to the Internet. Waiting for a turn on the computer or arranging to visit a computer lab or school library limits how much students use the Internet, no matter how valuable the Internet may be. In such cases, furthermore, computers tend to function in relatively traditional ways that do not take full advantage of the Internet: as a word processor (a "fancy typewriter"), for example, or as a reference book similar to an encyclopedia.

Even so, single-computer classrooms create new possibilities and challenges for teachers. A single computer can be used, for example, to present upcoming assignments or supplementary material to students, either one at a time or small groups. In functioning in this way, the computer gives students more flexibility about when to finish old tasks or to begin new ones. A single computer can also enrich the learning of individual students with special interests or motivation. And it can provide additional review to students who need extra help. These changes are not dramatic, but they lead to important revisions in teachers' roles: they move teachers away from simply delivering information to students, and toward facilitating students' own constructions of knowledge.

A shift from "full-frontal teaching" to "guide on the side" becomes easier as the amount and use of computer and Internet technologies increases. If a school (or better yet, a classroom) has numerous computers with full Internet access, then students' can in principle direct their own learning more independently than if computers are scarce commodities. With ample technology available, teachers can focus much more on helping individuals in developing and carrying out learning plans, as well as on assisting individuals with special learning problems. In these ways a strong shift to computers and the Internet can change a teacher's role significantly, and make the teacher more effective.

But technology also brings some challenges, or even creates problems. It costs money to equip classrooms and schools fully: often that money is scarce, and may therefore mean depriving students of other valuable resources, like additional staff or additional books and supplies. Other challenges are less tangible. In using the Internet, for example, students need help in sorting out trustworthy information or websites from the "fluff", websites that are unreliable or even damaging (Seiter, 2005). Providing this help can sometimes be challenging even for experienced teachers. And some educational activities simply do not lend themselves to computerized learning—sports, for example, driver education, or choral practice. As a new teacher, therefore, you will need not only to assess what technologies are possible in your particular classroom, but also what will actually be assisted by new technologies. Then be prepared for your decisions to affect *how* you teach—the ways you work with students.

New trend #3: accountability in education

In recent years, the public and its leaders have increasingly expected teachers and students to be *accountable* for their work, meaning that schools and teachers are held responsible for implementing particular curricula and goals, and that students are held responsible for learning particular knowledge. The trend toward accountability has increased the legal requirements for becoming and (sometimes) remaining certified as a teacher. In the United States in particular, preservice teachers need more subject-area and education-related courses than in the past. They must also spend more time practice teaching than in the past, and they must pass one or more examinations of knowledge of subject matter and teaching strategies. The specifics of these requirements vary among regions, but the general trend—toward more numerous and "higher" levels of requirements—has occurred broadly throughout the English-speaking world. The changes obviously affect individuals' experiences of becoming a teacher—especially the speed and cost of doing so.

Public accountability has led to increased use of *high-stakes testing,* which are tests taken by all students in a district or region that have important consequences for students' further education (Fuhrman & Elmore, 2004). High-stakes tests may influence grades that students receive in courses or determine whether students graduate or continue to the next level of schooling. The tests are often a mixture of essay and structured-response questions (such as multiple-choice items), and raise important issues about what teachers should teach, as well as how (and whether) teachers should help students to pass the examinations. It also raises issues about whether high-stakes testing is fair to all students and consistent with other ideals of public education, such as giving students the best possible start in life instead of disqualifying them from educational opportunities. Furthermore, since the results of high-stakes tests are sometimes also used to evaluate the performance of teachers, schools, or school districts, insuring students' success on them becomes an obvious concern for teachers—one that affects instructional decisions on a daily basis. For this reason we discuss the purpose, nature, and effects of high-stakes tests in detail in Chapter 12.

New trend #4: increased professionalism of teachers

Whatever your reactions to the first three trends, it is important to realize that they have contributed to a fourth trend, an increase in *professionalism* of teachers. By most definitions, an occupation (like medicine or law—or in this case teaching) is a profession if its members take personal responsibility for the quality of their work, hold each other accountable for its quality, and recognize and require special training in order to practice it.

By this definition, teaching has definitely become *more* professional than in the past (Cochran-Smith & Fries, 2005). Increased expectations of achievement by students mean that teachers have increased responsibility not only for their students' academic success, but also for their own development as teachers. Becoming a new teacher now requires *more* specialized work than in the past, as reflected in the increased requirements for certification and licensing in many societies and regions. The increased requirements are partly a response to the complexities created by the increasing diversity of students and increasing use of technology in classrooms.

Greater professionalism has also been encouraged by initiatives from educators themselves to study and improve their own practice. One way to do so, for example, is through **action research** (sometimes also called **teacher research**), a form of investigation carried out by teachers about their own students or their own teaching.

1. The changing teaching profession and you

Action research studies lead to concrete decisions that improve teaching and learning in particular educational contexts (Mertler, 2006; Stringer, 2004). The studies can take many forms, but here are a few brief examples:

- How precisely do individual children learn to read? In an action research study, the teacher might observe and track one child's reading progress carefully for an extended time. From the observations she can get clues about how to help not only that particular child to read better, but also other children in her class or even in colleagues' classes.

- Does it really matter if a high school social studies teacher uses more, rather than fewer, open-ended questions? As an action of research study, the teacher might videotape his own lessons, and systematically compare students' responses to his open-ended questions compared to their responses to more closed questions (the ones with more fixed answers). The analysis might suggest when and how much it is indeed desirable to use open-ended questions.

- Can an art teacher actually entice students to take more creative risks with their drawings? As an action research study, the teacher might examine the students' drawings carefully for signs of visual novelty and innovation, and then see if the signs increase if she encourages novelty and innovation explicitly.

Table 1: Examples of action research project

Steps in action research Project	Example 1: students' use of the Internet	Example 2: a teacher's helpfulness to ESL students
Purpose of the research (as expressed by the teacher doing the research)	"In doing assignments, how successful are my students at finding high-quality, relevant information?"	"Am I responding to my ESL students as fully and helpfully as to my English-speaking students, and why or why not?"
Who is doing the study?	Classroom teacher (elementary level) and school computer specialist teacher	Classroom teacher (senior high level)—studying self; Possibly collaborating with other teachers or with ESL specialist.
How information is gathered and recorded	Assessing students' assignments; Observing students while they search the Internet. Interviewing students about their search experiences	Videotaping of self interacting during class discussions; Journal diary by teacher of experiences with ESL vs other students; Interviews with teacher's ESL students
How information is analyzed	Look for obstacles and "search tips" expressed by several students;	Look for differences in type and amount of interactions with ESL vs.

	Look for common strengths and problems with research cited on assignments.	other students; Look for patterns in the differences; Try altering the patterns of interaction and observe the result.
How information is reported and communicated	Write a brief report of results for fellow staff; Give a brief oral report to fellow staff about results	Write a summary of the results in teacher's journal diary; Share results with fellow staff; Share results with teacher's students.

Two other, more complete examples of action research are summarized in Table 1. Although these examples, like many action research studies, resemble "especially good teaching practice", they are planned more thoughtfully than usual, carried out and recorded more systematically, and shared with fellow teachers more thoroughly and openly. As such, they yield special benefits to teachers as professionals, though they also take special time and effort. For now, the important point is that use of action research simultaneously reflects the increasing professionalism of teachers, but at the same time creates higher standards for teachers when they teach.

How educational psychology can help

All things considered, then, times have changed for teachers. But teaching remains an attractive, satisfying, and worthwhile profession. The recent trends mean simply that you need to prepare for teaching differently than you might have in the past, and perhaps differently than your own school teachers did a generation ago. Fortunately, there are ways to do this. Many current programs in teacher education provide a balance of experiences in tune with current and emerging needs of teachers. They offer more time for practice teaching in schools, for example, and teacher education instructors often make deliberate efforts to connect the concepts and ideas of education and psychology to current best practices of education. These and other features of contemporary teacher education will make it easier for you to become the kind of teacher that you not only want to be, but also will need to be.

This book—about educational psychology and its relation to teaching and learning—can be one of your supports as you get started. To make it as useful as possible, we have written about educational psychology while keeping in mind the current state of teaching, as well as your needs as a unique future teacher. The text draws heavily on concepts, research and fundamental theories from educational psychology. But these are selected and framed around the problems, challenges, and satisfactions faced by teachers daily, and especially as faced by teachers new to the profession. We have selected and emphasized topics in proportion to two factors: (1) their importance as reported by teachers and other educational experts, and (2) the ability of educational psychology to comment on particular problems, challenges, and satisfactions helpfully.

There is a lot to learn about teaching, and much of it comes from educational psychology. As a career, teaching has distinctive features now that it did not have a generation ago. The new features make it more exciting in some ways, as well as more challenging than in the past. The changes require learning teaching skills that were less important in earlier times. But the new skills are quite learnable. Educational psychology, and this text, will get you started at that task.

Chapter summary

Teaching in the twenty-first century offers a number of satisfactions—witnessing and assisting the growth of young people, lifelong learning, the challenge and excitement of designing effective instruction. Four trends have affected the way that these satisfactions are experienced by classroom teachers: (1) increased diversity of students, (2) the spread of instructional technology in schools and classrooms, (3) increased expectations for accountability in education, and (4) the development of increased professionalism among teachers. Each trend presents new opportunities to students and teachers, but also raises new issues for teachers. Educational psychology, and this textbook, can help teachers to make constructive use of the new trends as well as deal with the dilemmas that accompany them. It offers information, advice, and useful perspectives specifically in three areas of teaching: (1) students as learners, (2) instruction and assessment, and (3) the psychological and social awareness of teachers.

On the Internet

<**www.ets.org/praxis**> Try this website of the Educational Testing Service if you are curious to learn more about licensing examinations for teachers, including the PRAXIS II test that is prominent in the United States (see pp. xxx). As you will see, specific requirements vary somewhat by state and region.

<**portal.unesco.org/education/en**> This is the website for the education branch of UNESCO, which is the abbreviation for the "United Nations Educational, Scientific, and Cultural Organization." It has extensive information and news about all forms of diversity in education, viewed from an *inter*national perspective. The challenges of teaching diverse classrooms, it seems, are not restricted to the United States, though as the new items on the website show, the challenges take different forms in different countries.

<**www.edchange.org**> <**www.cec.sped.org**> These two websites have numerous resources about diversity for teachers from a North American (USA and Canada) perspective. They are both useful for planning instruction. The first one—maintained by a group of educators and calling itself EdChange—focuses on culturally related forms of diversity, and the second one—by the Council for Exceptional Children—focuses on children with special educational needs.

Key terms

Accountability in education	Instructional technology
Action research	Lifelong learning
Assessment	Professionalism
Diversity	Teacher research
High-stakes testing	

References

Bash, L. (Ed.). (2005). *Best practices in adult learning*. Boston: Anker Publications.

Bredekamp, S. & Copple, C. (1997). *Developmentally appropriate practice, Revised edition*. Washington, D.C.: National Association for the Education of Young Children.

Cochran-Smith, M. (2003). Assessing assessment in teacher education. *Journal of Teacher Education, 54*(3), 187-191.

Cochran-Smith, M. & Fries, K. (2005). Research teacher education in changing times: Politics and paradigms. In M. Cochran-Smith & K. Zeichner (Eds.), *Studying teacher education: The report of the AERA Panel on Research and Teacher Education,* 69-110.

Cuban, L. (2001). *Oversold and underused: Computers in the classroom.* Cambridge, MA: Harvard University Press.

Educational Testing Service. (2004). *Study guide for <u>Principles of Learning and Teaching,</u> 2nd edition.* Princeton, NJ: Author.

Fuhrman, S. & Elmore, R. (2004). *Redesigning accountability systems for education.* New York: Teachers College Press.

Gebhard, L. (2006). *Teaching English as a second or foreign language: A teacher self-development and methodology guide, 2nd edition.* Ann Arbor, MI: University of Michigan Press.

Glassford, L. (2005). Triumph of politics over pedagogy? The case of the Ontario Teacher Qualifying Test. *Canadian Journal of Educational Administration and Policy, Issue #45.* Online at <<u>www.umanitoba.ca/publications/cjeap/articles/glassford.html</u>>.

Haertel, G. & Means, B. (2003). *Evaluating educational technology: Effective research designs for improving learning.* New York: Teachers College Press.

Harris, D. & Herrington, C. (2006). Accountability, standards, and the growing achievement gap: Lessons from the past half-century. *American Journal of Education, 112*(2), 163-208.

Harvard Educational Review. (2005). Interview: United States Secretary of Education Margaret Spellings. *Harvard Educational Review, 75*(4), 364-382.

Kushner, H. (1983). *When bad things happen to good people.* New York: Schocken Books.

Lubienski, C. (2005). Public schools in marketized environments: Shifting incentives and unintended consequences of competition-based educational reforms. *American Journal of Education, 111*(4), 464-486.

Mertler, C. (2006). *Action research: Teachers as researchers in the classroom.* Thousand Oaks, CA: Sage.

National Institute for Early Education Research. (2006). *Percent of population age 3 and 4 who are enrolled in school: Census 2000.* Retrieved on March 21, 2006 from <www.nieer.org/resources/facts>.

Neil, M. (2003). The dangers of testing. *Educational Leadership, 60*(5), 43-46.

Pitt, K. (2005). *Debates in ESL teaching and learning: Culture, communities, and classrooms.* London, UK: Routledge.

Rudalevige, A. (2005, August). Reform or séance? Seeking the "spirit" of the No Child Left Behind. *Teachers College Record.* Online at <<u>www.tcrecord.org</u>>, ID# 12112.

1. The changing teaching profession and you

Seiter, E. (2005). *The INTERNET playground: Children's access, entertainment, and miseducation.* New York: Peter Lang.

Stringer, E. (2004). *Action research in education.* Upper Saddle River, NJ: Pearson Education.

Sutton, R. (2004). Teaching under high-stakes testing: Dilemmas and decisions of a teacher educator. *Journal of Teacher Education, 55*(5), 463-475.

United States Census Bureau. (2005). *The Hispanic population in the United States: 2004.* Retrieved on March 21, 2006 from <http://www.census.gov/population/www/socdemo/hispanic/cps2004.html>.

United States Government Printing Office. (2002). *No Child Left Behind Act: A desktop reference.* Washington, D.C.: Author.

Federal Registry. (2005, June 21). *Assistance To States for the Education of Children with Disabilities.* United States Government Printing Office: Author.

Volante, L. (2004). Teaching to the test: What every educator and policy-maker should know. *Canadian Journal of Educational Administration and Policy, Issue #35.* Online at <www.umanitoba.ca/publications/cjeap/articles/volante.html>.

2. The learning process

When my son Michael was old enough to talk, and being an eager but naïve dad, I decided to bring Michael to my educational psychology class to demonstrate to my students "how children learn". In one task I poured water from a tall drinking glass to a wide glass pie plate, which according to Michael changed the "amount" of water—there was less now than it was in the pie plate. I told him that, on the contrary, the amount of water had stayed the same whether it was in the glass or the pie plate. He looked at me a bit strangely, but complied with my point of view—agreeing at first that, yes, the amount had stayed the same. But by the end of the class session he had reverted to his original position: there was less water, he said, when it was poured into the pie plate compared to being poured into the drinking glass. So much for demonstrating "learning"!

(Kelvin Seifert)

Learning is generally defined as relatively permanent changes in behavior, skills, knowledge, or attitudes resulting from identifiable psychological or social experiences. A key feature is permanence: changes do not count as learning if they are temporary. You do not "learn" a phone number if you forget it the minute after you dial the number; you do not "learn" to eat vegetables if you only do it when forced. The change has to last. Notice, though, that learning can be physical, social, or emotional as well as cognitive. You do not "learn" to sneeze simply by catching cold, but you do learn many skills and behaviors that are physically based, such as riding a bicycle or throwing a ball. You can also learn to like (or dislike) a person, even though this change may not happen deliberately.

Each year after that first visit to my students, while Michael was still a preschooler, I returned with him to my ed-psych class to do the same "learning demonstrations". And each year Michael came along happily, but would again fail the task about the drinking glass and the pie plate. He would comply briefly if I "suggested" that the amount of water stayed the same no matter which way it was poured, but in the end he would still assert that the amount had changed. He was not learning this bit of conventional knowledge, in spite of my repeated efforts.

But the year he turned six, things changed. When I told him it was time to visit my ed-psych class again, he readily agreed and asked: "Are you going to ask me about the water in the drinking glass and pie plate again?" I said yes, I was indeed planning to do that task again. "That's good", he responded, "because I know that the amount stays the same even after you pour it. But do you want me to fake it this time? For your students' sake?"

Teachers' perspectives on learning

For teachers, learning usually refers to things that happen in schools or classrooms, even though every teacher can of course describe examples of learning that happen outside of these places. Even Michael, at age 6, had begun realizing that what counted as "learning" in his dad's educator-type mind was something that happened in a classroom, under the supervision of a teacher (me). For me, as for many educators, the term has a more specific meaning than for many people less involved in schools. In particular, teachers' perspectives on learning often emphasize three ideas, and sometimes even take them for granted: (1) curriculum content and academic achievement, (2) sequencing and readiness, and (3) the importance of transferring learning to new or future situations.

Viewing learning as dependent on curriculum

When teachers speak of learning, they tend to emphasize whatever is taught in schools deliberately, including both the official curriculum and the various behaviors and routines that make classrooms run smoothly. In practice, defining learning in this way often means that teachers equate learning with the major forms of academic achievement—especially language and mathematics—and to a lesser extent musical skill, physical coordination, or social sensitivity (Gardner, 1999, 2006). The imbalance occurs not because the goals of public education make teachers responsible for certain content and activities (like books and reading) and the skills which these activities require (like answering teachers' questions and writing essays). It does happen not (thankfully!) because teachers are biased, insensitive, or unaware that students often learn a lot outside of school.

A side effect of thinking of learning as related only to curriculum or academics is that classroom social interactions and behaviors become issues for teachers—become things that they need to manage. In particular, having dozens of students in one room makes it more likely that I, as a teacher, think of "learning" as something that either takes concentration (to avoid being distracted by others) or that benefits from collaboration (to take advantage of their presence). In the small space of a classroom, no other viewpoint about social interaction makes sense. Yet in the wider world outside of school, learning often does happen incidentally, "accidentally" and without conscious interference or input from others: I "learn" what a friend's personality is like, for example, without either of us deliberately trying to make this happen. As teachers, we sometimes see incidental learning in classrooms as well, and often welcome it; but our responsibility for curriculum goals more often focuses our efforts on what students can learn through conscious, deliberate effort. In a classroom, unlike in many other human settings, it is always necessary to ask whether classmates are helping or hindering individual students' learning.

Focusing learning on changes in classrooms has several other effects. One, for example, is that it can tempt teachers to think that what is taught is equivalent to what is learned—even though most teachers know that doing so is a mistake, and that teaching and learning can be quite different. If I assign a reading to my students about the Russian Revolution, it would be nice to assume not only that they have read the same words, but also learned the same content. But that assumption is not usually the reality. Some students may have read and learned all of what I assigned; others may have read everything but misunderstood the material or remembered only some of it; and still others, unfortunately, may have neither read nor learned much of anything. Chances are that my students would confirm this picture, if asked confidentially. There are ways, of course, to deal helpfully with such diversity of outcomes; for suggestions, see especially Chapter 10 "Planning instruction" and Chapter 11 "Teacher-made assessment strategies". But whatever instructional strategies I adopt, they cannot include assuming that what I teach is the same as what students understand or retain of what I teach.

Viewing learning as dependent on sequencing and readiness

The distinction between teaching and learning creates a secondary issue for teachers, that of educational **readiness**. Traditionally the concept referred to students' preparedness to cope with or profit from the activities and expectations of school. A kindergarten child was "ready" to start school, for example, if he or she was in good health, showed moderately good social skills, could take care of personal physical needs (like eating lunch or going to the bathroom unsupervised), could use a pencil to make simple drawings, and so on. Table 3 shows a similar set of criteria for determining whether a child is "ready" to learn to read (Copple & Bredekamp, 2006). At older ages (such as in high school or university), the term readiness is often replaced by a more specific term, prerequisites. To take a course in physics, for example, a student must first have certain prerequisite experiences, such as studying advanced algebra or calculus. To begin work as a public school teacher, a person must first engage in practice teaching for a period of time (not to mention also studying educational psychology!).

Table 2: Reading readiness in students vs in teachers

Signs of readiness in the child or student	Signs of readiness to teach reading
• productive (speaking) vocabulary of 5,000-8,000 words • child understands and uses complete sentences • child's questions tend to be relevant to the task at hand • child's correctly using most common grammatical constructions • child can match some letters to some sounds • child can string a few letters together to make a few simple words • child can tell and retell stories, poems, and songs	• teacher answers children's questions when possible • teacher encourages child to find out more through other means in addition to asking teacher • teacher asks questions designed to elaborate or expand child's thinking • teacher highlights letters and sounds in the classroom • teacher provides lots of paper and marking tools • teacher assists child with initial writing of letters • teacher encourages children to enact stories, poems, and songs
Source: Copple & Bredekamp, 2006.	

Note that this traditional meaning, of readiness as preparedness, focuses attention on students' adjustment to school and away from the reverse: the possibility that schools and teachers also have a responsibility for adjusting to students. But the latter idea is in fact a legitimate, second meaning for **readiness:** If 5-year-old children normally need to play a lot and keep active, then it is fair to say that their kindergarten teacher needs to be "ready" for this behavior by planning for a program that allows a lot of play and physical activity. If she cannot or will not do so (whatever the reason may be), then in a very real sense this failure is not the children's responsibility. Among older students, the second, teacher-oriented meaning of readiness makes sense as well. If a teacher has a student with a disability (for example, the student is visually impaired), then the teacher has to adjust her approach in appropriate ways—not simply expect a visually impaired child to "sink or swim". As you might expect, this sense of *readiness* is very important for special education, so I discuss it further in Chapter 5 "Students with special educational needs". But the issue of readiness also figures importantly whenever students are diverse (which is most of the time), so it also comes up in Chapter 4 "Student diversity".

Viewing transfer as a crucial outcome of learning

Still another result of focusing the concept of learning on classrooms is that it raises issues of usefulness or transfer, which is the ability to use knowledge or skill in situations beyond the ones in which they are acquired. Learning to read and learning to solve arithmetic problems, for example, are major goals of the elementary school curriculum because those skills are meant to be used not only inside the classroom, but outside as well. We teachers intend, that is, for reading and arithmetic skills to "transfer", even though we also do our best to make the skills enjoyable while they are still being learned. In the world inhabited by teachers, even more than in other worlds, making learning fun is certainly a good thing to do, but making learning useful as well as fun is even better. Combining enjoyment and usefulness, in fact, is a "gold standard" of teaching: we generally seek it for students, even though we may not succeed at providing it all of the time.

Major theories and models of learning

Several ideas and priorities, then, affect how we teachers think about learning, including the curriculum, the difference between teaching and learning, sequencing, readiness, and transfer. The ideas form a "screen" through which to understand and evaluate whatever psychology has to offer education. As it turns out, many theories, concepts, and ideas from educational psychology *do* make it through the "screen" of education, meaning that they are consistent with the professional priorities of teachers and helpful in solving important problems of classroom teaching. In the case of issues about classroom learning, for example, educational psychologists have developed a number of theories and concepts that are relevant to classrooms, in that they describe at least *some* of what usually happens there and offer guidance for assisting learning. It is helpful to group the theories according to whether they focus on changes in behavior or in thinking. The distinction is rough and inexact, but a good place to begin. For starters, therefore, consider two perspectives about learning, called behaviorism (learning as changes in overt behavior) and constructivism, (learning as changes in thinking). The second category can be further divided into psychological constructivism (changes in thinking resulting from individual experiences), and social constructivism, (changes in thinking due to assistance from others). The rest of this chapter describes key ideas from each of these viewpoints. As I hope you will see, each describes some aspects of learning not just in general, but as it happens in classrooms in particular. So each perspective suggests things that *you* might do in *your* classroom to make students' learning more productive.

Behaviorism: changes in what students do

Behaviorism is a perspective on learning that focuses on changes in individuals' observable behaviors—changes in what people say or do. At some point we all use this perspective, whether we call it "behaviorism" or something else. The first time that I drove a car, for example, I was concerned primarily with whether I could actually do the driving, not with whether I could describe or explain how to drive. For another example: when I reached the point in life where I began cooking meals for myself, I was more focused on whether I could actually produce edible food in a kitchen than with whether I could explain my recipes and cooking procedures to others. And still another example—one often relevant to new teachers: when I began my first year of teaching, I was more focused on doing the job of teaching—on day-to-day survival—than on pausing to reflect on what I was doing.

Note that in all of these examples, focusing attention on behavior instead of on "thoughts" may have been desirable at that moment, but not necessarily desirable indefinitely or all of the time. Even as a beginner, there are times when it *is* more important to be able to describe how to drive or to cook than to actually do these things. And there definitely are many times when reflecting on and thinking about teaching can improve teaching itself. (As a teacher-friend once said to me: "Don't just *do* something; *stand* there!") But neither is focusing on behavior which is not necessarily less desirable than focusing on students' "inner" changes, such as gains in their knowledge or their personal attitudes. If you are teaching, you will need to attend to all forms of learning in students, whether inner or outward.

In classrooms, behaviorism is most useful for identifying relationships between specific actions by a student and the immediate precursors and consequences of the actions. It is less useful for understanding changes in students' thinking; for this purpose we need a more *cognitive* (or thinking-oriented) theory, like the ones described later in this chapter. This fact is not really a criticism of behaviorism as a perspective, but just a clarification of its particular strength or source of usefulness, which is to highlight observable relationships among actions, precursors and consequences. Behaviorists use particular terms (or "lingo", some might say) for these relationships. They also rely primarily on two basic images or models of behavioral learning, called *respondent (or "classical") conditioning* and

operant conditioning. The names are derived partly from the major learning mechanisms highlighted by each type, which I describe next.

Respondent conditioning: learning new associations with prior behaviors

As originally conceived, **respondent conditioning** (sometimes also called *classical conditioning*) begins with the involuntary responses to particular sights, sounds, or other sensations (Lavond, 2003). When I receive an injection from a nurse or doctor, for example, I cringe, tighten my muscles, and even perspire a bit. Whenever a contented, happy baby looks at me, on the other hand, I invariably smile in response. I cannot help myself in either case; both of the responses are automatic. In humans as well as other animals, there is a repertoire or variety of such specific, involuntary behaviors. At the sound of a sudden loud noise, for example, most of us show a "startle" response—we drop what we are doing (sometimes literally!), our heart rate shoots up temporarily, and we look for the source of the sound. Cats, dogs and many other animals (even fish in an aquarium) show similar or equivalent responses.

Involuntary stimuli and responses were first studied systematically early in the twentieth-century by the Russian scientist Ivan Pavlov (1927). Pavlov's most well-known work did not involve humans, but dogs, and specifically their involuntary tendency to salivate when eating. He attached a small tube to the side of dogs' mouths that allowed him to measure how much the dogs salivated when fed (Exhibit 1 shows a photograph of one of Pavlov's dogs). But he soon noticed a "problem" with the procedure: as the dogs gained experience with the experiment, they often salivated *before* they began eating. In fact the most experienced dogs sometimes began salivating before they even saw any food, simply when Pavlov himself entered the room! The sight of the experimenter, which had originally been a neutral experience for the dogs, became associated with the dogs' original salivation response. Eventually, in fact, the dogs would salivate at the sight of Pavlov even if he did *not* feed them.

This *change* in the dogs' involuntary response, and especially its growing independence from the food as stimulus, eventually became the focus of Pavlov's research. Psychologists named the process *respondent conditioning* because it describes changes in *responses* to stimuli (though some have also called it "classical conditioning" because it was historically the first form of behavioral learning to be studied systematically). Respondent conditioning has several elements, each with a special name. To understand these, look at and imagine a dog (perhaps even mine, named Ginger) prior to any conditioning. At the beginning Ginger salivates (an **unconditioned response (UR)**) only when she actually tastes her dinner (an **unconditioned stimulus (US)**). As time goes by, however, a neutral stimulus—such as the sound of opening a bag containing fresh dog food —is continually paired with the eating/tasting experience. Eventually the neutral stimulus becomes able to elicit salivation even *before* any dog food is offered to Ginger, or even if the bag of food is empty! At this point the neutral stimulus is called a **conditioned stimulus (UCS)** and the original response is renamed as a **conditioned response (CR).** Now, after conditioning, Ginger salivates merely at the sound of opening *any* large bag, regardless of its contents. (I might add that Ginger also engages in other conditioned responses, such as looking hopeful and following me around the house at dinner time.)

Before Conditioning:

(*UCS*) **Food**→ **Salivation** (UR)

(*UCS*) **Bell**→ **No response** (UR)

During Conditioning:

Bell + Food→ **Salivation**

After Conditioning:

(*CS*) **Bell only**→ **Salivation** (CR)

Exhibit 1: Classical conditioning of Ginger, the dog. *Before conditioning, Ginger salivates only to the taste of food and the bell has no effect. After conditioning, she salivates even when the bell is presented by itself.*

Respondent Conditioning and Students

"OK," you may be thinking, "Respondent conditioning may happen to animals. But does anything like it happen in classrooms?" It might seem like not much would, since teaching is usually about influencing students' conscious words and thoughts, and not their involuntary behaviors. But remember that schooling is not just about encouraging thinking and talking. Teachers, like parents and the public, also seek positive changes in students' attitudes and feelings—attitudes like a love for learning, for example, and feelings like self-confidence. It turns out that respondent conditioning describes these kinds of changes relatively well.

Consider, for example, a child who responds happily whenever meeting a new person who is warm and friendly, but who also responds cautiously or at least neutrally in any new situation. Suppose further that the "new, friendly person" in question is you, his teacher. Initially the child's response to you is like an unconditioned stimulus: you smile (the unconditioned stimulus) and in response he perks up, breathes easier, and smiles (the unconditioned response). This exchange is not the whole story, however, but merely the setting for an important bit of behavior change: suppose you smile at him while standing in your classroom, a "new situation" and therefore one to which he normally responds cautiously. Now respondent learning can occur. The initially neutral stimulus (your classroom) becomes associated repeatedly with the original unconditioned stimulus (your smile) and the child's unconditioned response (his smile). Eventually, if all goes well, the classroom becomes a conditioned stimulus in its own right: it can elicit the child's smiles and other "happy behaviors" even without your immediate presence or stimulus. Exhibit 2 diagrams the situation graphically. When the change in behavior happens, you might say that the child has "learned" to like being in your classroom. Truly a pleasing outcome for both of you!

Before Conditioning:

(UCS) **Seeing Teacher Smile** → **Student Smiles** (UR)

(UCS) **Seeing Classroom** → **No response** (UR)

During Conditioning:

Seeing Teaching Smile + Seeing Classroom → **Student Smiles**

After Conditioning:

(CS) **Seeing Classroom → Student Smiles** (CR)

Exhibit 2: Respondent conditioning of student to classroom. *Before conditioning, the student smiles only when he sees the teacher smile, and the sight of the classroom has no effect. After conditioning, the student smiles at the sight of the classroom even without the teacher present.*

But less positive or desirable examples of respondent conditioning also can happen. Consider a modification of the example that I just gave. Suppose the child that I just mentioned did *not* have the good fortune of being placed in *your* classroom. Instead he found himself with a less likeable teacher, whom we could simply call Mr Horrible. Instead of smiling a lot and eliciting the child's unconditioned "happy response", Mr Horrible often frowns and scowls at the child. In this case, therefore, the child's initial *unconditioned* response is negative: whenever Mr Horrible directs a frown or scowl at the child, the child automatically cringes a little, his eyes widen in fear, and his heart beat races. If the child sees Mr Horrible doing most of his frowning and scowling *in* the classroom, eventually the classroom itself will acquire power as a negative conditioned stimulus. Eventually, that is, the child will not need Mr Horrible to be present in order to feel apprehensive; simply being in the classroom will be enough. Exhibit 3 diagrams this unfortunate situation. Obviously it is an outcome to be avoided, and in fact does not usually happen in such an extreme way. But hopefully it makes the point: any stimulus that is initially neutral, but that gets associated with an unconditioned stimulus and response, can eventually acquire the ability to elicit the response by itself. *Anything*—whether it is desirable or not.

Before Conditioning:

(UCS) **Mr Horrible Frowns** → **Student Cringes** (UCR)

Mr Horrible's Classroom → **No response**

During Conditioning:

Mr Horrible Frowns + Sight of Classroom → **Student Cringes**

After Conditioning:

(CS) **Seeing Classroom** → **Student Cringes** (CR)

Exhibit 3: Respondent conditioning of student to classroom. *Before conditioning, the student cringes only when he sees Mr Horrible smile, and the sight of the classroom has no effect. After conditioning, the student cringes at the sight of the classroom even without Mr Horrible present.*

The changes described in these two examples are important because they can affect students' attitude about school, and therefore also their *motivation* to learn. In the positive case, the child becomes more inclined to please the teacher and to attend to what he or she has to offer; in the negative case, the opposite occurs. Since the changes in attitude happen "inside" the child, they are best thought of as one way that a child can acquire *i* **intrinsic motivation,** meaning a desire or tendency to direct attention and energy in a particular way that originates from the child himself or herself. Intrinsic motivation is sometimes contrasted to **extrinsic motivation,** a tendency to direct attention and energy that originates from *outside* of the child. As we will see, classical conditioning can influence students' intrinsic motivation in directions that are either positive or negative. As you might suspect, there are other ways to influence motivation as well. Many of these are described in Chapter 6 ("Student motivation"). First, though, let us look at three other features of classical conditioning that complicate the picture a bit, but also render conditioning a bit more accurate, an appropriate description of students' learning.

Three key ideas about respondent conditioning

Extinction: This term does not refer to the fate of dinosaurs, but to the *disappearance* of a link between the conditioned stimulus and the conditioned response. Imagine a third variation on the conditioning "story" described above. Suppose, as I suggested above, that the child begins by associating your happy behaviors—your smiles—to his being present in the classroom, so that the classroom itself becomes enough to elicit his own smiles. But now suppose there is a sad turn of events: you become sick and must therefore leave the classroom in the middle of the school year. A substitute is called in who is not Mr Horrible, but simply someone who is not very expressive, someone we can call Ms Neutral. At first the child continues to feel good (that is, to smile) whenever present in the classroom. But because the link between the classroom and your particular smile is no longer repeated or associated, the child's response gradually *extinguishes,* or fades until it has disappeared entirely. In a sense the child's initial learning is "unlearned".

Extinction can also happen with negative examples of classical conditioning. If Mr Horrible leaves mid-year (perhaps because no one could stand working with him any longer!), then the child's negative responses (cringing, eyes widening, heart beat racing, and so on) will also extinguish eventually. Note, though, that whether the conditioned stimulus is positive or negative, extinction does not happen suddenly or immediately, but unfolds over time. This fact can sometimes obscure the process if you are a busy teacher attending to many students.

Generalization: When Pavlov studied conditioning in dogs, he noticed that the original conditioned stimulus was not the only neutral stimulus that elicited the conditioned response. If he paired a particular bell with the sight of food, for example, so that the bell became a conditioned stimulus for salivation, then it turned out that *other* bells, perhaps with a different pitch or type or sound, also acquired some ability to trigger salivation—though not as much as the original bell. Psychologists call this process generalization, or the tendency for similar stimuli to elicit a conditioned response. The child being conditioned to your smile, for example, might learn to associate your smile not only with being present in *your* classroom, but also to being present in other, similar classrooms. His conditioned smiles may be strongest where he learned them initially (that is, in your own room), but nonetheless visible to a significant extent in other teachers' classrooms. To the extent that this happens, he has *generalized* his learning. It is of course good news; it means that we can say that the child is beginning to "learn to like school" in general, and not just your particular room. Unfortunately, the opposite can also happen: if a child learns negative associations from Mr Horrible, the child's fear, caution, and stress might generalize to other classrooms as well. The lesson for teachers is therefore clear: we have a responsibility, wherever possible, to make classrooms pleasant places to be.

Discrimination: Generalization among similar stimuli can be reduced if only *one* of the similar stimuli is associated consistently with the unconditioned response, while the others are not. When this happens, psychologists say that **discrimination learning** has occurred, meaning that the individual has learned to distinguish or respond differently to one stimulus than to another. From an educational point of view, discrimination learning can be either desirable or not, depending on the particulars of the situation. Imagine again (for the fourth time!) the child who learns to associate your classroom with your smiles, so that he eventually produces smiles of his own whenever present in your room. But now imagine yet another variation on his story: the child is old enough to attend *middle school,* and therefore has several teachers across the day. You—with your smiles—are one, but so are Mr Horrible and Ms Neutral. At first the child may generalize his classically conditioned smiles to the other teachers' classrooms. But the other teachers do not smile like you do, and this fact causes the child's smiling to extinguish somewhat in their rooms. Meanwhile, you keep smiling in your room. Eventually the child is smiling *only* in your room and not in the other rooms. When this happens, we say that **discrimination** has occurred, meaning that the conditioned associations happen only to a single version of the unconditioned stimuli—in this case, only to *your* smiles, and not to the (rather rare) occurrences of smiles in the other classrooms. Judging by his behavior, the child is making a distinction between your room and others.

In one sense the discrimination in this story is unfortunate in that it prevents the child from acquiring a liking for school that is generalized. But notice that an opposing, more desirable process is happening at the same time: the child is also *prevented* from acquiring a generalized *dislike* of school. The fear-producing stimuli from Mr Horrible, in particular, become discriminated from the happiness-producing smiles from you, so the child's learns to confine his fearful responses to that particular classroom, and does not generalize them to other "innocent" classrooms, including your own. This is still not an ideal situation for the student, but maybe it is more desirable than disliking school altogether.

Operant conditioning: new behaviors because of new consequences

Instead of focusing on associations between stimuli and responses, **operant conditioning** focuses on how the effects of consequences on behaviors. The operant model of learning begins with the idea that certain consequences tend to make certain behaviors happen more frequently. If I compliment a student for a good comment during a discussion, there is more of a chance that I will hear comments from the student more often in the future (and hopefully they will also be good ones!). If a student tells a joke to several classmates and they laugh at it, then the student is more likely to tell additional jokes in the future and so on.

As with respondent conditioning, the original research about this model of learning was not done with people, but with animals. One of the pioneers in the field was a Harvard professor named B. F. Skinner, who published numerous books and articles about the details of the process and who pointed out many parallels between operant conditioning in animals and operant conditioning in humans (1938, 1948, 1988). Skinner observed the behavior of rather tame laboratory rats (not the unpleasant kind that sometimes live in garbage dumps). He or his assistants would put them in a cage that contained little except a lever and a small tray just big enough to hold a small amount of food. (Exhibit 4 shows the basic set-up, which is sometimes nicknamed a "Skinner box".) At first the rat would sniff and "putter around" the cage at random, but sooner or later it would happen upon the lever and eventually happen to press it. Presto! The lever released a small pellet of food, which the rat would promptly eat. Gradually the rat would spend more time near the lever and press the lever more frequently, getting food more frequently. Eventually it would spend *most* of its time at the lever and eating its fill of food. The rat had "discovered" that the consequence of pressing the level was to receive food. Skinner called the changes in the rat's behavior an example of **operant conditioning,** and gave special names to the different parts of the process. He called the food pellets the **reinforcement** and the lever-pressing the **operant** (because it "operated" on the rat's environment). See below.

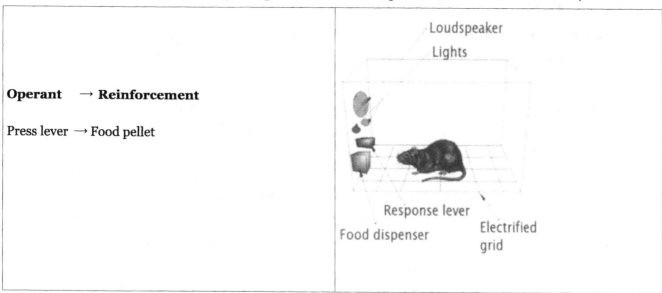

Operant → **Reinforcement**

Press lever → Food pellet

Loudspeaker

Lights

Response lever

Food dispenser

Electrified grid

Exhibit 4: Operant conditioning with a laboratory rat

Skinner and other behavioral psychologists experimented with using various reinforcers and operants. They also experimented with various patterns of reinforcement (or **schedules of reinforcement**), as well as with various

cues or signals to the animal about when reinforcement was available. It turned out that all of these factors—the operant, the reinforcement, the schedule, and the cues—affected how easily and thoroughly operant conditioning occurred. For example, reinforcement was more effective if it came immediately after the crucial operant behavior, rather than being delayed, and reinforcements that happened intermittently (only part of the time) caused learning to take longer, but also caused it to last longer.

Operant conditioning and students' learning: As with respondent conditioning, it is important to ask whether operant conditioning also describes learning in human beings, and especially in students in classrooms. On this point the answer seems to be clearly "yes". There are countless classroom examples of consequences affecting students' behavior in ways that resemble operant conditioning, although the process certainly does not account for all forms of student learning (Alberto & Troutman, 2005). Consider the following examples. In most of them the operant behavior tends to become more frequent on repeated occasions:

- A seventh-grade boy makes a silly face (the operant) at the girl sitting next to him. Classmates sitting around them giggle in response (the reinforcement).

- A kindergarten child raises her hand in response to the teacher's question about a story (the operant). The teacher calls on her and she makes her comment (the reinforcement).

- Another kindergarten child blurts out her comment without being called on (the operant). The teacher frowns, ignores this behavior, but before the teacher calls on a different student, classmates are listening attentively (the reinforcement) to the student even though he did not raise his hand as he should have.

- A twelfth-grade student—a member of the track team—runs one mile during practice (the operant). He notes the time it takes him as well as his increase in speed since joining the team (the reinforcement).

- A child who is usually very restless sits for five minutes doing an assignment (the operant). The teaching assistant compliments him for working hard (the reinforcement).

- A sixth-grader takes home a book from the classroom library to read overnight (the operant). When she returns the book the next morning, her teacher puts a gold star by her name on a chart posted in the room (the reinforcement).

Hopefully these examples are enough to make four points about operant conditioning. First, the process is widespread in classrooms—probably more widespread than respondent conditioning. This fact makes sense, given the nature of public education: to a large extent, teaching is about making certain consequences for students (like praise or marks) depend on students' engaging in certain activities (like reading certain material or doing assignments). Second, learning by operant conditioning is not confined to any particular grade, subject area, or style of teaching, but by nature happens in nearly every imaginable classroom. Third, teachers are not the only persons controlling reinforcements. Sometimes they are controlled by the activity itself (as in the track team example), or by classmates (as in the "giggling" example). A result of all of the above points is the fourth: that multiple examples of operant conditioning often happen at the same time. The skill builder for this chapter *(The decline and fall of Jane Gladstone)* suggests how this happened to someone completing student teaching.

2. The learning process

Because operant conditioning happens so widely, its effects on motivation are a bit more complex than the effects of respondent conditioning. As in respondent conditioning, operant conditioning can encourage **intrinsic motivation** to the extent that the reinforcement for an activity can sometimes be the activity itself. When a student reads a book for the sheer enjoyment of reading, for example, he is reinforced by the reading itself; then we often say that his reading is "intrinsically motivated". More often, however, operant conditioning stimulates *both* intrinsic *and* extrinsic motivation at the same time. The combining of both is noticeable in the examples that I listed above. In each example, it is reasonable to assume that the student felt intrinsically motivated to some partial extent, even when reward came from outside the student as well. This was because *part* of what reinforced their behavior was the behavior itself—whether it was making faces, running a mile, or contributing to a discussion. At the same time, though, note that each student probably was also **extrinsically motivated,** meaning that another part of the reinforcement came from consequences or experiences *not* inherently part of the activity or behavior itself. The boy who made a face was reinforced not only by the pleasure of making a face, for example, but *also* by the giggles of classmates. The track student was reinforced not only by the pleasure of running itself, but *also* by knowledge of his improved times and speeds. Even the usually restless child sitting still for five minutes may have been reinforced partly by this brief experience of unusually focused activity, even if he was *also* reinforced by the teacher aide's compliment. Note that the extrinsic part of the reinforcement may sometimes be more easily observed or noticed than the intrinsic part, which by definition may sometimes only be experienced within the individual and not also displayed outwardly. This latter fact may contribute to an impression that sometimes occurs, that operant conditioning is really just "bribery in disguise", that only the *external* reinforcements operate on students' behavior. It is true that external reinforcement may sometimes alter the nature or strength of internal (or intrinsic) reinforcement, but this is not the same as saying that it destroys or replaces intrinsic reinforcement. But more about this issue later! (See especially Chapter 6, "Student motivation".)

Comparing operant conditioning and respondent conditioning: Operant conditioning is made more complicated, but also more realistic, by many of the same concepts as used in respondent conditioning. In most cases, however, the additional concepts have slightly different meanings in each model of learning. Since this circumstance can make the terms confusing, let me explain the differences for three major concepts used in both models—extinction, generalization, and discrimination. Then I will comment on two additional concepts— schedules of reinforcement and cues—that are sometimes also used in talking about both forms of conditioning, but that are important primarily for understanding operant conditioning. The explanations and comments are also summarized in Table 2.

Table 3: Comparison of terms common to operant and respondent conditioning

Term	As defined in respondent conditioning	As defined in operant conditioning
Extinction	Disappearance of an association between a conditioned stimulus and a conditioned response	Disappearance of the operant behavior due to lack of reinforcement
Generalization	Ability of stimulus similar to the conditioned stimulus to elicit the conditioned response	Tendency of behaviors similar to operant to be conditioned along with

		the original operant
Discrimination	Learning **not** to respond to stimuli that are similar to the originally conditioned stimulus	Learning **not** to emit behaviors that are similar to the originally conditioned operant
Schedule of Reinforcement	The pattern or frequency by which a CS is paired with the UCS during learning	The pattern or frequency by which a reinforcement is a consequence of an operant during learning
Cue	Not applicable	Stimulus prior to the operant that signals the availability or not of reinforcement

In both respondent and operant conditioning, **extinction** refers to the disappearance of "something". In operant conditioning, what disappears is the *operant behavior* because of a lack of reinforcement. A student who stops receiving gold stars or compliments for prolific reading of library books, for example, may extinguish (i.e. decrease or stop) book-reading behavior. In respondent conditioning, on the other hand, what disappears is association between the conditioned stimulus (the CS) and the conditioned response (CR). If you stop smiling at a student, then the student may extinguish her association between you and her pleasurable response to your smile, or between your classroom and the student's pleasurable response to your smile.

In both forms of conditioning, **generalization** means that something "extra" gets conditioned if it is somehow similar to "something". In operant conditioning, the extra conditioning is to behaviors similar to the original *operant*. If getting gold stars results in my reading more library books, then I may generalize this behavior to other similar activities, such as reading the newspaper, even if the activity is not reinforced directly. In respondent conditioning, however, the extra conditioning refers to *stimuli* similar to the original conditioned stimulus. If I am a student and I respond happily to my teacher's smiles, then I may find myself responding happily to other people (like my other teachers) to some extent, even if they do not smile at me. Generalization is a lot like the concept of *transfer* that I discussed early in this chapter, in that it is about extending prior learning to new situations or contexts. From the perspective of operant conditioning, though, what is being extended (or "transferred" or generalized) is a behavior, not knowledge or skill.

In both forms of conditioning, **discrimination** means learning **not** to generalize. In operant conditioning, though, what is **not** being overgeneralized is the operant behavior. If I am a student who is being complimented (reinforced) for contributing to discussions, I must also learn to discriminate when to make verbal contributions from when **not** to make verbal contributions—such as when classmates or the teacher are busy with other tasks. In respondent conditioning, what are **not** being overgeneralized are the conditioned stimuli that elicit the conditioned response. If I, as a student, learn to associate the mere sight of a smiling teacher with my own happy, contented behavior, then I also have to learn *not* to associate this same happy response with similar, but slightly different sights, such as a teacher looking annoyed.

In both forms of conditioning, the **schedule of reinforcement** refers to the pattern or frequency by which "something" is paired with "something else". In operant conditioning, what is being paired is the pattern by which reinforcement is linked with the operant. If a teacher praises me for my work, does she do it every time, or only sometimes? Frequently or only once in awhile? In respondent conditioning, however, the schedule in question is the pattern by which the conditioned stimulus is paired with the unconditioned stimulus. If I am student with Mr Horrible as my teacher, does he scowl every time he is in the classroom, or only sometimes? Frequently or rarely?

Behavioral psychologists have studied schedules of reinforcement extensively (for example, Ferster, et al., 1997; Mazur, 2005), and found a number of interesting effects of different schedules. For teachers, however, the most important finding may be this: partial or intermittent schedules of reinforcement generally cause learning to take longer, but also cause extinction of learning to take longer. This dual principle is important for teachers because so much of the reinforcement we give is partial or intermittent. Typically, if I am teaching, I can compliment a student a lot of the time, for example, but there will inevitably be occasions when I cannot do so because I am busy elsewhere in the classroom. For teachers concerned both about motivating students and about minimizing inappropriate behaviors, this is both good news and bad. The good news is that the benefits of my praising students' constructive behavior will be more lasting, because they will not extinguish their constructive behaviors immediately if I fail to support them every single time they happen. The bad news is that students' negative behaviors may take longer to extinguish as well, because those too may have developed through partial reinforcement. A student who clowns around inappropriately in class, for example, may not be "supported" by classmates' laughter every time it happens, but only some of the time. Once the inappropriate behavior is learned, though, it will take somewhat longer to disappear even if everyone—both teacher and classmates—make a concerted effort to ignore (or extinguish) it.

Finally, behavioral psychologists have studied the effects of **cues.** In operant conditioning, a cue is a stimulus that happens just prior to the operant behavior and that signals that performing the behavior may lead to reinforcement. Its effect is much like discrimination learning in respondent conditioning, except that what is "discriminated" in this case is not a conditioned behavior that is reflex-like, but a voluntary action, the operant. In the original conditioning experiments, Skinner's rats were sometimes cued by the presence or absence of a small electric light in their cage. Reinforcement was associated with pressing a lever when, and only when, the light was on. In classrooms, cues are sometimes provided by the teacher or simply by the established routines of the class. Calling on a student to speak, for example, can be a cue that *if* the student *does* say something at that moment, then he or she *may* be reinforced with praise or acknowledgment. But if that cue does *not* occur—if the student is *not* called on—speaking may *not* be rewarded. In more everyday, non-behaviorist terms, the cue allows the student to learn when it is acceptable to speak, and when it is not.

Constructivism: changes in how students think

Behaviorist models of learning may be helpful in understanding and influencing what students do, but teachers usually also want to know what students are *thinking,* and how to enrich what students are thinking. For this goal of teaching, some of the best help comes from **constructivism,** which is a perspective on learning focused on how students actively create (or "construct") knowledge out of experiences. Constructivist models of learning differ about how much a learner constructs knowledge independently, compared to how much he or she takes cues from people who may be more of an expert and who help the learner's efforts (Fosnot, 2005; Rockmore, 2005). For convenience these are called **psychological constructivism** and **social constructivism,** even though both versions are in a sense explanations about thinking within individuals.

Psychological constructivism: the independent investigator

The main idea of psychological constructivism is that a person learns by mentally organizing and reorganizing new information or experiences. The organization happens partly by relating new experiences to prior knowledge that is already meaningful and well understood. Stated in this general form, individual constructivism is sometimes associated with a well-known educational philosopher of the early twentieth century, **John Dewey** (1938-1998). Although Dewey himself did not use the term constructivism in most of his writing, his point of view amounted to a type of constructivism, and he discussed in detail its implications for educators. He argued, for example, that if students indeed learn primarily by building their own knowledge, then teachers should adjust the curriculum to fit students' prior knowledge and interests as fully as possible. He also argued that a curriculum could only be justified if it related as fully as possible to the activities and responsibilities that students will probably have *later,* after leaving school. To many educators these days, his ideas may seem merely like good common sense, but they were indeed innovative and progressive at the beginning of the twentieth century.

A more recent example of psychological constructivism is the cognitive theory of **Jean Piaget** (Piaget, 2001; Gruber & Voneche, 1995). Piaget described learning as interplay between two mental activities that he called *assimilation* and *accommodation.* **Assimilation** is the interpretation of new information in terms of pre-existing concepts, information or ideas. A preschool child who already understands the concept of *bird,* for example, might initially label any flying object with this term—even butterflies or mosquitoes. Assimilation is therefore a bit like the idea of *generalization* in operant conditioning, or the idea of *transfer* described at the beginning of this chapter. In Piaget's viewpoint, though, what is being transferred to a new setting is not simply a behavior (Skinner's "operant" in operant conditioning), but a mental representation for an object or experience.

Assimilation operates jointly with **accommodation,** which is the revision or modification of pre-existing concepts in terms of new information or experience. The preschooler who initially generalizes the concept of *bird* to include any flying object, for example, eventually revises the concept to include only particular kinds of flying objects, such as robins and sparrows, and not others, like mosquitoes or airplanes. For Piaget, assimilation and accommodation work together to enrich a child's thinking and to create what Piaget called **cognitive equilibrium**, which is a balance between reliance on prior information and openness to new information. At any given time, cognitive equilibrium consists of an ever-growing repertoire of mental representations for objects and experiences. Piaget called each mental representation a **schema** (all of them together—the plural—was called **schemata**). A schema was not merely a concept, but an elaborated mixture of vocabulary, actions, and experience related to the concept. A child's schema for *bird,* for example, includes not only the relevant verbal knowledge (like knowing how to define the word "bird"), but also the child's experiences with birds, pictures of birds, and conversations about birds. As assimilation and accommodation about birds and other flying objects operate together over time, the child does not just revise and add to his vocabulary (such as acquiring a new word, "butterfly"), but also adds and remembers relevant new experiences and actions. From these collective revisions and additions the child gradually constructs whole new schemata about birds, butterflies, and other flying objects. In more everyday (but also less precise) terms, Piaget might then say that "the child has learned more about birds".

2. The learning process

The upper part of Exhibit 5 diagrams the relationships among the Piagetian version of psychological constructivist learning. Note that the model of learning in the Exhibit is rather "individualistic", in the sense that it does not say much about how *other* people involved with the learner might assist in assimilating or accommodating information. Parents and teachers, it would seem, are left lingering on the sidelines, with few significant responsibilities for helping learners to construct knowledge. But the Piagetian picture does nonetheless imply a role for helpful others: someone, after all, has to tell or model the vocabulary needed to talk about and compare birds from airplanes and butterflies! Piaget did recognize the importance of helpful others in his writings and theorizing, calling the process of support or assistance *social transmission*. But he did not emphasize this aspect of constructivism. Piaget was more interested in what children and youth could figure out on their own, so to speak, than in how teachers or parents might be able to help the young to figure out (Salkind, 2004). Partly for this reason, his theory is often considered less about learning and more about *development,* which is long-term change in a person resulting from multiple experiences. For the same reason, educators have often found Piaget's ideas especially helpful for thinking about students' *readiness* to learn, another one of the lasting educational issues that I discussed at the beginning of this chapter. I will therefore return to Piaget later to discuss development and its importance for teaching in more detail.

Learning According to Piaget:
Assimilation + Accommodation → Equilibrium → Schemata
Learning According to Vygotsky:
Novice → Zone of Proximal Development ← Expert (ZPD)

Exhibit 5: Constructivist models of learning

Social Constructivism: assisted performance

Unlike Piaget's rather individually oriented version of constructivism, some psychologists and educators have explicitly focused on the relationships and interactions between a learner and more knowledgeable and experienced individuals. One early expression of this viewpoint came from the American psychologist **Jerome Bruner** (1960, 1966, 1996), who became convinced that students could usually learn more than had been traditionally expected as long as they were given appropriate guidance and resources. He called such support **instructional scaffolding**—literally meaning a temporary framework, like one used in constructing a building, that allows a much stronger structure to be built within it. In a comment that has been quoted widely (and sometimes disputed), he wrote: "We [constructivist educators] begin with the hypothesis that any subject can be taught effectively in some intellectually honest form to any child at any stage of development." (1960, p. 33). The reason for such a bold assertion was Bruner's belief in scaffolding—his belief in the importance of providing guidance in the right way and at the right time. When scaffolding is provided, students seem more competent and "intelligent," and they learn more.

Similar ideas were proposed independently by the Russian psychologist **Lev Vygotsky** (1978), whose writing focused on how a child's or novice's thinking is influenced by relationships with others who are more capable, knowledgeable, or expert than the learner. Vygotsky proposed that when a child (or any novice) is learning a new skill or solving a new problem, he or she can perform *better* if accompanied and helped by an expert than if performing alone—though still not as well as the expert. Someone who has played very little chess, for example, will probably compete against an opponent better if helped by an expert chess player than if competing alone against an opponent. Vygotsky called the difference between solo performance and assisted performance the **zone of proximal development** (or **ZPD** for short)—meaning the place or area (figuratively speaking) of immediate change. From this perspective learning is like *assisted performance* (Tharp & Gallimore, 1991). Initially during learning, knowledge or skill is found mostly "in" the expert helper. If the expert is skilled and motivated to help, then the expert arranges experiences that allow the novice to practice crucial skills or to construct new knowledge. In this regard the expert is a bit like the coach of an athlete—offering help and suggesting ways of practicing, but never doing the actual athletic work himself or herself. Gradually, by providing continued experiences matched to the novice learner's emerging competencies, the expert-coach makes it possible for the novice or apprentice to **appropriate** (or make his or her own) the skills or knowledge that originally resided only with the expert. These relationships are diagrammed in the lower part of Exhibit 5.

In both the psychological and social versions of constructivist learning, the novice is not really "taught" so much as just allowed to learn. The social version of constructivism, however, highlights the responsibility of the expert for making learning possible. He or she must not only have knowledge and skill, but also know how to arrange experiences that make it easy and safe for learners to gain knowledge and skill themselves. These requirements sound, of course, a lot like the requirements for classroom teaching. In addition to knowing what is to be learned, the expert (i.e. the teacher) also has to break the content into manageable parts, offer the parts in a sensible sequence, provide for suitable and successful practice, bring the parts back together again at the end, and somehow relate the entire experience to knowledge and skills already meaningful to the learner. But of course, no one said that teaching is easy!

Implications of constructivism for teaching

Fortunately there are strategies that teachers can use for giving students this kind of help—in fact they constitute a major portion of this book, and are a major theme throughout the entire preservice teacher education programs. For now, let me just point briefly to two of them, saving a complete discussion for later. One strategy that teachers often find helpful is to organize the content to be learned as systematically as possible, because doing this allows the teacher to select and devise learning activities that are more effective. One of the most widely used frameworks for organizing content, for example, is a classification scheme proposed by the educator Benjamin Bloom, published with the somewhat imposing title of *Taxonomy of Educational Objectives: Handbook #1: Cognitive Domain* (Bloom, et al., 1956; Anderson & Krathwohl, 2001). **Bloom's taxonomy**, as it is usually called, describes six kinds of learning goals that teachers can in principle expect from students, ranging from simple recall of knowledge to complex evaluation of knowledge. (The levels are defined briefly in Table 2.3 with examples from *Goldilocks and the Three Bears*.)

Bloom's taxonomy makes useful distinctions among possible kinds of knowledge needed by students, and therefore potentially helps in selecting activities that truly target students' "zones of proximal development" in the sense meant by Vygotsky. A student who knows few terms for the species studied in biology unit (a problem at Bloom's *knowledge* and *comprehension* levels), for example, may initially need support at remembering and defining the terms before he or she can make useful comparisons among species (Bloom's *analysis* level). Pinpointing the most appropriate learning activities to accomplish this objective remains the job of the teacher-expert (that's *you*), but the learning itself has to be accomplished by the student. Put in more social constructivist terms, the teacher arranges a zone of proximal development that allows the student to compare species successfully, but the student still has to construct or appropriate the comparisons for him or herself.

Table 4: Bloom's taxonomy of educational objectives: cognitive domain

Category or type of thinking	Definition	Example (with apologies to Goldilocks and her bear friends!)
Knowledge	Remembering or recalling facts, information, or procedures	List three things Goldilocks did in the three bears' house.
Comprehension	Understanding facts, interpreting information	Explain why Goldilocks liked the little bear's chair the best.
Application	Using concepts in new situations, solving particular problems	Predict some of the things that Goldilocks might have used if she had entered *your* house.
Analysis	Distinguish parts of information, a concept, or a procedure	Select the part of the story where Goldilocks seemed most comfortable.
Synthesis	Combining elements or parts into a new object, idea, or procedure	Tell how the story would have been different if it had been about three fishes.
Evaluation	Assessing and judging the value or ideas, objects, or materials in a particular situation	Decide whether Goldilocks was a bad girl, and justify your position.

A second strategy may be coupled with the first. As students gain experience as students, they become able to think about how they *themselves* learn best, and you (as the teacher) can encourage such self-reflection as one of your goals for their learning. These changes allow you to transfer some of your responsibilities for *arranging* learning to the students themselves. For the biology student mentioned above, for example, you may be able not only to plan activities that support comparing species, but also to devise ways for the student to think about how he or she might learn the same information independently. The resulting self-assessment and self-direction of learning often goes by the name of **metacognition**—an ability to think about and regulate one's own thinking (Israel, 2005). Metacognition can sometimes be difficult for students to achieve, but it is an important goal for social constructivist learning because it gradually frees learners from dependence on expert teachers to guide their learning. Reflective learners, you might say, become their own expert guides. Like with using Bloom's taxonomy, though, promoting metacognition and self-directed learning is important enough that I will come back to it later in more detail (especially in Chapter 9, "Facilitating complex thinking").

By assigning a more visible role to expert helpers—and by implication also to teachers—than does the psychological constructivism, social constructivism is seemingly more complete as a description of what teachers usually do in classrooms, and of what they usually hope students will experience there. As we will see in the next chapter, however, there are more uses to a theory than whether it describes the moment-to-moment interactions between teacher and students. As I explain there, some theories can be helpful for planning instruction rather than for doing it. It turns out that this is the case for psychological constructivism, which offers important ideas about the appropriate sequencing of learning and development. This fact makes the psychological constructivism valuable in its own way, even though it (and a few other learning theories as well) seem to "omit" mentioning teachers, parents, or experts in detail. So do not make up your mind about the relative merits of different learning theories yet!

Chapter summary

Although the term learning has many possible meanings, the term as used by teachers emphasizes its relationship to curriculum, to teaching, and to the issues of sequencing, readiness, and transfer. Viewed in this light, the two major psychological perspectives of learning—behaviorist and constructivist—have important ideas to offer educators. Within the behaviorist perspective are two major theories or models of learning, called respondent conditioning and operant conditioning. Respondent conditioning describes how previously neutral associations can acquire the power to elicit significant responses in students. Operant conditioning describes how the consequences and cues for a behavior can cause the behavior to become more frequent. In either case, from a teacher's point of view, the learned behaviors or responses can be either desirable or unwanted.

The other major psychological perspective—constructivism—describes how individuals build or "construct" knowledge by engaging actively with their experiences. The psychological version of constructivism emphasizes the learners' individual responses to experience—their tendency both to assimilate it and to accommodate to it. The social version of constructivism emphasizes how other, more expert individuals can create opportunities for the learner to construct new knowledge. Social constructivism suggests that a teacher's role must include deliberate instructional planning, such as facilitated by Bloom's taxonomy of learning objectives, but also that teachers need to encourage metacognition, which is students' ability to monitor their own learning.

On the Internet

<**http://seab.envmed.rochester.edu/jaba**> This is the website for the Journal of Applied Behavior Analysis, and as such it is an excellent source of examples of how behaviorist learning principles can be applied to a wide variety of behavior-related difficulties. Any article older than one year is available in full-text, free of charge from the website. (If it is from the most recent three issues, however, you have to subscribe to the journal.)

<**www.piaget.org**> This is the website for the Jean Piaget Society, which in spite of its name is not just about Piaget, but about all forms of constructivist research about learning and development, including social constructivist versions. They have excellent brief publications about this perspective, available free of charge at the website, as well as information about how to find additional information.

2. The learning process

Key terms

Appropriate (verb)
Behaviorism
Bloom's taxonomy
Classical conditioning
Constructivism
   Psychological constructivism
      John Dewey
      Jean Piaget
         Assimilation
         Accommodation
         Equilibrium
         Schema
   Social constructivism
      Jerome Bruner
         Instructional scaffolding
      Lev Vygotsky
         Zone of proximal development
Discrimination
Extinction

Extrinsic motivation
Generalization
Learning
Intrinsic motivation
Metacognition
Operant conditioning
   Cue
   Operant
   Reinforcement
   Schedule of reinforcement
Ivan Pavlov
Readiness
Respondent conditioning
   Conditioned response
   Conditioned stimulus
   Unconditioned response
   Unconditioned stimulus
B. F. Skinner
Transfer

References

Alberto, P. & Troutman, A. (2005). *Applied behavior analysis for teachers, 7th edition*. Upper Saddle River, NJ: Prentice Hall.

Anderson, L. & Krathwohl, D. (Eds.). (2001). *A taxonomy for learning, teaching, and assessing: A revision of Bloom's taxonomy of educational objectives*. New York: Longman.

Bruner, J. (1960). *The process of education*. Cambridge, MA: Harvard University Press.

Bruner, J. (1966). *Toward a theory of instruction*. Cambridge, MA: Harvard University Press.

Bruner, J. (1996). *The culture of education*. Cambridge, MA: Harvard University Press.

Copple, C. & Bredekamp, S. (2006). *Basics of developmentally appropriate practice*. Washington, D.C.: National Association for the Education of Young Children.

Dewey, J. (1938/1998). *How we think*. Boston: Houghton Mifflin.

Ferster, C., Skinner, B. F., Cheney, C., Morse, W., & Dews, D. *Schedules of reinforcement*. New York: Copley Publishing Group.

Fosnot, C. (Ed.). (2005). *Constructivism: Theory, perspectives, and practice, 2nd edition*. New York: Teachers College Press.

Gardner, H. (1999). *Intelligence reframed: Multiple intelligences for the 21st century*. New York: Basic Books.

Gardner, H. (2006). *The development and education of the mind*. New York: Routledge.

Goldman, J. (2006). Web-based designed activities for young people in health education: A constructivist approach. *Health Education Journal 65*(1), 14-27.

Gruber, H. & Voneche, J. (Eds.). (1995). *The essential Piaget.* New York: Basic Books.

Israel, S. (Ed.). (2005). *Metacognition in literacy learning.* Mahwah, NJ: Erlbaum.

Lavond, D. & Steinmetz, J. (2003). *Handbook of classical conditioning.* Boston: Kluwer Academic Publishing.

Mazur, J. (2005). *Learning and behavior, 6th edition.* Upper Saddle River, NJ: Prentice Hall.

Onslow, M., Menzies, R., & Packman, A. (2001). An operant intervention for early stuttering. *Behavior modification 25*(1), 116-139.

Pavlov, I. (1927). *Conditioned reflexes.* London, UK: Oxford University Press.

Piaget, J. (2001). *The psychology of intelligence.* London, UK: Routledge.

Rockmore, T. (2005). *On constructivist epistemology.* Lanham, MD: Rowman & Littlefield Publishers.

Salkind, N. (2004). *An introduction to theories of human development.* Thousand Oaks, CA: Sage Publications.

Skinner, B. F. (1938). *The behavior of organisms.* New York: Appleton-Century-Crofts.

Skinner, B. F. (1948). *Walden Two.* New York: Macmillan.

Skinner, B. F. (1988). *The selection of behavior: The operant behaviorism of B. F. Skinner.* New York: Cambridge University Press.

Tharp, R. & Gallimore, R. (1991). *Rousing minds to life: Teaching, learning, and schooling in social context.* Cambridge, UK: Cambridge University Press.

Vygotsky, L. (1978). *Mind in society: The development of higher psychological processes.* Cambridge, MA: Harvard University Press.

3. Student development

When one of our authors (Kelvin Seifert) was growing up, he was provided with piano lessons. Daily practice was a staple of childhood--365 days a year, and in a home that was deliberately kept quiet to facilitate practice. Music—especially the piano—defined a major part of his emerging self-identity. Altogether he studied piano for 13 years, from age 4 to the end of high school, with only occasional interruptions.

At any one time, Kelvin witnessed small changes in his skills. He performed a simple piece a bit better than he had the previous week, or he played more of it from memory. There were direct, obvious connections between his skills at one moment and at the moment just before or after. Back then, if you had asked him what accounted for the changes, he would have stated without hesitation that they were because he was "learning" specific piano pieces.

Across broader spans of time, however, he noticed changes that were more dramatic. Kelvin learned much more complex pieces than he had several years earlier, for example. He also played with significantly more "finesse", sensitivity and polish than as a young child. He was even listening to classical music on the radio some of the time! Kelvin's musical talent became transformed over the long term, and in some sense he did not have the "same" talent that he had had as a beginner.

*If you had asked what accounted for these longer-term changes, he would have had a harder time answering than when asked about the short-term changes. He might have said simply and a bit vaguely: "I have been getting better at piano." If you ask the same question now, however, he would say that his music skills had **developed**, that their development had been slow and gradual, and that the changes resulted not just from simple practice, but also from becoming more widely skilled about music in general.*

Development refers to long-term personal changes that have multiple sources and multiple effects. It is like the difference between Kelvin's music at age fifteen compared to his music at age five, rather than the difference between his music one week and his music the next. Some human developments are especially broad and take years to unfold fully; a person's ever-evolving ability to "read" other's moods, for example, may take a lifetime to develop fully. Other developments are faster and more focused, like a person's increasing skill at solving crossword puzzles. The faster and simpler is the change, the more likely we are to call the change "learning" instead of development. The difference between *learning* and *development* is a matter of degree. When a child learns to name the planets of the solar system, for example, the child may not need a lot of time, nor does the learning involve a multitude of experiences. So it is probably better to think of that particular experience—learning to name the planets—as an example of *learning* rather than of *development* (Salkind, 2004; Lewis, 1997).

Why development matters

Students' development matters for teachers, but the *way* it matters depends partly on how schooling is organized. In teaching a single, "self-contained" grade-level, the benefits of knowing about development will be less explicit, but just as real, as if you teach many grade levels. Working exclusively with a single grade (like, say, a third-grade classroom) highlights *differences* among students that happen *in spite of* their similar ages, and obscures *similarities* that happen *because of* having similar ages. Under these conditions it is still easy to notice students' diversity, but harder to know how much of it comes from differences in long-term development, compared to differences in short-term experiences. Knowledge about long term changes is still useful, however, in planning appropriate activities and in holding appropriate expectations about students. What changes in students can you expect relatively soon simply from your current program of activities, and which ones may take a year or more to show up? This is a question that developmental psychology can help to answer.

If you teach multiple grade levels, as often is true of specialists or teachers in middle school or high school, then your need for developmental knowledge will be more obvious because you will confront wide age differences on a daily basis. As a physical education teacher, for example, you may teach kindergarten children at one time during the day, but sixth-graders at another time, or teach seventh-graders at one time but twelfth-graders at another. Students will differ more obviously because of age, in addition to differing because of other factors like their skills or knowledge learned recently. Nonetheless, the instructional challenge will be the same as the one faced by teachers of single-grade classes: you will want to know what activities and expectations are appropriate for your students. To answer this question, you will need to know something not only about how your students are unique, but also about general trends of development during childhood and adolescence.

Note that developmental trends vary in two important ways. The first, as indicated already, is in their generality. Some theories or models of development boldly assert that certain changes happen to virtually every person on the planet, and often at relatively predictable points in life. For example, a theory might assert that virtually *every* toddler acquires a spoken language, or that *every* teenager forms a sense of personal identity. Individuals who do not experience these developments would be rare, though not necessarily disabled as a result. Other theories propose developmental changes that are more limited, claiming only that the changes happen to *some* people or only under certain conditions. Developing a female gender role, for example, does not happen to everyone, but only to the females in a population, and the details vary according to the family, community, or society in which a child lives.

The second way that developmental trends vary is in how strictly they are sequenced and hierarchical. In some views of development, changes are thought to happen in a specific order and to build on each other—sort of a "staircase" model of development (Case, 1991, 1996). For example, a developmental psychologist (and many of the rest of us) might argue that young people must have tangible, hands-on experience with new materials before they can reason about the materials in the abstract. The order cannot be reversed. In other views of development, change happens, but not with a sequence or end point that is uniform. This sort of change is more like a "kaleidoscope" than a staircase (Levinson, 1990; Lewis, 1997; Harris, 2006). A person who becomes permanently disabled, for example, may experience complex long-term changes in personal values and priorities that are different both in timing and content from most people's developmental pathway.

In general, educational psychologists have tended to emphasize explanations of development that are relatively general, universal and sequential, rather than specific to particular cultures or that are unsequenced and kaleidoscopic (see, for example, Woolfolk, 2006, Chapter 3; or Slavin, 2005, Chapters 8 and 9). Such models (sometimes called "grand theories") have the advantage of concisely integrating many features of development, while also describing the kind of people children or adolescents usually end up to be. The preference for integrative perspectives makes sense given educators' need to work with and teach large numbers of diverse students both efficiently and effectively. But the approach also risks *over*generalizing or *over*simplifying the experiences of particular children and youth. It can also confuse what *does* happen as certain children (like the middle-class ones) develop with what *should* happen to children. To understand this point, imagine two children of about the same age who have dramatically very different childhood experiences—for example, one who grows up in poverty and another who grows up financially well-off. In what sense can we say that these two children experience the *same* underlying developmental changes as they grow up? And how much should they even be expected to do so? Developmental psychology, and especially the broad theories of developmental psychology, highlight the "sameness" or common ground between these two children. As such, it serves as counterpoint to knowledge of their obvious uniqueness, and places their uniqueness in broader perspective.

Physical development during the school years

Although it may be tempting to think that physical development is the concern of physical education teachers only, it is actually a foundation for many academic tasks. In first grade, for example, it is important to know whether children can successfully manipulate a pencil. In later grades, it is important to know how long students can be expected to sit still without discomfort—a real physical challenge. In all grades, it is important to have a sense of students' health needs related to their age or maturity, if only to know who may become ill, and with what illness, and to know what physical activities are reasonable and needed.

Trends in height and weight

Typical height and weight for well-nourished, healthy students are shown in Table 9. The figure shows averages for several ages from preschool through the end of high school. But the table does not show the diversity among children. At age 6, for example, when children begin school, the average boy or girl is about 115 centimeters tall, but some are 109 and others are 125 centimeters. Average weight at age 6 is about 20 kilograms, but ranges between about 16 and 24 kilograms—about 20% variation in either direction.

Table 5: Average height and weight of well-nourished children

Age	Height (cm)	Weight (kg)
2	85	7.0
6	115	20.0
10	135	31.0
14	162	52.0
18	169	60.5

3. Student development

There are other points to keep in mind about average height and weight that are not evident from Table 9. The first is that boys and girls, on average, are quite similar in height and weight during childhood, but diverge in the early teenage years, when they reach puberty. For a time (approximately age 10-14), the average girl is taller, but not much heavier, than the average boy. After that the average boy becomes both taller and heavier than the average girl—though there remain individual exceptions (Malina, et al., 2004). The pre-teen difference can therefore be awkward for some children and youth, at least among those who aspire to looking like older teenagers or young adults. For young teens less concerned with "image", though, the fact that girls are taller may not be especially important, or even noticed (Friedman, 2000).

A second point is that as children get older, individual differences in weight diverge more radically than differences in height. Among 18-year-olds, the heaviest youngsters weigh almost twice as much as the lightest, but the tallest ones are only about 10 per cent taller than the shortest. Nonetheless, both height and weight can be sensitive issues for some teenagers. Most modern societies (and the teenagers in them) tend to favor relatively short women and tall men, as well as a somewhat thin body build, especially for girls and women. Yet neither "socially correct" height nor thinness is the destiny for many individuals. Being overweight, in particular, has become a common, serious problem in modern society (Tartamella, et al., 2004) due to the prevalence of diets high in fat and lifestyles low in activity. The educational system has unfortunately contributed to the problem as well, by gradually restricting the number of physical education courses and classes in the past two decades.

The third point to keep in mind is that average height and weight is related somewhat to racial and ethnic background. In general, children of Asian background tend to be slightly shorter than children of European and North American background. The latter in turn tend to be shorter than children from African societies (Eveleth & Tanner, 1990). Body shape differs slightly as well, though the differences are not always visible until after puberty. Asian youth tend to have arms and legs that are a bit short relative to their torsos, and African youth tend to have relatively long arms and legs. The differences are only *averages;* there are large individual differences as well, and these tend to be more relevant for teachers to know about than broad group differences.

Puberty and its effects on students

A universal physical development in students is **puberty,** which is the set of changes in early adolescence that bring about sexual maturity. Along with internal changes in reproductive organs are outward changes such as growth of breasts in girls and the penis in boys, as well as relatively sudden increases in height and weight. By about age 10 or 11, most children experience increased sexual attraction to others (usually heterosexual, though not always) that affects social life both in school and out (McClintock & Herdt, 1996). By the end of high school, more than half of boys and girls report having experienced sexual intercourse at least once—though it is hard to be certain of the proportion because of the sensitivity and privacy of the information. (Center for Disease Control, 2004b; Rosenbaum, 2006).

At about the same time that puberty accentuates gender, role differences also accentuate for at least some teenagers. Some girls who excelled at math or science in elementary school may curb their enthusiasm and displays of success at these subjects for fear of limiting their popularity or attractiveness as girls (Taylor & Gilligan, 1995; Sadker, 2004). Some boys who were not especially interested in sports previously may begin dedicating themselves to athletics to affirm their masculinity in the eyes of others. Some boys and girls who once worked together

44

successfully on class projects may no longer feel comfortable doing so—or alternatively may now seek to be working partners, but for social rather than academic reasons. Such changes do not affect all youngsters equally, nor affect any one youngster equally on all occasions. An individual student may act like a young adult on one day, but more like a child the next. When teaching children who are experiencing puberty, , teachers need to respond flexibly and supportively.

Development of motor skills

Students' fundamental motor skills are already developing when they begin kindergarten, but are not yet perfectly coordinated. Five-year-olds generally can walk satisfactorily for most school-related purposes (if they could not, schools would have to be organized very differently!). For some fives, running still looks a bit like a hurried walk, but usually it becomes more coordinated within a year or two. Similarly with jumping, throwing, and catching: most children can do these things, though often clumsily, by the time they start school, but improve their skills noticeably during the early elementary years (Payne & Isaacs, 2005). Assisting such developments is usually the job either of physical education teachers, where they exist, or else of classroom teachers during designated physical education activities. Whoever is responsible, it is important to notice if a child does not keep more-or-less to the usual developmental timetable, and to arrange for special assessment or supports if appropriate. Common procedures for arranging for help are described in Chapter 5 ("Special education").

Even if physical skills are not a special focus of a classroom teacher,, they can be quite important to students themselves. Whatever their grade level, students who are clumsy are aware of that fact and how it could potentially negatively effect respect from their peers. In the long term, self-consciousness and poor self-esteem can develop for a child who is clumsy, especially if peers (or teachers and parents) place high value on success in athletics. One research study found, for example, what teachers and coaches sometimes suspect: that losers in athletic competitions tend to become less sociable and are more apt to miss subsequent athletic practices than winners (Petlichkoff, 1996).

Health and illness

By world standards, children and youth in economically developed societies tend, on average, to be remarkably healthy. Even so, much depends on precisely how well-off families are and on how much health care is available to them. Children from higher-income families experience far fewer serious or life-threatening illnesses than children fromlower-income families. Whatever their income level, parents and teachers often rightly note that children—especially the youngest ones—get far more illnesses than do adults. In 2004, for example, a government survey estimated that children get an average of 6-10 colds per year, but adults get only about 2-4 per year (National Institute of Allergies and Infectious Diseases, 2004). The difference probably exists because children's immune systems are not as fully formed as adults', and because children at school are continually exposed to other children, many of whom may be contagious themselves. An indirect result of children's frequent illnesses is that teachers (along with airline flight attendants, incidentally!) also report more frequent minor illnesses than do adults in general—about five colds per year, for example, instead of just 2-4 (Whelen, et al., 2005). The "simple" illnesses are not life threatening, but they are responsible for many lost days of school, both for students and for teachers, as well as days when a student may be present physically, but functions below par while simultaneously infecting classmates. In these ways, learning and teaching often suffer because health is suffering.

3. Student development

The problem is not only the prevalence of illness as such (in winter, even in the United States, approximately one person gets infected with a minor illness every few *seconds)*, but the fact that illnesses are not distributed uniformly among students, schools, or communities. Whether it is a simple cold or something more serious, illness is particularly common where living conditions are crowded, where health care is scarce or unaffordable, and where individuals live with frequent stresses of any kind. Often, but not always, these are the circumstances of poverty. Table 6 summarizes these effects for a variety of health problems, not just for colds or flu.

Table 6: Health effects of children's economic level

Health program	Comparison: poor vs non-poor
Delayed immunizations	3 times higher
Asthma	Somewhat higher
Lead poisoning	3 times higher
Deaths in childhood from accidents	2-3 times higher
Deaths in childhood from disease	3-4 times higher
Having a condition that limits school activity	2-3 times higher
Days sick in bed	40 per cent higher
Seriously impaired vision	2-3 times higher
Severe iron-deficiency (anemia)	2 times higher
Source: Richardson, J> (2005). *The Cost of Being Poor*. New York: Praeger. Spencer, N. (2000). *Poverty and Child Health*, 2nd edition. Abington, UK: Radcliffe Medical Press. Allender, J. (2005). *Community Health Nursing*. Philadelphia: Lippinsott, Williams & Wilkins.	

As students get older, illnesses become less frequent, but other health risks emerge. The most widespread is the consumption of alcohol and the smoking of cigarettes. As of 2004, about 75 per cent of teenagers reported drinking an alcoholic beverage at least occasionally, and 22 per cent reported smoking cigarettes (Center for Disease Control, 2004a). The good news is that these proportions show a small, but steady *decline* in the frequencies over the past 10 years or so. The bad news is that teenagers also show *increases* in the abuse of some prescription drugs, such as inhalants, that act as stimulants (Johnston, et al., 2006). As with the prevalence of illnesses, the prevalence of drug use is not uniform, with a relatively small fraction of individuals accounting for a disproportionate proportion of usage. One survey, for example, found that a teenager was 3-5 times more likely to smoke or to use alcohol, smoke marijuana, or use drugs if he or she has a *sibling* who has also indulged these habits (Fagan & Najman, 2005). Siblings, it seems, are more influential in this case than parents.

Cognitive development: the theory of Jean Piaget

Cognition refers to thinking and memory processes, and **cognitive development** refers to long-term changes in these processes. One of the most widely known perspectives about cognitive development is the cognitive stage theory of a Swiss psychologist named **Jean Piaget.** Piaget created and studied an account of how children and youth gradually become able to think logically and scientifically. Because his theory is especially popular among educators, we focus on it in this chapter. We will look at other cognitive perspectives—ones that are not as fully "developmental", in later chapters, especially Chapter 9 ("Facilitating complex thinking").

In brief comments in Chapter 2 (see "Psychological constructivism") about how Piaget explained learning, we described Piaget as a *psychological constructivist:* in his view, learning proceeded by the interplay of assimilation (adjusting new experiences to fit prior concepts) and accommodation (adjusting concepts to fit new experiences). The to-and-fro of these two processes leads not only to short-term learning, as pointed out in Chapter 1, but also to long-term *developmental change*. The long-term developments are really the main focus of Piaget's cognitive theory.

After observing children closely, Piaget proposed that cognition developed through distinct stages from birth through the end of adolescence. By stages he meant a sequence of thinking patterns with four key features:

1. They always happen in the same order.

2. No stage is ever skipped.

3. Each stage is a significant transformation of the stage before it.

4. Each later stage incorporated the earlier stages into itself. Basically this is the "staircase" model of development mentioned at the beginning of this chapter. Piaget proposed four major stages of cognitive development, and called them (1) sensorimotor intelligence, (2) preoperational thinking, (3) concrete operational thinking, and (4) formal operational thinking. Each stage is correlated with an age period of childhood, but only approximately.

The sensorimotor stage: birth to age 2

In Piaget's theory, the **sensorimotor stage** is first, and is defined as the period when infants "think" by means of their senses and motor actions. As every new parent will attest, infants continually touch, manipulate, look, listen to, and even bite and chew objects. According to Piaget, these actions allow them to learn about the world and are crucial to their early cognitive development.

The infant's actions allow the child to represent (or construct simple concepts of) objects and events. A toy animal may be just a confusing array of sensations at first, but by looking, feeling, and manipulating it repeatedly, the child gradually organizes her sensations and actions into a stable concept, *toy animal*. The representation acquires a permanence lacking in the individual experiences of the object, which are constantly changing. Because the representation is stable, the child "knows", or at least believes, that *toy animal* exists even if the actual toy animal is temporarily out of sight. Piaget called this sense of stability **object permanence,** a belief that objects exist whether or not they are actually present. It is a major achievement of sensorimotor development, and marks a qualitative transformation in how older infants (24 months) think about experience compared to younger infants (6 months).

During much of infancy, of course, a child can only barely talk, so sensorimotor development initially happens without the support of language. It might therefore seem hard to know what infants are thinking, but Piaget devised several simple, but clever experiments to get around their lack of language, and that suggest that infants do indeed represent objects even without being able to talk (Piaget, 1952). In one, for example, he simply hid an object (like a toy animal) under a blanket. He found that doing so consistently prompts older infants (18-24 months) to search for the object, but fails to prompt younger infants (less than six months) to do so. (You can try this experiment yourself if you happen to have access to young infant.) "Something" motivates the search by the older infant even without the benefit of much language, and the "something" is presumed to be a permanent concept or representation of the object.

The preoperational stage: age 2 to 7

In the **preoperational stage,** children use their new ability to represent objects in a wide variety of activities, but they do not yet do it in ways that are organized or fully logical. One of the most obvious examples of this kind of cognition is **dramatic play,** the improvised make-believe of preschool children. If you have ever had responsibility for children of this age, you have likely witnessed such play. Ashley holds a plastic banana to her ear and says: "Hello, Mom? Can you be sure to bring me my baby doll? OK!" Then she hangs up the banana and pours tea for Jeremy into an invisible cup. Jeremy giggles at the sight of all of this and exclaims: "Rinnng! Oh Ashley, the phone is ringing again! You better answer it." And on it goes.

In a way, children immersed in make-believe seem "mentally insane", in that they do not think realistically. But they are not truly insane because they have not really taken leave of their senses. At some level, Ashley and Jeremy always know that the banana is still a banana and not *really* a telephone; they are merely *representing* it as a telephone. They are thinking on two levels at once—one imaginative and the other realistic. This dual processing of experience makes dramatic play an early example of **metacognition,** or reflecting on and monitoring of thinking itself. As we explained in Chapter 2, metacognition is a highly desirable skill for success in school, one that teachers often encourage (Bredekamp & Copple, 1997; Paley, 2005). Partly for this reason, teachers of young children (preschool, kindergarten, and even first or second grade) often make time and space in their classrooms for dramatic play, and sometimes even participate in it themselves to help develop the play further.

The concrete operational stage: age 7 to 11

As children continue into elementary school, they become able to represent ideas and events more flexibly and logically. Their rules of thinking still seem very basic by adult standards and usually operate unconsciously, but they allow children to solve problems more systematically than before, and therefore to be successful with many academic tasks. In the concrete operational stage, for example, a child may unconsciously follow the rule: "If nothing is added or taken away, then the amount of something stays the same." This simple principle helps children to understand certain arithmetic tasks, such as in adding or subtracting zero from a number, as well as to do certain classroom science experiments, such as ones involving judgments of the amounts of liquids when mixed. Piaget called this period the **concrete operational stage** because children mentally "operate" on concrete objects and events. They are not yet able, however, to operate (or think) systematically about *representations* of objects or events. Manipulating representations is a more abstract skill that develops later, during adolescence.

Concrete operational thinking differs from preoperational thinking in two ways, each of which renders children more skilled as students. One difference is **reversibility,** or the ability to think about the steps of a process in any order. Imagine a simple science experiment, for example, such as one that explores why objects sink or float by having a child place an assortment of objects in a basin of water. Both the preoperational and concrete operational child can recall and describe the steps in this experiment, but only the concrete operational child can recall them *in any order*. This skill is very helpful on any task involving multiple steps—a common feature of tasks in the classroom. In teaching new vocabulary from a story, for another example, a teacher might tell students: "First make a list of words in the story that you do not know, then find and write down their definitions, and finally get a friend to test you on your list". These directions involve repeatedly remembering to move back and forth between a second step and a first—a task that concrete operational students—and most adults—find easy, but that preoperational children often forget to do or find confusing. If the younger children are to do this task reliably, they may need external prompts, such as having the teacher remind them periodically to go back to the story to look for more unknown words.

The other new feature of thinking during the concrete operational stage is the child's ability to **decenter,** or focus on more than one feature of a problem at a time. There are hints of decentration in preschool children's dramatic play, which requires being aware on two levels at once—knowing that a banana can be both a banana and a "telephone". But the decentration of the concrete operational stage is more deliberate and conscious than preschoolers' make-believe. Now the child can attend to two things at once quite purposely. Suppose you give students a sheet with an assortment of subtraction problems on it, and ask them to do this: "Find all of the problems that involve two-digit subtraction *and* that involve borrowing' from the next column. Circle and solve *only* those problems." Following these instructions is quite possible for a concrete operational student (as long as they have been listening!) because the student can attend to the two subtasks simultaneously—finding the two-digit problems *and* identifying which actually involve borrowing. (Whether the student actually knows how to "borrow" however, is a separate question.)

In real classroom tasks, reversibility and decentration often happen together. A well-known example of joint presence is Piaget's experiments with **conservation,** the belief that an amount or quantity stays the same even if it changes apparent size or shape (Piaget, 2001; Matthews, 1998). Imagine two identical balls made of clay. Any child, whether preoperational or concrete operational, will agree that the two indeed have the same amount of clay in them simply because they look the same. But if you now squish one ball into a long, thin "hot dog", the preoperational child is likely to say that the amount of that ball has changed—either because it is longer or because it is thinner, but at any rate because it now looks different. The concrete operational child will not make this mistake, thanks to new cognitive skills of reversibility and decentration: for him or her, the amount is the same because "you could squish it back into a ball again" (reversibility) and because "it may be longer, but it is also thinner" (decentration). Piaget would say the concrete operational child "has conservation of quantity".

The classroom examples described above also involve reversibility and decentration. As already mentioned, the vocabulary activity described earlier requires reversibility (going back and forth between identifying words and looking up their meanings); but it can also be construed as an example of decentration (keeping in mind two tasks at once—word identification *and* dictionary search). And as mentioned, the arithmetic activity requires decentration (looking for problems that meet two criteria *and* also solving them), but it can also be construed as an example of reversibility (going back and forth between subtasks, as with the vocabulary activity). Either way, the development of concrete operational skills support students in doing many basic academic tasks; in a sense they make ordinary schoolwork possible.

The formal operational stage: age 11 and beyond

In the last of the Piagetian stages, the child becomes able to reason not only about tangible objects and events, but also about hypothetical or abstract ones. Hence it has the name **formal operational stage**—the period when the individual can "operate" on "forms" or representations. With students at this level, the teacher can pose hypothetical (or contrary-to-fact) problems: "What *if* the world had never discovered oil?" or "What *if* the first European explorers had settled first in California instead of on the East Coast of the United States?" To answer such questions, students must use **hypothetical reasoning,** meaning that they must manipulate ideas that vary in several ways at once, and do so entirely in their minds.

The hypothetical reasoning that concerned Piaget primarily involved scientific problems. His studies of formal operational thinking therefore often look like problems that middle or high school teachers pose in science classes. In one problem, for example, a young person is presented with a simple pendulum, to which different amounts of weight can be hung (Inhelder & Piaget, 1958). The experimenter asks: "What determines how fast the pendulum swings: the length of the string holding it, the weight attached to it, or the distance that it is pulled to the side?" The young person is not allowed to solve this problem by trial-and-error with the materials themselves, but must reason a way to the solution mentally. To do so systematically, he or she must imagine varying each factor separately, while also imagining the other factors that are held constant. This kind of thinking requires facility at manipulating mental representations of the relevant objects and actions—precisely the skill that defines formal operations.

As you might suspect, students with an ability to think hypothetically have an advantage in many kinds of school work: by definition, they require relatively few "props" to solve problems. In this sense they can in principle be more self-directed than students who rely only on concrete operations—certainly a desirable quality in the opinion of most teachers. Note, though, that formal operational thinking is desirable but not *sufficient* for school success, and that it is far from being the only way that students achieve educational success. Formal thinking skills do not insure that a student is motivated or well-behaved, for example, nor does it guarantee other desirable skills, such as ability at sports, music, or art. The fourth stage in Piaget's theory is really about a particular kind of formal thinking, the kind needed to solve scientific problems and devise scientific experiments. Since many people do not normally deal with such problems in the normal course of their lives, it should be no surprise that research finds that many people never achieve or use formal thinking fully or consistently, or that they use it only in selected areas with which they are very familiar (Case & Okomato, 1996). For teachers, the limitations of Piaget's ideas suggest a need for additional theories about development—ones that focus more directly on the social and interpersonal issues of childhood and adolescence. The next sections describe some of these.

Social development: relationships, personal motives, and morality

Social development refers to the long-term changes in relationships and interactions involving self, peers, and family. It includes both positive changes, such as how friendships develop, and negative changes, such as aggression or bullying. The social developments that are the most obviously relevant to classroom life fall into three main areas: (1) changes in self-concept and in relationships among students and teachers, (2) changes in basic needs or personal motives, and (3) changes in sense of rights and responsibilities. As with cognitive development, each of these areas has a broad, well-known theory (and theorist) that provides a framework for thinking about how the area relates to teaching. For development of self-concept and relationships, it is the theory of **Erik Erikson;** for development of personal motives, it is the theory of **Abraham Maslow;** and for development of ethical knowledge and beliefs, it is the work of **Lawrence Kohlberg** and his critic, **Carol Gilligan.** Their theories are definitely not the only ones related to social development of students, and their ideas are often debated by other researchers. But their accounts do explain much about social development that is relevant to teaching and education.

Erik Erikson: eight psychosocial crises of development

Like Piaget, Erik Erikson developed a theory of social development that relies on stages, except that Erikson thought of stages as a series of psychological or social (or **psychosocial**) **crises**—turning points in a person's relationships and feelings about himself or herself (Erikson, 1963, 1980). Each crisis consists of a dilemma or choice that carries both advantages and risks, but in which one choice or alternative is normally considered more desirable or "healthy". How one crisis is resolved affects how later crises are resolved. The resolution also helps to create an individual's developing personality. Erikson proposed eight crises that extend from birth through old age; they are summarized in Table 7. Four of the stages occur during the school years, so we give these special attention here, but it is helpful also to know what crises are thought to come both before and after those in the school years.

Table 7: Eight psychosocial crises according to Erikson

Psychosocial crisis	Approximate age	Description
Trust and mistrust	Birth to one year	Development of trust between caregiver and child
Autonomy and shame	Age 1-3	Development of control over bodily functions and activities
Initiative and guilt	Age 3-6	Testing limits of self-assertion and purposefulness
Industry and inferiority	Age 6-12	Development of sense of mastery and competence
Identity and role confusion	Age 12-19	Development of identity and acknowledge of identity by others
Intimacy and isolation	Age 19-25+	Formation of intimate relationships and commitments
Generativity and stagnation	Age 25-50+	Development of creative or productive activities that contribute to future generations
Integrity and despair	Age 50+	Acceptance of personal life history and forgiveness of self and others

Crises of infants and preschoolers: trust, autonomy, and initiative

Almost from the day they are born, infants face a crisis (in Erikson's sense) about **trust and mistrust.** They are happiest if they can eat, sleep, and excrete according to their own physiological schedules, regardless of whether their schedules are convenient for the caregiver (often the mother). Unfortunately, though, a young infant is in no position to control or influence a mother's care giving or scheduling needs; so the baby faces a dilemma about how much to *trust* or *mistrust* the mother's helpfulness. It is as if the baby asks, "If I demand food (or sleep or a clean diaper) *now*, will my mother actually be able to help me meet this need?" Hopefully, between the two of them, mother and child resolve this choice in favor of the baby's trust: the mother proves herself at least "good enough" in her attentiveness, and the baby risks trusting mother's motivation and skill at care giving.

Almost as soon as this crisis is resolved, however, a new one develops over the issue of **autonomy and shame.** The child (who is now a toddler) may now trust his or her caregiver (mother), but the very trust contributes to a desire to assert *autonomy* by taking care of basic personal needs, such as feeding, toileting, or dressing. Given the child's lack of experience in these activities, however, self-care is risky at first—the toddler may feed (or toilet or dress) clumsily and ineffectively. The child's caregiver, for her part, risks overprotecting the child and criticizing his early efforts unnecessarily and thus causing the child to feel *shame* for even trying. Hopefully, as with the earlier crisis of trust, the new crisis gets resolved in favor of autonomy through the combined efforts of the child to exercise autonomy and of the caregiver to support the child's efforts.

Eventually, about the time a child is of preschool age, the autonomy exercised during the previous period becomes more elaborate, extended, and focused on objects and people other than the child and basic physical needs. The child at a day care center may now undertake, for example, to build the "biggest city in the world" out of all available unit blocks—even if other children want some of the blocks for themselves. The child's projects and desires create a new crisis of **initiative and guilt,** because the child soon realizes that acting on impulses or desires can sometimes have negative effects on others—more blocks for the child may mean fewer for someone else. As with the crisis over autonomy, caregivers have to support the child's initiatives where possible, but also not make the child feel guilty just for *desiring* to have or to do something that affects others' welfare. By limiting behavior where necessary but not limiting internal feelings, the child can develop a lasting ability to take initiative. Expressed in Erikson's terms, the crisis is then resolved in favor of initiative.

Even though only the last of these three crises overlaps with the school years, all three relate to issues faced by students of any age, and even by their teachers. A child or youth who is fundamentally mistrustful, for example, has a serious problem in coping with school life. If you are a student, it is essential for your long-term survival to believe that teachers and school officials have your best interests at heart, and that they are not imposing assignments or making rules, for example, "just for the heck of it." Even though students are not infants any more, teachers function like Erikson's caregiving parents in that they need to prove worthy of students' trust through their initial flexibility and attentiveness.

Parallels from the classroom also exist for the crises of autonomy and of initiative. To learn effectively, students need to make choices and undertake academic initiatives at least some of the time, even though not every choice or initiative may be practical or desirable. Teachers, for their part, need to make true choices and initiatives possible, and refrain from criticizing, even accidentally, a choice or intention behind an initiative even if the teacher privately believes that it is "bound to fail". Support for choices and initiative should be focused on providing resources and on guiding the student's efforts toward more likely success. In these ways teachers function like parents of toddlers and preschoolers in Erikson's theory of development, regardless of the age of their students.

The crisis of childhood: industry and inferiority

Once into elementary school, the child is faced for the first time with becoming competent and worthy in the eyes of the world at large, or more precisely in the eyes of classmates and teachers. To achieve their esteem, he or she must develop skills that require effort that is sustained and somewhat focused. The challenge creates the crisis of **industry and inferiority.** To be respected by teachers, for example, the child must learn to read and to behave like a "true student". To be respected by peers, he or she must learn to cooperate and to be friendly, among other things. There are risks involved in working on these skills and qualities, because there can be no guarantee of success with them in advance. If the child does succeed, therefore, he or she experiences the satisfaction of a job well done and of skills well learned—a feeling that Erikson called *industry*. If not, however, the child risks feeling lasting *inferiority* compared to others. Teachers therefore have a direct, explicit role in helping students to resolve this crisis in favor of *industry* or success. They can set realistic academic goals for students—ones that tend to lead to success—and then provide materials and assistance for students to reach their goals. Teachers can also express their confidence that students can in fact meet their goals if and when the students get discouraged, and avoid hinting (even accidentally) that a student is simply a "loser". Paradoxically, these strategies will work best if the teacher is also tolerant of less-than-perfect performance by students. Too much emphasis on perfection can undermine some students' confidence—foster Erikson's *inferiority*—by making academic goals seem beyond reach.

The crisis of adolescence: identity and role confusion

As the child develops lasting talents and attitudes as a result of the crisis of industry, he begins to face a new question: what do all the talents and attitudes add up to be? Who is the "me" embedded in this profile of qualities? These questions are the crisis of **identity and role confusion.** Defining identity is riskier than it may appear for a person simply because some talents and attitudes may be poorly developed, and some even may be undesirable in the eyes of others. (If you are poor at math, how do you live with family and friends if they think you should be good at this skill?) Still others may be valuable but fail to be noticed by other people. The result is that who a person wants to be may not be the same as who he or she is in actual fact, nor the same as who other people want the person to be. In Erikson's terms, *role confusion* is the result.

Teachers can minimize role confusion in a number of ways. One is to offer students lots of diverse role models—by identifying models in students' reading materials, for example, or by inviting diverse guests to school. The point of these strategies would be to express a key idea: that there are many ways to be respected, successful, and satisfied with life. Another way to support students' identity development is to be alert to students' confusions about their futures, and refer them to counselors or other services outside school that can help sort these out. Still another strategy is to tolerate changes in students' goals and priorities—sudden changes in extra-curricular activities or in personal plans after graduation. Since students are still trying roles out, discouraging experimentation may not be in students' best interests.

The crises of adulthood: intimacy, generativity, and integrity

Beyond the school years, according to Erikson, individuals continue psychosocial development by facing additional crises. Young adults, for example, face a crisis of **intimacy and isolation.** This crisis is about the risk of establishing close relationships with a select number of others. Whether the relationships are heterosexual, homosexual, or not sexual at all, their defining qualities are depth and sustainability. Without them, an individual risks feeling isolated. Assuming that a person resolves this crisis in favor of intimacy, however, he or she then faces a crisis about **generativity and stagnation.** This crisis is characteristic of most of adulthood, and not surprisingly therefore is about caring for or making a contribution to society, and especially to its younger generation. Generativity is about making life productive and creative so that it matters to others. One obvious way for some to achieve this feeling is by raising children, but there are also many other ways to contribute to the welfare of others. The final crisis is about **integrity and despair,** and is characteristically felt during the final years of life. At the end of life, a person is likely to review the past and to ask whether it has been lived as well as possible, even if it was clearly not lived perfectly. Since personal history can no longer be altered at the end of life, it is important to make peace with what actually happened and to forgive oneself and others for mistakes that may have been made. The alternative is *despair,* or depression from believing not only that one's life was lived badly, but also that there is no longer any hope of correcting past mistakes.

Even though Erikson conceives of these crises as primarily concerns of adulthood, there are precursors of them during the school years. Intimacy, for example, is a concern of many children and youth in that they often desire, but do not always find, lasting relationships with others (Beidel, 2005; Zimbardo & Radl, 1999). Personal isolation is a particular risk for students with disabilities, as well as for students whose cultural or racial backgrounds differ from classmates' or the teacher's. Generativity—feeling helpful to others and to the young—is needed not only by many adults, but also by many children and youth; when given the opportunity as part of their school program, they frequently welcome a chance to be of authentic service to others as part of their school programs (Eyler & Giles, 1999; Kay, 2003). Integrity—taking responsibility for your personal past, "warts and all", is often a felt need for anyone, young or old, who has lived long enough to have a past on which to look. Even children and youth have a past in this sense, though their pasts are of course shorter than persons who are older.

Abraham Maslow: a hierarchy of motives and needs

Abraham Maslow's theory frames personal needs or motives as a hierarchy, meaning that basic or "lower-level" needs have to be satisfied before higher-level needs become important or motivating (1976, 1987). Compared to the stage models of Piaget and Erikson, Maslow's hierarchy is only loosely "developmental", in that Maslow was not concerned with tracking universal, irreversible changes across the lifespan. Maslow's stages are universal, but they are not irreversible; earlier stages sometimes reappear later in life, in which case they must be satisfied again before later stages can redevelop. Like the theories of Piaget and Erikson, Maslow's is a rather broad "story", one that has less to say about the effects of a person's culture, language, or economic level, than about what we all have in common.

In its original version, Maslow's theory distinguishes two types of needs, called **deficit needs** and **being needs** (or sometimes *deficiency needs* and *growth needs)*. Table 8 summarizes the two levels and their sublevels. Deficit needs are prior to being needs, not in the sense of happening earlier in life, but in that deficit needs must be satisfied *before* being needs can be addressed. As pointed out, deficit needs can reappear at any age, depending on circumstances. If that happens, they must be satisfied again before a person's attention can shift back to "higher" needs. Among students, in fact, deficit needs are likely to return chronically to those whose families lack economic or social resources or who live with the stresses associated with poverty (Payne, 2005).

Table 8: Maslow's hierarchy of motives and needs

Deficit Needs	Physiological needs
	Safety and security needs
	Love and belonging needs
	Cognitive needs

| Being Needs | Aesthetic needs |
| | Self-actualization needs |

Deficit needs: getting the basic necessities of life

Deficit needs are the basic requirements of physical and emotional well-being. First are *physiological needs*—food, sleep, clothing, and the like. Without these, nothing else matters, and especially nothing very "elevated" or self-fulfilling. A student who is not getting enough to eat is not going to feel much interest in learning! Once physiological needs are met, however, *safety and security needs* become important. The person looks for stability and protection, and welcomes a bit of structure and limits if they provide these conditions. A child from an abusive family, for example, may be getting enough to eat, but may worry chronically about personal safety. In school, the student may appreciate a well-organized classroom with rules that insures personal safety and predictability, whether or not the classroom provides much in the way of real learning.

After physiological and safety needs are met, *love and belonging needs* emerge. The person turns attention to making friends, being a friend, and cultivating positive personal relationships in general. In the classroom, a student motivated at this level may make approval from peers or teachers into a top priority. He or she may be provided for materially and find the classroom and family life safe enough, but still miss a key ingredient in life—love. If such a student (or anyone else) eventually does find love and belonging, however, then his or her motivation shifts again, this time to *esteem needs*. Now the concern is with gaining recognition and respect—and even more importantly, gaining self-respect. A student at this level may be unusually concerned with achievement, for example, though only if the achievement is visible or public enough to earn public recognition.

Being needs: becoming the best that you can be

Being needs are desires to become fulfilled as a person, or to be the best person that you can possibly be. They include *cognitive needs* (a desire for knowledge and understanding), *aesthetic needs* (an appreciation of beauty and order), and most importantly, *self-actualization needs* (a desire for fulfillment of one's potential). Being needs emerge only after all of a person's deficit needs have been largely met. Unlike deficit needs, being needs beget more being needs; they do not disappear once they are met, but create a desire for even more satisfaction of the same type. A thirst for knowledge, for example, leads to further thirst for knowledge, and aesthetic appreciation leads to more aesthetic appreciation. Partly because being needs are lasting and permanent once they appear, Maslow sometimes treated them as less hierarchical than deficit needs, and instead grouped cognitive, aesthetic, and self-actualization needs into the single category *self-actualization needs*.

People who are motivated by self-actualization have a variety of positive qualities, which Maslow went to some lengths to identify and describe (Maslow, 1976). Self-actualizing individuals, he argued, value deep personal relationships with others, but also value solitude; they have a sense of humor, but do not use it against others; they accept themselves as well as others; they are spontaneous, humble, creative, and ethical. In short, the self-actualizing person has just about every good quality imaginable! Not surprisingly, therefore, Maslow felt that true self-actualization is rare. It is especially unusual among young people, who have not yet lived long enough to satisfy earlier, deficit-based needs.

In a way this last point is discouraging news for teachers, who apparently must spend their lives providing as best they can for individuals—students—still immersed in deficit needs. Teachers, it seems, have little hope of ever meeting a student with fully fledged being needs. Taken less literally, though, Maslow's hierarchy is still useful for thinking about students' motives. Most teachers would argue that students—young though they are—*can* display positive qualities similar to the ones described in Maslow's self-actualizing person. However annoying students may sometimes be, there are also moments when they show care and respect for others, for example, and moments when they show spontaneity, humility, or a sound ethical sense. Self-actualization is an appropriate way to think about these moments—the times when students are at their best. At the same time, of course, students sometimes also have deficit needs. Keeping in mind the entire hierarchy outlined by Maslow can therefore deepen teachers' understanding of the full humanity of students.

Moral development: forming a sense of rights and responsibilities

Morality is a system of beliefs about what is right and good compared to what is wrong or bad. **Moral development** refers to changes in moral beliefs as a person grows older and gains maturity. Moral beliefs are related to, but not identical with, moral *behavior:* it is possible to know the right thing to do, but not actually do it. It is also not the same as knowledge of *social conventions,* which are arbitrary customs needed for the smooth operation of society. Social conventions may have a moral element, but they have a primarily practical purpose. Conventionally, for example, motor vehicles all keep to the same side of the street (to the right in the United States, to the left in Great Britain). The convention allows for smooth, accident-free flow of traffic. But following the convention also has a moral element, because an individual who chooses to drive on the wrong side of the street can cause injuries or even death. In this sense, choosing the wrong side of the street is wrong morally, though the choice is also unconventional.

When it comes to schooling and teaching, moral choices are not restricted to occasional dramatic incidents, but are woven into almost every aspect of classroom life. Imagine this simple example. Suppose that you are teaching, reading to a small group of second-graders, and the students are taking turns reading a story out loud. Should you give every student the same amount of time to read, even though some might benefit from having additional time? Or should you give more time to the students who need extra help, even if doing so bores classmates and deprives others of equal shares of "floor time"? Which option is more fair, and which is more considerate? Simple dilemmas like this happen every day at all grade levels simply because students are diverse, and because class time and a teacher's energy are finite.

Embedded in this rather ordinary example are moral themes about fairness or justice, on the one hand, and about consideration or care on the other. It is important to keep both themes in mind when thinking about how students develop beliefs about right or wrong. A **morality of justice** is about human rights—or more specifically, about respect for fairness, impartiality, equality, and individuals' independence. A **morality of care**, on the other hand, is about human responsibilities—more specifically, about caring for others, showing consideration for individuals' needs, and interdependence among individuals. Students and teachers need both forms of morality. In the next sections therefore we explain a major example of each type of developmental theory, beginning with the morality of justice.

Kohlberg's morality of justice

One of the best-known explanations of how morality of justice develops was developed by Lawrence Kohlberg and his associates (Kohlberg, Levine, & Hewer, 1983; Power, Higgins, & Kohlberg, 1991). Using a stage model similar to Piaget's, Kohlberg proposed six stages of moral development, grouped into three levels. Individuals experience the stages universally and in sequence as they form beliefs about justice. He named the levels simply preconventional, conventional, and (you guessed it) postconventional. The levels and stages are summarized in Table 5.

Table 9: Moral stages according to Kohlberg

Moral stage	Definition of what is "good"
Preconventional Level:	
Stage 1: Obedience and punishment	Action that is rewarded and *not* punished
Stage 2: Market exchange	Action that is agreeable to the child and child's partner
Conventional Level:	
Stage 3: Peer opinion	Action that wins approval from friends or peers
Stage 4: Law and order	Action that conforms to community customs or laws
Postconventional Level:	
Stage 5: Social contract	Action that follows social accepted ways of making decisions
Stage 6: Universal principles	Action that is consistent with self-chosen, general principles

Preconventional justice: obedience and mutual advantage

The *preconventional* level of moral development coincides approximately with the preschool period of life and with Piaget's preoperational period of thinking. At this age the child is still relatively self-centered and insensitive to the moral effects of actions on others. The result is a somewhat short-sighted orientation to morality. Initially (Kohlberg's Stage 1), the child adopts an **ethics of obedience and punishment**—a sort of "morality of keeping out of trouble". The rightness and wrongness of actions is determined by whether actions are rewarded or punished by authorities such as parents or teachers. If helping yourself to a cookie brings affectionate smiles from adults, then taking the cookie is considered morally "good". If it brings scolding instead, then it is morally "bad". The child does not think about why an action might be praised or scolded; in fact, says Kohlberg, he would be incapable at Stage 1 of considering the reasons even if adults offered them.

Eventually the child learns not only to respond to positive consequences, but also learns how to *produce* them by exchanging favors with others. The new ability creates Stage 2, an **ethics of market exchange.** At this stage the morally "good" action is one that favors not only the child, but another person directly involved. A "bad" action is one that lacks this reciprocity. If trading the sandwich from your lunch for the cookies in your friend's lunch is mutually agreeable, then the trade is morally good; otherwise it is not. This perspective introduces a type of fairness into the child's thinking for the first time. But it still ignores the larger context of actions—the effects on people not present or directly involved. In Stage 2, for example, it would also be considered morally "good" to pay a classmate to do another student's homework—or even to avoid bullying or to provide sexual favors—provided that both parties regard the arrangement as being fair.

Conventional justice: conformity to peers and society

As children move into the school years, their lives expand to include a larger number and range of peers and (eventually) of the community as a whole. The change leads to *conventional morality,* which are beliefs based on what this larger array of people agree on—hence Kohlberg's use of the term "conventional". At first, in Stage 3, the child's reference group are immediate peers, so Stage 3 is sometimes called the **ethics of peer opinion**. If peers believe, for example, that it is morally good to behave politely with as many people as possible, then the child is likely to agree with the group and to regard politeness as not merely an arbitrary social convention, but a moral "good". This approach to moral belief is a bit more stable than the approach in Stage 2, because the child is taking into account the reactions not just of one other person, but of many. But it can still lead astray if the group settles on beliefs that adults consider morally wrong, like "Shop lifting for candy bars is fun and desirable."

Eventually, as the child becomes a youth and the social world expands even more, he or she acquires even larger numbers of peers and friends. He or she is therefore more likely to encounter disagreements about ethical issues and beliefs. Resolving the complexities lead to Stage 4, the **ethics of law and order,** in which the young person increasingly frames moral beliefs in terms of what the majority of society believes. Now, an action is morally good if it is legal or at least customarily approved by most people, including people whom the youth does not know personally. This attitude leads to an even more stable set of principles than in the previous stage, though it is still not immune from ethical mistakes. A community or society may agree, for example, that people of a certain race should be treated with deliberate disrespect, or that a factory owner is entitled to dump waste water into a commonly shared lake or river. To develop ethical principles that reliably avoid mistakes like these require further stages of moral development.

Postconventional justice: social contract and universal principles

As a person becomes able to think abstractly (or "formally", in Piaget's sense), ethical beliefs shift from acceptance of what the community *does* believe to the *process* by which community beliefs are formed. The new focus constitutes Stage 5, the **ethics of social contract.** Now an action, belief, or practice is morally good if it has been created through fair, democratic processes that respect the rights of the people affected. Consider, for example, the laws in some areas that require motorcyclists to wear helmets. In what sense are the laws about this behavior ethical? Was it created by consulting with and gaining the consent of the relevant people? Were cyclists consulted and did they give consent? Or how about doctors or the cyclists' families? Reasonable, thoughtful individuals disagree about how thoroughly and fairly these *consultation* processes should be. In focusing on the processes by which the law was created, however, individuals are thinking according to Stage 5, the ethics of social contract, regardless of the position they take about wearing helmets. In this sense, beliefs on both sides of a debate about an issue can sometimes be morally sound even if they contradict each other.

Paying attention to due process certainly seems like it should help to avoid mindless conformity to conventional moral beliefs. As an ethical strategy, though, it too can sometimes fail. The problem is that an ethics of social contract places more faith in democratic process than the process sometimes deserves, and does not pay enough attention to the content of what gets decided. In principle (and occasionally in practice), a society could decide democratically to kill off every member of a racial minority, for example, but would deciding this by due process make it ethical? The realization that ethical means can sometimes serve unethical ends leads some individuals toward Stage 6, the **ethics of self-chosen, universal principles.** At this final stage, the morally good action is based on personally held principles that apply both to the person's immediate life as well as to the larger community and society. The universal principles may include a belief in democratic due process (Stage 5 ethics), but also other principles, such as a belief in the dignity of all human life or the sacredness of the natural environment. At Stage 6, the universal principles will guide a person's beliefs even if the principles mean disagreeing occasionally with what is customary (Stage 4) or even with what is legal (Stage 5).

Gilligan's morality of care

As logical as they sound, Kohlberg's stages of moral justice are not sufficient for understanding the development of moral beliefs. To see why, suppose that you have a student who asks for an extension of the deadline for an assignment. The justice orientation of Kohlberg's theory would prompt you to consider issues of whether granting the request is fair. Would the late student be able to put more effort into the assignment than other students? Would the extension place a difficult demand on you, since you would have less time to mark the assignments? These are important considerations related to the rights of students and the teacher. In addition to these, however, are considerations having to do with the responsibilities that you and the requesting student have for each other and for others. Does the student have a valid personal reason (illness, death in the family, etc.) for the assignment being late? Will the assignment lose its educational value if the student has to turn it in prematurely? These latter questions have less to do with fairness and rights, and more to do with taking care of and responsibility for students. They require a framework different from Kohlberg's to be understood fully.

One such framework has been developed by Carol Gilligan, whose ideas center on a **morality of care,** or system of beliefs about human responsibilities, care, and consideration for others. Gilligan proposed three moral positions that represent different extents or breadth of ethical care. Unlike Kohlberg, Piaget, or Erikson, she does not claim that the positions form a strictly developmental sequence, but only that they can be ranked hierarchically according to their depth or subtlety. In this respect her theory is "semi-developmental" in a way similar to Maslow's theory of motivation (Brown & Gilligan, 1992; Taylor, Gilligan, & Sullivan, 1995). Table 10 summarizes the three moral positions from Gilligan's theory

Table 10: Positions of moral development according to Gilligan

Moral position	Definition of what is morally good
Position 1: Survival orientation	Action that considers one's personal needs only
Position 2: Conventional care	Action that considers others' needs or preferences, but not one's own

Position 3: Integrated care	Action that attempts to coordinate one's own personal needs with those of others

Position 1: caring as survival

The most basic kind of caring is a **survival orientation,** in which a person is concerned primarily with his or her own welfare. If a teenage girl with this ethical position is wondering whether to get an abortion, for example, she will be concerned entirely with the effects of the abortion on herself. The morally good choice will be whatever creates the least stress for herself and that disrupts her own life the least. Responsibilities to others (the baby, the father, or her family) play little or no part in her thinking.

As a moral position, a survival orientation is obviously not satisfactory for classrooms on a widespread scale. If every student only looked out for himself or herself, classroom life might become rather unpleasant! Nonetheless, there are situations in which focusing primarily on yourself is both a sign of good mental health and relevant to teachers. For a child who has been bullied at school or sexually abused at home, for example, it is both healthy and morally desirable to speak out about how bullying or abuse has affected the victim. Doing so means essentially looking out for the victim's own needs at the expense of others' needs, including the bully's or abuser's. Speaking out, in this case, requires a survival orientation and is healthy because the child is taking caring of herself.

Position 2: conventional caring

A more subtle moral position is **caring for others,** in which a person is concerned about others' happiness and welfare, and about reconciling or integrating others' needs where they conflict with each other. In considering an abortion, for example, the teenager at this position would think primarily about what other people prefer. Do the father, her parents, and/or her doctor want her to keep the child? The morally good choice becomes whatever will please others the best. This position is more demanding than Position 1, ethically and intellectually, because it requires coordinating several persons' needs and values. But it is often morally insufficient because it ignores one crucial person: the self.

In classrooms, students who operate from Position 2 can be very desirable in some ways; they can be eager to please, considerate, and good at fitting in and at working cooperatively with others. Because these qualities are usually welcome in a busy classroom, teachers can be tempted to reward students for developing and using them. The problem with rewarding Position 2 ethics, however, is that doing so neglects the student's development—his or her own academic and personal goals or values. Sooner or later, personal goals, values, and identity need attention and care, and educators have a responsibility for assisting students to discover and clarify them.

Position 3: integrated caring

The most developed form of moral caring in Gilligan's model is **integrated caring,** the coordination of personal needs and values with those of others. Now the morally good choice takes account of everyone *including* yourself, not everyone *except* yourself. In considering an abortion, a woman at Position 3 would think not only about the consequences for the father, the unborn child, and her family, but also about the consequences for herself. How would bearing a child affect her own needs, values, and plans? This perspective leads to moral beliefs that are more comprehensive, but ironically are also more prone to dilemmas because the widest possible range of individuals are being considered.

In classrooms, integrated caring is most likely to surface whenever teachers give students wide, sustained freedom to make choices. If students have little flexibility about their actions, there is little room for considering *anyone's* needs or values, whether their own or others'. If the teacher says simply: "Do the homework on page 50 and turn it in tomorrow morning", then the main issue becomes compliance, not moral choice. But suppose instead that she says something like this: "Over the next two months, figure out an inquiry project about the use of water resources in our town. Organize it any way you want—talk to people, read widely about it, and share it with the class in a way that all of us, including yourself, will find meaningful." An assignment like this poses moral challenges that are not only educational, but also moral, since it requires students to make value judgments. Why? For one thing, students must decide what aspect of the topic really matters to them. Such a decision is partly a matter of personal values. For another thing, students have to consider how to make the topic meaningful or important to *others* in the class. Third, because the time line for completion is relatively far in the future, students may have to weigh personal priorities (like spending time with friends or family) against educational priorities (working on the assignment a bit more on the weekend). As you might suspect, some students might have trouble making good choices when given this sort of freedom—and their teachers might therefore be cautious about giving such an assignment. But the difficulties in making choices are part of Gilligan's point: integrated caring is indeed more demanding than the caring based only on survival or on consideration of others. Not all students may be ready for it.

Understanding "the typical student" versus understanding students

In this chapter, in keeping with the general nature of developmental theory, we have often spoken of students in a generalized way, referring to "the" child, student, or youngster, as if a single typical or average individual exists and develops through single, predictable pathways. As every teacher knows, however, development is not that simple. A class of 25 or 30 students will contain 25 or 30 individuals each learning and developing along distinct pathways. Why then study developmental patterns at all? Because underlying their obvious diversity, students indeed show important similarities. This chapter has indicated some of the similarities and how they relate to the job of teaching. Our references to "the" student should *not* be understood, therefore, as supporting simple-minded stereotypes; they refer instead to common tendencies of real, live children and youth. Pointing to developmental changes is like pointing to a flock of birds in flight: the flock has a general location, but individual birds also have their own locations and take individual flight paths. Development and diversity therefore have to be understood jointly, not separately. There are indeed similarities woven among the differences in students, but also differences woven among students' commonalities. We recommend therefore that you read this chapter on development together with the next one, which looks explicitly at student diversity.

Chapter summary

Understanding development, or the long-term changes in growth, behavior, and knowledge, helps teachers to hold appropriate expectations for students as well as to keep students' individual diversity in perspective. From kindergarten through the end of high school, students double their height, triple their weight, experience the social and hormonal effects of puberty, and improve basic motor skills. Their health is generally good, though illnesses are affected significantly by students' economic and social circumstances.

Cognitively, students develop major new abilities to think logically and abstractly, based on a foundation of sensory and motor experiences with the objects and people around them. Jean Piaget has one well-known theory detailing how these changes unfold.

3. Student development

Socially, students face and resolve a number of issues—especially the issue of industry (dedicated, sustained work) during childhood and the issue of identity during adolescence. Erik Erikson has described these crises in detail, as well as social crises that precede and follow the school years. Students are motivated both by basic human needs (food, safety, belonging, esteem) and by needs to enhance themselves psychologically (self-actualization). Abraham Maslow has described these motivations and how they relate to each other.

Morally, students develop both a sense of justice and of care for others, and their thinking in each of these realms undergoes important changes as they mature. Lawrence Kohlberg has described changes in children and youth's beliefs about justice, and Carol Gilligan has described changes in their beliefs about care.

On the Internet

<**www.srcd.org/press**> This is part of the website for the Society for Research in Child Development, an organization that supports research about children and youth, and that advocates for government policies on their behalf. The specific web page recommended here contains their press releases, which summarize findings from current research and their implications for children's welfare. You will need to register to use this page, but registration is free.

<**www.apa.org**> This is the website for the American Psychological Association, the largest professional association of psychologists in the English-speaking world. From the homepage you can go to a section called "psychology topics", which offers a variety of interesting articles and press releases free of charge. Among other topics, for example, there are articles about obesity and its effects, as well as about factors that support (and/or detract from) children's well-being.

Key terms

Development
  Puberty
  Cognition
  Cognitive stages
    Jean Piaget
    Sensorimotor stage
      Object permanence
    Preoperational stage
      Dramatic play
    Concrete operational stage
      Decenter
      Conservation
    Formal operational stage
      Hypothetical reasoning
  Social development
    Erik Erikson
    Abraham Maslow
    Lawrence Kohlberg
    Carol Gilligan
    Psychosocial crises
      Trust, autonomy, and initiative
      Industry

Identity
  Intimacy, generativity, and integrity
  Maslow's hierarchy of needs
    Deficit needs
    Being needs
      Self-actualization
Moral development
  Lawrence Kohlberg
  Carol Gilligan
  Morality of justice
    Preconventional justice
      Ethics of obedience
  Ethics of mutual advantage
    Conventional justice
      Ethics of peer opinion
      Ethics of law and order
    Postconventional justice
      Ethics of social contract
      Ethics of universal principles
  Morality of care
    Survival Orientation
    Conventional care

Integrated care

References

Allender, J. (2005). *Community health nursing, 6th edition*. Philadelphia: Lippincott, Williams, & Wilkins.

Bawa, S. (2005). The role of the consumption of beverages in the obesity epidemic. *Journal of the Royal Society for the Promotion of Health, 125*(3), 124-128.

Beidel, B. (2005). *Childhood anxiety disorders*. Oxford, UK: Brunner-Routledge.

Bredekamp, S. & Copple, C. (1997). *Developmentally appropriate practice, Revised edition*. Washington, D.C.: National Association for the Education of Young Children.

Brown, L. & Gilligan, C. (1992). *Meeting at the crossroads: Women's psychology and girls' development*. Cambridge, MA: Harvard University Press.

Case, R. (1991). *The mind's staircase: Exploring the conceptual underpinnings of children's thought and knowledge*. Hillsdale, NJ: Erlbaum.

Case, R. & Okamoto, Y. (1996). *The role of central conceptual structures in children's thought*. Chicago: Society for Research on Child Development.

Center for Disease Control. (2004a). *National survey on drug use and health*. Bethesda, MD: Department of Health and Human Services.

Center for Disease Control (2004b). *Trends in the prevalence of sexual behaviors, 1991-2003*. Bethesda, MD: Author.

Eveleth, P. & Tanner, J. (1990). *Worldwide variation in human growth* (2nd edition). New York: Cambridge University Press.

Eyler, J. & Giles, D. (1999). *Where's the learning in service learning?* San Francisco: Jossey-Bass.

Fagan, A. & Najman, J. (2005). The relative contribution of parental and sibling substance use to adolescent alcohol, tobacco, and other drug use. *Journal of Drug Issues, 35*, 869-883.

Friedman, S. (2000). *When girls feel fat: Helping girls through adolescence*. Toronto: Firefly Books.

Harris, J. (2006). *No two alike: Human nature and human individuality*. New York: Norton.

Inhelder, B. & Piaget, J. (1958). *The growth of logical thinking from childhood to adolescence: An essay on the growth of formal operational structures*. New York: Basic Books.

Johnston, L., O'Malley, P., Bachman, J., & Schulenberg, J. (2006). *Monitoring the future: National results on adolescent drug use: Overview of key findings, 2005*. Bethesda, MD: National Institute on Drug Abuse.

Kay, C. (2003). *The complete guide to service learning*. New York: Free Spirit Publishing.

Kohlberg, L., Levine, C., & Hewer, A. (1983). *Moral stages: A current formulation and a response to critics*. Basel: S. Karger.

Lewis, M. (1997). *Altering fate: Why the past does not predict the future*. New York: Guilford Press.

3. Student development

Malina, R., Bouchard, C., & Bar-Or O. (2004). *Growth, maturation, and physical activity*. Champaign, IL: Human Kinetics Press.

Maslow, A. (1987). *Motivation and personality, 3rd edition*. New York: Harper & Row.

Maslow, A. (1976). *The Farther Reaches of Human Nature, 2nd edition*. New York: Penguin Books.

Matthews, G. (1998). *The philosophy of childhood*. Cambridge, MA: Harvard University Press.

McClintock, M. & Herdt, G. (1996). Rethinking puberty: The development of sexual attraction. *Current Directions in Psychological Science, 5*, 178-183.

Narayan, K., Boyle, J., Thompson, T., Sorensen, S., & Williamson, D. (2003). Lifetime risk for diabetes mellitus in the United States. *Journal of the American Medical Association, 290*(14), 1884-1890.

National Institute of Allergies and Infectious Diseases. (2005). *The common cold*. Bethesda, MD: Author. Also available at <http://www.niaid.nih.gov/facts/cold.htm>.

Ogden, C., Flega, K., Carroll, M. & Johnson, C. (2002). Prevalence and trends in overweight among U.S. children and adolescents, 1999-2000. *Journal of the American Medical Association, 288*(14), 1728-1732.

Paley, V. (2005). *A child's work: The importance of fantasy play*. Chicago: University of Chicago Press.

Payne, R. (2005). *A framework for understanding poverty*. Highlands, TX: aha!Process, Inc.

Payne, V. & Isaacs, L. (2005). *Human motor development: A lifespan approach, 6th edition*. Boston: McGraw-Hill.

Piaget, J. (1952). *The origins of intelligence in children*. New York: International Universities Press.

Piaget, J. (1983). Piaget's theory. In P. Mussen (Ed.), *Handbook of child psychology, volume 1*. New York: Wiley.

Piaget, J. (2001). *The psychology of intelligence*. Oxford, UK: Routledge.

Petlichkoff, L. (1996). The drop-out dilemma in youth sports. In O. Bar-Or (Ed.), *The child and adolescent athlete* (pp. 418-432). Oxford, UK: Blackwell.

Power, F., Higgins, A., & Kohlberg, L. (1991). *Lawrence Kohlberg's approach to moral education*. New York: Columbia University Press.

Richardson, J. (2005). *The cost of being poor*. Westport, CN: Praeger.

Rosenbaum, J. (2006). Reborn a Virgin: Adolescents' Retracting of Virginity Pledges and Sexual Histories. *American Journal of Public Health, 96*(6), xxx-yyy.

Sadker, M. (2004). Gender equity in the classroom: The unfinished agenda. In M. Kimmel (Ed.), *The gendered society reader, 2nd edition*. New York: Oxford University Press.

Salkind, N. (2004). *An introduction to theories of human development*. Thousand Oaks, CA: Sage Publications.

Slavin, R. (2005). *Educational psychology, 7th edition*. Boston: Allyn & Bacon.

Spencer, N. (2000). *Poverty and child health, 2nd edition.* Abingdon, UK: Radcliffe Medical Press.

Tartamella, L., Herscher, E., Woolston, C. (2004). *Generation extra large: Rescuing our children from the obesity epidemic.* New York: Basic Books.

Taylor, J. & Gilligan, C., & Sullivan, A. (1995). *Between voice and silence: Women and girls, race and relationship.* Cambridge, MA: Harvard University Press.

United States Government Printing Office. (2002). *No Child Left Behind Act: A desktop reference.* Washington, D.C.: Author.

Whelen, E., Lawson, C., Grajewski, B., Petersen, M., Pinkerton, L., Ward, E., & Schnorr, T. (2003). Prevalence of respiratory symptoms among female flight attendants and teachers. *Occupational and Environmental Medicine, 60,* 929-934.

Woolfolk, A. (2006). *Educational psychology, 10th edition.* Boston: Allyn & Bacon.

Yin, Z., Hanes, J., Moore, J., Humbles, P., Barbeau, & Gutin, B. (2005). An after-school physical activity program for obesity prevention in children. *Evaluation and the Health Professions, 28*(1), 67-89.

Zimbardo, P. & Radl, S. (1999). *The shy child: Overcoming and preventing shyness from birth to adulthood.* Cambridge, MA: Malor Books.

4. Student diversity

I'll tell you this: There are some people, and then there are others.

(Anna Harris)

Anna Harris was Kelvin Seifert's grandmother as well as a schoolteacher from about 1910 to 1930. She used to make comments, like the one above, that sounded odd but that also contained a grain of wisdom. In this case her remark makes a good theme for this chapter—and even for teaching in general. Students do differ in a multitude of ways, both individually and because of memberships in families, communities or cultural groups. Sometimes the differences can make classroom-style teaching more challenging, but other times, as Anna Harris implied, they simply enrich classroom life. To teach students well, we need to understand the important ways that they differ among themselves, and when or how the differences really matter for their education. This chapter offers some of that understanding and suggests how you might use it in order to make learning effective and enjoyable for everyone, including yourself.

*For convenience we will make a major distinction between differences among individuals and differences among groups of students. As the term implies, **individual differences** are qualities that are unique; just one person has them at a time. Variation in hair color, for example, is an individual difference; even though some people have nearly the same hair color, no two people are exactly the same. **Group differences** are qualities shared by members of an identifiable group or community, but not shared by everyone in society. An example is gender role: for better or for worse, one portion of society (the males) is perceived differently and expected to behave a bit differently than another portion of society (the females). Notice that distinguishing between individual and group differences is convenient, but a bit arbitrary. Individuals with similar, but nonetheless unique qualities sometimes group themselves together for certain purposes, and groups unusually contain a lot of individual diversity within them. If you happen to enjoy playing soccer and have some talent for it (an individual quality), for example, you may end up as a member of a soccer team or club (a group defined by members' common desire and ability to play soccer). But though everyone on the team fits a "soccer player's profile" at some level, individual members will probably vary in level of skill and motivation. The group, by its very nature, may obscure these signs of individuality.*

To begin, then, we look at several differences normally considered to be individually rather than group based. This discussion will necessarily be incomplete simply because individual differences are so numerous and important in teaching that some of them are also discussed in later chapters. Later sections of this chapter deal with three important forms of group diversity: gender differences, cultural differences, and language differences.

Individual styles of learning and thinking

All of us, including our students, have preferred ways of learning. Teachers often refer to these differences as **learning styles,** though this term may imply that students are more consistent across situations than is really the case. One student may like to make diagrams to help remember a reading assignment, whereas another student may prefer to write a sketchy outline instead. Yet in many cases, the students could in principle reverse the strategies and still learn the material: if coaxed (or perhaps required), the diagram-maker could take notes for a change and the note-taker could draw diagrams. Both would still learn, though neither might feel as comfortable as when using the strategies that they prefer. This reality suggests that a balanced, middle-of-the-road approach may be a teacher's best response to students' learning styles. Or put another way, it is good to support students' preferred learning strategies where possible and appropriate, but neither necessary nor desirable to do so all of the time (Loo, 2004; Stahl, 2002). Most of all, it is neither necessary nor possible to classify or label students according to seemingly fixed learning styles and then allow them to learn only according to those styles. A student may prefer to hear new material rather than see it; he may prefer for you to explain something orally, for example, rather than to see it demonstrated in a video. But he may nonetheless tolerate or sometimes even prefer to see it demonstrated. In the long run, in fact, he may learn it best by encountering the material in both ways, regardless of his habitual preferences.

That said, there is evidence that individuals, including students, do differ in how they habitually think. These differences are more specific than learning styles or preferences, and psychologists sometimes call them **cognitive styles,** meaning typical ways of perceiving and remembering information, and typical ways of solving problems and making decisions (Zhang & Sternberg, 2006). In a style of thinking called **field dependence,** for example, individuals perceive patterns as a whole rather than focus on the parts of the pattern separately. In a complementary tendency, called **field independence,** individuals are more inclined to analyze overall patterns into their parts. Cognitive research from the 1940s to the present has found field dependence/independence differences to be somewhat stable for any given person across situations, though not completely so (Witkin, Moore, Goodenough, & Cox, 1977; Zhang & Sternberg, 2005). Someone who is field dependent (perceives globally or "wholistically") in one situation, tends to a modest extent to perceive things globally or wholistically in other situations. Field dependence and independence can be important in understanding students because the styles affect students' behaviors and preferences in school and classrooms. Field dependent persons tend to work better in groups, it seems, and to prefer "open-ended" fields of study like literature and history. Field *independent* persons, on the other hand, tend to work better alone and to prefer highly analytic studies like math and science. The differences are only a tendency, however, and there are a lot of students who contradict the trends. As with the broader notion of learning styles, the cognitive styles of field dependence and independence are useful for tailoring instruction to particular students, but their guidance is only approximate. They neither can nor should be used to "lock" students to particular modes of learning or to replace students' own expressed preferences and choices about curriculum.

Another cognitive style is **impulsivity** as compared to **reflectivity.** As the names imply, an *impulsive* cognitive style is one in which a person reacts quickly, but as a result makes comparatively more errors. A *reflective* style is the opposite: the person reacts more slowly and therefore makes fewer errors. As you might expect, the reflective style would seem better suited to many academic demands of school. Research has found that this is indeed the case for academic skills that clearly benefit from reflection, such as mathematical problem solving or certain reading tasks (Evans, 2004). Some classroom or school-related skills, however, may actually develop better if a student is relatively impulsive. Being a good partner in a cooperative learning group, for example, may depend partly on responding spontaneously (i.e. just a bit "impulsively") to others' suggestions; and being an effective member of an athletic team may depend on *not* taking time to reflect carefully on every move that you or your team mates make.

There are two major ways to use knowledge of students' cognitive styles (Pritchard, 2005). The first and the more obvious is to build on students' existing style strengths and preferences. A student who is field independent and reflective, for example, can be encouraged to explore tasks and activities that are relatively analytic and that require relatively independent work. One who is field dependent and impulsive, on the other hand, can be encouraged and supported to try tasks and activities that are more social or spontaneous. But a second, less obvious way to use knowledge of cognitive styles is to encourage more balance in cognitive styles for students who need it. A student who *lacks* field independence, for example, may need explicit help in organizing and analyzing key academic tasks (like organizing a lab report in a science class). One who is already highly reflective may need encouragement to try ideas spontaneously, as in a creative writing lesson.

Multiple intelligences

For nearly a century, educators and psychologists have debated the nature of intelligence, and more specifically whether intelligence is just one broad ability or can take more than one form. Many classical definitions of the concept have tended to define **intelligence** as a single broad ability that allows a person to solve or complete many sorts of tasks, or at least many academic tasks like reading, knowledge of vocabulary, and the solving of logical problems (Garlick, 2002). There is research evidence of such a global ability, and the idea of general intelligence often fits with society's everyday beliefs about intelligence. Partly for these reasons, an entire mini-industry has grown up around publishing tests of intelligence, academic ability, and academic achievement. Since these tests affect the work of teachers, I return to discussing them later in this book.

But there are also problems with defining intelligence as one general ability. One way of summing up the problems is to say that conceiving of intelligence as something general tends to put it beyond teachers' influence. When viewed as a single, all-purpose ability, students either have a lot of intelligence or they do not, and strengthening their intelligence becomes a major challenge, or perhaps even an impossible one (Gottfredson, 2004; Lúbinski, 2004). This conclusion is troubling to some educators, especially in recent years as testing school achievements have become more common and as students have become more diverse.

But alternate views of intelligence also exist that portray intelligence as having multiple forms, whether the forms are subparts of a single broader ability or are multiple "intelligences" in their own right. For various reasons such this perspective has gained in popularity among teachers in recent years, probably because it reflects many teachers' beliefs that students cannot simply be rated along a single scale of ability, but are fundamentally diverse (Kohn, 2004).

One of the most prominent of these models is **Howard Gardner's theory of multiple intelligences** (Gardner, 1983, 2003). Gardner proposes that there are eight different forms of intelligence, each of which functions independently of the others. (The eight intelligences are summarized in Table 11. Each person has a mix of all eight abilities—more of one and less of another—that helps to constitute that person's individual cognitive profile. Since most tasks—including most tasks in classrooms—require several forms of intelligence and can be completed in more than one way, it is possible for people with various profiles of talents to succeed on a task equally well. In writing an essay, for example, a student with high interpersonal intelligence but rather average verbal intelligence might use his or her interpersonal strength to get a lot of help and advice from classmates and the teacher. A student with the opposite profile might work well alone, but without the benefit of help from others. Both students might end up with essays that are good, but good for different reasons.

Table 11: Multiple intelligences according to Howard Gardner

Form of intelligence	Examples of activities using the intelligence
Linguistic: verbal skill; ability to use language well	• verbal persuasion • writing a term paper skillfully
Musical: ability to create and understand music	• singing, playing a musical instrument • composing a tune
Logical: Mathematical: logical skill; ability to reason, often using mathematics	• solving mathematical problems easily and accurately • developing and testing hypotheses
Spatial: ability to imagine and manipulate the arrangement of objects in the environment	• completing a difficult jigsaw puzzle • assembling a complex appliance (e.g. a bicycle)
Bodily: kinesthetic: sense of balance; coordination in use of one's body	• dancing • gymnastics
Interpersonal: ability to discern others' nonverbal feelings and thoughts	• sensing when to be tactful • sensing a "subtext" or implied message in a person's statements
Intrapersonal: sensitivity to one's own thoughts and feelings	• noticing complex of ambivalent feelings in oneself • identifying true motives for an action in oneself
Naturalist: sensitivity to subtle differences and patterns found in the natural environment	• identifying examples of species of plants or animals • noticing relationships among species and natural processes in the environment

Source: Gardner, 1983, 2003

As evidence for the possibility of multiple intelligences, Gardner cites descriptions of individuals with exceptional talent in one form of intelligence (for example, in playing the piano) but who are neither above nor below average in other areas. He also cites descriptions of individuals with brain damage, some of whom lose one particular form of intelligence (like the ability to talk) but retain other forms. In the opinion of many psychologists, however, the evidence for multiple intelligences is not strong enough to give up the "classical" view of general intelligence. Part of the problem is that the evidence for multiple intelligences relies primarily on anecdotes— examples or descriptions of particular individuals who illustrate the model—rather than on more widespread information or data (Eisner, 2004).

Nonetheless, whatever the status of the research evidence, the model itself can be useful as a way for teachers to think about their work. Multiple intelligences suggest the importance of diversifying instruction in order to honor and to respond to diversity in students' talents and abilities. Viewed like this, whether Gardner's classification scheme is actually accurate is probably less important than the fact there is (or may be) more than one way to be "smart". In the end, as with cognitive and learning styles, it may not be important to label students' talents or intellectual strengths. It may be more important simply to provide important learning and knowledge in several modes or styles, ways that draw on more than one possible form of intelligence or skill. A good example of this principle is your own development in learning to teach. It is well and good to read books about teaching (like this one, perhaps), but it is even better to read books and talk with classmates and educators about teaching and getting actual experience in classrooms. The combination both invites and requires a wide range of your talents and usually proves more effective than any single type of activity, whatever your profile of cognitive styles or intellectual abilities happens to be.

Gifted and talented students

The idea of multiple intelligences leads to new ways of thinking about students who have special gifts and talents. Traditionally, the term *gifted* referred only to students with unusually high verbal skills. Their skills were demonstrated especially well, for example, on standardized tests of general ability or of school achievement, like those described in Chapter 12 ("Standardized and other formal assessments"). More recently, however, the meaning of *gifted* has broadened to include unusual talents in a range of activities, such as music, creative writing, or the arts (G. Davis & Rimm, 2004). To indicate the change, educators often use the dual term *gifted and talented*.

Qualities of the gifted and talented

What are students who are gifted and talented like? Generally they show some combination of the following qualities:

- They learn more quickly and independently than most students their own age.

- They often have well-developed vocabulary, as well as advanced reading and writing skills.

- They are very motivated, especially on tasks that are challenging or difficult.

- They hold themselves to higher than usual standards of achievement.

Contrary to a common impression, students who are gifted or talented are *not* necessarily awkward socially, less healthy, or narrow in their interests—in fact, quite the contrary (Steiner & Carr, 2003). They also come from all economic and cultural groups.

Ironically, in spite of their obvious strengths as learners, such students often languish in school unless teachers can provide them with more than the challenges of the usual curriculum. A kindergarten child who is precociously advanced in reading, for example, may make little further progress at reading if her teachers do not recognize and develop her skill; her talent may effectively disappear from view as her peers gradually catch up to her initial level. Without accommodation to their unusual level of skill or knowledge, students who are gifted or talented can become bored by school, and eventually the boredom can even turn into behavior problems.

Partly for these reasons, students who are gifted or talented have sometimes been regarded as the responsibility of special education, along with students with other sorts of disabilities. Often their needs are discussed, for example, in textbooks about special education, alongside discussions of students with intellectual disabilities, physical impairments, or major behavior disorders (Friend, 2008). There is some logic to this way of thinking about their needs; after all, they *are* quite exceptional, and they do require modifications of the usual school programs in order to reach their full potential. But it is also misleading to ignore obvious differences between exceptional giftedness and exceptional disabilities of other kinds. The key difference is in students' potential. By definition, students with gifts or talents are capable of creative, committed work at levels that often approach talented adults. Other students—including students with disabilities—may reach these levels, but not as soon and not as frequently. Many educators therefore think of the gifted and talented not as examples of students with disabilities, but as examples of diversity. As such they are not so much the responsibility of special education specialists, as the responsibility of all teachers to differentiate their instruction.

Supporting students who are gifted and talented

Supporting the gifted and talented usually involves a mixture of *acceleration* and *enrichment* of the usual curriculum (Schiever & Maker, 2003). **Acceleration** involves either a child's skipping a grade, or else the teacher's redesigning the curriculum within a particular grade or classroom so that more material is covered faster. Either strategy works, but only up to a point: children who have skipped a grade usually function well in the higher grade, both academically and socially. Unfortunately skipping grades cannot happen repeatedly unless teacher, parents, and the students themselves are prepared to live with large age and maturity differences within single classrooms. In itself, too, there is no guarantee that instruction in the new, higher-grade classroom will be any more stimulating than it was in the former, lower-grade classroom. Redesigning the curriculum is also beneficial to the student, but impractical to do on a widespread basis; even if teachers had the time to redesign their programs, many non-gifted students would be left behind as a result.

Enrichment involves providing additional or different instruction added on to the usual curriculum goals and activities. Instead of books at more advanced reading levels, for example, a student might read a wider variety of types of literature at the student's current reading level, or try writing additional types of literature himself. Instead of moving ahead to more difficult kinds of math programs, the student might work on unusual logic problems not assigned to the rest of the class. Like acceleration, enrichment works well up to a point. Enrichment curricula exist to help classroom teachers working with gifted students (and save teachers the time and work of creating enrichment materials themselves). Since enrichment is not part of the normal, officially sanctioned curriculum, however, there is a risk that it will be perceived as busywork rather than as intellectual stimulation, particularly if the teacher herself is not familiar with the enrichment material or is otherwise unable to involve herself in the material fully.

Obviously acceleration and enrichment can sometimes be combined. A student can skip a grade and also be introduced to interesting "extra" material at the new grade level. A teacher can move a student to the next unit of study faster than she moves the rest of the class, while at the same time offering additional activities not related to the unit of study directly. For a teacher with a student who is gifted or talented, however, the real challenge is not simply to choose between acceleration and enrichment, but to observe the student, get to know him or her as a unique individual, and offer activities and supports based on that knowledge. This is essentially the challenge of *differentiating instruction,* something needed not just by the gifted and talented, but by students of all sorts. As you might suspect, differentiating instruction poses challenges about managing instruction; we discuss it again in more detail in Chapter 9 ("Facilitating complex thinking") and Chapter 10 ("Instructional planning").

Gender differences in the classroom

Gender roles are the patterns of behaviors, attitudes, and expectations associated with a particular sex—with being either male or female. For clarity, psychologists sometimes distinguish *gender differences,* which are related to social roles, from *sex differences,* which are related only to physiology and anatomy. Using this terminology, gender matters in teaching more than sex (in spite of any jokes told about the latter!).

Although there are many exceptions, boys and girls do differ on average in ways that parallel conventional gender stereotypes and that affect how the sexes behave at school and in class. The differences have to do with physical behaviors, styles of social interaction, academic motivations, behaviors, and choices. They have a variety of sources—primarily parents, peers, and the media. Teachers are certainly not the primary cause of gender role differences, but sometimes teachers influence them by their responses to and choices made on behalf of students.

Physical differences in gender roles

Physically, boys tend to be more active than girls, and by the same token more restless if they have to sit for long periods. They are also more prone than girls to rely on physical aggression if they are frustrated (Espelage & Swearer, 2004). Both tendencies are inconsistent with the usual demands of classroom life, of course, and make it a little more likely that school will be a difficult experience for boys, even for boys who never actually get in trouble for being restless or aggressive.

During the first two or three years of elementary school, gross motor skills develop at almost the same average rate for boys and girls. As a *group*, both sexes can run, jump, throw a ball, and the like with about equal ease, though there are of course wide significant differences among *individuals* of both sexes. Toward the end of elementary school, however, boys pull ahead of girls at these skills even though neither sex has begun yet to experience puberty. The most likely reason is that boys participate more actively in formal and informal sports because of expectations and support from parents, peers, and society (Braddock, Sokol-Katz, Greene, & Basinger-Fleischman, 2005; Messner, Duncan, & Cooky, 2003). Puberty eventually adds to this advantage by making boys taller and stronger than girls, on average, and therefore more suited at least for sports that rely on height and strength.

In thinking about these differences, keep in mind that they refer to average trends and that there are numerous individual exceptions. Every teacher knows of individual boys who are not athletic, for example, or of particular girls who are especially restless in class. The individual differences mean, among other things, that it is hard to justify providing different levels of support or resources to boys than to girls for sports, athletics, or physical education. The differences also suggest, though, that individual students who *contradict* gender stereotypes about physical abilities may benefit from emotional support or affirmation from teachers, simply because they may be less likely than usual to get such affirmation from elsewhere.

Social differences in gender roles

When relaxing socially, boys more often gravitate to large groups. Whether on the playground, in a school hallway, or on the street, boys' social groups tend literally to fill up a lot of space, and often include significant amounts of roughhousing as well as organized and "semi-organized" competitive games or sports (Maccoby, 2002). Girls, for their part, are more likely to seek and maintain one or two close friends and to share more intimate information and feelings with these individuals. To the extent that these gender differences occur, they can make girls less visible or noticeable than boys, at least in leisure play situations where children or youth choose their companions freely. As with physical differences, however, keep in mind that differences in social interactions do *not* occur uniformly for all boys and girls. There are boys with close friends, contradicting the general trend, and girls who play primarily in large groups.

Differences in social interaction styles happen in the classroom as well. Boys, on average, are more likely to speak up during a class discussion—sometimes even if not called on, or even if they do not know as much about the topic as others in the class (Sadker, 2002). When working on a project in a small co-ed group, furthermore they have a tendency to ignore girls' comments and contributions to the group. In this respect co-ed student groups parallel interaction patterns in many parts of society, where men also have a tendency to ignore women's comments and contributions (Tannen, 2001).

Academic and cognitive differences in gender

On average, girls are more motivated than boys to perform well in school, at least during elementary school. By the time girls reach high school, however, some may try to down play their own academic ability in order make themselves more likeable by both sexes (Davies, 2005). Even if this occurs, though, it does not affect their grades: from kindergarten through twelfth grade, girls earn slightly higher average grades than boys (Freeman, 2004). This fact does not lead to similar achievement, however, because as youngsters move into high school, they tend to choose courses or subjects conventionally associated with their gender—math and science for boys, in particular, and literature and the arts for girls. By the end of high school, this difference in course selection makes a measurable difference in boys' and girls' academic performance in these subjects.

But again, consider my caution about stereotyping: there are individuals of both sexes whose behaviors and choices run counter to the group trends. (I have made this point as well in "Preparing for Licensure: Interpreting Gender-Related Behavior" by deliberately concealing the gender of a student described.) Differences within each gender group generally are far larger than any differences between the groups. A good example is the "difference" in cognitive ability of boys and girls. Many studies have found none at all. A few others have found small differences, with boys slightly better at math and girls slightly better at reading and literature. Still other studies have found the differences not only are small, but have been getting smaller in recent years compared to earlier studies. Collectively the findings about cognitive abilities are virtually "non-findings", and it is worth asking why gender differences have therefore been studied and discussed so much for so many years (Hyde, 2005). How teachers influence gender roles?

Teachers often intend to interact with both sexes equally, and frequently succeed at doing so. Research has found, though, that they do sometimes respond to boys and girls differently, perhaps without realizing it. Three kinds of differences have been noticed. The first is the overall amount of attention paid to each sex; the second is the visibility or "publicity" of conversations; and the third is the type of behavior that prompts teachers to support or criticize students.

Attention paid

In general, teachers interact with boys more often than with girls by a margin of 10 to 30 percent, depending on the grade level of the students and the personality of the teacher (Measor & Sykes, 1992). One possible reason for the difference is related to the greater assertiveness of boys that I already noted; if boys are speaking up more frequently in discussions or at other times, then a teacher may be "forced" to pay more attention to them. Another possibility is that some teachers may feel that boys are especially prone to getting into mischief, so they may interact with them more frequently to keep them focused on the task at hand (Erden & Wolfgang, 2004). Still another possibility is that boys, compared to girls, may interact in a wider variety of styles and situations, so there may simply be richer opportunities to interact with them. This last possibility is partially supported by another gender difference in classroom interaction, the amount of public versus private talk.

Public talk versus private talk

Teachers have a tendency to talk to boys from a greater physical distance than when they talk to girls (Wilkinson & Marrett, 1985). The difference may be both a cause and an effect of general gender expectations, expressive nurturing is expected more often of girls and women, and a businesslike task orientation is expected more often of boys and men, particularly in mixed-sex groups (Basow & Rubenfeld, 2003; Myaskovsky, Unikel, & Dew, 2005). Whatever the reason, the effect is to give interactions with boys more "publicity". When two people converse with each other from across the classroom, many others can overhear them; when they are at each other's elbows, though, few others can overhear.

Distributing praise and criticism

In spite of most teachers' desire to be fair to all students, it turns out that they sometimes distribute praise and criticism differently to boys and girls. The differences are summarized in Table 4.2. The tendency is to praise boys more than girls for displaying knowledge *correctly,* but to criticize girls more than boys for displaying knowledge *incorrectly* (Golombok & Fivush, 1994; Delamont, 1996). Another way of stating this difference is by what teachers tend to overlook: with boys, they tend to overlook *wrong* answers, but with girls, they tend to overlook *right* answers. The result (which is probably unintended) is a tendency to make boys' knowledge seem more important and boys themselves more competent. A second result is the other side of this coin: a tendency to make girls' knowledge *less* visible and girls themselves *less* competent.

Table 12: Gender differences in how teachers praise and criticize students

Type of response from	Boys	Girls

teacher		
Praises	Correct knowledge	"Good" or compliant behavior
Overlooks or ignores	"Good" or compliant behavior; *in*correct knowledge	*Mis*behavior; correct knowledge
Criticizes	*Mis*behavior	*In*correct knowledge
Source: Golobuk & Fivush, 1994		

Gender differences also occur in the realm of classroom behavior. Teachers tend to praise girls for "good" behavior, regardless of its relevance to content or to the lesson at hand, and tend to criticize boys for "bad" or inappropriate behavior (Golombok & Fivush, 1994). This difference can also be stated in terms of what teachers overlook: with girls, they tend to overlook behavior that is not appropriate, but with boys they tend to overlook behavior that is appropriate. The net result in this case is to make girls' seem more good than they may really be, and also to make their "goodness" seem more important than their academic competence. By the same token, the teacher's patterns of response imply that boys are more "bad" than they may really be.

At first glance, the gender differences in interaction can seem discouraging and critical of teachers because they imply that teachers as a group are biased about gender. But this conclusion is too simplistic for a couple of reasons. One is that like all differences between groups, interaction patterns are trends, and as such they hide a lot of variation within them. The other is that the trends suggest what often tends in fact to happen, not what can in fact happen if a teacher consciously sets about to avoid interaction patterns like the ones I have described. Fortunately for us all, teaching does not need to be unthinking; we have choices that we can make, even during a busy class!

Differences in cultural expectations and styles

A culture is the system of attitudes, beliefs, and behaviors that constitute the distinctive way of life of a people. Although sometimes the term is also used to refer specifically to the artistic, intellectual and other "high-brow" aspects of life, I use it here more broadly to refer to everything that characterizes a way of life—baseball games as well as symphony concerts, and McDonald's as well as expensive restaurants. In this broad sense culture is nearly synonymous with ethnicity, which refers to the common language, history, and future experienced by a group within society. Culture has elements that are obvious, like unique holidays or customs, but also features that are subtle or easy for outsiders to overlook, like beliefs about the nature of intelligence or about the proper way to tell a story. When a classroom draws students from many cultures or ethnic groups, therefore, the students bring to it considerable diversity. Teachers need to understand that diversity—understand how students' habitual attitudes, beliefs, and behaviors differ from each other, and especially how they differ from the teacher's.

But this kind of understanding can get complicated. To organize the topic, therefore, I will discuss aspects of cultural diversity according to how directly they relate to language differences compared to differences in other social and psychological features of culture. The distinction is convenient, but it is also a bit arbitrary because, as you will see, the features of a culture overlap and influence each other.

Bilingualism: language differences in the classroom

Although monolingual speakers often do not realize it, the majority of children around the world are bilingual, meaning that they understand and use two languages (Meyers-Scotton, 2005). Even in the United States, which is a relatively monolingual society, more than 47 million people speak a language other than English at home, and about 10 million of these people were children or youths in public schools (United States Department of Commerce, 2003). The large majority of bilingual students (75 per cent) are Hispanic, but the rest represent more than a hundred different language groups from around the world. In larger communities throughout the United States, it is therefore common for a single classroom to contain students from several language backgrounds at once.

In classrooms as in other social settings, bilingualism exists in different forms and degrees. At one extreme are students who speak both English and another language fluently; at the other extreme are those who speak only limited versions of both languages. In between are students who speak their home (or heritage) language much better than English, as well as others who have partially lost their heritage language in the process of learning English (Tse, 2001). Commonly, too, a student may speak a language satisfactorily, but be challenged by reading or writing it—though even this pattern has individual exceptions. Whatever the case, each bilingual student poses unique challenges to teachers.

Balanced or fluent bilingualism

The student who speaks both languages fluently has a definite cognitive advantage. As you might suspect and as research has confirmed, a fully fluent bilingual student is in a better position than usual to express concepts or ideas in more than one way, and to be aware of doing so (Jimenez, et al. 1995; Francis, 2006). The question: "What if a dog were called a cat?" is less likely to confuse even a very young bilingual child. Nor will the follow-up question: "Could the 'cat' meow?" confuse them. Such skill in reflecting on language is a form of **metacognition**, which I discussed in Chapter 2 and defined as using language as an *object* of thought. Metacognition can be helpful for a variety of academic purposes, such as writing stories and essays, or interpreting complex text materials.

Unbalanced bilingualism

Unfortunately, the bilingualism of many students is "unbalanced" in the sense that they are either still learning English, or else they have lost some earlier ability to use their original, heritage language—or occasionally a bit of both. The first sort of student—sometimes called an *English language learner* (**ELL**) or *limited English learner* (**LEL**)—has received the greatest attention and concern from educators, since English is the dominant language of instruction and skill and obviously helps prepare a student for life in American society. ELL students essentially present teachers with this dilemma: how to respect the original language and culture of the student while *also* helping the student to join more fully in the mainstream—i.e. English-speaking—culture? Programs to address this question have ranged from total immersion in English from a young age (the "sink or swim" approach) to phasing in English over a period of several years (sometimes called an *additive* approach to bilingual education). In general, evaluations of bilingual programs have favored the more additive approaches (Beykont, 2002). Both languages are developed and supported, and students ideally become able to use either language permanently, though often for different situations or purposes. A student may end up using English in the classroom or at work, for example, but continue using Spanish at home or with friends, even though he or she is perfectly capable of speaking English with them.

Language loss

What about the other kind of imbalance, in which a student is acquiring English but losing ability with the student's home or heritage language? This sort of bilingualism is quite common in the United States and other nations with immigrant populations (Tse, 2001). Imagine this situation: First-generation immigrants arrive, and they soon learn just enough English to manage their work and daily needs, but continue using their original language at home with family and friends from their former country. Their children, however, experience strong expectations and pressure to learn and use English, and this circumstance dilutes the children's experience with the heritage language. By the time the children become adults, they are likely to speak and write English better than their heritage language, and may even be unable or unwilling to use the heritage language with their own children (the grandchildren of the original immigrants).

This situation might not at first seem like a problem for which we, as teachers, need to take responsibility, since the children immigrants, as students, are acquiring the dominant language of instruction. In fact, however, things are not that simple. Research finds that language loss limits students' ability to learn English as well or as quickly as they otherwise can do. Having a large vocabulary in a first language, for example, has been shown to save time in learning vocabulary in a second language (Hansen, Umeda & McKinney, 2002). But students can only realize the savings if their first language is preserved. Preserving the first language is also important if a student has impaired skill in *all* languages and therefore needs intervention or help from a speech-language specialist. Research has found, in such cases, that the specialist can be more effective if the specialist speaks and uses the first language as well as English (Kohnert, et al., 2005). Generally, though also more indirectly, minimizing language loss helps all bilingual students' education because preservation tends to enrich students' and parents' ability to communicate with each other. With two languages to work with, parents can stay "in the loop" better about their children's educations and support the teacher's work—for example, by assisting more effectively with homework (Ebert, 2005).

Note that in the early years of schooling, language loss can be minimized to some extent by the additive or parallel-track bilingual programs that I mentioned above. For a few years, though not forever, young students are encouraged to use *both* of their languages. In high school, in addition, some conventional foreign language classes— notably in Spanish—can be adjusted to include and support students who are already native speakers of the language alongside students who are learning it for the first time (Tse, 2001). But for heritage languages not normally offered as "foreign" languages in school, of course, this approach will not work. Such languages are especially at risk for being lost.

Cultural differences in language use

Cultures and ethnic groups differ not only in languages, but also in how languages are used. Since some of the patterns differ from those typical of modern classrooms, they can create misunderstandings between teachers and students (Cazden, 2001; Rogers, et al., 2005). Consider these examples: In some cultures, it is considered polite or even intelligent not to speak unless you have something truly important to say. "Chitchat", or talk that simply affirms a personal tie between people, is considered immature or intrusive (Minami, 2002). In a classroom, this habit can make it easier for a child to learn not to interrupt others, but it can also make the child seem unfriendly.

- *Eye contact* varies by culture. In many African American and Latin American communities, it is considered appropriate and respectful for a child not to look directly at an adult who is speaking to them (Torres-Guzman, 1998). In classrooms, however, teachers often expect a lot of eye contact (as in "I want all eyes on me!") and may be tempted to construe lack of eye contact as a sign of indifference or disrespect.

- *Social distance* varies by culture. In some cultures, it is common to stand relatively close when having a conversation; in others, it is more customary to stand relatively far apart (Beaulieu, 2004). Problems may happen when a teacher and a student prefer different social distances. A student who expects a closer distance than does the teacher may seem overly familiar or intrusive, whereas one who expects a longer distance may seem overly formal or hesitant.

- *Wait time* varies by culture. Wait time is the gap between the end of one person's comment or question and the next person's reply or answer. In some cultures wait time is relatively long—as long as three or four seconds (Tharp & Gallimore, 1989). In others it is a "negative" gap, meaning that it is acceptable, even expected, for a person to interrupt before the end of the previous comment. In classrooms the wait time is customarily about one second; after that, the teacher is likely to move on to another question or to another student. A student who habitually expects a wait time long than one second may seem hesitant, and not be given many chances to speak. A student who expects a "negative" wait time, on the other hand, may seem overeager or even rude.

- In most non-Anglo cultures, *questions* are intended to gain information, and it is assumed that a person asking the question truly does not have the information requested (Rogoff, 2003). In most classrooms, however, teachers regularly ask *test questions,* which are questions to which the teacher already knows the answer and that simply assess whether a student knows the answer as well (Macbeth, 2003). The question: *"How much is 2 + 2?"* for example, is a test question. If the student is not aware of this purpose, he or she may become confused, or think that the teacher is surprisingly ignorant! Worse yet, the student may feel that the teacher is trying deliberately to shame the student by revealing the student's ignorance or incompetence to others.

Cultural differences in attitudes and beliefs

In addition to differences in language and in practices related to language, cultural groups differ in a variety of other attitudes and beliefs. Complete descriptions of the details of the differences have filled entire books of encyclopedias (see, for example, Birx, 2005). For teachers, however, the most important ones center on beliefs about **identity,** or the sense of self, or of "who you are". A number of other cultural beliefs and practices can be understood as resulting from how members of a culture think about personal identity.

In white, middle-class American culture, the self is usually thought of as unique and independent—a unitary, living source of decisions, choices, and actions that stands (or should eventually stand) by itself (Greenfield, et al., 2003; Rogoff, 2003). This view of the self is well entrenched in schools, as for example when students are expected to take responsibility for their own successes or failures and when they are tested and evaluated individually rather than as a group or team. As teachers, furthermore, most of us subscribe to the idea that all students are unique, even if we cannot implement this idea fully in teaching because of the constraints of large classes. Whatever the circumstances, teachers tend to believe in an **independent self.**

4. Student diversity

To a greater or lesser extent, however, the majority of non-white cultures and ethnic groups believe in something closer to an **interdependent self,** or a belief that it is your relationships and responsibilities, and not uniqueness and autonomy, that defines a person (Greenfield, 1994; Greenfield, et al., 2003). In these cultures, the most worthy person is not the one who is unusual or who stands out in a crowd. Such a person might actually be regarded as lonely or isolated. The worthy person is instead the one who gets along well with family and friends, and who meets obligations to them reliably and skillfully. At some level, of course, we *all* value interpersonal skill and to this extent think of ourselves as interdependent. The difference between individual and interdependent self is one of emphasis, with many non-white cultures emphasizing interdependence significantly more than white middle-class society in general and more than schools in particular.

There can be consequences of the difference in how the students respond to school. Here are some of the possibilities—though keep in mind that there are also differences among students as individuals, whatever their cultural background. I am talking about tendencies, not straightforward predictions.

- *Preference for activities that are cooperative rather than competitive:* Many activities in school are competitive, even when teachers try to de-emphasize the competition. Once past the first year or second year of school, students often become attentive to who receives the highest marks on an assignment, for example, or who is the best athlete at various sports or whose contributions to class discussion the most verbal recognition from the teacher (Johnson & Johnson, 1998). Suppose, in addition, that a teacher deliberately organizes important activities or assignments competitively (as in "Let's see who finishes the math sheet first."). Classroom life can then become explicitly competitive, and the competitive atmosphere can interfere with cultivating supportive relationships among students or between students and the teacher (Cohen, 2004). For students who give priority to these relationships, competition can seem confusing at best and threatening at worst. What sort of sharing or helping with answers, the student may ask, is truly legitimate? If the teacher answers this question more narrowly than does the student, then what the student views as cooperative sharing may be seen by the teacher as laziness, "freeloading", or even cheating.

- *Avoidance of standing out publicly:* Even when we, as teachers, avoid obvious forms of competition, we may still interact frequently with students one at a time while allowing or inviting many others to observe the conversation. An especially common pattern for such conversations is sometimes called the **IRE** cycle, an abbreviation for the teacher *initiating,* a student *responding,* and the teacher then *evaluating* the response (Mehan, 1979). What is sometimes taken for granted is how often IRE cycles are witnessed publicly, and how much the publicity can be stressful or embarrassing for students who do *not* value standing out in a group but who *do* value belonging to the group. The embarrassment can be especially acute if they feel unsure about whether they have correct knowledge or skill to display. To keep such students from "clamming up" completely, therefore, teachers should consider limiting IRE cycles to times when they are truly productive. IRE conversations may often work best when talking with a student privately, or when confirming knowledge that the student is likely to be able to display competently already, or when "choral" speaking (responding together in unison) is appropriate.

- *Interpersonal time versus clock time:* In order to function, all schools rely on fairly precise units of time as measured on clocks. Teachers typically allot a fixed number of minutes to one lesson or class, another fixed number of minutes for the next, another for recess or lunch time, and so on. In more ways than one, therefore, being on time becomes especially valued in schools, as it is in many parts of society. Punctuality is not always conducive, however, to strong personal relationships, which develop best when individuals do not end joint activities unilaterally or arbitrarily, but allow activities to "finish themselves", so to speak—to finish naturally. If personal relationships are a broad, important priority for a student, therefore, it may take effort and practice by the student to learn the extent to which schools and teachers expect punctuality. Punctuality includes the obvious, like showing up for school when school is actually scheduled to begin. But it also includes subtleties, like starting and finishing tasks when the teacher tells students to do so, or answering a question promptly at the time it is asked rather than sometime later when discussion has already moved on.

Accommodating diversity in practice

Hopefully I have persuaded you—if you did need persuading—that students are indeed diverse. The important question that follows from this point is what to do about the diversity. I have begun answering that question by including a number of suggestions in the sections and paragraphs of this chapter. But there is obviously more to be said about *accommodating* diversity—about actually working with students' diversity and turning it into a resource rather than a burden or challenge. In the rest of this book therefore I offer more suggestions not only about knowing how different one student can be from another, but also about diversifying teaching to acknowledge this fact. Differences among students remain a challenge during all phases of teaching, from planning instruction, to implementing lessons and activities, to assessing students' learning after lessons or activities are all finished. In the next chapter, I illustrate this reality by describing how students with disabilities can be included in classroom life— one of the more telling examples of accommodating to diversity.

Chapter summary

Students differ in a multitude of ways, both individually and as groups. Individually, for example, students have a preferred learning style as well as preferred cognitive or thinking styles. They also have unique profiles or intelligence or competence that affect how and what they learn most successfully.

In addition to individual diversity, students tend to differ according to their gender, although there are numerous individual exceptions. Motor abilities as well as motivation and experience with athletics gradually differentiate boys and girls, especially when they reach and begin high school. Socially, boys tend to adopt relationships that are more active and wide-ranging than do girls. Academically, girls tend to be a bit more motivated to receive slightly higher marks in school. Teachers sometimes contribute to gender role differences— perhaps without intending—by paying attention to boys more frequently and more publicly in class, and by distributing praise and criticism in ways differentiated by sex.

Students also differ according to cultures, language, and ethnic groups of their families. Many students are bilingual, with educational consequences that depend on their fluency in each of their two languages. If they have more difficulty with English, then programs that add their first language together with English have proved to be helpful. If they have more difficulty with their first language, they are risk for language loss, and the consequences are also negative even if more hidden from teachers' views.

In addition to language differences as such, students differ according to culture in how language is used or practiced—in taking turns at speaking, in eye contact, social distance, wait time, and the use of questions. Some of these differences in practice stem from cultural differences in attitudes about self-identity, with non-Anglo culturally tending to support a more interdependent view of the self than Anglo culture or the schools. Differences in attitudes and in use of language have several consequences for teachers. In particular—where appropriate—they should consider using cooperative activities, avoid highlighting individuals' accomplishments or failures, and be patient about students' learning to be punctual.

On the Internet

<**www.nabe.org**> This is the website for the National Association of Bilingual Educators, which represents both English Language Learners and their teachers. The website offers a variety of information, free of charge, about all aspects of bilingual education, including introductory summaries of the field, position papers released to the government and the press, and research articles from their journals.

<**www.singlesexschools.org**> This website represents the National Association for Single Sex Public Education, which as its name implies advocates for all-girl and all-boy classes and schools. The website contains thoughtful summaries of the advantages to both boys and girls if they are educated separately and in public schools. Whether you agree with their point of view or not, their point of view is worth considering; though keep in mind that their supporting information tends to come from media sources (e.g. newspapers) instead of full-fledged research studies.

Key terms

African-American English	Impulsivity
Balanced bilingualism	Independent self
Bilingual	Individual differences
Cognitive styles	Interdependent self
Culture	IRE cycle
Dialect	Language loss
Ebonics	Learning styles
English language learner (ELL)	Limited English learner (LEL)
Ethnicity	Metacognition
Eye contact	Multiple intelligences
Field dependence	Reflectivity
Field independence	Social distance
Gender roles	Test questions
Group differences	Unbalanced bilingualism
Identity	Wait time

References

Basow, S. & Rubenfeld, K. (2003). "Troubles talk": Effects of gender and gender-typing. *Sex Roles, 48*(3/4), 183-188.

Beykont, Z. (Ed.). (2002). *The power of culture: Teaching across language difference.* Cambridge, MA: Harvard Education Publishing Group.

Beaulieu, C. (2004). Intercultural study of personal space: A case study. *Journal of Applied Social Psychology, 34*(4), 794-805.

Birx, H. J. (2005). *Encyclopedia of human anthropology*. Thousand Oaks, CA: Sage Publications.

Bohn, A. (2003). Familiar voices: Using Ebonics communication techniques in the primary classroom. *Urban Education, 38*(6), 688-707.

Braddock, J., Sokol-Katz, J., Greene, A., & Basinger-Fleischman, L. (2005). Uneven playing fields: State variations in boys' and girls' access to and participation in high school interscholastic sports. *Sociological Spectrum,* 25(2), 231-250.

Cazden, C. (2001). *Classroom discourse, 2nd edition*. Portsmouth, NH: Heineman Publishers.

Cohen, E. (2004). *Teaching cooperative learning: The challenge for teacher education*. Albany, NY: State University of New York Press.

Davies, J. (2005). Expressions of gender: An analysis of pupils' gendered discourse styles in small group classroom discussions. *Discourse and Society, 14*(2), 115-132.

Davis, G. & Rimm, S. (2004). *Education of the gifted and talented, 5th edition*. Boston: Allyn & Bacon.

Delamont, S. (1996). *Women's place in education*. Brookfield, MA: Avebury Publishers.

Ebert, J. (2005). Linguistics: Tongue tied. *Nature, 438,* 148-149.

Erden, F. & Wolfgang, C. (2004). An exploration of the differences in teachers' beliefs related to discipline when dealing with male and female students. *Early Child Development and Care, 174*(1), 3-11.

Eisner, E. (2004). Multiple intelligences: Its tensions and possibilities. *Teachers College Record, 106*(1), 31.

Espelage, D. & Swearer, S. (2004). *Bullying in American schools: A socio-ecological perspective on prevention and intervention*. Mahwah, NJ: Erlbaum.

Evans, C. (2004). Exploring the relationship between cognitive style and teaching style. *Educational psychology, 24*(4), 509-530.

Francis, N. (2006). The development of secondary discourse ability and metalinguistic awareness in second language learners. *International Journal of Applied Linguistics, 16,* 37-47.

Freeman, D. (2004). *Trends in educational equity of girls and women*. Washington, D.C.: United States Department of Education, National Center for Educational Statistics.

Friend, M. (2007). *Special education: Contemporary perspectives for school professionals, 2nd edition*. Boston: Allyn & Bacon.

Gardner, H. (1983). *Frames of mind: The theory of multiple intelligences*. New York: Basic Books.

Gardner, H. (2003, April 21). *Multiple intelligences after twenty years*. Paper presented at the American Educational Research Association, Chicago, IL.

Garlick, K. (2002). Understanding the nature of the general factor of intelligence. *Psychological review, 109*(1), 116-136.

Golombok, S. & Fivush, R. (1994). *Gender development*. New York: Cambridge University Press.

4. Student diversity

Greenfield, P. (1994). Independence and interdependence as cultural scripts. In P. Greenfield & R. Cocking (Eds.), *Cross-cultural roots of minority child development,* pp. 1-40. Mahwah, NJ: Erlbaum.

Greenfield, P., Keller, H., Fuligni, A., & Maynard, A. (2003). Cultural pathways through universal development. *Annual Review of Psychology, 54,* 461-490.

Gottfredson, L. (2004). Intelligence: Is it the epidemiologists' elusive "fundamental cause" of social class inequalities in health? *Journal of Personality and Social Psychology, 86*(1), 174-199.

Hansen, L., Umeda, Y., & McKinney, M. (2002). Savings in the relearning of second language vocabulary: The effects of time and proficiency. *Language Learning, 52,* 653-663.

Hyde, J. (2005). The gender similarities hypothesis. *American Psychologist, 60*(6), 581-592.

Jimenez, R., Garcia, G., & Pearson. D. (1995). Three children, two languages, and strategic reading: Case studies in bilingual/monolingual reading. *American Educational Research Journal, 32*(1), 67-97.

Johnson, D. & Johnson, R. (1998). *Learning together and alone: Cooperative, competitive, and individualistic learning, 5ᵗʰ edition.* Boston: Allyn & Bacon.

Kohn, A. (2004). Test today, privatize tomorrow. *Phi Delta Kappan, 85*(8), 568-577.

Kohnert, K., Yim, D., Nett, K., Kan, P., & Duran, L. (2005). Intervention with linguistically diverse preschool children. *Language, Speech, and Hearing Services in Schools, 36,* 251-263.

Loo, R. (2004). Kolb's learning styles and learning preferences: Is there a linkage? *Educational psychology, 24*(1), 99-108.

Lubinski, D. (2004). 100 years after Spearman's "'General Intelligence,' Objectively Determined and Measured". *Journal of Personality and Social Psychology, 86*(1), 96-111.

Macbeth, D. (2003). Hugh Mehan's "Learning Lessons" reconsidered: On the differences between naturalistic and critical analysis of classroom discourse. *American Educational Research Journal, 40*(1), 239-280.

Maccoby, E. (2002). *Gender and social exchange: A developmental perspective.* San Francisco: Jossey-Bass.

Martinez-Roldan, C. & Malave, G. (2004). Language ideologies mediating literacy and identity in bilingual contexts. *Journal of early childhood literacy, 4*(2), 155-180.

Measor, L. & Sykes, P. (1992). *Gender and schools.* New York: Cassell.

Mehan, H. (1979). *Learning lessons: social organization in the classroom.* Cambridge, MA: Harvard University Press.

Messner, M., Dunca, M., & Cooky, C. (2003). Silence, sports bras, and wrestling porn. *Journal of Sport and Social Issues, 27*(1), 38-51.

Meyers-Sutton, C. (2005). *Multiple voices: An introduction to bilingualism.* Malden, MA: Blackwell Publishers.

Minami, M. (2002). *Culture-specific language styles: The development of oral narrative and literacy.* Clevedon, UK: Multilingual Matters.

Myaskovsky, L, Unikel, E., & Dew, M. (2005). Effects of gender diversity on performance and interpersonal behavior in small work groups. *Sex Roles, 52*(9/10), 645-657.

Pritchard, A. (2005). *Ways of learning: Learning theories and learning styles in the classroom.* London, UK: David Fulton.

Rogers, R., Malancharuvil-Berkes, E., Mosely, M., Hui, D., & O'Garro, G. (2005). Critical discourse analysis in education: A review of the literature. *Review of Educational Research, 75*(3), 365-416.

Rogoff, B. (2003). *The culture of human development.* New York: Oxford University Press.

Sadker, D. (2002). An educator's primer on the gender war. *Phi Delta Kappan, 84*(3), 235-240.

Shiever, S. & Maker, C. (2003). New directions in enrichment and acceleration. In N. Colangelo & G. Davis (Eds.), *Handbook fo gifted education, 3rd edition* (pp. 163-173). Boston: Allyn & Bacon.

Stahl, S. (2002). Different strokes for different folks? In L. Abbeduto (Ed.), *Taking sides: Clashing on controversial issue sin educational psychology* (pp. 98-107). Guilford, CT: McGraw Hill.

Steiner, H. & Carr, M. (2003). Cognitive development in gifted children: Toward a more precise understanding of emerging differences in intelligence. *Educational Psychology Review, 15,* 215-246.

Tannen, D. (2001). *You just don't understand: Men and women in conversation.* New York: Quill.

Tharp, R. & Gallimore, R. (1989). *Rousing minds to life.* New York: Cambridge University Press.

Torres-Guzman, M. (1998). Language culture, and literacy in Puerto Rican communities. In B. Perez (Ed.), *Sociocultural contexts of language and literacy.* Mahwah, NJ: Erlbaum.

Tse, L. (2001). *Why don't they learn English?* New York: Teachers' College Press.

United States Department of Commerce, Bureau of the Census. (2003). *American community survey.* Washington, D.C.: Author.

Wilkinson, L. & Marrett, C. (Eds.). (1985). *Gender influences in classroom interaction.* Orlando, FL: Academic Press.

Zhang, L. & Sternberg, R. (2005). Three-fold model of intellectual styles. *Educational psychology review, 17*(1).

Zhang, L. & Sternberg, R. (2006). The nature of intellectual styles. Mahwah, NJ: Erlbaum

5. Students with special educational needs

Three people on the margins

The first person: In 1761 a six-year-old girl was captured from West Africa, given the name Phillis Wheatley, and sold into slavery in the City of Boston in Colonial America. By the time she was 17, Phillis had taught herself to read and write and had developed a special love and talent for poetry. Her owner was a wealthy businessman and sought to improve his reputation by publishing an anthology of her poems. Unfortunately he encountered stiff resistance from publishers because few people at that time believed Africans to be capable of the thought and imagination needed to write poetry. People who heard of her poetry were skeptical and inclined to think that it was faked. Eventually, to save his own reputation, the owner assembled a tribunal of 18 prominent judges—including the governor of Massachusetts and John Hancock, one of the signers of the Declaration of Independence—to assess the young woman's mental capacity. After cross-examining her, the judges finally decided that Ms Wheatley was, after all, capable of writing poetry (Robinson, 1982).

The second person: A century later, a child named Helen Keller lost her sight and hearing as a result of illness during infancy. In spite of this misfortune, though, Helen devised a language of gestural signs for communicating with a tutor, and was soon also using Braille to study both French and Latin. At ten, she wrote and published a short story. Yet like Ms Wheatley, Ms Keller also faced substantial, chronic skepticism about her capacities. Prominent educators accused her of plagiarizing others' writings and merely "parroting" others' ideas without understanding them (Keller, 1954; Bogdan, 2006). Eventually, as with Wheatley, a panel was assembled—though this time the members were professional experts about disabilities—to determine whether Ms Keller was in fact capable of writing what she published. The panel decided that she was indeed capable, though only by a slim margin (five judges vs four).

The third person: In 1978, Sue Rubin was born with a disability that limited her speech to disordered bursts of sound and occasionally echoing phrases of other people. She was labeled *autistic* because of her symptoms, and assumed to be profoundly retarded. With support and encouragement from her mother and others, however, Sue eventually learned to type on a keyboard without assistance. She learned to communicate effectively when she was about 13 and was able to go to school. Since then she has made many presentations about autism at conferences and recently co-edited a book about autism, titled *Autism: The Myth of the Person Alone* (Bogdan, et al., 2005).

One of these individuals experienced racial discrimination and the other two experienced physical disabilities, but notice something important: that all three were defined by society as disabled intellectually. Initially, their achievements were dismissed because of widespread assumptions—whether about race or disability—of their inherent incompetence. All three had to work harder than usual, not only to acquire literacy itself, but also to prove that their literacy was genuine and worthy of respect.

Since the time of Phillis Wheatley, North American society has eliminated slavery and made some progress at reducing certain forms of racism, though much remains to be done. In 1954, for example, the United States Supreme Court ruled that public schools could not be segregated by race, and in doing so recognized, at least legally, the intellectual competence of African-Americans as well as the moral obligation of society to provide all citizens with the best possible education. It has taken longer to recognize legally the rights and competence of persons with disabilities, but events and trends beginning in the 1970s have begun to make it happen. This chapter begins by explaining some of these and how they have altered the work of teachers.

Growing support for people with disabilities: legislation and its effects

Since the 1970s political and social attitudes have moved increasingly toward including people with disabilities into a wide variety of "regular" activities. In the United States, the shift is illustrated clearly in the Federal legislation that was enacted during this time. The legislation partly stimulated the change in attitudes, but at the same time they partly resulted from the change. Three major laws were passed that guaranteed the rights of persons with disabilities, and of children and students with disabilities in particular. Although the first two affected teachers' work in the classroom, the third has had the biggest impact on education.

Rehabilitation Act of 1973, Section 504

This law—the first of its kind—required that individuals with disabilities be accommodated in any program or activity that receives Federal funding (PL 93-112, 1973). Although this law was not intended specifically for education, in practice it has protected students' rights in some extra-curricular activities (for older students) and in some child care or after-school care programs (for younger students). If those programs receive Federal funding of any kind, the programs are not allowed to exclude children or youths with disabilities, and they have to find reasonable ways to accommodate the individuals' disabilities.

Americans with Disabilities Act of 1990 (or ADA).

This legislation also prohibited discrimination on the basis of disability, just as Section 504 of the Rehabilitation Act had done (PL 101-336, 1990). Although the ADA also applies to all people (not just to students), its provisions are more specific and "stronger" than those of Section 504. In particular, ADA extends to *all* employment and jobs, not just those receiving Federal funding. It also specifically requires accommodations to be made in public facilities such as with buses, restrooms, and telephones. ADA legislation is therefore responsible for some of the "minor" renovations in schools that you may have noticed in recent years, like wheelchair-accessible doors, ramps, and restrooms, and public telephones with volume controls.

Individuals with Disabilities Education Act (or IDEA)

As its name implied this legislation was more focused on education than either Section 504 or ADA. It was first passed in 1975 and has been amended several times since, including most recently in 2004 (PL 108-446, 2004). In its current form, the law guarantees the following rights related to education for anyone with a disability from birth to age 21. The first two influence schooling in general, but the last three affect the work of classroom teachers rather directly:

- *Free, appropriate education:* An individual or an individual's family should not have to pay for education simply because the individual has a disability, and the educational program should be truly educational (i.e. not merely care-taking or "babysitting" of the person).

- *Due process:* In case of disagreements between an individual with a disability and the schools or other professionals, there must be procedures for resolving the disagreements that are fair and accessible to all parties—including the person himself or herself or the person's representative.

- *Fair evaluation of performance in spite of disability:* Tests or other evaluations should not assume test-taking skills that a person with a disability cannot reasonably be expected to have, such as holding a pencil, hearing or seeing questions, working quickly, or understanding and speaking orally. Evaluation procedures should be modified to allow for these differences. This provision of the law applies *both* to evaluations made by teachers and to school-wide or "high-stakes" testing programs.

- *Education in the "least restrictive environment":* Education for someone with a disability should provide as many educational opportunities and options for the person as possible, both in the short term and in the long term. In practice this requirement has meant including students in regular classrooms and school activities as much as possible, though often not totally.

- *An individualized educational program:* Given that every disability is unique, instructional planning for a person with a disability should be unique or individualized as well. In practice this provision has led to classroom teachers planning individualized programs jointly with other professionals (like reading specialists, psychologists, or medical personnel) as part of a team.

Considered together, these provisions are both a cause and an effect of basic democratic philosophy. The legislation says, in effect, that all individuals should have access to society in general and to education in particular. Although teachers certainly support this philosophy in broad terms, and many have welcomed the IDEA legislation, others have found the prospect of applying it in classrooms leads to a number of questions and concerns. Some ask, for example, whether a student with a disability will disrupt the class; others, whether the student will interfere with covering the curriculum; still others, whether the student might be teased by classmates. Since these are legitimate concerns, I will return to them at the end of this chapter. First, however, let me clarify exactly how the IDEA legislation affects the work of teachers, and then describe in more detail the major disabilities that you are likely to encounter in students.

Responsibilities of teachers for students with disabilities

The IDEA legislation has affected the work of teachers by creating three new expectations. The first expectation is to provide alternative methods of assessment for students with disabilities; the second is to arrange a learning environment that is as normal or as "least restrictive" as possible; and the third is to participate in creating individual educational plans for students with disabilities.

Alternative assessments

In the context of students with disabilities, **assessment** refers to gathering information about a student in order both to identify the strengths of the student, and to decide what special educational support, if any, the student needs. In principle, of course, these are tasks that teachers have for *all* students: assessment is a major reason why we give tests and assignments, for example, and why we listen carefully to the quality of students' comments during class discussions. For students with disabilities, however, such traditional or conventional strategies of assessment often seriously underestimate the students' competence (Koretz & Barton, 2003/2004; Pullin, 2005). Depending on the disability, a student may have trouble with (a) holding a pencil, (b) hearing a question clearly, (c) focusing on a picture, (d) marking an answer in time even when he or she knows the answer, (e) concentrating on a task in the presence of other people, or (f) answering a question at the pace needed by the rest of the class. Traditionally, teachers have assumed that all students either have these skills or can learn them with just modest amounts of coaching, encouragement, and will power. For many other students, for example, it may be enough to say something like: "Remember to listen to the question carefully!" For students with disabilities, however, a comment like this may not work and may even be insensitive. A student with visual impairment does not need be reminded to "look closely at what I am writing on the board"; doing so will not cause the student to see the chalkboard more clearly—though the reminder might increase the student's anxiety and self-consciousness.

There are a number of strategies for modifying assessments in ways that attempt to be fair and that at the same time recognize how busy teachers usually are. One is to consider supplementing conventional assignments or tests with **portfolios**, which are collections of a student's work that demonstrate a student's development over time, and which usually include some sort of reflective or evaluative comments from the student, the teacher, or both (Carothers & Taylor, 2003; Wesson & King, 1996). Another is to devise a system for observing the student regularly, even if briefly, and informally recording notes about the observations for later consideration and assessment. A third strategy is to recruit help from teacher assistants, who are sometimes present to help a student with a disability; an assistant can often conduct a brief test or activity with the student, and later report on and discuss the results with you.

If you reflect on these strategies, you may realize that they may sometimes create issues about fairness. If a student with a disability demonstrates competence one way but other students demonstrate it another, should they be given similar credit? On the other hand, is it fair for one student to get a lower mark because the student lacks an ability—such as normal hearing—that teachers cannot, in principle, ever teach? These ethical issues are legitimate and important, and I therefore return to them in Chapters 11 and 12, which discuss assessment in much more detail.

Least restrictive environment

The IDEA legislation calls for placing students with disabilities in the **least restrictive environment** (or **LRE**), defined as the combination of settings that involve the student with regular classrooms and school programs as much as possible. The precise combination is determined by the circumstances of a particular school and of the student. A kindergarten child with a mild cognitive disability, for example, may spend the majority of time in a regular kindergarten class, working alongside and playing with non-disabled classmates and relying on a teacher assistant for help where needed. An individual with a similar disability in high school, however, might be assigned primarily to classes specially intended for slow learners, but nonetheless participate in some school-wide activities alongside non-disabled students. The difference in LREs might reflect teachers' perceptions of how difficult it is to modify the curriculum in each case; rightly or wrongly, teachers are apt to regard adaptation as more challenging at "higher" grade levels. By the same token, a student with a disability that is strictly physical might spend virtually all his or her time in regular classes throughout the student's school career; in this case, adjustment of the curriculum would not be an issue.

For you, the policy favoring the least restrictive environment means that if you continue teaching long enough, you will very likely encounter a student with a disability in one or more of your classes, or at least have one in a school-related activity for which you are responsible. It also means that the special educational needs of these students will most often be the "mildest". Statistically, the most frequent forms of special needs are *learning disabilities,* which are impairments in specific aspects of learning, and especially of reading. Learning disabilities account for about half of all special educational needs—as much as all other types put together. Somewhat less common are *speech and language disorders, cognitive disabilities,* and *attention deficit hyperactivity disorders* (or *ADHD)*. Because of their frequency and of the likelihood that you will meet students for whom these labels have been considered, I describe them more fully later in this chapter, along with other disability conditions that you will encounter much less frequently.

Individual educational plan

The third way that IDEA legislation and current educational approaches affect teachers is by requiring teachers and other professional staff to develop an annual **individual educational plan** (or **IEP**) for each student with a disability. The plan is created by a team of individuals who know the student's strengths and needs; at a minimum it includes one or more classroom teachers, a "resource" or special education teacher, and the student's parents or guardians. Sometimes, too, the team includes a school administrator (like a vice-principal) or other professionals from outside the school (like a psychologist or physician), depending on the nature of the child's disability. An IEP can take many forms, but it always describes a student's current social and academic strengths as well as the student's social or academic needs. It also specifies educational goals or objectives for the coming year, lists special services to be provided, and describes how progress toward the goals will be assessed at the end of the year. Exhibit 6 shows a simple, imaginary IEP. (But keep in mind that the actual visual formats of IEP plans vary widely among states, provinces, and school jurisdictions.) This particular plan is for a student named Sean, a boy having difficulties with reading. IEPs, like the one in the figure, originally served mainly students in the younger grades, but more recently they have been extended and modified to serve **transition planning** for adolescents with disabilities who are approaching the end of their public schooling (West, et al., 1999). For these students, the goals of the plan often include activities (like finding employment) to extend beyond schooling. See below.

5. Students with special educational needs

Student: Sean Cortinez	Birth Date: 26 May 2002	Period Covered by IEP: September 20xx – July 20xy
Address:		Phone:
School: Grant Park Middle School	Grade Level: 3	Teacher(s): G. Eidse

Support Team

List specialists (educational, medical, or other) involved in assisting the student:

Resource teacher, instructional aide (part time):

Special Curriculum Needs to be Addressed:

List general needs here; use separate sheet(s) for specific, short-term objectives as appropriate:

Sean can read short, familiar words singly, but cannot read connected text even when familiar. Needs help especially with decoding and other "word attack" skills. Some trouble focusing on reading tasks. Sean speaks clearly and often listens well when the topic interests him.

Special Materials or Equipment Needed:

Modified test procedures and reading materials as required.

Signatures:

Parent or guardian: K. Cortinez

Teacher(s): G. Eidse

Principal: L. Stauffer

Date of IEP Meeting: 26 October 20xx

Exhibit 6: A sample individual educational plan. (Note that actual visual formats of IEP plans vary.)

If you have a student with an IEP, you can expect two consequences for teaching. The first is that you should expect to make definite, clear plans for the student, and to put the plans in writing. This consequence does not, of course, prevent you from taking advantage of unexpected or spontaneous classroom events as well in order to enrich the curriculum. But it does mean that an educational program for a student with a disability cannot consist *only* of the unexpected or spontaneous. The second consequence is that you should not expect to construct an educational plan alone, as is commonly done when planning regular classroom programs. When it comes to students with disabilities, expect instead to plan as part of a team. Working with others ensures that everyone who is concerned about the student has a voice. It also makes it possible to improve the quality of IEPs by pooling ideas from many sources—even if, as you might suspect, it also challenges professionals to communicate clearly and cooperate respectfully with team members in order to serve a student as well as possible.

Categories of disabilities—and their ambiguities

So far I have said a lot about why inclusion has come to be important for teachers, but not much about the actual nature of students' disabilities. Part of the reason for delaying was because, to put it simply, disabilities are inherently ambiguous. Naming and describing "types" of them implies that disabilities are relatively fixed, stable, and distinct, like different kinds of fruit or vegetables. As many teachers discover, though, the reality is somewhat different. The behavior and qualities of a particular student with a disability can be hard to categorize. The student may be challenged not only by the disability, but also by experiences common to all students, disabled or not. Any particular disability, furthermore, poses problems more in some situations than in others. A student with a reading difficulty may have trouble in a language arts class, for example, but not in a physical education class; a student with a hearing impairment may have more trouble "hearing" a topic that he *dis*likes compared to one that he likes. Because official descriptions of types or categories of disabilities overlook these complexities, they risk stereotyping the real, live people to whom they are applied (Green, et al., 2005). Even the simplifications might not be a serious problem if the resulting stereotypes were complimentary—most of us would not mind being called a "genius", for example, even if the description is not always true. Stereotypes about disabilities, however, are usually stigmatizing, not complimentary.

Still, categories of disabilities do serve useful purposes by giving teachers, parents, and other professionals a language or frame of reference for talking about disabilities. They also can help educators when arranging special support services for students, since a student has to "have" an identifiable, nameable need if professionals are to provide help. Educational authorities have therefore continued to use categories (or "labels") to classify disabilities in spite of expressing continuing concern about whether the practice hurts students' self-esteem or standing in the eyes of peers (Biklen & Kliewer, 2006). For classroom teachers, the best strategy may be simply to understand how categories of disabilities are defined, while also keeping their limitations in mind and being ready to explain their limitations (tactfully, of course) to parents or others who use the labels *in*appropriately.

That said, what in fact are the major types of disabilities encountered by teachers? Let us take them one at a time, beginning with the more common ones.

Learning disabilities

A **learning disability** (or **LD**) is a specific impairment of academic learning that interferes with a specific aspect of schoolwork and that reduces a student's academic performance significantly. An LD shows itself as a major discrepancy between a student's ability and some feature of achievement: the student may be delayed in reading, writing, listening, speaking, or doing mathematics, but not in all of these at once. A learning problem is not considered a *learning* disability if it stems from physical, sensory, or motor handicaps, or from generalized intellectual impairment (or mental retardation). It is also not an LD if the learning problem really reflects the challenges of learning English as a second language. Genuine LDs are the learning problems left over after these other possibilities are accounted for or excluded. Typically, a student with an LD has not been helped by teachers' ordinary efforts to assist the student when he or she falls behind academically—though what counts as an "ordinary effort", of course, differs among teachers, schools, and students. Most importantly, though, an LD relates to a fairly specific area of academic learning. A student may be able to read and compute well enough, for example, but not be able to write.

LDs are by far the most common form of special educational need, accounting for half of all students with special needs in the United States and anywhere from 5 to 20 per cent of all students, depending on how the numbers are estimated (United States Department of Education, 2005; Ysseldyke & Bielinski, 2002). Students with LDs are so common, in fact, that most teachers regularly encounter at least one per class in any given school year, regardless of the grade level they teach.

Defining learning disabilities clearly

With so many students defined as having learning disabilities, it is not surprising that the term itself becomes ambiguous in the truest sense of "having many meanings". Specific features of LDs vary considerably. Any of the following students, for example, qualify as having a learning disability, assuming that they have no other disease, condition, or circumstance to account for their behavior:

- Albert, an eighth-grader, has trouble solving word problems that he reads, but can solve them easily if he hears them orally.

- Bill, also in eighth grade, has the reverse problem: he can solve word problems only when he can read them, not when he hears them.

- Carole, a fifth-grader, constantly makes errors when she reads textual material aloud, either leaving out words, adding words, or substituting her own words for the printed text.

- Emily, in seventh grade, has terrible handwriting; her letters vary in size and wobble all over the page, much like a first- or second-grader.

- Denny reads very slowly, even though he is in fourth grade. His comprehension suffers as a result, because he sometimes forgets what he read at the beginning of a sentence by the time he reaches the end.

- Garnet's spelling would have to be called "inventive", even though he has practiced conventionally correct spelling more than other students. Garnet is in sixth grade.

- Harmin, a ninth-grader has particular trouble decoding individual words and letters if they are unfamiliar; he reads *conceal* as "concol" and *alternate* as "alfoonite".

- Irma, a tenth-grader, adds multiple-digit numbers as if they were single-digit numbers stuck together: *42 + 59* equals *911* rather than *101,* though *23 + 54* correctly equals *77.*

With so many expressions of LDs, it is not surprising that educators sometimes disagree about their nature and about the kind of help students need as a consequence. Such controversy may be inevitable because LDs by definition are learning problems with no obvious origin. There is good news, however, from this state of affairs, in that it opens the way to try a variety of solutions for helping students with learning disabilities.

Assisting students with learning disabilities

There are various ways to assist students with learning disabilities, depending not only on the nature of the disability, of course, but also on the concepts or theory of learning guiding you. Take Irma, the girl mentioned above who adds two-digit numbers as if they were one digit numbers. Stated more formally, Irma adds two-digit numbers without carrying digits forward from the ones column to the tens column, or from the tens to the hundreds column. Exhibit 7 shows the effect that her strategy has on one of her homework papers. What is going on here and how could a teacher help Irma?

Directions: Add the following numbers.

42	23	11	47	97	41
+59	+54	+48	+23	+64	+27
911	77	59	610	1511	68

Three out of the six problems are done correctly, even though Irma seems to use an incorrect strategy systematically on all six problems.

Exhibit 7: Irma's math homework about two-digit addition

Behaviorism: reinforcement for wrong strategies

One possible approach comes from the behaviorist theory discussed in Chapter 2. Irma may persist with the single-digit strategy because it has been reinforced a lot in the past. Maybe she was rewarded so much for adding single-digit numbers (3+5, 7+8 etc.) correctly that she generalized this skill to two-digit problems—in fact *over* generalized it. This explanation is plausible because she would still get many two-digit problems right, as you can confirm by looking at it. In behaviorist terms, her incorrect strategy would still be reinforced, but now only on a "partial schedule of reinforcement". As I pointed out in Chapter 2, partial schedules are especially slow to extinguish, so Irma persists seemingly indefinitely with treating two-digit problems as if they were single-digit problems.

From the point of view of behaviorism, changing Irma's behavior is tricky since the desired behavior (borrowing correctly) rarely happens and therefore cannot be reinforced very often. It might therefore help for the teacher to reward behaviors that compete directly with Irma's inappropriate strategy. The teacher might reduce credit for simply finding the correct answer, for example, and increase credit for a student showing her work—including the work of carrying digits forward correctly. Or the teacher might make a point of discussing Irma's math work with Irma frequently, so as to create more occasions when she can praise Irma for working problems correctly.

Metacognition and responding reflectively

Part of Irma's problem may be that she is thoughtless about doing her math: the minute she sees numbers on a worksheet, she stuffs them into the first arithmetic procedure that comes to mind. Her learning style, that is, seems too impulsive and not reflective enough, as discussed in Chapter 4. Her style also suggests a failure of metacognition (remember that idea from Chapter 2?), which is her self-monitoring of her own thinking and its effectiveness. As a solution, the teacher could encourage Irma to think out loud when she completes two-digit problems—literally get her to "talk her way through" each problem. If participating in these conversations was sometimes impractical, the teacher might also arrange for a skilled classmate to take her place some of the time. Cooperation between Irma and the classmate might help the classmate as well, or even improve overall social relationships in the classroom.

Constructivism, mentoring, and the zone of proximal development

Perhaps Irma has in fact learned how to carry digits forward, but not learned the procedure well enough to use it reliably on her own; so she constantly falls back on the earlier, better-learned strategy of single-digit addition. In that case her problem can be seen in the constructivist terms, like those that I discussed in Chapter 2. In essence, Irma has lacked appropriate mentoring from someone more expert than herself, someone who can create a "zone of proximal development" in which she can display and consolidate her skills more successfully. She still needs mentoring or "assisted coaching" more than independent practice. The teacher can arrange some of this in much the way she encourages to be more reflective, either by working with Irma herself or by arranging for a classmate or even a parent volunteer to do so. In this case, however, whoever serves as mentor should not only listen, but also actively offer Irma help. The help has to be just enough to insure that Irma completes two-digit problems correctly —neither more nor less. Too much help may prevent Irma from taking responsibility for learning the new strategy, but too little may cause her to take the responsibility prematurely.

Attention deficit hyperactivity disorder

Attention deficit hyperactivity disorder (or **ADHD**) is a problem with sustaining attention and controlling impulses. As students, almost all of us have these problems at one time or another, but a student with ADHD shows them much more frequently than usual, and often at home as well as at school. In the classroom, the student with ADHD may fidget and squirm a lot, or have trouble remaining seated, or continually get distracted and off task, or have trouble waiting for a turn, or blurt out answers and comments. The student may shift continually from one activity to another, or have trouble playing quietly, or talk excessively without listening to others. Or the student may misplace things and seem generally disorganized, or be inclined to try risky activities without enough thought to the consequences. Although the list of problem behaviors is obviously quite extensive, keep in mind that the student will not do *all* of these things. It is just that over time, the student with ADHD is likely to do several of them chronically or repeatedly, and in more than one setting (American Psychiatric Association, 2000). In the classroom, of course, the behaviors may annoy classmates and frustrate teachers.

Differences in perceptions: ADHD versus high activity

It is important to note that classrooms are places that make heavy demands on *not* showing ADHD-like behaviors: students are often supposed to sit for long periods, avoid interrupting others, finish tasks after beginning them, and keep their minds (and materials) organized. Ironically, therefore, classroom life may sometimes aggravate ADHD without the teacher intending for it to do so. A student with only a mild or occasional tendency to be restless, for example, may fit in well outdoors playing soccer, but feel unusually restless indoors during class. It also should not be surprising that teachers sometimes mistake a student who is merely rather active for a student with ADHD, since any tendency to be physically active may contribute to problems with classroom management.

The tendency to "over-diagnose" is more likely for boys than for girls (Maniadaki, et al., 2003), presumably because gender role expectations cause teachers to be especially alert to high activity in boys. Over-diagnosis is also especially likely for students who are culturally or linguistically non-Anglo (Chamberlain, 2005), presumably because cultural and language differences may sometimes lead teachers to misinterpret students' behavior. To avoid making such mistakes, it is important to keep in mind that in true ADHD, restlessness, activity, and distractibility are widespread and sustained. A student who shows such problems at school but never at home, for example, may not have ADHD; he may simply not be getting along with his teacher or classmates.

Causes of ADHD

Most psychologists and medical specialists agree that true ADHD, as opposed to "mere" intermittent distractibility or high activity, reflects a problem in how the nervous system functions, but they do not know the exact nature or causes of the problem (Rutter, 2004, 2005). Research shows that ADHD tends to run in families, with children—especially boys—of parents who had ADHD somewhat more likely than usual to experience the condition themselves. The association does not necessarily mean, though, that ADHD is inborn or genetic. Why? It is because it is possible that parents who formerly had ADHD may raise their children more strictly in an effort to prevent their own condition in their children; yet their strictness, ironically, may trigger a bit more tendency, rather than less, toward the restless distractibility characteristic of ADHD. On the other hand (or is it "on the third hand"?), the parents' strictness may also be a *result,* as well as a cause of, a child's restlessness. The bottom line for teachers: sorting out causes from effects is confusing, if not impossible, and in any case may not help much to determine actual teaching strategies to help the students learn more effectively.

Teaching students with ADHD

Research also shows that ADHD can be reduced for many students if they take certain medications, of which the most common is *methylphenidate,* commonly known by the name Ritalin (Wilens, 2005; Olfson, 2003). This drug and others like it act by stimulating the nervous system, which reduces symptoms by helping a student pay better attention to the choices he or she makes and to the impact of actions on others. Unfortunately the medications do not work on all students with ADHD, especially after they reach adolescence, and in any case has certain practical problems. Drugs cost money, for one thing, which is a problem for a family without much money to begin with, or for a family lacking medical insurance that pays for medications—a particularly common situation in the United States. For another thing, drugs must be taken regularly in order to be effective, including on weekends. Keeping a regular schedule can be difficult if parents' own schedules are irregular or simply differ from the child's, for example because of night shifts at work or because parents are separated and share custody of the child.

In any case, since teachers are not doctors and medications are not under teachers' control, it may be more important simply to provide an environment where a student with ADHD can organize choices and actions easily and successfully. Clear rules and procedures, for example, can reduce the "noise" or chaotic quality in the child's classroom life significantly. The rules and procedures can be generated jointly with the child; they do not have to be imposed arbitrarily, as if the student were incapable of thinking about them reasonably. Sometimes a classmate can be enlisted to model slower, more reflective styles of working, but in ways that do not imply undue criticism of the student with ADHD. The more reflective student can complete a set of math problems, for example, while explaining what he or she is thinking about while doing the work. Sometimes the teacher can help by making lists of tasks or of steps in long tasks. It can help to divide focused work into small, short sessions rather than grouping it into single, longer sessions. Whatever the strategies that you use, they should be consistent, predictable, and generated by the student as much as possible. By having these qualities, the strategies can strengthen the student's self-direction and ability to screen out the distractions of classroom life. The goal for teachers, in essence, is to build the student's metacognitive capacity, while at the same time, of course, treating the student with respect.

Intellectual disabilities

An **intellectual disability** is a significant limitation in a student's cognitive functioning and daily adaptive behaviors (Schalock & Luckasson, 2004; American Association on Mental Retardation, 2002). The student may have limited language or impaired speech and may not perform well academically. Compared to students with learning disabilities discussed earlier, students with intellectual disabilities have impairments to learning that are broader and more significant. They score poorly on standardized tests of intelligence (like the ones discussed later, in Chapter 12). Everyday tasks that most people take for granted, like getting dressed or eating a meal, may be possible, but they may also take more time and effort than usual. Health and safety can sometimes be a concern (for example, knowing whether it is safe to cross a street). For older individuals, finding and keeping a job may require help from supportive others. The exact combination of challenges varies from one person to another, but it always (by definition) involves limitations in *both* intellectual and daily functioning.

As a teacher, you may hear more than one term for describing students with intellectual disabilities. If the disability is mild, teachers sometimes refer to a student with the disability simply as a **slow learner**, particularly if the student has no formal, special supports for the disability, such as a teaching assistant hired specifically to assist the student. If the disability is more marked, then the student is more likely to be referred to either as having an **intellectual disability** or as having **mental retardation**. In this chapter I primarily use the term *intellectual disability*, because it has fewer negative connotations while still describing one key educational aspect of the disability, cognitive impairment. Keep in mind, however, that actual intellectual disabilities are always more than cognitive: they also involve challenges about adapting to everyday living.

Levels of support for individuals with intellectual disabilities

Intellectual disabilities happen in different degrees or amounts, though most often are relatively mild. Traditionally the intensity or "amount" of the disability was defined by scores on a standardized test of scholastic aptitude (or "IQ test"), with lower scores indicating more severe disability. (More about these tests in Chapter 12.) Because of the insensitivity of such tests to individuals' daily social functioning, however, current trends are toward defining intensities by the amount of support needed by the individual. Table 13 summarizes the most commonly used scheme for this purpose, one created by the American Association on Intellectual and Developmental Disabilities (AAMR, 2002). Levels of support range from *intermittent* (just occasional or "as needed" for specific activities) to *pervasive* (continuous in all realms of living).

Table 13: Levels and areas of support for intellectual disabilities

Level of support	Duration of support	Frequency of support	Setting of support	Amount of professional assistance
Intermittent	Only as needed	Occasional or	Usually only one	Occasional

		infrequent	or two (e.g. 1-2 classes or activities)	consultation or monitoring by professional
Limited	As needed, but sometimes continuing	Regular, but frequency varies	Several settings, but not usually all	Occasional or regular contact with professionals
Extensive	Usually continuing	Regular, but frequency varies	Several settings, but not usually all	Regular contact with professionals at least once a week
Pervasive	May be lifelong	Frequent or continuous	Nearly all settings	Continuous contact and monitoring by professionals

Source: American Association on Mental Retardation, 2002: Schalock & Luckassen, 2004.

As a classroom teacher, the intellectual disabilities that you are most likely to see are the ones requiring the least support in your classroom. A student requiring only intermittent support may require special help with some learning activities or classroom routines, but not others; he or she might need help with reading or putting on winter clothes, for example, but primarily on occasions when there is pressure to do these things relatively quickly. Students requiring somewhat more support are likely to spend somewhat less time in your classroom and more time receiving special help from other professionals, such as a special education teacher, a speech and language specialist, or an assistant to these professionals. These circumstances have distinct implications for ways of teaching these students.

Teaching students with intellectual disabilities

There are many specific techniques that can help in teaching students with mild or moderate intellectual disabilities, but most can be summarized into three more general strategies. The first is to give more time and practice than usual; the second is to embed activities into the context of daily life or functioning where possible; and the third is to include the child both in social and in academic activities, rather than just one or the other. Let us look briefly at each of these ideas.

Giving more time and practice than usual

If a student has only a mild intellectual disability, he or she can probably learn important fundamentals of the academic curriculum—basic arithmetic, for example, and basic reading. Because of the disability, though, the student may need more time or practice than most other students. He or she may be able to read many words by sight *(day, night, morning, afternoon, etc.),* but need longer than other students to recognize and say them. Or the student may know that *2 + 3 = 5,* but need help applying this math fact to real objects; you (or a helper) might need to show the student that two *pencils* plus three *pencils* make five *pencils.*

Giving extra help takes time and perseverance, and can try the patience of the student (and of you, too). To deal with this problem, it may help to reward the student frequently for effort and successes with well-timed praise, especially if it is focused on specific, actual achievements; "You added that one correctly", may be more helpful than "You're a hard worker", even if both comments are true. Giving appropriate praise is in turn easier if you set reasonable, "do-able" goals by breaking skills or tasks into steps that the student is likely to learn without becoming overly discouraged. At the same time, it is important not to insult the student with goals or activities that are *too* easy or by using curriculum materials clearly intended for children who are much younger. Setting expectations too low actually deprives a student with an intellectual disability of rightful opportunities to learn—a serious ethical and professional mistake (Bogdan, 2006). In many curriculum areas, fortunately, there already existing materials that are simplified, yet also appropriate for older students (Snell, et al., 2005). Special education teacher-specialists can often help in finding them and in devising effective ways of using them.

Adaptive and functional skills

Students with intellectual disabilities present especially clear examples of a universal dilemma of teaching: since there is not enough time to teach everything, how do we choose what to teach? One basis for selecting activities is to relate learning goals to students' everyday lives and activities, just as you would with all students. This strategy addresses the other defining feature of mental retardation, the student's difficulties with adapting to and functioning in everyday living. In teaching addition and subtraction, for example, you can create examples about the purchasing of common familiar objects (e.g. food) and about the need to make or receive change for the purchases. Similar considerations apply to learning new reading or oral language vocabulary. Instead of simply learning words in a "basic reading" series (or reading textbook), try encouraging the student to learn words that are especially useful to the student's own life. Often the student, not you yourself, is the best person to decide what these words actually are.

An adaptive, functional approach can help in nonacademic areas as well. In learning to read or "tell time" on a clock, for example, try focusing initially on telling the times important to the student, such as when he or she gets up in the morning or when schools starts. As you add additional times that are personally meaningful to the student, he or she works gradually towards full knowledge of how to read the hands on a clock. Even if the full knowledge proves slow to develop, however, the student will at least have learned the most useful clock knowledge first.

Include the student deliberately in group activities

The key word here is *inclusion:* the student should participate in and contribute to the life of the class as much as possible. This means that wherever possible, the student attends special events (assemblies, field days) with the class; that if the class plays a group game, then the student with the disability is part of the game; that if classmates do an assignment as a group, then if at all possible the student is assigned to one of the groups. The changes resulting from these inclusions are real, but can be positive for everyone. On the one hand, they foster acceptance and helpfulness toward the child with the disability; classmates learn that school is partly about providing opportunities for everyone, and not just about evaluating or comparing individuals' skills. On the other hand, the changes caused by inclusion stimulate the student with the disability to learn as much as possible from classmates, socially and academically. Among other benefits, group activities can give the student chances to practice "belonging" skills—how to greet classmates appropriately, or when and how to ask the teacher a question. These are skills, I might add, that are beneficial for everyone to learn, disabled or not. (I discuss group work more thoroughly in Chapter 9, "Facilitating complex thinking")

Behavioral disorders

Behavioral disorders are a diverse group of conditions in which a student chronically performs highly inappropriate behaviors. A student with this condition might seek attention, for example, by acting out disruptively in class. Other students with the condition might behave aggressively, be distractible and overly active, seem anxious or withdrawn, or seem disconnected from everyday reality. As with learning disabilities, the sheer range of signs and symptoms defies concise description. But the problematic behaviors do have several general features in common (Kauffman, 2005; Hallahan & Kauffman, 2006):

- they tend to be extreme

- they persist for extended periods of time

- they tend to be socially unacceptable (e.g. unwanted sexual advances or vandalism against school property)

- they affect school work

- they have no other obvious explanation (e.g. a health problem or temporary disruption in the family)

The variety among behavioral disorders means that estimates of their frequency also tend to vary among states, cities, and provinces. It also means that in some cases, a student with a behavioral disorder may be classified as having a different condition, such as ADHD or a learning disability. In other cases, a behavioral problem shown in one school setting may seem serious enough to be labeled as a behavioral disorder, even though a similar problem occurring in another school may be perceived as serious, but not serious enough to deserve the label. In any case, available statistics suggest that only about one to two per cent of students, or perhaps less, have true behavioral disorders—a figure that is only about one half or one third of the frequency for intellectual disabilities (Kauffman, 2005). Because of the potentially disruptive effects of behavioral disorders, however, students with this condition are of special concern to teachers. Just one student who is highly aggressive or disruptive can interfere with the functioning of an entire class, and challenge even the best teacher's management skills and patience.

Strategies for teaching students with behavioral disorders

The most common challenges of teaching students with behavioral disorders have to do with classroom management—a topic discussed more thoroughly in Chapter 7 ("Classroom management"). Three important ideas discussed there, however, also deserve special emphasis here: (1) identifying circumstances that trigger inappropriate behaviors, (2) teaching of interpersonal skills explicitly, and (3) disciplining a student fairly.

Identifying circumstances that trigger inappropriate behaviors

Dealing with a disruption is more effective if you can identify the specific circumstances or event that triggers it, rather than focusing on the personality of the student doing the disrupting. A wide variety of factors can trigger inappropriate behavior (Heineman, Dunlap, & Kincaid, 2005):

- physiological effects—including illness, fatigue, hunger, or side-effects from medications

- physical features of the classroom—such as the classroom being too warm or too cold, the chairs being exceptionally uncomfortable for sitting, or seating patterns that interfere with hearing or seeing

• instructional choices or strategies that frustrate learning—including restricting students' choices unduly, giving instructions that are unclear, choosing activities that are too difficult or too long, or preventing students from asking questions when they need help

By identifying the specific variables often associated with disruptive behaviors, it is easier to devise ways to prevent the behaviors, either by avoiding the triggers if this is possible, or by teaching the student alternative but quite specific ways of responding to the triggering circumstance.

Teaching interpersonal skills explicitly

Because of their history and behavior, some students with behavior disorders have had little opportunity to learn appropriate social skills. Simple courtesies (like remembering to say *please* or *thanks)* may not be totally unknown, but may be unpracticed and seem unimportant to the student, as might body language (like eye contact or sitting up to listen to a teacher rather than slouching and looking away). These skills can be taught in ways that do not make them part of punishment, make them seem "preachy", or put a student to shame in front of classmates. Depending on the age or grade-level of the class, one way is by reading or assigning books and stories in which the characters model good social skills. Another is through games that require courteous language to succeed; one that I recall from my own school days, for example, was called "Mother, May I?" (Sullivan & Strang, 2002). Still another is through programs that link an older student or adult from the community as a partner to the student at risk for behavior problems; a prominent example of such a program in the United States is Big Brothers Big Sisters of America, which arranges for older individuals to act as mentors for younger boys and girls (Tierney, Grossman, & Resch, 1995; Newburn & Shiner, 2006).

In addition, strategies based on behaviorist theory have proved effective for many students, especially if the student needs opportunities simply to practice social skills that he has learned only recently and may still feel awkward or self-conscious in using (Algozzine & Ysseldyke, 2006). Several behaviorist techniques were discussed in Chapter 2, including the use of positive reinforcement, extinction, generalization, and the like. In addition to these, teachers can arrange for **contingency contracts,** which are agreements between the teacher and a student about exactly what work the student will do, how it will be rewarded, and what the consequences will be if the agreement is *not* fulfilled (Wilkinson, 2003). An advantage of all such behaviorist techniques is their precision and clarity: there is little room for misunderstanding about just what your expectations are as the teacher. The precision and clarity in turn makes it less tempting or necessary for you, as teacher, to become angry about infractions of rules or a student's failure to fulfill contracts or agreements, since the consequences tend already to be relatively obvious and clear. "Keeping your cool" can be especially helpful when dealing with behavior that is by nature annoying or disrupting.

Fairness in disciplining

Many strategies for helping a student with a behavior disorder may be spelled out in the student's *individual educational plan,* such as discussed earlier in this chapter. The plan can (and indeed is supposed to) serve as a guide in devising daily activities and approaches with the student. Keep in mind, however, that since an IEP is akin to a legal agreement among a teacher, other professionals, a student and the student's parents, departures from it should be made only cautiously and carefully, if ever. Although such departures may seem unlikely, a student with a behavior disorder may sometimes be exasperating enough to make it tempting to use stronger or more sweeping punishments than usual (for example, isolating a student for extended times). In case you are tempted in this direction, remember that every IEP also guarantees the student and the student's parents *due process* before an IEP can be changed. In practice this means consulting with everyone involved in the case—especially parents, other specialists, and the student himself—and reaching an agreement before adopting new strategies that differ significantly from the past.

Instead of "increasing the volume" of punishments, a better approach is to *keep careful records* of the student's behavior and of your own responses to it, documenting the reasonableness of your rules or responses to any major disruptions. By having the records, collaboration with parents and other professionals can be more productive and fair-minded, and increase others' confidence in your judgments about what the student needs in order to fit in more comfortably with the class. In the long term, more effective collaboration leads both to better support and to more learning for the student (as well as to better support for you as teacher!).

Physical disabilities and sensory impairments

A few students have serious physical, medical, or sensory challenges that interfere with their learning. Usually, the physical and medical challenges are medical conditions or diseases that require ongoing medical care. The sensory challenges are usually a loss either in hearing or in vision, or more rarely in both. Whatever the specific problem, it is serious enough to interfere with activities in regular classroom programs and to qualify the student for special educational services or programs.

Physical challenges that are this serious are relatively infrequent compared to some of the other special needs discussed in this chapter, though they are of course important in the lives of the students and their families, as well as important for teachers to accommodate. Only about one per cent of US students have a hearing loss serious enough to be served by special programs for such students (United States Department of Education, 2005). Only about half that number have visual impairments that lead them to be served by special programs. For two reasons, though, these figures are a bit misleading. One reason is that many more students have vision or hearing problems that are too mild (such as wearing eyeglasses for "ordinary" nearsightedness). Another is that some students with serious sensory impairments may also have other disabilities and therefore not be counted in statistics about sensory impairments.

Hearing loss

A child can acquire a hearing loss for a variety of reasons, ranging from disease early in childhood, to difficulties during childbirth, to reactions to toxic drugs. In the classroom, however, the cause of the loss is virtually irrelevant because it makes little difference in how to accommodate a student's educational needs. More important than the cause of the loss is its extent. Students with only mild or moderate loss of hearing are sometimes called *hearing impaired* or *hard of hearing;* only those with nearly complete loss are called *deaf.* As with other sorts of disabilities, the milder the hearing loss, the more likely you are to encounter the student in a regular classroom, at least for part of the day.

Signs of hearing loss

Although determining whether a student has a hearing loss may seem straightforward ("Just give a hearing test!"), the assessment is often not clear cut if it takes the student's daily experiences into account. A serious or profound hearing loss tends to be noticed relatively quickly and therefore often receive special help (or at least receives additional diagnosis) sooner. Mild or moderate hearing loss is much more common, however, and is more likely to be overlooked or mistaken for some other sort of learning problem (Sherer, 2004). Students with a mild hearing loss sometimes have somewhat depressed (or lowered) language and literacy skills—though not always, and in any case so do some students *without* any loss. They may also seem not to listen or attend to a speaker because of trouble in locating the source of sounds—but then again, sometimes students *without* loss also fail to listen, though for entirely different reasons. Students with hearing loss may frequently give incorrect answers to questions—but so do certain other students with normal hearing. In addition, partial hearing loss can be hidden if the student teaches himself or herself to lip read, for example, or is careful in choosing which questions to answer in a class discussion. And so on. Systematic hearing tests given by medical or hearing specialists can resolve some of these ambiguities. But even they can give a misleading impression, since students' true ability to manage in class depends on how well they combine cues and information from the entire context of classroom life.

In identifying a student who may have a hearing loss, therefore, teachers need to observe the student over an extended period of time and in as many situations as possible. In particular, look for a persistent combination of some of the following, but look for them over repeated or numerous occasions (Luckner & Carter, 2001):

- delayed language or literacy skills, both written and oral

- some ability (usually partial) to read lips

- less worldly knowledge than usual because of lack of involvement with oral dialogue and/or delayed literacy

- occasionally, tendency to social isolation because of awkwardness in communication

Teaching students with hearing loss

In principle, adjustments in teaching students with hearing loss are relatively easy to make though they do require deliberate actions or choices by the teacher and by fellow students. Interestingly, many of the strategies make good advice for teaching *all* students!

- *Take advantage of the student's residual hearing.* Seat the student close to you if you are doing the talking, or close to key classmates if the students are in a work group. Keep competing noise, such as unnecessary talking or whispering, to a minimum (because such noise is especially distracting to someone with a hearing loss). Keep instructions concise and to-the-point. Ask the student occasionally whether he or she is understanding.

- *Use visual cues liberally.* Make charts and diagrams wherever appropriate to illustrate what you are saying. Look directly at the student when you are speaking to him or her (to facilitate lip reading). Gesture and point to key words or objects—but within reason, not excessively. Provide handouts or readings to review visually the points that you make orally.

- *Include the student in the community of the classroom.* Recruit one or more classmates to assist in "translating" oral comments that the student may have missed. If the student uses American Sign Language (ASL) at home or elsewhere, then learn a few basic, important signs of ASL yourself ("Hello" "thank you" "How are you?"). Teach them to classmates as well.

Visual impairment

Students with visual impairments have difficulty seeing even with corrective lenses. Most commonly the difficulty has to do with refraction (the ability to focus), but some students may also experience a limited field of view (called *tunnel vision)* or be overly sensitive to light in general. As with hearing loss, labels for visual impairment depend somewhat on the extent and nature of the problem. *Legal blindness* means that the person has significant tunnel vision or else visual acuity (sharpness of vision) of 20/200 or less, which means that he or she must be 20 feet away from an object that a person with normal eyesight can see at 200 feet. *Low vision* means that a person has some vision usable for reading, but often needs a special optical device such as a magnifying lens for doing so. As with hearing loss, the milder the impairment, the more likely that a student with a vision problem will spend some or even all the time in a regular class.

Signs of visual impairment

Students with visual impairments often show some of the same signs as students with simple, common nearsightedness. The students may rub their eyes a lot, for example, blink more than usual, or hold books very close to read them. They may complain of itchiness in their eyes, or of headaches, dizziness, or even nausea after doing a lot of close eye work. The difference between the students with visual impairment and those with "ordinary" nearsightedness is primarily a matter of degree: the ones with impairment show the signs more often and more obviously. If the impairment is serious enough or has roots in certain physical conditions or disease, they may also have additional symptoms, such as crossed eyes or swollen eyelids. As with hearing loss, the milder forms ironically can be the most subtle to observe and therefore the most prone to being overlooked at first. For classroom teachers, the best strategy may be to keep track of a student whose physical signs happen in *combination* with learning difficulties, and for whom the combination persists for many weeks.

Teaching students with visual impairment

In general, advice for teaching students with mild or moderate visual impairment parallels the advice for teaching students with hearing loss, though with obvious differences because of the nature of the students' disabilities.

- *Take advantage of the student's residual vision.* If the student still has some useful vision, place him or her where he can easily see the most important parts of the classroom—whether that is you, the chalkboard, a video screen, or particular fellow students. Make sure that the classroom, or at least the student's part of it, is well lit (because good lighting makes reading easier with low vision). Make sure that handouts, books and other reading materials have good, sharp contrast (also helpful with a visual impairment).

- *Use non-visual information liberally.* Remember not to expect a student with visual impairment to learn information that is by nature *only* visual, such as the layout of the classroom, the appearance of photographs in a textbook or of story lines in a video. Explain these to the student somehow. Use hands-on materials wherever they will work, such as maps printed in three-dimensional relief or with different textures. If the student knows how to read Braille (an alphabet for the blind using patterns of small bumps on a page), allow him to do so.

- *Include the student in the community of the classroom.* Make sure that the student is accepted as well as possible into the social life of the class. Recruit classmates to help explain visual material when necessary.

Learn a bit of basic Braille and encourage classmates to do the same, even if none of you ever become as skilled with it as the student himself or herself.

The value of including students with special needs

I have hinted at it already in this chapter, but it is worth saying again: including students with disabilities in regular classrooms is valuable for everyone concerned. The students with disabilities themselves tend to experience a richer educational environment, both socially and academically. Just as with racial segregation, separate education is not equal education, or at least cannot be counted on to be equal. But classmates of students with disabilities also experience a richer educational environment; they potentially meet a wider range of classmates and to see a wider range of educational purposes in operation. Teachers also experience these benefits, but their programs often benefit in other ways as well. The most notable additional benefit is that many teaching strategies that are good for students with disabilities also turn out to benefit all students—benefits like careful planning of objectives, attention to individual differences among students, and establishment of a positive social atmosphere in the classroom. Later (in Chapters 9 and 10) we will return to these topics because of their importance for high-quality teaching. But at that point we will frame the topics around the needs of *all* students, whatever their individual qualities.

Chapter summary

Since the 1970s support for people with disabilities has grown significantly, as reflected in the United States by three key pieces of legislation: the Rehabilitation Act of 1973, Americans with Disabilities Act of 1990, and the Individuals with Disabilities Education Act (IDEA). The support has led to new educational practices, including alternative assessments for students with disabilities, placement in the least restrictive environment, and individual educational plans.

There are many ways of classifying people with disabilities, all of which carry risks of stereotyping and oversimplifying individuals' strengths and needs. For the purposes of education, the most frequent category is learning disabilities, which are difficulties with specific aspects of academic work. The high prevalence of learning disabilities makes this category especially ambiguous as a description of particular students. Assistance for students with learning disabilities can be framed in terms of behaviorist reinforcement, metacognitive strategies, or constructivist mentoring.

Attention deficit hyperactivity disorder (ADHD) is a problem in sustaining attention and controlling impulses. It can often be controlled with medications, but usually it is also important for teachers to provide a structured environment for the student as well.

Intellectual disabilities (or mental retardation) are general limitations in cognitive functioning as well as in the tasks of daily living. Contemporary experts tend to classify individuals with these disabilities according to the amount and frequency of support they need from others. Teachers can assist these students by giving more time and practice than usual, by including adaptive and functional skills in what they teach, and by making sure that the student is included in the daily life of the classroom.

Behavioral disorders are conditions in which students chronically perform highly inappropriate behaviors. Students with these problems present challenges for classroom management, which teachers can meet by identifying circumstances that trigger inappropriate behaviors, by teaching interpersonal skills explicitly, and by making sure that punishments or disciplinary actions are fair and have been previously agreed upon.

Physical and sensory disabilities are significant limitations in health, hearing, or vision. The signs both of hearing loss and of vision loss can be subtle, but can sometimes be observed over a period of time. Teaching students with either a hearing loss or a vision loss primarily involves making use of the students' residual sensory abilities and insuring that the student is included in and supported by the class as well as possible.

Key terms

Alternative assessment	Least restrictive environment (LRE)
Americans with Disabilities Act of 1990	Learning disabilities
Attention deficit hyperactivity disorder (ADHD)	Mental retardation
Behavioral disorders	Portfolio assessment
Contingency contracts	Rehabilitation Act of 1973
Hearing loss	Sensory impairment
Individuals with Disabilities Education Act	Transition planning
Individual educational plan (IEP)	Visual impairment
Intellectual disabilities	

On the Internet

Each of the following websites represents an organization focused on the needs of people with one particular type of disability. Each includes free access to archives of non-current journals and other publications, as well as information about conferences, professional training events, and political news relevant to persons with disabilities. (Note that the sponsoring organizations about hearing loss and about intellectual disabilities changed their names recently, though not their purposes, so their websites may eventually change names as well.)

<**www.ldanatl.org**> This is primarily about learning disabilities, but also somewhat about ADHD.

<**www.add.org**> This website is primarily about ADHD. Note that its website name uses an older terminology for this disability, ADD (no "H") for *attention deficit disorder* (with the term *hyperactivity)*.

<**www.shhh.org**> This one primarily discusses about hearing loss.

<**www.navh.org**> This website is primarily about visual impairment.

<**www.aamr.org**> This one is primarily about intellectual disabilities or mental retardation.

References

Algozzine, R. & Ysseldyke, J. (2006). *Teaching students with emotional disturbance: A practical guide for every teacher*. Thousand Oaks, CA: Corwin Press.

American Association on Mental Retardation. (2002). *Definition, classification, and system of supports, 10th edition*. Washington, D.C.: Author.

American Psychiatric Association. (2000). *Diagnostic and statistical manual of mental disorders, DSM-IV-TR (text revision)*. Arlington, VA: American Psychiatric Association.

Biklen, S. & Kliewer, C. (2006). Constructing competence: Autism, voice and the "disordered" body. *International Journal of Inclusive Education, 10*(2/3), 169-188.

5. Students with special educational needs

Bogdan, D., Attfield, R., Bissonnette, L., Blackman, L., Burke, J., Mukopadhyay, T., & Rubin, S. (Eds.). (2005). *Autism: The myth of the person alone.* New York: New York University Press.

Bogdan, D. (2006). Who may be literate? Disability and resistance to the cultural denial of competence. *American Educational Research Journal, 43*(2), 163-192.

Bradley, M. & Mandell, D. (2005). Oppositional defiant disorder: A systematic review of the evidence of intervention effectiveness. *Journal of Experimental Criminology, 34*(1), 343-365.

Carothers, D. & Taylor, R. (2003). Use of portfolios for students with autism. *Focus on Autism and Other Developmental Disorders, 18*(2), 121-124.

Chamberlain, S. (2005). Recognizing and responding to cultural differences in the education of culturally and linguistically diverse learners. *Intervention in School and Clinic, 40*(4), 195-211.

Green, S., Davis, C., Karshmer, E., March, P. & Straight, B. (2005). Living stigma: The impact of labeling, stereotyping, separation, status loss, and discrimination in the lives of individuals with disabilities and their families. *Sociological Inquiry, 75*(2), 197-215.

Hallahan, D. & Kauffman, J. (2006). *Exceptional learners: Introduction to special education, 10th edition.* Boston: Allyn & Bacon.

Heineman, M., Dunlap, G., & Kincaid, D. (2005). Positive support strategies for students with behavioral disorders in regular classrooms. *Psychology in the Schools, 42*(8), 779-794.

Kauffman, J. (2005). *Characteristics of children with emotional and behavioral disorders, 8th edition.* Upper Saddle River, NJ: Pearson/Merrill Prentice Hall.

Keller, H. (1952). *The story of my life.* New York: Doubleday.

Kelly, S. (2004). Are teachers tracked? On what basis and with what consequences. *Social psychology in education, 7*(1), 55-72.

Koretz, D. & Barton, K. (2003/2004). Assessing students with disabilities: Issues and evidence. *Assessment and Evaluation, 9*(1 & 2), 29-60.

Luckner, J. L. & Carter, K. (2001). *Essential Competencies for Teaching Students with Hearing Loss and Additional Disabilities.* 146(1), 7-15.

Newburn, T. & Shiner, M. (2006). Young people, mentoring and social inclusion. *Youth Justice, 6*(1), 23-41.

Oakes, J. (2005). *Keeping track: How schools structure inequality, 2nd edition.* New Haven, CT: Yale University Press.

Olfson, M., Gameroff, M., Marcus, S., & Jensen, P. (2003). National trends in the treatment of ADHD. *American Journal of Psychiatry, 160,* 1071-1077.

Public Law 93-112, 87 Stat. 394 (Sept. 26, 1973). *Rehabilitation Act of 1973.* Washington, D.C.: United States Government Printing Office.

Public Law 101-336, 104 Stat. 327 (July 26, 1990). *Americans with Disabilities Act of 1990*. Washington, D.C.: United States Government Printing Office.

Public Law 108-446, 118 Stat. 2647 (December 3, 2004). *Individuals with Disabilities Education Improvement Act*. Washington, D.C.: United States Government Printing Office.

Pullin, D. (2005). When one size does not fit all: The special challenges of accountability testing for students with disabilities. *Yearbook of the National Society for Studies in Education, 104*(2), 199.

Quinn, M. (2002). Changing antisocial behavior patterns in young boys: a structured cooperative learning approach. *Education and treatment of young children, 25*(4), 380-395.

Robinson, W. (1982). *Critical essays on Phillis Wheatley*. Boston: Hall Publishers.

Rutter, M. (2004). Pathways of genetic influences in psychopathology. *European Review, 12*, 19-33.

Rutter, M. (2005). Multiple meanings of a developmental perspective on psychopathology. *European Journal of Developmental Psychology, 2*(3), 221-252.

Schalock, R. & Luckasson, R. (2004). American Association on Mental Retardation's *Definition, Classification, & System of Supports, 10th edition. Journal of Policy and Practice in Intellectual Disabilities, 1*(3/4), 136-146.

Sherer, M. (2004). *Connecting to learn: Educational and assistive technology for people with disabilities*. Washington, D.C.: American Psychological Association.

Snell, M., Janney, R., Elliott, J., Beck, M., Colley, K., & Burton, C. (2005). *Collaborative teaming: Teachers' guide to inclusive practices*. Baltimore, MD: Brookes Publishing Co.

Stowitschek, J., Lovitt, T., & Rodriguez, J. (2001). Patterns of collaboration in secondary education for youth with special needs: Profiles of three high schools. *Urban Education, 36*(1), 93-128.

Sullivan, A. K. & Strang, H. R. (2002/2003). Bibliotherapy in the Classroom: Using Literature to Promote the Development of Emotional Intelligence. *Childhood Education 79*(2), 74-80.

Tierney, J., Grossman, J., & Resch, N. (1995). *Making a difference: An impact study of big brothers big sisters*. Philadelphia: Public/Private Ventures.

United States Department of Education. (2005). *27th Annual Report to Congress on the implementation of the Individuals with Disabilities Education Act*. Washington, D.C.: Author.

Wesson, C. & King, R. (1996). Portfolio assessment and special education students. *Teaching Exceptional Children, 28*(2), 44-48.

West, L., Corbey, S., Boyer-Stephens, A., Jones, B. Miller, R., & Sarkees-Wircenski, M. (1999). *Integrating transition planning into the IEP process, 2nd edition*. Alexandria, VA: Council for Exceptional Children.

Wilens, T., McBurnett, K., Stein, M., Lerner, M., Spencer, T., & Wolraich, M. (2005). ADHD treatment with once-daily methylphenidate. *Journal of American Academy of Child & Adolescent Psychiatry, 44*(10), 1015-1023.

5. Students with special educational needs

Wilkinson, L. (2003). Using behavioral consultation to reduce challenging behavior in the classroom. *Psychology in the schools, 47*(3), 100-105.

Ysseldyke, J. & Bielinski, J. (2002). Effect of different methods of reporting and reclassification on trends in test scores for students with disabilities. *Exceptional Children, 68*(2), 189-201.

6. Student motivation

Not so long ago, a teacher named Barbara Fuller taught general science to elementary years students, and one of her units was about insects and spiders. As part of the unit she had students search for insects and spiders around their own homes or apartments. They brought the creatures to school (safely in jars), answered a number of questions about them in their journals, and eventually gave brief oral reports about their findings to the class. The assignment seemed straightforward, but Barbara found that students responded to it in very different ways. Looking back, here is how Barbara described their responses:

"I remember Jose couldn't wait to get started, and couldn't bear to end the assignment either! Every day he brought more bugs or spiders—eventually 25 different kinds. Every day he drew pictures of them in his journal and wrote copious notes about them. At the end he gave the best oral presentation I've ever seen from a third-grader; he called it 'They Have Us Outnumbered!' I wish I had filmed it, he was so poised and so enthusiastic.

"Then there was Lindsey—the one who was always wanted to be the best in everything, regardless of whether it interested her. She started off the work rather slowly—just brought in a few bugs and only one spider. But she kept an eye on what everyone else was bringing, and how much. When she saw how much Jose was doing, though, she picked up her pace, like she was trying to match his level. Except that instead of bringing a diversity of creatures as Jose was doing, she just brought more and more of the same ones—almost twenty dead house flies, as I recall! Her presentation was OK—I really could not give her a bad mark for it—but it wasn't as creative or insightful as Jose's. I think she was more concerned about her mark than about the material.

"And there was Tobias—discouraging old Tobias. He did the work, but just barely. I noticed him looking a lot at other students' insect collections and at their journal entries. He wasn't cheating, I believe, just figuring out what the basic level of work was for the assignment—what he needed to do simply to avoid failing it. He brought in fewer bugs than most others, though still a number that was acceptable. He also wrote shorter answers in his journal and gave one of the shortest oral reports. It was all acceptable, but not much more than that.

"And Zoey: she was quite a case! I never knew whether to laugh or cry about her. She didn't exactly resist doing the assignment, but she certainly liked to chat with other students. So she was easily distracted, and that cut down on getting her work done, especially about her journal entries. What really saved her—what kept her work at a reasonably high level of quality—were the two girls she ended up chatting with. The other two were already pretty motivated to do a lot with the assignment —create fine looking bug collections, write good journal entries, and make interesting oral presentations. So when Zoey attempted chitchat with them, the conversations often ended up

focusing on the assignment anyway! She had them to thank for keeping her mind on the work. I don't know what Zoey would have done without them."

As Barbara Fuller's recollections suggest, students assign various meanings and attitudes to academic activities —personal meanings and attitudes that arouse and direct their energies in different ways. We call these and their associated energizing and directing effects by the term **motivation,** or sometimes **motivation to learn.** As you will see, differences in motivation are an important source of diversity in classrooms, comparable in importance to differences in prior knowledge, ability, or developmental readiness. When it comes to school learning, furthermore, students' motivations take on special importance because students' mere presence in class is (of course) no guarantee that students really want to learn. It is only a sign that students live in a society requiring young people to attend school. Since modern education is compulsory, teachers cannot take students' motivation for granted, and they have a responsibility to insure students' motivation to learn. Somehow or other, teachers must persuade students to want to do what students have to do anyway. This task—understanding and therefore influencing students' motivations to learn—is the focus of this chapter. Fortunately, as you will see, there are ways of accomplishing this task that respect students' choices, desires, and attitudes.

Like motivation itself, theories of it are full of diversity. For convenience in navigating through the diversity, we have organized the chapter around six major theories or perspectives about motives and their sources. We call the topics (1) motives as behavior change, (2) motives as goals, (3) motives as interests, (4) motives as attributions about success, (5) motives as beliefs about self-efficacy, and (6) motives as self-determination. We end with a perspective called *expectancy-value theory* which integrates ideas from some of the other six theories, and partly as a result implies some additional suggestions for influencing students' motivations to learn in positive ways.

Motives as behavior

Sometimes it is useful to think of motivation not as something "inside" a student driving the student's behavior, but as *equivalent* to the student's outward behaviors. This is the perspective of behaviorism, which we discussed in Chapter 1 ("Student learning") as a way to think about the learning process. In its most thorough-going form, behaviorism focuses almost completely on what can be directly seen or heard about a person's behavior, and has relatively few comments about what may lie behind (or "underneath" or "inside") the behavior. When it comes to motivation, this perspective means minimizing or even ignoring the distinction between the inner drive or energy of students, and the outward behaviors that express the drive or energy. The two are considered the same, or nearly so.

Equating the inner and the outward might seem to violate common sense. How can a student do something without some sort of feeling or thought to make the action happen? As we will explain, this very question has led to alternative models of motivation that are based on cognitive rather than behaviorist theories of learning. We will explain some of these later in this chapter. Before getting to them, however, we encourage you to consider the advantages of a behaviorist perspective on motivation.

Sometimes the circumstances of teaching limit teachers' opportunities to distinguish between inner motivation and outward behavior. Certainly teachers see plenty of student behaviors—signs of motivation of some sort. But the multiple demands of teaching can limit the time needed to determine what the behaviors mean. If a student asks a lot of questions during discussions, for example, is he or she curious about the material itself, or just wanting to look intelligent in front of classmates and the teacher? In a class with many students and a busy agenda, there may not be a lot of time for a teacher to decide between these possibilities. In other cases, the problem may not be limited time as much as communication difficulties with a student. Consider a student who is still learning English, or who belongs to a cultural community that uses patterns of conversation that are unfamiliar to the teacher, or who has a disability that limits the student's general language skill. In these cases discerning the student's inner motivations may take more time and effort. It is important to invest the extra time and effort for such students, but while a teacher is doing so, it is also important for her to guide and influence the students' behavior in constructive directions. That is where behaviorist approaches to motivation can help.

Operant conditioning as a way of motivating

The most common version of the behavioral perspective on motivation is the theory of *operant conditioning* associated with B. F. Skinner (1938, 1957), which we discussed in Chapter 1 ("Learning process"). The description in that chapter focused on behavioral learning, but the same operant model can be transformed into an account of motivation. In the operant model, you may recall, a behavior being learned (the "operant") increases in frequency or likelihood because performing it makes a reinforcement available. To understand this model in terms of motivation, think of the *likelihood* of response as the motivation and the *reinforcement* as the motivator. Imagine, for example, that a student learns by operant conditioning to answer questions during class discussions: each time the student answers a question (the operant), the teacher praises (reinforces) this behavior. In addition to thinking of this situation as behavioral *learning*, however, you can also think of it in terms of *motivation:* the likelihood of the student answering questions (the motivation) is increasing because of the teacher's praise (the motivator).

Many concepts from operant conditioning, in fact, can be understood in motivational terms. Another one, for example, is the concept of *extinction,* which we defined in Chapter 1 as the tendency for learned behaviors to become less likely when reinforcement no longer occurs—a sort of "unlearning", or at least a decrease in performance of previously learned. The decrease in performance frequency can be thought of as a loss of motivation, and removal of the reinforcement can be thought of as removal of the motivator. Table 14 summarizes this way of reframing operant conditioning in terms of motivation, both for the concepts discussed in Chapter 1 and for other additional concepts.

Table 14: Operant conditioning as learning and as motivation

Concept	Definition phrased in terms of learning	Definition phrased in terms of motivation	Classroom example
Operant	Behavior that becomes more likely because of reinforcement	Behavior that suggests an increase in motivation	Student listens to teacher's comments during lecture or discussion
Reinforcement	Stimulus that increases likelihood of a behavior	Stimulus that motivates	Teacher praises student for listening
Positive reinforcement	Stimulus that *increases* likelihood of a behavior by being *introduced* or *added*	Stimulus that motivates by its *presence*; an "incentive"	Teacher makes encouraging remarks about student's homework

6. Student motivation

	to a situation		
Negative reinforcement	Stimulus that *increases* the likelihood of a behavior by being *removed* or taken away from a situation	Stimulus that motivates by its *absence* or *avoidance*	Teacher stops nagging student about late homework
Punishment	Stimulus that *decreases* the likelihood of a behavior by being *introduced* or *added* to a situation	Stimulus that *decreases* motivation by its *presence*	Teacher deducts points for late homework
Extinction	Removal of reinforcement for a behavior	Removal of motivating stimulus that leads to decrease in motivation	Teacher stops commenting altogether about student's homework
Shaping successive approximations	Reinforcements for behaviors that gradually resemble (approximate) a final goal behavior	Stimuli that gradually shift motivation toward a final goal motivation	Teacher praises student for returning homework a bit closer to the deadline; gradually she praises for actually being on time
Continuous reinforcement	Reinforcement that occurs *each* time that an operant behavior occurs	Motivator that occurs *each* time that a behavioral sign of motivation occurs	Teacher praises highly active student for *every* time he works for five minutes without interruption
Intermittent reinforcement	Reinforcement that *sometimes* occurs following an operant behavior, but not on every occasion	Motivator that occurs *sometimes* when a behavioral sign of motivation occurs, but not on every occasion	Teacher praises highly active student *sometimes* when he works without interruption, but not every time

Cautions about behavioral perspectives on motivation

As we mentioned, behaviorist perspectives about motivation do reflect a classroom reality: that teachers sometimes lack time and therefore must focus simply on students' appropriate outward behavior. But there are nonetheless cautions about adopting this view. An obvious one is the ambiguity of students' specific behaviors; what looks like a sign of one motive to the teacher may in fact be a sign of some other motive to the student (DeGrandpre, 2000). If a student looks at the teacher intently while she is speaking, does it mean the student is motivated to learn, or only that the student is daydreaming? If a student invariably looks away while the teacher is speaking, does it mean that the student is disrespectful of the teacher, or that student comes from a family or cultural group where *avoiding* eye contact actually shows more respect for a speaker than direct eye contact?

Another concern about behaviorist perspectives, including operant conditioning, is that it leads teachers to ignore students' choices and preferences, and to "play God" by making choices on their behalf (Kohn, 1996). According to this criticism, the distinction between "inner" motives and expressions of motives in outward behavior does not disappear just because a teacher (or a psychological theory) chooses to treat a motive and the behavioral expression of a motive as equivalent. Students usually *do* know what they want or desire, and their wants or desires may not always correspond to what a teacher chooses to reinforce or ignore. This, in a new guise, is once again the issue of *intrinsic* versus *extrinsic* motivation that we discussed in Chapter 1. Approaches that are exclusively behavioral, it is argued, are not sensitive enough to students' *intrinsic,* self-sustaining motivations.

As we pointed out in Chapter 1, there is truth to this allegation if a teacher actually does rely on rewarding behaviors that she alone has chosen, or even if she persists in reinforcing behaviors that students already find motivating without external reinforcement. In those cases reinforcements can backfire: instead of serving as an incentive to desired behavior, reinforcement can become a reminder of the teacher's power and of students' lack of control over their own actions. A classic research study of intrinsic motivation illustrated the problem nicely. In the study, researchers rewarded university students for two activities—solving puzzles and writing newspaper headlines —that they already found interesting. Some of the students, however, were *paid* to do these activities, whereas others were not. Under these conditions, the students who were paid were *less* likely to engage in the activities following the experiment than were the students who were not paid, even though both groups had been equally interested in the activities to begin with (Deci, 1971). The extrinsic reward of payment, it seemed, interfered with the intrinsic reward of working the puzzles.

Later studies confirmed this effect in numerous situations, though they have also found certain conditions where extrinsic rewards do *not* reduce intrinsic rewards. Extrinsic rewards are not as harmful, for example, if a person is paid "by the hour" (i.e. by a flat rate) rather than piecemeal (by the number of items completed) (Cameron & Pierce, 1994; Eisenberger & Cameron, 1996). They also are less harmful if the task itself is relatively well-defined (like working math problems or playing solitaire) and high-quality performance is expected at all times. So there are still times and ways when externally determined reinforcements are useful and effective. In general, however, extrinsic rewards do seem to undermine intrinsic motivation often enough that they need to be used selectively and thoughtfully (Deci, Koestner, & Ryan, 2001). As it happens, help with being selective and thoughtful can be found in the other, more cognitively oriented theories of motivation. These use the goals, interests, and beliefs of students as ways of explaining differences in students' motives and in how the motives affect engagement with school. We turn to these cognitively oriented theories next, beginning with those focused on students' goals.

Motives as goals

One way motives vary is by the kind of goals that students set for themselves, and by how the goals support students' academic achievement. As you might suspect, some goals encourage academic achievement more than others, but even motives that do not concern academics explicitly tend to affect learning indirectly.

Goals that contribute to achievement

What kinds of achievement goals do students hold? Imagine three individuals, Maria, Sara, and Lindsay, who are taking algebra together. Maria's main concern is to learn the material as well as possible because she finds it interesting and because she believes it will be useful to her in later courses, perhaps at university. Hers is a mastery goal because she wants primarily to learn or master the material. Sara, however, is concerned less about algebra than about getting top marks on the exams and in the course. Hers is a performance goal because she is focused primarily on looking successful; learning algebra is merely a vehicle for performing well in the eyes of peers and teachers. Lindsay, for her part, is primarily concerned about avoiding a poor or failing mark. Hers is a performance-avoidance goal or failure-avoidance goal because she is not really as concerned about learning algebra, as Maria is, or about competitive success, as Sara is; she is simply intending to avoid failure.

As you might imagine, mastery, performance, and performance-avoidance goals often are not experienced in pure form, but in combinations. If you play the clarinet in the school band, you might want to improve your technique simply because you enjoy playing as well as possible—essentially a mastery orientation. But you might also want to look talented in the eyes of classmates—a performance orientation. Another part of what you may wish, at least privately, is to avoid looking like a complete failure at playing the clarinet. One of these motives may predominate over the others, but they all may be present.

Mastery goals tend to be associated with enjoyment of learning the material at hand, and in this sense represent an outcome that teachers often seek for students. By definition therefore they are a form of *intrinsic motivation*. As such mastery goals have been found to be better than performance goals at sustaining students' interest in a subject. In one review of research about learning goals, for example, students with primarily mastery orientations toward a course they were taking not only tended to express greater interest in the course, but also continued to express interest well beyond the official end of the course, and to enroll in further courses in the same subject (Harackiewicz, et al., 2002; Wolters, 2004).

Performance goals, on the other hand, imply *extrinsic motivation,* and tend to show the mixed effects of this orientation. A positive effect is that students with a performance orientation do tend to get higher grades than those who express primarily a mastery orientation. The advantage in grades occurs both in the short term (with individual assignments) and in the long term (with overall grade point average when graduating). But there is evidence that performance oriented students do not actually learn material as deeply or permanently as students who are more mastery oriented (Midgley, Kaplan, & Middleton, 2001). A possible reason is that measures of performance—such as test scores—often reward relatively shallow memorization of information and therefore guide performance-oriented students away from processing the information thoughtfully or deeply. Another possible reason is that a performance orientation, by focusing on gaining recognition as the best among peers, encourages competition among peers. Giving and receiving help from classmates is thus not in the self-interest of a performance-oriented student, and the resulting isolation limits the student's learning.

Goals that affect achievement indirectly
Failure-avoidant goals

As we mentioned, failure-avoidant goals by nature undermine academic achievement. Often they are a negative byproduct of the competitiveness of performance goals (Urdan, 2004). If a teacher (and sometimes also fellow students) put too much emphasis on being the best in the class, and if interest in learning the material as such therefore suffers, then some students may decide that success is beyond their reach or may not be desirable in any case. The alternative—simply avoiding failure—may seem wiser as well as more feasible. Once a student adopts this attitude, he or she may underachieve more or less deliberately, doing only the minimum work necessary to avoid looking foolish or to avoid serious conflict with the teacher. Avoiding failure in this way is an example of **self-handicapping**—deliberate actions and choices that the reduce chances of success. Students may self-handicap in a number of ways; in addition to not working hard, they may procrastinate about completing assignments, for example, or set goals that are unrealistically high.

Social goals

Most students need and value relationships, both with classmates and with teachers, and often (though not always) they get a good deal of positive support from the relationships. But the effects of social relationships are complex, and at times can work both for and against academic achievement. If a relationship with the teacher is important and reasonably positive, then the student is likely to try pleasing the teacher by working hard on assignments (Dowson & McInerney, 2003). Note, though, that this effect is closer to performance than mastery; the student is primarily concerned about looking good to someone else. If, on the other hand, a student is especially concerned about relationships with peers, the effects on achievement depend on the student's motives for the relationship, as well as on peers' attitudes. Desiring to be close to peers personally may lead a student to ask for help from, and give help to peers—a behavior that may support higher achievement, at least up to a point. But desiring to impress peers with skills and knowledge may lead to the opposite: as we already mentioned, the competitive edge of such a performance orientation may keep the student from collaborating, and in this indirect way reduce a student's opportunities to learn. The abilities and achievement motivation of peers themselves can also make a difference, but once again the effects vary depending on the context. Low achievement and motivation by peers affects an individual's academic motivation more in elementary school than in high school, more in learning mathematics than learning to read, and more if their is a wide *range* of abilities in a classroom than if there is a more narrow range (Burke & Sass, 2006).

In spite of these complexities, social relationships are valued so highly by most students that teachers should generally facilitate them, though also keep an eye on their nature and their consequent effects on achievement. As we explain further, many assignments can be accomplished productively in groups, for example, as long as the groups are formed thoughtfully; in that chapter we discuss some ways of insuring that such groups are successful, such as by choosing group tasks wisely and recognizing all members' contributions are fully as possible. Relationships can also be supported with activities that involve students or adults from another class or from outside the school, as often happens with school or community service projects. These can provide considerable social satisfaction and can sometimes be connected to current curriculum needs (Butin, 2005). But the majority of students' social contacts are likely always to come from students' own initiatives with each other in simply taking time to talk and interact. The teacher's job is to encourage these informal contacts, especially when they happen at times that support rather than interfere with learning.

Encouraging mastery goals

Even though a degree of performance orientation may be inevitable in school because of the mere presence of classmates, it does not have to take over students' academic motivation completely. Teachers can encourage mastery goals in various ways, and should in fact do so because a mastery orientation leads to more sustained, thoughtful learning, at least in classrooms, where classmates may sometimes debate and disagree with each other (Darnon, Butera, & Harackiewicz, 2006).

How can teachers do so? One way is to allow students to choose specific tasks or assignments for themselves, where possible, because their choices are more likely than usual to reflect prior personal interests, and hence be motivated more intrinsically than usual. The limitation of this strategy, of course, is that students may not see some of the connections between their prior interests and the curriculum topics at hand. In that case it also helps for the teacher to look for and point out the relevance of current topics or skills to students' personal interests and goals. Suppose, for example, that a student enjoys the latest styles of music. This interest may actually have connections with a wide range of school curriculum, such as:

- biology (because of the physiology of the ear and of hearing)

- physics or general science (because of the nature of musical acoustics)

- history (because of changes in musical styles over time)

- English (because of relationships of musical lyrics and themes with literary themes)

- foreign languages (because of comparisons of music and songs among cultures)

Still another way to encourage mastery orientation is to focus on students' individual effort and improvement as much as possible, rather than on comparing students' successes to each other. You can encourage this orientation by giving students detailed feedback about how they can improve performance, or by arranging for students to collaborate on specific tasks and projects rather than to compete about them, and in general by showing your own enthusiasm for the subject at hand.

Motives as interests

In addition to holding different kinds of goals—with consequent differences in academic motivation—students show obvious differences in levels of interest in the topics and tasks of the classroom. Suppose that two high school classmates, Frank and Jason, both are taking chemistry, and specifically learning how to balance chemical equations. Frank finds the material boring and has to force himself to study it; as a result he spends only the time needed to learn the basic material and to complete the assignments at a basic level. Jason, on the other hand, enjoys the challenges of balancing chemical equations. He thinks of the task as an intriguing puzzle; he not only solves each of them, but also compares the problems to each other as he goes through them.

Frank's learning is based on *effort* compared to Jason's, whose learning is based more fully on *interest*. As the example implies, when students learn from interest they tend to devote more attention to the topic than if they learn from effort (Hidi & Renninger, 2006). The finding is not surprising since interest is another aspect of *intrinsic motivation*—energy or drive that comes from within. A distinction between effort and interest is often artificial, however, because the two motives often get blended or combined in students' personal experiences. Most of us can remember times when we worked at a skill that we enjoyed and found interesting, but that also required effort to learn. The challenge for teachers is therefore to draw on and encourage students' interest as much as possible, and thus keep the required effort within reasonable bounds—neither too hard nor too easy.

Situational interest versus personal interest

Students' interests vary in how deeply or permanently they are located within students. **Situational interests** are ones that are triggered temporarily by features of the immediate situation. Unusual sights, sounds, or words can stimulate situational interest. A teacher might show an interesting image on the overhead projector, or play a brief bit of music, or make a surprising comment in passing. At a more abstract level, unusual or surprising topics of discussion can also arouse interest when they are first introduced. **Personal interests** are relatively permanent preferences of the student, and are usually expressed in a variety of situations. In the classroom, a student may (or may not) have a personal interest in particular topics, activities, or subject matter. Outside class, though, he or she usually has additional personal interests in particular non-academic activities (e.g. sports, music) or even in particular people (a celebrity, a friend who lives nearby). The non-academic personal interests may sometimes conflict with academic interest; it may be more interesting to go to the shopping mall with a friend than to study even your most favorite subject.

Benefits of personal interest

In general, personal interest in an academic topic or activity tends to correlate with achievement related to the topic or activity. As you might suppose, a student who is truly interested is more likely to focus on the topic or activity more fully, to work at it for longer periods, to use more thoughtful strategies in learning—and to enjoy doing so (Hidi, 2001; Hidi & Renninger, 2006). Small wonder that the student achieves more! Note, though, a persistent ambiguity about this benefit: it is often not clear whether personal interest leads to higher achievement, or higher achievement leads to stronger interest. Either possibility seems plausible. Research to sort them out, however, has suggested that at least some of the influence goes in the direction from interest to achievement; when elementary students were given books from which to learn about a new topic, for example, they tended to learn more from books which they chose themselves than from books that were simply assigned (Reynolds & Symons, 2001). So interest seemed to lead to learning. But this conclusion does not rule out its converse, that achievement may stimulate interest as well. As Joe learns more about history, he steadily finds history more interesting; as McKenzie learns more about biology, she gradually wants to learn more of it.

Stimulating situational interests

If a student has little prior personal interest in a topic or activity, the teacher is faced with stimulating initial, situational interest, in hopes that the initial interest will gradually become more permanent and personal. There are a number of strategies for meeting this challenge:

- It helps to include surprises in your comments and in classroom activities from time to time: tell students facts that are true but counter-intuitive, for example, or demonstrate a science experiment that turns out differently than students expect (Guthrie, Wigfield, & Humenick, 2006).

- It also helps to relate new material to students' prior experiences even if their experiences are not related to academics or to school directly. The concepts of gravitation and acceleration, for example, operate every time a ball is hit or thrown in a softball game. If this connection is pointed out to a student who enjoys playing a lot of softball, the concepts can make concepts more interesting.

- It helps to encourage students to respond to new material actively. By having students talk about the material together, for example, students can begin making their own connections to prior personal interests, and the social interaction itself helps to link the material to their personal, social interests as well.

A caution: seductive details

Even though it is important to stimulate interest in new material somehow, it is also possible to mislead or distract students accidentally by adding inappropriate, but stimulating features to new material (Garner, et al., 1992; Harp & Mayer, 1998). Distractions happen a number of ways, such as any of these among others:

- deliberately telling jokes in class

- using colorful illustrations or pictures

- adding interesting bits of information to a written or verbal explanation

When well chosen, all of these moves can indeed arouse students' interest in a new topic. But if they do not really relate to the topic at hand, they may simply create misunderstandings or prevent students from focusing on key material. As with most other learning processes, however, there are individual differences among students in distractability, students who are struggling, and are more prone to distraction and misunderstanding than students who are already learning more successfully (Sanchez & Wiley, 2006). On balance the best advice is probably therefore to use strategies to arouse situational interest, but to assess students' responses to them continually and as honestly as possible. The key issue is whether students seem to learn because of stimulating strategies that you provide, or in spite of them.

Motives related to attributions

Attributions are perceptions about the causes of success and failure. Suppose that you get a low mark on a test and are wondering what caused the low mark. You can construct various explanations for—make various attributions about—this failure. Maybe you did not study very hard; maybe the test itself was difficult; maybe you were unlucky; maybe you just are not smart enough. Each explanation attributes the failure to a different factor. The explanations that you settle upon may reflect the truth accurately—or then again, they may not. What is important about attributions is that they reflect personal beliefs about the sources or causes of success and failure. As such, they tend to affect motivation in various ways, depending on the nature of the attribution (Weiner, 2005).

Locus, stability, and controllability

Attributions vary in three underlying ways: locus, stability, and controllability. **Locus** of an attribution is the location (figuratively speaking) of the source of success or failure. If you attribute a top mark on a test to your ability, then the locus is *internal;* if you attribute the mark to the test's having easy questions, then the locus is *external.* The **stability** of an attribution is its relative permanence. If you attribute the mark to your ability, then the source of success is relatively *stable*—by definition, ability is a relatively lasting quality. If you attribute a top mark to the effort you put in to studying, then the source of success is *unstable*—effort can vary and has to be renewed on each occasion or else it disappears. The **controllability** of an attribution is the extent to which the individual can influence it. If you attribute a top mark to your effort at studying, then the source of success is relatively *controllable*—you can influence effort simply by deciding how much to study. But if you attribute the mark to simple luck, then the source of the success is *uncontrollable*—there is nothing that can influence random chance.

As you might suspect, the way that these attributions combine affects students' academic motivations in major ways. It usually helps both motivation and achievement if a student attributes academic successes and failures to factors that are internal and controllable, such as effort or a choice to use particular learning strategies (Dweck, 2000). Attributing successes to factors that are internal but stable or controllable (like ability), on the other hand, is both a blessing and a curse: sometimes it can create optimism about prospects for future success ("I always do well"), but it can also lead to indifference about correcting mistakes (Dweck, 2006), or even create pessimism if a student happens not to perform at the accustomed level ("Maybe I'm not as smart as I thought"). Worst of all for academic motivation are attributions, whether stable or not, related to external factors. Believing that performance depends simply on luck ("The teacher was in a bad mood when marking") or on excessive difficulty of material removes incentive for a student to invest in learning. All in all, then, it seems important for teachers to encourage internal, stable attributions about success.

Influencing students' attributions

How can they do so? One way or another, the effective strategies involve framing teachers' own explanations of success and failure around internal, controllable factors. Instead of telling a student: "Good work! You're smart!", try saying: "Good work! Your effort really made a difference, didn't it?" If a student fails, instead of saying,"Too bad! This material is just too hard for you," try saying, "Let's find a strategy for practicing this more, and then you can try again." In both cases the first option emphasizes uncontrollable factors (effort, difficulty level), and the second option emphasizes internal, controllable factors (effort, use of specific strategies).

Such attributions will only be convincing, however, if teachers provide appropriate conditions for students to learn—conditions in which students' efforts really do pay off. There are three conditions that have to be in place in particular. First, academic tasks and materials actually have to be at about the right level of difficulty. If you give problems in advanced calculus to a first-grade student, the student will not only fail them but also be justified in attributing the failure to an external factor, task difficulty. If assignments are assessed in ways that produce highly variable, unreliable marks, then students will rightly attribute their performance to an external, unstable source: luck. Both circumstances will interfere with motivation.

Second, teachers also need to be ready to give help to individuals who need it—even if they believe that an assignment is easy enough or clear enough that students should not need individual help. Readiness to help is always essential because it is often hard to know in advance exactly how hard a task will prove to be for particular students. Without assistance, a task that proves difficult initially may remain difficult indefinitely, and the student will be tempted to make unproductive, though correct, attributions about his or her failure ("I will never understand this", "I'm not smart enough", or "It doesn't matter how hard I study").

Third, teachers need to remember that ability—usually considered a relatively stable factor—often actually changes *incrementally* over the long term. Recognizing this fact is one of the best ways to bring about actual increases in students' abilities (Blackwell, Trzniewski, & Dweck, 2007; Schunk, Pintrich, & Meese, 2008). A middle-years student might play the trumpet in the school band at a high level of ability, but this ability actually reflects a lot of previous effort and a gradual increase in ability. A second grade student who reads fluently, in this sense may have high current ability to read; but at some point in the distant past that same student could not read as well, and even further back he may not have been able to read at all. The increases in ability have happened at least in part because of effort. While these ideas may seem obvious, they can easily be forgotten in the classroom because effort and ability evolve according to very different time frames. Effort and its results appear relatively immediately; a student expends effort this week, this day, or even at this very moment, and the effort (if not the results) are visible right away. But ability may take longer to show itself; a student often develops it only over many weeks, months, or years.

Motivation as self-efficacy

In addition to being influenced by their goals, interests, and attributions, students' motives are affected by *specific* beliefs about the student's personal capacities. In **self-efficacy theory** the beliefs become a primary, explicit explanation for motivation (Bandura, 1977, 1986, 1997). **Self-efficacy** is the belief that you are capable of carrying out a specific task or of reaching a specific goal. Note that the belief and the action or goal are *specific*. Self-efficacy is a belief that you can write an acceptable term paper, for example, or repair an automobile, or make friends with the new student in class. These are relatively specific beliefs and tasks. Self-efficacy is not about whether you believe that you are intelligent in general, whether you always like working with mechanical things, or think that you are generally a likeable person. These more general judgments are better regarded as various mixtures of *self-concepts* (beliefs about general personal identity) or of *self-esteem* (evaluations of identity). They are important in their own right, and sometimes influence motivation, but only indirectly (Bong & Skaalvik, 2004). Self-efficacy beliefs, furthermore, are not the same as "true" or documented skill or ability. They are *self-constructed*, meaning that they are personally developed perceptions. There can sometimes therefore be discrepancies between a person's self-efficacy beliefs and the person's abilities. You can believe that you can write a good term paper, for example, without actually being able to do so, and vice versa: you can believe yourself *in*capable of writing a paper, but discover that you *are* in fact able to do so. In this way self-efficacy is like the everyday idea of *confidence,* except that it is defined more precisely. And as with confidence, it is possible to have either too much or too little self-efficacy. The optimum level seems to be either at or slightly above true capacity (Bandura, 1997). As we indicate below, large discrepancies between self-efficacy and ability can create motivational problems for the individual.

Effects of self-efficacy on students' behavior

Self-efficacy may sound like a uniformly desirable quality, but research as well as teachers' experience suggests that its effects are a bit more complicated than they first appear. Self-efficacy has three main effects, each of which has both a "dark" or undesirable side and a positive or desirable side.

Choice of tasks

The first effect is that self-efficacy makes students more willing to choose tasks where they already feel confident of succeeding. This effect is almost inevitable, given the definition of the concept of self-efficacy, it has also been supported by research on self-efficacy beliefs (Pajares & Schunk, 2001). For teachers, the effect on choice can be either welcome or not, depending on circumstances. If a student believes that he or she can solve mathematical problems, then the student is more likely to attempt the mathematics homework that the teacher assigns. Unfortunately the converse is also true. If a student believes that he or she is *in*capable of math, then the student is *less* likely to attempt the math homework (perhaps telling himself, "What's the use of trying?"), regardless of the student's actual ability in math.

Since self-efficacy is self-constructed, furthermore, it is also possible for students to miscalculate or misperceive their true skill, and the misperceptions themselves can have complex effects on students' motivations. From a teacher's point of view, all is well even if students overestimate their capacity but actually do succeed at a relevant task anyway, or if they underestimate their capacity, yet discover that they *can* succeed and raise their self-efficacy beliefs as a result. All may not be well, though, if students do not believe that they can succeed and therefore do not even try, or if students overestimate their capacity by a wide margin, but are disappointed unexpectedly by failure and lower their self-efficacy beliefs.

Persistence at tasks

A second effect of high self-efficacy is to increase a persistence at relevant tasks. If you believe that you can solve crossword puzzles, but encounter one that takes longer than usual, then you are more likely to work longer at the puzzle until you (hopefully) really do solve it. This is probably a desirable behavior in many situations, unless the persistence happens to interfere with other, more important tasks (what if you should be doing homework instead of working on crossword puzzles?). If you happen to have low self-efficacy for crosswords, on the other hand, then you are more likely to give up early on a difficult puzzle. Giving up early may often be undesirable because it deprives you of a chance to improve your skill by persisting. Then again (on the third hand?), the consequent lack of success because of giving up may provide a useful incentive to improve your crossword skills. And again, misperceptions of capacity make a difference. Overestimating your capacity by a lot (excessively high self-efficacy) might lead you not to prepare for or focus on a task properly, and thereby impair your performance. So as with choosing tasks, the effects of self-efficacy vary from one individual to another and one situation to another. The teacher's task is therefore two-fold: first, to discern the variations, and second, to encourage the positive self-efficacy beliefs. Table 15 offers some additional advice about how to do this.

Table 15: Ways of encouraging self-efficacy beliefs

Strategy	Example of what the teacher might say
1. Set goals with students, and get a commitment from them to reach the goals.	"By the end of the month, I want you to know *all* of the times table up to 25 x 25. Can I count on you to do that?"
2. Encourage students to compare their performance with their own previous performance, not with other students.	"Compare that drawing against the one that you made last semester. I think you'll find improvements!"
3. Point out links between effort and improvement.	"I saw you studying for this test more this week. No wonder you did better this time!"
4. In giving feedback about performance, focus on information, not evaluative judgments.	"Part 1 of the lab write-up was very detailed, just as the assignment asked. Part 2 has a lot of good ideas in it, but it needs to be more detailed and stated more explicitly."

5. Point out that increases in knowledge or skill happen gradually by sustained effort, not because of inborn ability.	"Every time I read another one of your essays, I see more good ideas than the last time. They are so much more complete than when you started the year."

Response to failure

High self-efficacy for a task not only increases a person's persistence at the task, but also improves their ability to cope with stressful conditions and to recover their motivation following outright failures. Suppose that you have two assignments—an essay and a science lab report—due on the same day, and this circumstance promises to make your life hectic as you approach the deadline. You will cope better with the stress of multiple assignments if you already believe yourself capable of doing both of the tasks, than if you believe yourself capable of doing just one of them or (especially) of doing neither. You will also recover better in the unfortunate event that you end up with a poor grade on one or even both of the tasks.

That is the good news. The bad news, at least from a teacher's point of view, is that the same resilience can sometimes also serve non-academic and non-school purposes. How so? Suppose, instead of two school assignments due on the same day, a student has only one school assignment due, but also holds a part-time evening job as a server in a local restaurant. Suppose, further, that the student has high self-efficacy for both of these tasks; he believes, in other words, that he is capable of completing the assignment as well as continuing to work at the job. The result of such resilient beliefs can easily be a student who devotes *less* attention to school work than ideal, and who even ends up with a *lower* grade on the assignment than he or she is capable of.

Learned helplessness and self-efficacy

If a person's sense of self-efficacy is very low, he or she can develop **learned helplessness,** a perception of complete *lack* of control in mastering a task. The attitude is similar to depression, a pervasive feeling of apathy and a belief that effort makes no difference and does not lead to success. Learned helplessness was originally studied from the behaviorist perspective of classical and operant conditioning by the psychologist Martin Seligman (1995). The studies used a somewhat "gloomy" experimental procedure in which an animal, such as a rat or a dog, was repeatedly shocked in a cage in a way that prevented the animal from escaping the shocks. In a later phase of the procedure, conditions were changed so that the animal could avoid the shocks by merely moving from one side of the cage to the other. Yet frequently they did not bother to do so! Seligman called this behavior *learned helplessness*.

In people, learned helplessness leads to characteristic ways of dealing with problems. They tend to attribute the source of a problem to themselves, to generalize the problem to many aspects of life, and to see the problem as lasting or permanent. More optimistic individuals, in contrast, are more likely to attribute a problem to outside sources, to see it as specific to a particular situation or activity, and to see it as temporary or time-limited. Consider, for example, two students who each fail a test. The one with a lot of learned helplessness is more likely to explain the failure by saying something like: "I'm stupid; I never perform well on any schoolwork, and I never will perform well at it." The other, more optimistic student is more likely to say something like: "The teacher made the test too hard this time, so the test doesn't prove anything about how I will do next time or in other subjects."

What is noteworthy about these differences in perception is how much the more optimistic of these perspectives resembles high self-efficacy and how much learned helplessness seems to contradict or differ from it. As already noted, high self-efficacy is a strong belief in one's capacity to carry out a *specific* task successfully. By definition therefore self-efficacy focuses attention on a temporary or time-limited activity (the task), even though the cause of successful completion (oneself) is "internal". Teachers can minimize learned helplessness in students, therefore, by encouraging their self-efficacy beliefs. There are several ways of doing this, as we explain next.

Sources of self-efficacy beliefs

Psychologists who study self-efficacy have identified four major sources of self-efficacy beliefs (Pajares & Schunk, 2001, 2002). In order of importance they are (1) prior experiences of mastering tasks, (2) watching others' mastering tasks, (3) messages or "persuasion" from others, and (4) emotions related to stress and discomfort. Fortunately the first three can be influenced by teachers directly, and even the fourth can sometimes be influenced indirectly by appropriate interpretive comments from the teacher or others.

Prior experiences of mastery

Not surprisingly, past successes at a task increase students' beliefs that they will succeed again in the future. The implication of this basic fact means that teachers need to help students build a history of successes. Whether they are math problems, reading assignments, or athletic activities, tasks have to end with success more often than with failure. Note, though, that the successes have to represent mastery that is genuine or competence that is truly authentic. Success at tasks that are trivial or irrelevant do not improve self-efficacy beliefs, nor does praise for successes that a student has not really had (Erikson, 1968/1994).

As a practical matter, creating a genuine history of success is most convincing if teachers also work to broaden a student's vision of "the past". Younger students (elementary-age) in particular have relatively short or limited ideas of what counts as "past experience"; they may go back only a few occasions when forming impressions of whether they can succeed again in the future (Eccles, et al., 1998). Older students (secondary school) gradually develop longer views of their personal "pasts", both because of improvements in memory and because of accumulating a personal history that is truly longer. The challenge for working with any age, however, is to insure that students base self-efficacy beliefs on *all* relevant experiences from their pasts, not just on selected or recent experiences.

Watching others' experiences of mastery

A second source of efficacy beliefs comes from *vicarious experience of mastery,* or observing others' successes (Schunk & Zimmerman, 1997). Simply seeing someone else succeed at a task, in other words, can contribute to believing that you, too, can succeed. The effect is stronger when the observer lacks experience with the task and therefore may be unsure of his or her own ability. It is also stronger when the model is someone respected by the observer, such as a student's teacher, or a peer with generally comparable ability. Even under these conditions, though, vicarious experience is not as influential as direct experience. The reasons are not hard to imagine. Suppose, for example, you witness both your teacher and a respected friend succeed at singing a favorite tune, but you are unsure whether you personally can sing. In that case you may feel encouraged about your own potential, but are likely still to feel somewhat uncertain of your own efficacy. If on the other hand you do *not* witness others' singing, but you have a history of singing well yourself, it is a different story. In that case you are likely to believe in your efficacy, regardless of how others perform.

All of which suggests that to a modest extent, teachers may be able to enhance students' self-efficacy by modeling success at a task or by pointing out classmates who are successful. These strategies can work because they not only show how to do a task, but also communicate a more fundamental message, the fact that the task *can* in fact be done. If students are learning a difficult arithmetic procedure, for example, you can help by demonstrating the procedure, or by pointing out classmates who are doing it. Note, though, that vicarious mastery is helpful only if backed up with real successes performed by the students themselves. It is also helpful only if the "model classmates" are perceived as truly comparable in ability. Overuse of vicarious models, especially in the absence of real success by learners, can cause learners to disqualify a model's success; students may simply decide that the model is "out of their league" in skills and is therefore irrelevant to judging their own potential.

Social messages and persuasion

A third source of efficacy beliefs are encouragements, both implied and stated, that persuade a person of his or her capacity to do a task. Persuasion does not create high efficacy by itself, but it often increases or supports it when coupled with either direct or vicarious experience, especially when the persuasion comes from more than one person (Goddard, Hoy, & Hoy, 2004).

For teachers, this suggests two things. The first, of course, is that encouragement can motivate students, especially when it is focused on achievable, specific tasks. It can be motivating to say things like: "I think you can do it" or "I've seen you do this before, so I know that you can do it again". But the second implication is that teachers should arrange wherever possible to support their encouragement by designing tasks at hand that are in fact achievable by the student. Striking a balance of encouragement and task difficulty may seem straightforward, but sometimes it can be challenging because students can sometimes perceive teachers' comments and tasks quite differently from how teachers intend. Giving excessive amounts of detailed help, for example, may be intended as support for a student, but be taken as a lack of confidence in the student's ability to do the task independently.

Emotions related to success, stress or discomfort

The previous three sources of efficacy beliefs are all rather cognitive or "thinking oriented", but emotions also influence expectations of success or failure. Feeling nervous or anxious just before speaking to a large group (sometimes even just a class full of students!) can function like a message that says "I'm not going to succeed at doing this", even if there is in fact good reason to expect success. But positive feelings can also raise beliefs about efficacy. When recalling the excitement of succeeding at a previous, unrelated task, people may overestimate their chances of success at a new task with which they have no previous experience, and are therefore in no position to predict their efficacy.

For teachers, the most important implication is that students' motivation can be affected when they generalize from past experience which they believe, rightly or wrongly, to be relevant. By simply announcing a test, for example, a teacher can make some students anxious even before the students find out anything about the test—whether it is easy or difficult, or even comparable in any way to other experiences called "tests" in their pasts. Conversely, it can be misleading to encourage students on the basis of their success at past academic tasks if the earlier tasks were not really relevant to requirements of the new tasks at hand. Suppose, for example, that a middle-years student has previously written only brief opinion-based papers, and never written a research-based paper. In that case boosting the student's confidence by telling him that "it is just like the papers you wrote before" may not be helpful or even honest.

A caution: motivation as content versus motivation as process

A caution about self-efficacy theory is its heavy emphasis on just the process of motivation, at the expense of the content of motivation. The basic self-efficacy model has much to say about how beliefs affect behavior, but relatively little to say about which beliefs and tasks are especially satisfying or lead to the greatest well-being in students. The answer to this question is important to know, since teachers might then select tasks as much as possible that are intrinsically satisfying, and not merely achievable.

Another way of posing this concern is by asking: "Is it possible to feel high self-efficacy about a task that you do not enjoy?" It does seem quite possible for such a gap to exist. As a youth, for example, one of us (Kelvin Seifert) had considerable success with solving mathematics problems in high school algebra, and expended considerable effort doing algebra assignments as homework. Before long, he had developed high self-efficacy with regard to solving such problems. But Kelvin never really enjoyed solving the algebra problems, and later even turned away permanently from math or science as a career (much to the disappointment of his teachers and family). In this case self-efficacy theory nicely explained the process of his motivation—Kelvin's belief in his capacity led to persistence at the tasks. But it did not explain the content of his motivation—his growing dislike of the tasks. Accounting for such a gap requires a different theory of motivation, one that includes not only specific beliefs, but "deeper" personal needs as well. An example of this approach is self-determination theory, where we turn next.

Motivation as self-determination

Common sense suggests that human motivations originate from some sort of inner "need". We all think of ourselves as having various "needs", a need for food, for example, or a need for companionship—that influences our choices and activities. This same idea also forms part of some theoretical accounts of motivation, though the theories differ in the needs that they emphasize or recognize. In Chapter 2, for example, we talked about Maslow's hierarchy of needs as an example of motivations that function like needs that influence long-term personal development. According to Maslow, individuals must satisfy physical survival needs before they seek to satisfy needs of belonging, they satisfy belonging needs before esteem needs, and so on. In theory, too, people have both deficit needs and growth needs, and the deficit needs must be satisfied before growth needs can influence behavior (Maslow, 1970). In Maslow's theory, as in others that use the concept, a need is a relatively lasting condition or feeling that requires relief or satisfaction and that tends to influence action over the long term. Some needs may decrease when satisfied (like hunger), but others may not (like curiosity). Either way, needs differ from the self-efficacy beliefs discussed earlier, which are relatively specific and cognitive, and affect particular tasks and behaviors fairly directly.

A recent theory of motivation based on the idea of needs is self-determination theory, proposed by the psychologists Edward Deci and Richard Ryan (2000), among others. The theory proposes that understanding motivation requires taking into account three basic human needs:

- autonomy—the need to feel free of external constraints on behavior

- competence—the need to feel capable or skilled

- relatedness—the need to feel connected or involved with others

Note that these needs are all psychological, not physical; hunger and sex, for example, are not on the list. They are also about personal growth or development, not about deficits that a person tries to reduce or eliminate. Unlike food (in behaviorism) or safety (in Maslow's hierarchy), you can never get enough of autonomy, competence, or relatedness. You (and your students) will seek to enhance these continually throughout life.

The key idea of self-determination theory is that when persons (such as you or one of your students) feel that these basic needs are reasonably well met, they tend to perceive their actions and choices to be intrinsically motivated or "self-determined". In that case they can turn their attention to a variety of activities that they find attractive or important, but that do not relate directly to their basic needs. Among your students, for example, some individuals might read books that you have suggested, and others might listen attentively when you explain key concepts from the unit that you happen to be teaching. If one or more basic needs are not met well, however, people will tend to feel coerced by outside pressures or external incentives. They may become preoccupied, in fact, with satisfying whatever need has not been met and thus exclude or avoid activities that might otherwise be interesting, educational, or important. If the persons are students, their learning will suffer.

Self-determination and intrinsic motivation

In proposing the importance of needs, then, self-determination theory is asserting the importance of intrinsic motivation, an idea that has come up before in this book (see especially Chapter 1, about learning theory), and that will come again later (see especially Chapter 9, about planning instruction). The self-determination version of intrinsic motivation, however, emphasizes a person's perception of freedom, rather than the presence or absence of "real" constraints on action. Self-determination means a person feels free, even if the person is also operating within certain external constraints. In principle, a student can experience self-determination even if the student must, for example, live within externally imposed rules of appropriate classroom behavior. To achieve a feeling of self-determination, however, the student's basic needs must be met—needs for autonomy, competence, and relatedness. In motivating students, then, the bottom line is that teachers have an interest in helping students to meet their basic needs, and in not letting school rules or the teachers' own leadership styles interfere with or block satisfaction of students' basic needs.

"Pure" self-determination may be the ideal for most teachers and students, of course, but the reality is usually different. For a variety of reasons, teachers in most classrooms cannot be expected to meet all students' basic needs at all times. One reason is the sheer number of students, which makes it impossible to attend to every student perfectly at all times. Another reason is teachers' responsibility for a curriculum, which can require creating expectations for students' activities that sometimes conflict with students' autonomy or makes them feel (temporarily) less than fully competent. Still another reason is students' personal histories, ranging from divorce to poverty, which may create needs in some individuals which are beyond the power of teachers to remedy.

The result from students' point of view is usually only a partial perception of self-determination, and therefore a simultaneous mix of intrinsic and extrinsic motivations. Self-determination theory recognizes this reality by suggesting that the "intrinsic-ness" of motivation is really a matter of degree, extending from highly *extrinsic*, through various mixtures of intrinsic and extrinsic, to highly *intrinsic* (Koestner & Losier, 2004). At the extrinsic end of the scale is learning that is regulated primarily by external rewards and constraints, whereas at the intrinsic end is learning regulated primarily by learners themselves. Table 16 summarizes and gives examples of the various levels and their effects on motivation. By assuming that motivation is often a mix of the intrinsic and extrinsic, the job of the teacher becomes more realistic; the job is not to expect purely intrinsic motivation from students all the time, but simply to arrange and encourage motivations that are as intrinsic as possible. To do this, the teacher needs to support students' basic needs for autonomy, competence, and relatedness.

Table 16: Combinations of intrinsic and extrinsic motivation

Source of regulation of action	Description	Example
"Pure" extrinsic motivation	Person lacks the intention to take any action, regardless of pressures or incentives	Student completes *no* work even when pressured or when incentives are offered
Very external to person	Actions regulated only by outside pressures and incentives, and controls	Student completes assignment *only* if reminded explicitly of the incentive of grades and/or negative consequences of failing
Somewhat external	Specific actions regulated internally, but without reflection or connection to personal needs	Student completes assignment independently, but only because of fear of shaming self or because of guilt about consequences of not completing assignment
Somewhat internal	Actions recognized by individual as important or as valuable as a means to a more valued goal	Student generally completes school work independently, but only because of its value in gaining admission to college
Very internal	Actions adopted by individual as integral to self-concept and to person's major personal values	Student generally completes school work independently, because being well educated is part of the student's concept of himself
"Pure" intrinsic regulation	Actions practiced solely because they are enjoyable and valued for their own sake	Student enjoys every topic, concept, and assignment that every teacher ever assigns, and completes school work solely because of his enjoyment

Using self-determination theory in the classroom

What are some teaching strategies for supporting students' needs? Educational researchers have studied this question from a variety of directions, and their resulting recommendations converge and overlap in a number of ways. For convenience, the recommendations can be grouped according to the basic need that they address, beginning with the need for autonomy.

Supporting autonomy in learners

A major part of supporting autonomy is to give students *choices* wherever possible (Ryan & Lynch, 2003). The choices that encourage the greatest feelings of self-control, obviously, are ones that are about relatively major issues or that have relatively significant consequences for students, such as whom to choose as partners for a major group project. But choices also encourage some feeling of self-control even when they are about relatively minor issues, such as how to organize your desk or what kind of folder to use for storing your papers at school. It is important, furthermore, to offer choices to *all* students, including students needing explicit directions in order to work successfully; avoid reserving choices for only the best students or giving up offering choices altogether to students who fall behind or who need extra help. All students will feel more self-determined and therefore more motivated if they have choices of some sort.

Teachers can also support students' autonomy more directly by minimizing external rewards (like grades) and comparisons among students' performance, and by orienting and responding themselves to students' expressed goals and interests. In teaching elementary students about climate change, for example, you can support autonomy by exploring which aspects of this topic have *already* come to students' attention and aroused their concern. The point of the discussion would not be to find out "who knows the most" about this topic, but to build and enhance students' intrinsic motivations as much as possible. In reality, of course, it may not be possible to succeed at this goal fully—some students may simply have no interest in the topic, for example, or you may be constrained by time or resources from individualizing certain activities fully. But any degree of attention to students' individuality, as well as any degree of choice, will support students' autonomy.

Supporting the need for competence

The most obvious way to make students feel competent is by selecting activities which are challenging but nonetheless achievable with reasonable effort and assistance (Elliott, McGregor, & Thrash, 2004). Although few teachers would disagree with this idea, there are times when it is hard to put into practice, such as when you first meet a class at the start of a school year and therefore are unfamiliar with their backgrounds and interests. But there are some strategies that are generally effective even if you are not yet in a position to know the students well. One is to emphasize activities that require active response from students. Sometimes this simply means selecting projects, experiments, discussions and the like that require students to do more than simply listen. Other times it means expecting active responses in all interactions with students, such as by asking questions that call for "divergent" (multiple or elaborated) answers. In a social studies class, for example, try asking "What are some ways we could find out more about our community?" instead of "Tell me the three best ways to find out about our community." The first question invites more divergent, elaborate answers than the second.

Another generally effective way to support competence is to respond and give feedback as immediately as possible. Tests and term papers help subsequent learning more if returned, with comments, sooner rather than later. Discussions teach more if you include your own ideas in them, while still encouraging students' input. Small group and independent activities are more effective if you provide a convenient way for students to consult authoritative sources for guidance when needed, whether the source is you personally, a teaching assistant, a specially selected reading, or even a computer program. In addition, you can sometimes devise tasks that create a feeling of competence because they have a "natural" solution or ending point. Assembling a jigsaw puzzle of the community, for example, has this quality, and so does *creating* a jigsaw puzzle of the community if the students need a greater challenge.

Supporting the need to relate to others

The main way of support students' need to relate to others is to arrange activities in which students work together in ways that are mutually supportive, that recognize students' diversity, and minimize competition among individuals. We will have more to say about this strategy in Chapter 8 ("Instructional strategies"), where we describe several varieties of cooperative learning, as well as some of their pitfalls to be avoided. For now, simply note that having students work together can happen in many ways. You can, for example, deliberately arrange projects that require a variety of talents; some educators call such activities "rich group work" (Cohen, 1994; Cohen, Brody, & Sapon-Shevin, 2004). In studying in small groups about medieval society, for example, one student can contribute his drawing skills, another can contribute his writing skills, and still another can contribute his dramatic skills. The result can be a multi-faceted presentation—written, visual, and oral. The groups needed for rich group work provide for students' relationships with each other, whether they contain six individuals or only two.

There are other ways to encourage relationships among students. In the jigsaw classroom (Aronson & Patnoe, 1997), for example, students work together in two phases. In the first phase, groups of "experts" work together to find information on a specialized topic. In a second phase the expert groups split up and reform into "generalist" groups containing one representative from each former expert group. In studying the animals of Africa, for example, each expert group might find information about a different particular category of animal or plant; one group might focus on mammal, another on bird, a third on reptiles, and so on. In the second phase of the jigsaw, the generalist groups would pool information from the experts to get a more well-rounded view of the topic. The generalist groups would each have an expert about mammals, for example, but also an expert about birds and about reptiles.

As a teacher, you can add to these organizational strategies by encouraging the development of your own relationships with class members. Your goal, as teacher, is to demonstrate caring and interest in your students not just as students, but as people. The goal also involves behaving as if good relationships between and among class members are not only possible, but ready to develop and perhaps even already developing. A simple tactic, for example, is to speak of "we" and "us" as much as possible, rather than speaking of "you students". Another tactic is to present cooperative activities and assignments without apology, as if they are in the best interests not just of students, but of "us all" in the classroom, yourself included.

Keeping self-determination in perspective

In certain ways self-determination theory provides a sensible way to think about students' intrinsic motivation and therefore to think about how to get them to manage their own learning. A particular strength of the theory is that it recognizes *degrees* of self-determination and bases many ideas on this reality. Most people recognize combinations of intrinsic and extrinsic motivation guiding particular activities in their own lives. We might enjoy teaching, for example, but also do this job partly to receive a paycheck. To its credit, self-determination theory also relies on a list of basic human needs—autonomy, competence, and relatedness—that relate comfortably with some of the larger purposes of education.

Although these are positive features for understanding and influencing students' classroom motivation, some educators and psychologists nonetheless have lingering questions about the limitations of self-determination theory. One is whether merely providing choices actually improves students' learning, or simply improves their *satisfaction* with learning. There is evidence supporting both possibilities (Flowerday & Schraw, 2003; Deci & Ryan, 2003), and it is likely that there are teachers whose classroom experience supports both possibilities as well. Another question is whether it is possible to *overdo* attention to students' needs—and again there is evidence for both favoring and contradicting this possibility. Too many choices can actually make anyone (not just a student) frustrated and dissatisfied with a choice the person actually *does* make (Schwartz, 2004). Furthermore, differentiating activities to students' competence levels may be impractical if students are functioning at extremely diverse levels within a single class, as sometimes happens. Differentiating may be inappropriate, too, if it holds a teacher back from covering key curriculum objectives which students need and which at least some students are able to learn. These are serious concerns, though in our opinion *not* serious enough to give up offering choices to students or to stop differentiating instruction altogether. In Chapter 7 ("Classroom management and the learning environment"), therefore, we explain the practical basis for this opinion, by describing workable ways for offering choices and recognizing students' diversity.

Expectancy x value: effects on students' motivation

As we have explained in this chapter, motivation is affected by several factors, including reinforcement for behavior, but especially also students' goals, interests, and sense of self-efficacy and self-determination. The factors combine to create two general sources of motivation: students' expectation of success and the value that students place on a goal. Viewing motivation in this way is often called the expectancy-value model of motivation (Wigfield & Eccles, 2002; Wigfield, Tonk, & Eccles, 2004), and sometimes written with a multiplicative formula: expectancy x value = motivation. The relationship between expectation and value is "multiplicative" rather than additive because in order to be motivated, it is necessary for a person to have at least a modest expectation of success and to assign a task at least some positive value. If you have high expectations of success but do not value a task at all (mentally assign it a "0" value), then you will not feel motivated at all. Likewise, if you value a task highly but have no expectation of success about completing it (assign it a "0" expectancy), then you also will not feel motivated at all.

Expectancies are the result of various factors, but particularly the goals held by a student, and the student's self-efficacy, which we discussed earlier in this chapter. A student with mastery goals and strong self-efficacy for a task, for example, is likely to hold high expectations for success—almost by definition. Values are also the result of various factors, but especially students' interests and feelings of self-determination. A student who has a lasting personal interest in a task or topic and is allowed to choose it freely is especially likely to value the task—and therefore to feel motivated.

Ideally both expectancies and values are high in students on any key learning task. The reality, however, is that students sometimes do not expect success, nor do they necessarily value it when success is possible. How can a teacher respond to low expectations and low valuing? We have offered a number of suggestions to meet this challenge throughout this chapter. In brief, raising low expectations depends on adjusting task difficulty so that success becomes a reasonable prospect: a teacher must make tasks neither too hard nor too easy. Reaching this general goal depends in turn on thoughtful, appropriate planning—selecting reasonable objectives, adjusting them on the basis of experience, finding supportive materials, and providing students with help when needed.

Raising the value of academic tasks is equally important, but the general strategies for doing so are different than for raising expectations. Increasing value requires linking the task to students' personal interests and prior knowledge, showing the utility of the task to students' future goals, and showing that the task is valuable to other people whom students' respect. Some of these strategies were discussed earlier in this chapter, but others (e.g. linking new learning with prior knowledge) are discussed in Chapter 2, which is called "The learning process".

TARGET: a model for integrating ideas about motivation

A model of motivation that integrates many ideas about motivation, including those in this chapter, has been developed by Carole Ames (1990, 1992). The acronym or abbreviated name for the program is TARGET, which stands for six elements of effective motivation:

- **Task**
- **Authority**
- **Recognition**
- **Grouping**
- **Evaluating**
- **Time**

Each of the elements contributes to students' motivation either directly or indirectly.

Task

As explained earlier, students experience tasks in terms of their value, their expectation of success, and their authenticity. The value of a task is assessed by its importance, interest to the student, usefulness or utility, and the cost in terms of effort and time to achieve it. Expectation of success is assessed by a student's perception of the difficulty of a task. Generally a middling level of difficulty is optimal for students; too easy, and the task seems trivial (not valuable or meaningful), and too hard, and the task seems unlikely to succeed and in this sense useless. Authenticity refers to how much a task relates to real-life experiences of students; the more it does so, the more it can build on students' interests and goals, and the more meaningful and motivating it becomes.

Autonomy

Motivation is enhanced if students feel a degree of autonomy or responsibility for a learning task. Autonomy strengthens self-efficacy and self-determination—two valued and motivating attitudes described earlier in this chapter. Where possible, teachers can enhance autonomy by offering students' choices about assignments and by encouraging them to take initiative about their own learning.

Recognition

Teachers can support students' motivation by recognizing their achievements appropriately. Much depends, however, on how this is done; as discussed earlier, praise sometimes undermines performance. It is not especially effective if praise is very general and lacking in detailed reasons for the praise; or if praise is for qualities which a student cannot influence (like intelligence instead of effort); or if praise is offered so widely that it loses meaning or even becomes a signal that performance has been substandard. Many of these paradoxical effects are described by self-determination and self-efficacy theory (and were explained earlier in this chapter).

Grouping

Motivation is affected by how students are grouped together for their work—a topic discussed in more detail in Chapter 8 ("Instructional Strategies"). There are many ways to group students, but they tend to fall into three types: cooperative, competitive, and individualistic (Johnson & Johnson, 1999). In cooperative learning, a set of students work together to achieve a common goal (for example, producing a group presentation for the class); often they receive a final grade, or part of a final grade, in common. In competitive learning, students work individually, and their grades reflect comparisons among the students (for example, their performances are ranked relative to each other, or they are "graded on a curve"). In individualistic learning, students work by themselves, but their grades are unrelated to the performance of classmates. Research that compares these three forms of grouping tends to favor cooperative learning groups, which apparently supports students' need for belonging—an idea important in self-determination theory discussed earlier in this chapter.

Evaluation

Grouping structures obviously affect how students' efforts are evaluated. A focus on comparing students, as happens with competitive structures, can distract students from thinking about the material to be learned, and to focus instead on how they appear to external authorities; the question shifts from "What am I learning?" to "What will the teacher think about my performance?" A focus on cooperative learning, on the other hand, can have double-edged effects: students are encouraged to help their group mates, but may also be tempted to rely excessively on others' efforts or alternatively to ignore each other's contributions and overspecialize their own contributions. Some compromise between cooperative and individualistic structures seems to create optimal motivation for learning (Slavin, 1995).

Time

As every teacher knows, students vary in the amount of time needed to learn almost any material or task. Accommodating the differences can be challenging, but also important for maximizing students' motivation. School days are often filled with interruptions and fixed intervals of time devoted to non-academic activities—facts that make it difficult to be flexible about granting individuals different amounts of time to complete academic tasks. Nonetheless a degree of flexibility is usually possible: larger blocks of time can sometimes be created for important activities (for example, writing an essay), and sometimes enrichment activities can be arranged for some students while others receive extra attention from the teacher on core or basic tasks. More about such strategies is discussed in Chapter 8 ("Instructional Strategies").

The bottom line about motivation: sustaining focus on learning

Sooner or later when you teach, there will be situations appropriate for each perspective about motivation described in this chapter. There will be times when focusing exclusively on students' appropriate behavior (or lack thereof) will be both necessary and sufficient evidence of motivation. But there will be other times when it is important to encourage students' beliefs that they can accomplish specific tasks, and still other times when providing for students' underlying needs for competence or social connection is important. Think of these perspectives as alternatives to be used either singly or in combination when the time is right.

Because of your own values, attitudes, or beliefs, you may find one perspective more personally compatible than another. Even if you settle on favorite ways of motivating students, though, we encourage you to keep the other, less favored approaches in reserve anyway, and to experiment with them. We believe that an eclectic approach to motivation will enrich your teaching the most, and enrich your students' motivation and learning as well. If there is a single lesson from the concepts about motivation outlined in this chapter, it is this: academic motivation has no single source, and teachers motivate students the best when they assume motivation is complex. The next two chapters look at ways of realizing such "broad-mindedness" in practice, first when you prepare activities and classes and later when you actually teach them.

Chapter summary

Motivation—the energy or drive that gives behavior direction and focus—can be understood in a variety of ways, each of which has implications for teaching. One perspective on motivation comes from behaviorism, and equates underlying drives or motives with their outward, visible expression in behavior. Most others, however, come from cognitive theories of learning and development. Motives are affected by the kind of goals set by students—whether they are oriented to mastery, performance, failure-avoidance, or social contact. They are also affected by students' interests, both personal and situational. And they are affected by students' attributions about the causes of success and failure—whether they perceive the causes are due to ability, effort, task difficulty, or luck.

A major current perspective about motivation is based on self-efficacy theory, which focuses on a person's belief that he or she is capable of carrying out or mastering a task. High self-efficacy affects students' choice of tasks, their persistence at tasks, and their resilience in the face of failure. It helps to prevent learned helplessness, a perception of complete lack of control over mastery or success. Teachers can encourage high self-efficacy beliefs by providing students with experiences of mastery and opportunities to see others' experiences of mastery, by offering well-timed messages persuading them of their capacity for success, and by interpreting students' emotional reactions to success, failure and stress.

An extension of self-efficacy theory is self-determination theory, which is based on the idea that everyone has basic needs for autonomy, competence, and relatedness to others. According to the theory, students will be motivated more intrinsically if these three needs are met as much as possible. A variety of strategies can assist teachers in doing so. As a practical matter, the strategies can encourage motivation that is more intrinsic to students, but usually not completely intrinsic.

On the Internet

<**www.des.emory.edu/mfp/self-efficacy.html**> This is a rather extensive site maintained about all aspects of self-efficacy theory. The site gives access to a number of published articles on the subject as well as to extensive "lecture" notes by Frank Pajares, who publishes and teaches about self-efficacy theory.

<**www.psych.rochester.edu/SDT/faculty/index.html**> This, too, is a rather extensive site, maintained at the University of Rochester by Edward Deci and Richard Ryan, two psychologists who have published extensively about self-determination theory. The site is especially thorough in reviewing evidence *contrary* to the theory and in offering many of the actual research questionnaires which have been used to study self-determination.

6. Student motivation

<**www.indiana.edu/~reading/ieo/bibs/mot-gen.html**> Here is a website that discusses many aspects of motivation in education. It is not limited to any one theory, perspective, or concept about this topic. Many of the references are to citations from the ERIC database (also available at <**www.eric.ed.gov**>), and there are links to bibliographies on additional topics about education.

Key terms

Albert Bandura	Mastery goals
Attributions of success or failure	Motivation
Autonomy, need for	Need for relatedness
Behaviorist perspective on motivation	Performance goals
Competence, need for	Personal interests
Failure-avoidant goals	Self-determination theory
Intrinsic motivation	Self-efficacy
Jigsaw classroom	Situational interests
Learned helplessness	TARGET

References

Allison, K., Dwyer, J., & Makin, S. (1999). Self-efficacy and participation in vigorous physical activity by high school students. *Health Education and Behavior, 26*(1), 12-24.

Ames, C. (1990). Motivation: What teachers need to know. *Teachers College Record, 91*, 409-421.

Ames. C. (1992). Classrooms: Goals, structures, and student motivation. *Journal of Educational Psychology, 84*, 261-271.

Aronson, E. & Patnoe, S. (1997). *The Jigsaw classroom: Building cooperation in the classroom, 2nd edition.* New York: Longman.

Bandura, A. (1977). Self-efficacy: Toward a unifying theory of behavioral change. *Psychological Review, 84*, 191-215.

Bandura, A. (1986). *Social foundations of thought and action: A social cognitive theory.* Englewood Cliffs, NJ: Prentice Hall.

Bandura, A. (1997). *Self-efficacy: The exercise of control.* New York: Freeman.

Blackwell, L., Trzniewski, K., & Dweck, C. (2007). Implicit theories predict achievement across an adolescent transition: a longitudinal study. *Child Development, 78*, 246-263.

Bong, M. & Skaalvik, E. (2004). Academic self-concept and self-efficacy: How different are they really? *Educational psychology review, 15*(1), 1-40.

Burke, M. & Sass, T. (2006). Classroom peer effects and student achievement. Paper presented at the annual meeting of the American Economic Association, Boston, USA.

Butin, D. (2005). *Service learning in higher education.* New York: Palgrave Macmillan.

Cameron, J. & Pierce, W. (1994). Reinforcement, reward, and intrinsic motivation: A meta-analysis. *Review of Educational Research, 64*, 363-423.

Cohen, E. (1994). *Designing groupwork: Strategies for the heterogeneous classroom, 2nd edition*. New York: Teachers' College Press.

Darnon, C., Butera, F., & Harackiewicz, J. (2006). Achievement goals in social interactions: Learning with mastery versus performance goals. *Motivation and Emotion, 31,* 61-70.

Deci, E. (1971). Effects of externally mediated rewards on intrinsic motivation. *Journal of Personality and Social Psychology, 18,* 105-115.

Deci, E., Koestner, R., & Ryan, R. (2001). Extrinsic rewards and intrinsic motivation in education: Reconsidered once again. *Review of Educational Research, 71*(1), 1-27.

Deci, E. & Ryan, R. (2003). The paradox of achievement: The harder you push, the worse it gets. In E. Aronson (Ed.), *Improving academic achievement: Impact of psychological factors in education* (pp. 62-90). Boston: Academic Press.

DeGranpre, R. (2000). A science of meaning: Can behaviorism bring meaning to psychological science? *American Psychologist, 55*(7), 721-736.

Dowson, M. & McInerney, D. (2003). What do students say about their motivational goals? Toward a more complex and dynamic perspective on student motivation. *Contemporary Educational Psychology, 28,* 91-113.

Dweck, C. (2000). *Self-theories: Their role in motivation, personality, and development*. Philadelphia: Psychology Press.

Dweck, C. (2006). *Mindset: The new psychology of success*. New York: Random House.

Eccles, J., Wigfield, A., & Schiefele, U. (1998). Motivation to succeed. In W. Damon & N. Eisenberg (Eds.), *Handbook of child psychology, Volume 3: Social, emotional, and personality development, 5th edition* (pp. 1017-1095). New York: Wiley.

Eisenberger, R. & Cameron, J. (1996). Detrimental effects of reward: Reality or myth? *American Psychologist, 51,* 1153-1166.

Elliott, A., McGregor, H., & Thrash, T. (2004). The need for competence. In E. Deci & R. Ryan (Eds.), *Handbook of self-determination research* (pp. 361-388). Rochester, NY: University of Rochester Press.

Erikson, E. (1968/1994). *Identity, youth, and crisis*. New York: Norton.

Flowerday, T., Shraw, G., & Stevens, J. (2004). Role of choice and interest in reader engagement. *Journal of Educational Research, 97,* 93-103.

Garner, R., Brown, R., Sanders, S. & Menke, D. (1992). "Seductive details" and learning from text. In A. Renninger, S. Hidi, & A. Krapp (Eds.), *The role of interest in learning and development,* pp. 239-254. Mahwah, NJ: Erlbaum.

Goddard, R., Hoy, W., & Hoy, A. (2004). Collective efficacy beliefs: Theoretical developments, empirical evidence, and future directions. *Educational Researcher, 33*(3), 3-13.

6. Student motivation

Guthrie, J., Wigfield, A., & Humenick, N. (2006). Influences of stimulating tasks on reading motivation and comprehension. *Journal of Educational Research, 99,* 232-245.

Harp, S. & Mayer, R. (1998). How seductive details do their damage. *Journal of Educational Psychology, 90,* 414-434.

Harzckiewicz, J., Barron, K., Tauer, J., & Elliot, A. (2002). Short-term and long-term consequences of achievement goals. *Journal of Educational Psychology, 92,* 316-320.

Hidi, S. & Renninger, A. (2006). A four-phase model of interest development. *Educational Psychology, 41,* 111-127.

Johnson, D. & Johnson, R. (1999). *Learning together and alone: Cooperative, competitive, and individualistic learning, 5th edition.* Boston: Allyn & Bacon.

Kohn, A. (1996). *No contest: The case against competition.* Boston: Houghton Mifflin.

Koestner, R. & Losier, G. (2004). Distinguishing three ways of being highly motivated: a closer look at introjection, identification, and intrinsic motivation. In E. Deci & R. Ryan (Eds.), *Handbook of self-determination research* (pp. 101-122). Rochester, NY: University of Rochester Press.

Lent, R., Brown, S., Nota, L., & Soresi, S. (2003). Teaching social cognitive interest and choice hypotheses across Holland types in Italian high school students. *Journal of Vocational Behavior, 62,* 101-118.

Lindley, L. (2006). The paradox of self-efficacy: Research with diverse populations. *Journal of Career Assessment, 14*(1), 143-160.

Mau, W.-C. (2003). Factors that influence persistence in science and engineering career aspirations. *Career Development Quarterly, 51,* 234-243.

Midgley, C., Kaplan, A., & Middleton, M. (2001). Performance-approach goals: Good for what, for whom, and under what conditions, and at what cost? *Journal of Educational Psychology, 93,* 77-86.

Pajares, F. & Schunk, D. (2001). Self-beliefs and school success: Self-efficacy, self-concept, and school achievement. In . Riding & S. Rayner (Eds.), *Perception* (pp. 239-266). London: Ablex Publishing.

Pajares, F. & Schunk, D. (2002). Self-beliefs in psychology and education: An historical perspective. In J. Aronson (Ed.), *Improving academic achievement* (pp. 3-21). New York: Academic Press.

Reynolds, P. & Symons, S. (2001). Motivational variables and children's text search. *Journal of Educational Psychology, 93,* 14-22.

Ryan, R. & Lynch, M. (2003). Philosophies of motivation and classroom management. In R. Curren (Ed.), *Blackwell companion to philosophy: A companion to the philosophy of education* (pp. 260-271). New York, NY: Blackwell.

Sanchez, C. & Wiley, J. (2006). An examination of the seductive details effect in terms of working memory capacity. *Memory and Cognition, 34,* 344-355.

Sapon-Shevin, M. & Cohen, E. (2004). Conclusion. In Cohen, E., Brody, C., & Sapon-Shevin, M. (Eds.), *Teaching cooperative learning: The challenge for teacher education* (pp. 217-224). Albany, NY: State University of New York Press.

Schunk, D. & Zimmerman, B. (1997). Social origins of self-regulatory competence. *Educational psychologist, 34*(4), 195-208.

Schwartz, B. (2004). *The paradox of choice: Why more is less.* New York: Ecco/Harper Collins.

Schunk, D., Pintrich, P., Meese, J. (2008). *Motivation in education: Theory, research and applications.* New York: Pearson Professional.

Skinner, B. F. (1938). *The behavior of organisms.* New York: Appleton-Century-Crofts.

Slavin, R. (1995). *Cooperative learning, 2nd edition.* Boston: Allyn & Bacon.

Skinner, B. F. (1957). *Verbal behavior.* New York: Appleton-Century-Crofts.

Urdan, T. (2004). Predictors of self-handicapping and achievement: Examining achievement goals, classroom goal structures, and culture. *Journal of Educational Psychology, 96,* 251-254.

Weiner, B. (2005). Motivation from an attribution perspective and the social psychology of perceived competence. In A. Elliot & C. Dweck (Eds.), *Handbook of Competence and Motivation,* pp. 73-84. New York: Guilford Press.

Wigfield, A. & Eccles, J. (2002). *The development of achievement motivation.* San Diego, CA: Academic Press.

Wigfield, A., Tonk, S., & Eccles, J. (2004). Expectancy-value theory in cross-cultural perspective. In D. McInerney & S. van Etten (Eds.), *Research on Sociocultural Influences on Motivation and Learning.* Greenwich, CT: Information Age Publishers.

Wolters, C. (2004). Advancing achievement goal theory: Using goal structures and goal orientations to predict students' motivation, cognition, and achievement. *Journal of Educational Psychology, 96,* 236-250.

7. Classroom management and the learning environment

This is an excerpt from a professional journal kept by one of us (Kelvin Seifert) when he was teaching kindergarten:

20xx-11-14: Today my student Carol sat in the circle, watching others while we all played Duck, Duck, Goose (in this game, one student is outside the circle, tags another student who then chases the first person around the circle). Carol's turn had already passed. Apparently she was bored, because she flopped on her back, smiling broadly, rolling around luxuriously on the floor in the path of the other runners. Several classmates noticed her, smiled or giggled, began flopping down as well. One chaser tripped over a "flopper".

"Sit up, Carol", said I, the ever-vigilant teacher. "You're in the way." But no result. I repeated this twice, firmly; then moved to pick her up.

Instantly Carol ran to the far side of the gym, still smiling broadly. Then her best friend ran off with her. Now a whole new game was launched, or really two games: "Run-from-the-teacher" and "Enjoy-being-watched-by-everybody". A lot more exciting, unfortunately, than Duck, Duck, Goose!

An excerpt from Kelvin's same journal several years later, when he was teaching math in high school:

20xx-3-4: The same four students sat in the back again today, as usual. They seem to look in every direction except at me, even when I'm explaining material that they need to know. The way they smile and whisper to each other, it seems almost like they are "in love" with each other, though I can't be sure who loves whom the most.

Others—students not part of the foursome—seem to react variously. Some seem annoyed, turn the other way, avoid talking with the group, and so on. But others seem almost envious—as if they want to be part of the "in" group, too, and were impressed with the foursome's ability to get away with being inattentive and almost rude. Either way, I think a lot of other students are being distracted.

Twice during the period today, I happened to notice members of the group passing a note, and then giggling and looking at me. By the end, I had had enough of this sort of thing, so I kept them in briefly after class and asked one of them to read the note. They looked a bit embarrassed and hesitant, but eventually one of them opened the note and read it out loud. "Choose one", it said. "Mr Seifert looks (1) old ____, (2) stupid____, or (3) clueless____."

Kelvin's experiences in managing these very different classrooms taught him what every teacher knows or else quickly learns: management matters a lot. But his experiences also taught him that management is about *more* than correcting the misbehaviors of individuals, *more* than just discipline. **Classroom management** is also about orchestrating or coordinating entire sets or sequences of learning activities so that *everyone,* misbehaving or not, learns as easily and productively as possible. Educators sometimes therefore describe good management as the **creation of a positive learning environment**, because the term calls attention to the totality of activities and people in a classroom, as well as to their goals and expectations about learning (Jones & Jones, 2007). When one of us (Kelvin) was teaching, he used both terms almost interchangeably, though in speaking of *management* he more often was referring to individual students' behavior and learning, and in speaking of the *learning environment* he more often meant the overall "feel" of the class as a whole.

Why classroom management matters

Managing the learning environment is both a major responsibility and an on-going concern for all teachers, even those with years of experience (Good & Brophy, 2002). There are several reasons. In the first place, a lot goes on in classrooms simultaneously, even when students seem to be doing only one task in common. Twenty-five students may all seem to be working on a sheet of math problems. But look more closely: several may be stuck on a particular problem, each for different reasons. A few others have worked only the first problem or two and are now chatting quietly with each other instead of continuing. Still others have finished and are wondering what to do next. At any one moment each student needs something different—different information, different hints, different kinds of encouragement. Such diversity increases even more if the teacher deliberately assigns multiple activities to different groups or individuals (for example, if some students do a reading assignment while others do the math problems).

Another reason that managing the environment is challenging is because a teacher can not predict everything that will happen in a class. A well-planned lesson may fall flat on its face, or take less time than expected, and you find yourself improvising to fill class time. On the other hand an unplanned moment may become a wonderful, sustained exchange among students, and prompt you to drop previous plans and follow the flow of discussion. Interruptions happen continually: a fire drill, a drop-in visit from another teacher or the principal, a call on the intercom from the office. An activity may indeed turn out well, but also rather differently than you intended; you therefore have to decide how, if at all, to adjust the next day's lesson to allow for this surprise.

A third reason for the importance of management is that students form opinions and perceptions about your teaching that are inconsistent with your own. What you intend as encouragement for a shy student may seem to the student herself like "forced participation". An eager, outgoing classmate watching your effort to encourage the shy student, moreover, may not see you as *either* encouraging or coercing, but as overlooking or ignoring *other* students who already want to participate. The variety of perceptions can lead to surprises in students' responses—most often small ones, but occasionally major.

At the broadest, society-wide level, classroom management challenges teachers because public schooling is not voluntary, and students' presence in a classroom is therefore not a sign, in and of itself, that they wish to learn. Instead, students' presence is just a sign that an *opportunity* exists for teachers to motivate students to learn. Some students, of course, do enjoy learning and being in school, almost regardless of what teachers do! Others do enjoy school, but only because teachers have worked hard to make classroom life pleasant and interesting. Those students become motivated because you have successfully created a positive learning environment and have sustained it through skillful management.

Fortunately it is possible to earn this sort of commitment from many students, and this chapter describes ways of doing so. We begin with ways of *preventing* management problems from happening by increasing students' focus on learning. The methods include ideas about arranging classroom space, about establishing procedures, routines, and rules, and about communicating the importance of learning to students and parents. After these prevention oriented discussions, we look at ways of *re*focusing students when and if their minds or actions stray from the tasks at hand. As you probably know from being a student, bringing students back on task can happen in many ways, and the ways vary widely in the energy and persistence required of the teacher. We try to indicate some of these variations, but because of space limitations and because of the richness of classroom life, we cannot describe them all.

Preventing management problems by focusing students on learning

The easiest management problems to solve are ones that do not happen in the first place! Even before the school year begins, you can minimize behavior problems by arranging classroom furniture and materials in ways that encourage a focus on learning as much as possible. Later, once school begins, you can establish procedures and rules that support a focus on learning even more.

Arranging classroom space

Viewed broadly, classrooms may seem to be arranged in similar ways, but there are actually important alternative arrangements to consider. Variations exist because of grade level, the subjects taught, the teacher's philosophy of education, and of course the size of the room and the furniture available. Whatever the arrangement that you choose, it should help students to focus on learning tasks as much as possible and minimize the chances of distractions. Beyond these basic principles, however, the "best" arrangement depends on what your students need and on the kind of teaching that you prefer and feel able to provide (Boyner, 2003; Nations & Boyett, 2002). The next sections describe some of the options. In considering them (and before moving too much furniture around your room!), you might want to try experimenting with spatial arrangements "virtually" by using one of the computer programs available on the Internet (see: http://teacher.scholastic.com/tools/class_setup/).

Displays and wall space

All classrooms have walls, of course, and how you fill them can affect the mood or feeling of a classroom. Ample displays make a room interesting and can be used to reinforce curriculum goals and display (and hence publicly recognize) students' work. But too many displays can also make a room seem "busy" or distracting as well as physically smaller. They can also be more work to maintain. If you are starting a new school year, then, a good strategy is to decorate some of the wall or bulletin board space, but not to fill it all immediately. Leaving some space open leaves flexibility to respond to ideas and curriculum needs that emerge after the year is underway. The same advice applies especially for displays that are high maintenance, such as aquariums, pets, and plants. These can serve wonderfully as learning aids, but do not have to be in place on the first day of school. Not only the students, but also you yourself, may already have enough to cope with at that time.

Computers in the classroom

If you are like the majority of teachers, you will have only one computer in your room, or at most just a few, and their placement may be pre-determined by the location of power and cable outlets. If so, you need to think about computer placement early in the process of setting up a room. Once the location of computers is set, locations for desks, high-usage shelves, and other moveable items can be chosen more sensibly—in general, as already mentioned, so as to minimize distractions to students and to avoid unnecessary traffic congestion.

Visibility of and interactions with students

Learning is facilitated if the furniture and space allow you to see all students and to interact with them from a comfortable distance. Usually this means that the main, central part of the room—where desks and tables are usually located—needs to be as open and as spacious as possible. While this idea may seem obvious, enacting it can be challenging in practice if the room itself is small or shaped unusually. In classrooms with young students (kindergarten), furthermore, open spaces tend to allow, if not invite, physical movement of children—a feature that you may consider either constructive or annoying, depending on your educational goals and the actual level of activity that occurs.

Spatial arrangements unique to grade levels or subjects

The best room arrangement sometimes depends on the grade level or subject area of the class. If you teach in elementary school, for example, you may need to think especially about where students can keep their daily belongings, such as coats and lunches. In some schools, these can be kept outside the classroom—but not necessarily. Some subjects and grade levels, furthermore, lend themselves especially well to small group interaction, in which case you might prefer not to seat students in rows, but instead around small-group tables or work areas. The latter arrangement is sometimes preferred by elementary teachers, but is also useful in high schools wherever students need lots of counter space, as in some shops or art courses, or where they need to interact, as in English as a Second Language courses (McCafferty, Jacobs, & Iddings, 2006). The key issue in deciding between tables and rows, however, is not grade level or subject as such, but the amount of small group interaction you want to encourage, compared to the amount of whole-group instruction. As a rule, tables make working with peers easier, and rows make listening to the teacher more likely and group work slightly more awkward physically.

Ironically, some teachers also experience challenges about room arrangement because they do not actually have a classroom of their own, because they must move each day among other teachers' rooms. "Floating" is especially likely for specialized teachers (e.g. music teachers in elementary schools, who move from class to class) and in schools have an overall shortage of classrooms. Floating can sometimes be annoying to the teacher, though it actually also has advantages, such as not having to take responsibility for how other teachers' rooms are arranged. If you find yourself floating, it helps to consider a few key strategies, such as:

- consider using a permanent cart to move crucial supplies from room to room

- make sure that every one of your rooms has an overhead projector (do not count on using chalkboards or computers in other teachers' rooms)

- talk to the other teachers about having at least one shelf or corner in each room designated for your exclusive use

Establishing daily procedures and routines

Procedures or **routines** are specific ways of doing common, repeated classroom tasks or activities. Examples include checking daily attendance, dealing with students who arrive late, or granting permission to leave the

141

classroom for an errand. Academically related procedures include ways of turning in daily homework (e.g. putting it on a designated shelf at a particular time), of gaining the teacher's attention during quiet seat work (e.g. raising your hand and waiting), and of starting a "free choice" activity after completing a classroom assignment.

Procedures serve the largely practical purpose of making activities and tasks flow smoothly—a valuable and necessary purpose in classrooms, where the actions of many people have to be coordinated within limited time and space. As such, procedures are more like social conventions than like moral expectations. They are only indirectly about what is ethically *right* or ethically *desirable* to do (Turiel, 2006). Most procedures or routines can be accomplished in more than one way, with only minor differences in outcomes. There is more than one way, for example, for the procedure of taking attendance: the teacher could call the role, delegate a student to call the role, or note students' presence on a seating chart. Each variation accomplishes essentially the same task, and the choice may be less important than the fact that the class coordinates its actions *somehow,* by committing to *some* sort of choice.

For teachers, of course, an initial management task is to establish procedures and routines as promptly as possible. Because of the conventional quality of procedures, some teachers find that it works well simply to announce and explain key procedures without inviting much discussion from students ("Here is how we will choose partners for the group work"). Other teachers prefer to invite input from students when creating procedures (asking the class, "What do *you* feel is the best way for students to get my attention during a quiet reading time?"). Both approaches have advantages as well as disadvantages. Simply announcing key procedures saves time and insures consistency in case you teach more than one class (as you would in high school). But it puts more responsibility on the teacher to choose procedures that are truly reasonable and practical. Inviting students' input, on the other hand, can help students to become aware of and committed to procedures, but at the cost of requiring more time to settle on them. It also risks creating confusion if you teach multiple classes, each of which adopts different procedures. Whatever approach you choose, of course, they have to take into account any procedures or rules imposed by the school or school district as a whole. A school may have a uniform policy about how to record daily attendance, for example, and that policy may determine, either partly or completely, how you take attendance with your particular students.

Establishing classroom rules

Unlike procedures or routines, **rules** express standards of behavior for which individual students need to take responsibility. Although they are like procedures in that they sometimes help in insuring the efficiency of classroom tasks, they are really about encouraging students to be responsible for learning and showing respect for each other. Exhibit 8 lists a typical set of classroom rules.

- Treat others with courtesy and politeness.

- Make sure to bring required materials to class and to activities.

- Be on time for class and other activities.

- Listen to the teacher and to others when they are speaking.

- Follow all school rules.

Exhibit 8: Sample set of classroom rules

Note three things about the examples in Exhibit 8. One is that the rules are not numerous; the table lists only five. Most educational experts recommend keeping the number of rules to a minimum in order to make them easier to remember (Thorson, 2003; Brophy, 2004). A second feature is that they are stated in positive terms ("Do X...") rather than negative terms ("Do not do Y..."), a strategy that emphasizes and clarifies what students should *do* rather than what they should avoid. A third feature is that each rule actually covers a collection of more specific behaviors. The rule "Bring all materials to class", for example, covers bringing pencils, paper, textbooks, homework papers, and permission slips—depending on the situation. As a result of their generality, rules often have a degree of ambiguity that sometimes requires interpretation. Infractions may occur that are marginal or "in a grey area", rather than clear cut. A student may bring a pen, for example, but the pen may not work properly. You may therefore wonder whether this incident is really a failure to follow the rule, or just an unfortunate (and in this case minor) fault of the pen manufacturer.

As with classroom procedures, rules can be planned either by the teacher alone, or by the teacher with advice from students. The arguments for each approach are similar to the arguments for procedures: rules "laid on" by the teacher may be more efficient and consistent, and in this sense more fair, but rules influenced by the students may be supported more fully by the students. Because rules focus strongly on personal responsibility, however, there is a stronger case for involving students in making them than in making classroom procedures (Brookfield, 2006; Kohn, 2006). In any case the question of who plans classroom rules is not necessarily an either/or choice. It is possible in principle to impose certain rules on students (for example, "Always be polite to each other") but let the students determine the consequences for violations of certain rules (for example, "If a student is discourteous to a classmate, he/she must apologize to the student in writing"). Some mixture of influences is probably inevitable, in fact, if only because the class needs to take into account your own moral commitments as the teacher as well as any imposed by the school (like "No smoking in the school" or "Always walk in the hallways").

Pacing and structuring lessons and activities

One of the best ways to prevent management problems is by pacing and structuring lessons or activities as smoothly and continuously as possible. This goal depends on three major strategies:

- selecting tasks or activities at an appropriate level of difficulty for your students

- providing a moderate level of structure or clarity to students about what they are supposed to do, especially during transitions between activities

- keeping alert to the flow and interplay of behaviors for the class as a whole and for individuals within it.

Each strategy presents special challenges to teachers, but also opportunities for helping students to learn.

Choosing tasks at an appropriate level of difficulty

As experienced teachers know and as research has confirmed, students are most likely to engage with learning when tasks are of moderate difficulty, neither too easy nor too hard and therefore neither boring nor frustrating (Britt, 2005). Finding the right level of difficulty, however, can be a challenge if you have little experience teaching a particular grade level or curriculum, or even if students are simply new to you and their abilities unknown. Whether familiar or not, members of any class are likely to have diverse skills and readiness—a fact that makes it challenging to determine what level of difficulty is appropriate. A common strategy for dealing with these challenges is to begin units, lessons, or projects with tasks that are relatively easy and familiar. Then, introduce more difficult material or tasks gradually until students seem challenged, but not overwhelmed. Following this strategy gives the teacher a chance to observe and diagnose students' learning needs before adjusting content, and it gives students a chance to orient themselves to the teacher's expectations, teaching style, and topic of study without becoming frustrated prematurely. Later in a unit, lesson, or project, students seem better able to deal with more difficult tasks or content (Van Merrionboer, 2003). The principle seems to help as well with "authentic" learning tasks—ones that resemble real-world activities, such as learning to drive an automobile or to cook a meal, and that present a variety of complex tasks simultaneously. Even in those cases it helps to isolate and focus on the simplest subtasks first (such as "put the key in the ignition") and move to harder tasks only later (such as parallel parking).

Sequencing instruction is only a partial solution to finding the best "level" of difficulty, however, because it does not deal with enduring individual differences among students. The fundamental challenge to teachers is to individualize or differentiate instruction fully: to tailor it not only to the class as a group, but to the lasting differences among members of the class. One way to approach this sort of diversity, obviously, is to plan different content or activities for different students or groups of students. While one group works on Task A, another group works on Task B; one group works on relatively easy math problems, for example, while another works on harder ones. Differentiating instruction in this way complicates a teacher's job, but it can be done, and has in fact been done by many teachers (it also makes teaching more interesting!). In the next chapter, we describe some classroom management strategies that help with such multi-tasking.

Providing moderate amounts of structure and detail

Chances are that at some point in your educational career you have wished that a teacher would clarify or explain an assignment more fully, and perhaps give it a clearer structure or organization. Students' desire for clarity is especially common with assignments that are by nature open-ended, such as long essays, large projects, or creative works. Simply being told to "write an essay critiquing the novel", for example, leaves more room for uncertainty (and worry) than being given guidelines about what questions the essay should address, what topics or parts it should have, and what its length or style should be (Chesebro, 2003). As you might suspect, some students desire clarity more than others, and improve their performance especially much when provided with plenty of structure and clarity. Students with certain kinds of learning difficulties, in particular, often learn effectively and stay on task only if provided with somewhat explicit, detailed instructions about the tasks expected of them (Marks, et al., 2003).

As a teacher, the challenge is to accommodate students' need for clarity without making guidance so specific or detailed that students do little thinking for themselves. As a (ridiculously extreme) example, consider a teacher gives "clear" instructions for an essay by announcing not only exactly which articles to read and cite in the essay and which topics or issues to cover, but even requires specific wording of sentences in their essays. This much specificity may reduce students' uncertainties and make the teacher's task of evaluating the essays relatively straightforward and easy. But it also reduces or even eliminates the educational value of the assignment—assuming, of course, that its purpose is to get students to think for themselves.

Ideally, then, structure should be moderate rather than extreme. There should be just enough to give students some sense of direction and to stimulate more accomplishment than if they worked with less structure or guidance. This ideal is an application of Vygotsky's idea of the zone of proximal development that we discussed in Chapter 2: a place (figuratively speaking) where students get more done with help than without it. The ideal amount of guidance —the "location" of the zone of proximal development—varies with the assignment and the student, and it (hopefully) decreases over time for all students. One student may need more guidance to do his or her best in math, but less guidance in order to write her or his best essay. Another student may need the reverse. But if all goes well, both students may need less at the end of the year than at the beginning.

Managing transitions

Transitions between activities is often full of distractions and "lost" time, and is a time when inappropriate behaviors are especially likely to occur. Part of the problem is intrinsic to transitions: students may have to wait before a new activity actually begins, and therefore get bored at the very moment when the teacher is preoccupied with arranging materials for the new activity. From the point of view of the students, transitions may seem essentially like unsupervised group time, when seemingly any behavior is tolerated.

Minimizing such problems requires two strategies, one of which is easier to implement than the other. The easier strategy is for you, as teacher, to organize materials as well as possible ahead of time, so that you minimize the time needed to begin a new activity. The advice sounds simple, and mostly is, but it sometimes takes a bit of practice to implement smoothly. When one of us (Kelvin) first began teaching university, for example, particular papers or overhead transparencies sometimes got lost in the wrong folder in spite of Kelvin's efforts to keep them where they were easy to find. The resulting delays about finding them slowed the pace of class and caused frustrations.

A second, more complex strategy is to teach students ways to manage their own behavior during transitions (Marzano & Marzano, 2004). If students talk too loudly at these times, for example, then discuss with them what constitutes appropriate levels or amounts of talk, and discuss the need for them to monitor their own sound level. Or if students stop work early in anticipation of ending an activity, then talk about—or even practice—waiting for a signal from yourself to indicate the true ending point for an activity. If certain students continue working *beyond* the end of an activity. On the other hand, try giving them warning of the impending end in advance, and remind them about to take responsibility for actually finishing work once they hear the advance warning, and so on. The point of these tactics is to encourage responsibility for behavior during transitions, and thereby reduce your own need to monitor students at that crucial time.

None of these ideas, of course, mean that you, as teacher, should give up monitoring students' behavior entirely. Chances are that you still will need to notice if and when someone talks too loudly, finishes too early, or continues too long, and you will still need to give some students appropriate reminders. But the amount of reminding will be less to the extent that students can remind and monitor themselves—a welcome trend at any time, but especially during transitions.

Maintaining the flow of activities

A lot of classroom management is really about keeping activities flowing smoothly, both during individual lessons and across the school day. The trouble is that there is never just "one" event happening at a time, even if only one activity has been formally planned and is supposed to be occurring. Imagine, for example, that everyone is supposed to be attending a single whole-class discussion on a topic; yet individual students will be having different experiences at any one moment. Several students may be listening and contributing comments, for example, but a few others may be planning what they want to say *next* and ignoring the current speakers, still others may be ruminating about what a previous speaker said, and still others may be thinking about unrelated matters--the restroom, food, or sex. Things get even more complicated if the teacher deliberately plans multiple activities: in that case some students may interact with the teacher, for example, while others do work in an unsupervised group or work independently in a different part of the room. How is a teacher to keep activities flowing smoothly in the face of such variety?

A common mistake of beginning teachers in multi-faceted settings like these is to pay too much attention to any *one* activity, student, or small group, at the expense of noticing and responding to all the others. If you are helping a student on one side of the room when someone on the other side disturbs classmates with off-task conversation, it can be less effective *either* to finish with the student you are helping before attending to the disruption, *or* to interrupt yourself to solve the disruption on the other side of the room. Although one of these responses may be necessary, either one involves disruption *somewhere*. There is a risk that either the student's chatting may spread to others, or the interrupted student may become bored with waiting for the teacher's attention and wander off-task herself.

A better solution, though one that at first may seem challenging, is to attend to *both* events at once—a strategy that was named **withitness** in a series of now-classic research studies several decades ago (Kounin, 1970). Withitness does not mean that you focus on all simultaneous activities with equal care, but only that you remain aware of multiple activities, behaviors, and events to some degree. At a particular moment, for example, you may be focusing on helping a student, but in some corner of your mind you also notice when chatting begins on the other side of the room. You have, as the saying goes, "eyes in the back of your head". Research has found that experienced teachers are much more likely to show withitness than inexperienced teachers, and that these qualities are associated with managing classrooms successfully (Emmer & Stough, 2001).

Simultaneous awareness—withitness—makes possible responses to the multiple events that are immediate and nearly simultaneous—what educators sometimes called **overlapping.** The teacher's responses to each event or behavior need not take equal time, nor even be equally noticeable to all students. If you are helping one student with seat work at the precise moment when another student begins chatting off-task, for example, a quick glance to the second student may be enough to bring the second one back to the work at hand, and may scarcely interrupt your conversation with the first student, or be noticed by others who are not even involved. The result is a smoother flow to activities overall.

As a new teacher, you may find that withitness and overlapping develop more easily in some situations than in others. It may be easier to keep an eye (or ear) on multiple activities during familiar routines, such as taking attendance, but harder to do the same during activities that are unfamiliar or complex, such as introducing a new topic or unit that you have never taught before. But skill at broadening your attention does increase with time and practice. It helps to keep trying. Merely demonstrating to students that you are "withit", in fact, even without making deliberate overlapping responses, can sometimes deter students from off-task behavior. Someone who is tempted to pass notes in class, for example, might not do so because she believes that you will probably notice her doing it anyway, whether or not you are able to notice in fact.

Communicating the importance of learning and of positive behavior

Altogether, the factors we have discussed—arranging space, procedures, and rules, and developing *withitness*—help communicate an important message: that in the classroom learning and positive social behavior are priorities. In addition, teachers can convey this message by offering timely feedback to students about performance, by keeping accurate records of the performance, and by deliberately communicating with parents or caregivers about their children and about class activities.

Communicating effectively is so important for all aspects of teaching, in fact, that we discuss it more fully later in this book (see Chapter 8, "The nature of classroom communication"). Here we focus on only one of its important aspects: how communication contributes to a smoothly functioning classroom and in this way helps prevent behavior problems.

Giving timely feedback

The term *feedback,* when used by educators, refers to responses to students about their behavior or performance. Feedback is essential if students are to learn and if they are to develop classroom behavior that is socially skilled and "mature". But feedback can only be fully effective if offered as soon as possible, when it is still relevant to the task or activity at hand (Reynolds, 1992). A score on a test is more informative immediately after a test than after a six-month delay, when students may have forgotten much of the content of the test. A teacher's comment to a student about an inappropriate, off-task behavior may not be especially welcome at the moment the behavior occurs, but it can be more influential and informative then; later, both teacher and student will have trouble remembering the details of the off-task behavior, and in this sense may literally "not know what they are talking about". The same is true for comments about a *positive* behavior by a student: hearing a compliment right away makes it easier to the comment with the behavior, and allows the compliment to influence the student more strongly. There are of course practical limits to how fast feedback can be given, but the general principle is clear: feedback tends to work better when it is timely.

The principle of timely feedback is consistent, incidentally, with a central principle of operant conditioning discussed in Chapter 2: reinforcement works best when it follows a to-be-learned operant behavior closely (Skinner, 1957). In this case a teacher's feedback serves as a form of reinforcement. The analogy is easiest to understand when the feedback takes the form of praise; in operant conditioning terms, the reinforcing praise then functions like a "reward". When feedback is negative, it functions as an "aversive stimulus" (in operant terms), shutting down the behavior criticized. At other times, though, criticism can also function as an unintended reinforcement. This happens, for example, if a student experiences criticism as a reduction in isolation and therefore as in increase in his importance in the class—a relatively desirable change. So the inappropriate behavior continues, or even increases, contrary to the teacher's intentions. Exhibit 9 diagrams this sequence of events.

Example of Unintended Negative Reinforcement in the Classroom:

Student is isolated socially → **Student publicly misbehaves** → **Student gains others' attention**

Reinforcement can happen in class if an undesirable behavior, leads to a less aversive state for a student. Social isolation can be reduced by public misbehavior, which stimulates attention that is reinforcing. Ironically, the effort to end misbehavior ends up stimulating the misbehavior.

Exhibit 9: Attracting attention as negative reinforcement

Maintaining accurate records

Although timeliness in responding to students can sometimes happen naturally during class, there are also situations where promptness depends on having organized key information ahead of time. Obvious examples are the scores, marks, and grades returned to students for their work. A short quiz (such as a weekly spelling test) may be possible to return quite soon after the quiz—sometimes you or even the students themselves can mark it during class. More often, though, assignments and tests require longer processing times: you have to read, score, or add comments to each paper individually. Excessive time to evaluate students' work can reduce the usefulness of a teacher's evaluations to students when she finally does return the work (Black, et al., 2004). During the days or weeks waiting for a test or assignment to be returned, students are left without information about the quality or nature of their performance; at the extreme they may even have to complete another test or do another assignment before getting information about an earlier one. (Perhaps you yourself have experienced this particular problem!)

Delays in providing feedback about academic performance can never be eliminated entirely, but they can be reduced by keeping accurate, well-organized records of students' work. A number of computer programs are available to help with this challenge; if your school does not already have one in use, then there are several downloadable either free or at low cost from the Internet (e.g. <<u>http://dmoz.org/Computers/Software/Educational/Teachers_Help/Gradebooks/</u>>). Describing these is beyond the scope of this book. For now we simply emphasize that grading systems benefit students' learning the most when they provide feedback as quickly and frequently as possible (McMillan, 2001), precisely the reason why accurate, well-organized record-keeping is important to keep.

Accurate records are helpful not only for scores on tests, quizzes, or assignments, but also for developing descriptive summaries of the nature of students' academic skills or progress. A common way to develop a description is the student portfolio, which is a compilation of the student's work and on-going assessments of it created by the teacher or in some cases by the student (Moritz & Christie, 2005; White, 2005). To know how a student's science project evolved from its beginning, for example, a teacher and student can keep a portfolio of lab notes, logs, preliminary data, and the like. To know how a student's writing skills developed, they could keep a portfolio of early drafts on various writing assignments. As the work accumulates, the student can discuss it with the teacher, and write brief reflections on its strengths thus far or on the steps needed to improve the work further. By providing a way to respond to work as it evolves, and by including students in making the assessments, portfolios provide relatively prompt feedback, and in any case provide it sooner than by waiting for the teacher to review work that is complete or final.

Communicating with parents and caregivers

Since parents and caregivers in a sense "donate" their children to schools (at least figuratively speaking), teachers are responsible for keeping them informed and involved to whatever extent is practical. Virtually all parents understand and assume that schools are generally intended for learning. Detailed communication can enrich parents' understanding, of how learning is addressed with their particular child's classroom, and show them more precisely what their particular child is doing. The better such understanding in turn encourages parents and caregivers to support their child's learning more confidently and "intelligently". In this sense it contributes indirectly to a positive learning environment in their child's class.

There are various ways to communicate with parents, each with advantages and limitations. Here are three common examples:

- *A regular classroom newsletter:* A newsletter establishes a link with parents or caregivers with comparatively little effort on the part of the teacher. At the beginning of the year, for example, a newsletter can tell about special materials that students will need, important dates to remember (like professional development days when there is no school), or about curriculum plans for the next few weeks. But newsletters also have limitations. They can seem impersonal, and they may get lost on the way home and never reach parents or caregivers. They can also be impractical for teachers with multiple classes, as in high school or in specialist subjects (like music or physical education), where each class follows a different program or curriculum.

- *Telephone calls:* The main advantage of phoning is its immediacy and individuality. Teacher and parent or caregiver can talk about a particular student, behavior, or concern, and do it *now*. By the same token, however, phone calls are not an efficient way for informing parents about events or activities that affect everyone in common. The individuality of phoning may explain why teachers often use this method when a student has a problem that is urgent or unusual—as when he has failed a test, missed classes, or misbehaved seriously. Rightly or wrongly, a student's successes tend not to prompt phone calls to the student's home (though in fairness students may be more likely to tell parents about their successes themselves, making it less essential for the teacher to do so).

- *Parent-teacher conferences:* Most schools schedule periodic times—often a day or evening per term—when teachers meet briefly with parents or caregivers who wish to meet. Under good conditions, the conferences have the individuality of phone calls, but also the richness of communication possible only in face-to-face meetings. Since conferences are available to all parents, they need not focus on behavior or academic problems, but often simply help to build rapport and understanding between parents or caregivers and the teacher. Sometimes too, particularly at younger grade levels, teachers involve students in leading their own conferences; the students display and explain their own work using a portfolio or other archive of accumulated materials (Benson & Barnett, 2005; Stiggins & Chappuis, 2005). In spite of all of these advantages, though, parent-teacher conferences have limitations. Some parents cannot get to conferences because of work schedules, child care, or transportation problems. Others may feel intimated by any school-sponsored event because they speak limited English or because they remember painful experiences from their own school days.

Even if you make several efforts to communicate, some parents may remain out of contact. In these cases it is important to remember that the parents may *not* be indifferent to their child or to the value of education. Other possibilities exist, as some of our comments above imply: parents may have difficulties with child care, for example, have inconvenient work schedules, or feel self-conscious about their own communication skills (Stevens & Tollafield, 2003). Even so, there are ways to encourage parents who may be shy, hesitant, or busy. One is to think about how they can assist the school even from home—for example, by making materials to be used in class or (if they are comfortable using English) phoning other parents about class events. A second way is to have a specific task for the parents in mind—one with clear structure, such as photocopying materials to be used by students later. A third is to remember to encourage, support, and respect the parents' presence and contributions when they *do* show up at school functions. Keep in mind that parents are experts about their own particular children, and without them, you would have no students to teach!

Responding to student misbehavior

So far we have focused on preventing behaviors that are inappropriate or annoying. The advice has all been pro-active or forward-looking: plan classroom space thoughtfully, create reasonable procedures and rules, pace lessons and activities appropriately, and communicate the importance of learning clearly. Although we consider these ideas important, it would be naïve to imply they are enough to prevent all behavior problems. For various reasons, students sometimes still do things that disrupt other students or interrupt the flow of activities. At such moments the challenge is not about long-term planning but about making appropriate, but prompt responses. Misbehaviors left alone can be contagious, a process educators sometimes call the **ripple effect** (Kounin, 1970). Chatting between two students, for example, can gradually spread to six students; rudeness by one can eventually become rudeness by several; and so on. Because of this tendency, delaying a response to inappropriate behavior can make the job of getting students back on track harder than responding to it as immediately as possible.

There are many ways to respond to inappropriate behaviors, of course, and they vary in how much they focus on the immediate behavior compared to longer-term features or patterns of a student's behavior. There are so many ways to respond, in fact, that we can describe only a sample of the possibilities here. None are effective all of the time, though all do work at least some of the time. We start with a response that may not seem on the surface like a remedy at all—simply ignoring misbehaviors.

Ignoring misbehaviors

A lot of misbehaviors are not important or frequent enough to deserve any response at all. They are likely to disappear (or *extinguish,* in behaviorist terms) simply if left alone. If a student who is usually quiet during class happens to whisper to a neighbor once in awhile, it is probably less disruptive and just as effective to ignore the infraction than to respond to it. Some misbehaviors may not be worth a response even if they are frequent, as long as they do not seem to bother others. Suppose, for example, that a certain student has a habit of choosing quiet seat-work times to sharpen her pencil. She is continually out of her seat to go to the sharpener. Yet this behavior is not really noticed by others. Is it then really a problem, however unnecessary or ill-timed it may be? In both examples ignoring the behavior may be wise because there is little danger of the behavior disrupting other students or of becoming more frequent. Interrupting your activities—or the students'—might cause more disruption than simply ignoring the problem.

That said, there can still be problems in deciding whether a particular misbehavior is truly minor, infrequent, or unnoticed by others. Unlike in our example above, students may whisper to each other more than "rarely" but less than "often": in that case, when do you decide that the whispering is in fact *too* frequent and needs a more active response from you? Or the student who sharpens her pencil, mentioned above, may not bother most others, but she may nonetheless bother a few. In that case how many bothered classmates are "too many"? Five, three, just one, or...? In these ambiguous cases, you may need more active ways of dealing with an inappropriate behavior, like the ones described in the next sections.

Gesturing nonverbally

Sometimes it works to communicate using gestures, eye contact, or "body language" that involve little or no speaking. Nonverbal cues are often appropriate if a misbehavior is just a bit too serious or frequent to ignore, but not serious or frequent enough to merit taking the time deliberately to speak to or talk with the student. If two students are chatting off-task for a relatively extended time, for example, sometimes a glance in their direction, a frown, or even just moving closer to the students is enough of a reminder to get them back on task. Even if these responses prove *not* to be enough, they may help to keep the off-task behavior from spreading to other students.

A risk of relying on nonverbal cues, however, is that some students may not understand their meaning, or may even fail to notice them. If the two chatting students mentioned above are engrossed in their talking, for example, they may not see you glance or frown at them. Or they might notice but not interpret your cue as a reminder to get back on task. Misinterpretation of nonverbal gestures and cues is more likely with young children, who are still learning the subtleties of adults' nonverbal "language" (Guerrero & Floyd, 2005; Heimann, et al., 2006). It is also more likely with students who speak limited English or whose cultural background differs significantly from your own. These students may have learned different nonverbal gestures from your own as part of their participation in their original culture (Marsh, Elfenbein, & Ambady, 2003).

Natural and logical consequences

Consequences are the outcomes or results of an action. When managing a classroom, two kinds of consequences are especially effective for influencing students' behavior: natural consequences and logical consequences. As the term implies, **natural consequences** happen "naturally", without deliberate intention by anyone. If a student is late for class, for example, a natural consequence is that he misses information or material that needed to do an assignment. **Logical consequences** are ones that happen because of the responses of or decisions by others, but that also have an obvious or "logical" relationship to the original action. If one student steals another's lunch, for example, a logical consequence might be for the thief to reimburse the victim for the cost of the lunch. Natural and logical consequences are often woven together and thus hard to distinguish: if one student picks a fight with another student, a natural consequence might be injury not only to the victim, but also to the aggressor (an inherent byproduct of fighting), but a *logical* consequence might be to lose friends (the response of others to fighting). In practice both may occur.

In general research has found that both natural and logical consequences can be effective for minimizing undesirable behaviors, provided they are applied in appropriate situations (Weinstein, Tomlinson-Clarke, & Curran, 2004). Consider a student who runs impulsively down school hallways. The student is likely to have "traffic accidents", and thus (hopefully) to see that running is not safe and to reduce the frequency of running. Or consider a student who chronically talks during class instead of working on an assigned task. The student may have to make up the assignment later, possibly as homework. Because the behavior and the consequence are connected logically, the student is relatively likely to see the drawback of choosing to talk, and to reduce how much he or she talks on subsequent occasions. In either case, whether natural or logical, the key features that make consequences work are (a) that they are appropriate to the misbehavior and (b) that the student understands the connection between the consequences and the original behavior.

Notice, though, that natural and logical consequences do not always work; if they did, there would be no further need for management strategies! One limitation is that misbehaviors can sometimes be so serious that no natural or logical consequence seems sufficient or appropriate. Suppose, for example, that one student deliberately breaks another student's eyeglasses. There may be a natural consequence for the *victim* (he or she will not be able to see easily), but not for the student who broke the glasses. There may also be no consequences for the aggressor that are both logical and fully satisfactory: the aggressor student will not be able to repair the broken glasses himself, and may not be able to pay for new glasses either.

Another limitation of natural and logical consequences is that their success depends on the motives of the misbehaving student. If the student is seeking attention or acceptance by others, then consequences often work well. Bullying in order to impress others, for example, is more likely to *lose* friends than to win them—so bullying motivated in this way is self-limiting. If a student is seeking power over others, on the other hand, then the consequences of bullying may not reduce the behavior. Bullying in order to control others' actions by definition actually achieves its own goal, and its "natural" result (losing friends) would be irrelevant. Of course, a bully might also act from a combination of motives, so that natural and logical consequences limit bullying behavior, but only partially.

A third problem with natural and logical consequences is that they can easily be confused with deliberate punishment (Kohn, 2006). The difference is important. Consequences are focused on repairing damage and restoring relationships, and in this sense they focus on the future. Punishments highlight a mistake or wrongdoing and in this sense focus on the past. Consequences tend to be more solution focused. Punishments tend to highlight the person who committed the action, and they often shame or humiliate the wrong doer. (Table 17 summarizes these and other differences.)

Table 17: Differences between consequences and punishments

Focused on future solutions	Focused on past mistakes
Focused on individual's actions	Focused on character of student or child
Focused on repairing mistakes	Focused on establishing blame

Focused on restoring positive relationships	Focused on isolating wrong-doer
Tend to reduce emotional pain and conflict	Tend to impose emotional pain or conflict

Classroom examples of the differences between consequences and punishment are plentiful. If a student fails to listen to the teacher's instructions, then a consequence is that he or she misses important information, but a punishment may be that the teacher criticizes or reprimands the student. If a student speaks rudely to the teacher, a consequence may be that the teacher does not respond to the comment, or simply reminds the student to speak courteously. A punishment may be that the teacher scolds the student in the presence of others , or even imposes a detention ("Stay after school for 15 minutes").

Conflict resolution and problem solving

When a student misbehaves persistently and disruptively, you will need strategies that are more active and assertive than the ones discussed so far, and that focus on **conflict resolution**—the reduction of disagreements that persist over time. Conflict resolution strategies that educators and teachers tend to use usually have two parts (Jones, 2004). First, they involve ways of identifying what "the" problem is precisely. Second, they remind the student of classroom expectations and rules with simple clarity and assertiveness, but *without* apology or harshness. When used together, the two strategies not only reduce conflicts between a teacher and an individual student, but also provide a model for other students to follow when they have disagreements of their own. The next sections discuss the nature of assertion and clarification for conflict resolution in more detail.

Step 1: clarifying and focusing: problem ownership

Classrooms can be emotional places even though their primary purpose is to promote thinking rather than expression of feelings. The emotions can be quite desirable: they can give teachers and students "passion" for learning and a sense of care among members of the class. But feelings can also cause trouble if students misbehave: at those moments negative feelings—annoyance, anger, discomfort—can interfere with understanding exactly what is wrong and how to set things right again. Gaining a bit of distance from the negative feelings is exactly what those moments need, especially on the part of the teacher, the person with (presumably) the greatest maturity.

In a widely cited approach to conflict resolution called *Teacher Effectiveness Training,* the educator Thomas Gordon describes this challenge as an issue of **problem ownership,** or deciding whose problem a behavior or conflict it really is (Gordon, 2003). The "owner" of the problem is the primary person who is troubled or bothered by it. The owner can be the student committing the behavior, the teacher, or another student who merely happens to see the behavior. Since the owner of a problem needs to take primary responsibility for solving it, identifying ownership makes a difference in how to deal with the behavior or problem effectively.

Suppose, for example, that a student named David makes a remark that the teacher finds offensive (like "Sean is fat"). Is this remark the student's problem or the teacher's? If David made the comment privately to the teacher and is unlikely to repeat it, then maybe it is only the teacher's problem. If he is likely to repeat it to other students or to Sean himself, however, then maybe the problem is really David's. On the other hand, suppose that a different student, Sarah, complains repeatedly that classmates refuse to let her into group projects. This is less likely to be the teacher's problem rather than Sarah's: her difficulty may affect her ability to do her own work, but not really affect the teacher or classmates directly. As you might suspect, too, a problem may sometimes affect several people at once. David, who criticized Sean, may discover that he offended not only the teacher, but also classmates, who therefore avoid working with him. At that point the whole class begins to share in some aspect of "the" problem: not only is David prevented from working with others comfortably, but also classmates *and* the teacher begin dealing with bad feelings about David.

Step 2: active, empathetic listening

Diagnosing accurately who really has a problem with a behavior—who "owns" it—is helped by a number of strategies. One is **active listening**—attending carefully to all aspects of what a student says and attempting to understand or empathize as fully as possible, even if you do not agree with what is being said (Cooper & Simonds, 2003). Active listening involves asking questions in order continually to check your understanding. It also involves encouraging the student to elaborate on his or her remarks, and paraphrasing and summarizing what the student says in order to check your perceptions of what is said. It is important *not* to move too fast toward solving the problem with advice, instructions, or scolding, even if these are responses that you might, as a teacher, feel responsible for making. Responding too soon with solutions can shut down communication prematurely, and leave you with inaccurate impressions of the source or nature of the problem.

Step 3: assertive discipline and I-messages

Once you have listened well to the student's point of view, it helps to frame your responses and comments in terms of how the student's behavior affects you in particular, especially in your role as the teacher. The comments should have several features:

- They should be *assertive*—neither passive and apologetic, nor unnecessarily hostile and aggressive (Cantor, 1996). State the problem as matter-of-factly as possible: "Joe, you are talking while I'm explaining something", instead of either "Joe, do you think you could be quiet now?" or "Joe, be quiet!"

- The comments should emphasize **I-messages** (Gordon, 1981), which are comments that focus on how the problem behavior is affecting the teacher's ability to teach, as well as how the behavior makes the teacher feel. They are distinct from *you-messages*, which focus on evaluating the mistake or problem which the student has created. An I-message might be, "Your talking is making it hard for me to remember what I'm trying to say." A you-message might be, "Your talking is rude."

- The comments should encourage the student to think about the effects of his or her actions on others—a strategy that in effect encourages the student to consider the ethical implications of the actions (Gibbs, 2003). Instead of simply saying: "When you cut in line ahead of the other kids, that was not fair to them", you can try saying, "How do you think the other kids feel when you cut in line ahead of them?"

Step 4: negotiation

The first three steps describe ways of interacting that are desirable, but also fairly specific in scope and limited in duration. But in themselves, they may not be enough when conflict persists over time and develops a number of complications or confusing features. A student may persist in being late for class, for example, in spite of efforts by the teacher to modify this behavior. Or two students may repeatedly speak rudely to each other, even though the teacher has mediated this conflict in the past. Or a student may fail to complete homework, time after time. Because these problems develop over time, and because they may involve repeated disagreements, they can eventually become stressful for the teacher, the student, and any classmates who may be affected. Their persistence can tempt a teacher simply to dictate a resolution—a decision that can leave everyone feeling defeated, including the teacher.

Often in these situations it is better to **negotiate** a solution, which means systematically discussing options and compromising on one if possible. Although negotiation always requires time and effort, it is often less time or effort than continuing to cope with the original problem, and the results can be beneficial to everyone. A number of experts on conflict resolution have suggested strategies for negotiating with students about persistent problems (Davidson & Wood, 2004). The suggestions vary in detail, but usually include some combination of the steps we have already discussed above, along with a few others:

- *Decide as accurately as possible what the problem is.* Usually this step involves a lot of the active listening described above.

- *Brainstorm possible solutions, and **then** consider their effectiveness.* Remember to include students in this step; otherwise you end up simply imposing a solution on others, which is *not* what negotiation is supposed to achieve.

- *If possible, choose a solution by consensus.* Complete agreement on the choice may not be possible, but strive for it as best you can. Remember that taking a vote may be a democratic, acceptable way to settle differences in some situations, but if feelings are running high, voting does not work as well. In that case voting may simply allow the majority to impose its will on the minority, leaving the underlying conflict unresolved.

- *Pay attention to how well the solution works after it is underway.* For many reasons, things may not work out the way you or students hope or expect. You may need to renegotiate the solution at a later time.

Keeping management issues in perspective

There are two primary messages from this chapter. One is that management issues are important, complex, and deserving of serious attention. The other is that strategies exist that can reduce, if not eliminate, management problems when and if they occur. We have explained some of those strategies—including some intended to prevent problems and others intended to remedy problems.

But there is an underlying assumption about management that this chapter emphasized fully: that good classroom management is not an end in itself, but a means for creating a classroom where learning happens and students are motivated. Amidst the stresses of handling a problem behavior, there is a risk of losing sight of this idea. Telling a student to be quiet is never a goal in itself, for example; it is desirable only because (or when) it allows all students to hear the teacher's instructions or classmates' spoken comments, or because it allows students to concentrate on their work. There may actually be moments when students' keeping quiet is *not* appropriate, such as during a "free choice" time in an elementary classroom or during a group work task in a middle school classroom. As teachers, we need to keep this perspective firmly in mind. Classroom management should serve students' learning, and not the other way around. The next chapter is based on this idea, because it discusses ways not just to set the stage for learning, as this chapter has done, but ways to plan directly for students' learning.

Chapter summary

Classroom management is the coordination of lessons and activities to make learning as productive as possible. It is important because classrooms are complex and somewhat unpredictable, because students respond to teachers' actions in diverse ways, and because society requires that students attend school. There are two major features of management: preventing problems before they occur and responding to them after they occur. Many management problems can be prevented by attending to how classroom space is used, by establishing daily procedures, routines, and rules, by pacing and structuring activities appropriately, and by communicating the importance of learning and of positive behavior to students and parents. There are several ways of dealing with a management problem after it occurs, and the choice depends on the nature of the problem. A teacher can simply ignore a misbehavior, gesture or cue students nonverbally, rely on natural and logical consequences, or engage conflict resolution strategies. Whatever tactics the teacher uses, it is important to keep in mind their ultimate purpose: to make learning possible and effective.

On the Internet

<www.theteachersguide.com/ClassManagement.htm> This is part of a larger website for teachers containing resources of all kinds. This section—about classroom management—has several articles with very "nuts and bolts" tips about management. You may also find their page of resources for substitute teachers useful.

<www.teachnet.com> Another website for teachers with lots of resources of all kinds. A section called "Power Tools" has dozens of brief articles about various aspects of classroom management.

Key terms

Active listening	Overlapping
Classroom management	Portfolio
Conflict resolution	Problem ownership
I-messages	Procedures
Learning environment	Ripple effect
Logical consequences	Rules
Natural consequences	Withitness
Negotiation	

References

Benson, B. & Barnett, S. (2005). *Student-led conferencing using showcase portfolios*. Thousand Oaks, CA: Corwin Press.

Black, P., Harrison, C., Lee C., Marshall, B., & Wiliam, D. (2004). Working inside the black box: Assessment for learning in the classroom. *Phi Delta Kappan, 86*(1), 8-21.

Bothmer, S. (2003). *Creating the peaceable classroom*. Tuscon, AZ: Zephyr Press.

Britt, T. (2005). Effects of identity-relevance and task difficulty on task motivation, stress, and performance. *Motivation and Emotion, 29*(3), 189-202.

Brophy, J. (2004). *Motivating students to learn, 2nd edition*. Mahwah, NJ: Erlbaum.

Brookfield, S. (2006). *The skillful teacher: On technique, trust, and responsiveness in the classroom, 2nd edition*. San Francisco: Jossey-Bass.

7. Classroom management and the learning environment

Brown, D. (2004). Urban teachers' professed classroom management strategies: Reflections of culturally responsive teaching. *Urban Education, 39*(3), 266-289.

Chesebro, J. (2003). Effects of teacher clarity and nonverbal immediacy on student learning, receiver apprehension, and affect. *Communication Education, 52*(2), 135-147.

Cooper, P. & Simonds, C. (2003). *Communication for the classroom teacher, 7th edition.* Boston: Allyn & Bacon.

Davidson, J. & Wood, C. (2004). A conflict resolution model. *Theory into Practice, 43*(1), 6-13.

Emmer, E. & Stough, L. (2001). Classroom management: A critical part of educational psychology, with implications for teacher education. *Educational Psychologist, 36*(2), 103-112.

Gibbs, J. (2003). *Moral development and reality: Beyond the theories of Kohlberg and Hoffman.* Thousand Oaks, CA: Sage.

Good, T. & Brophy, J. (2002). *Looking in classrooms, 9th edition.* Boston: Allyn & Bacon.

Gordon, T. (2003). *Teacher effectiveness training.* New York: Three Rivers Press.

Guerrero, L. & Floyd, K. (2005). *Nonverbal communication in close relationships.* Mahwah, NJ: Erlbaum.

Heimann, M. Strid, K., Smith, L., Tjus, T., Ulvund, S. & Meltzoff, A. (2006). Exploring the relation between memory, gestural communication, and the emergence of language in infancy: a longitudinal study. *Infant and Child Development,* 15(3), 233-249.

Jones, T. (2004). Conflict resolution education: The field, the findings, and the future. *Conflict Resolution Quarterly, 22*(1-2), 233-267.

Jones, V. & Jones, L. (2006). *Comprehensive classroom management: Creating communities of support and solving problems, 6th edition.* Boston: Allyn & Bacon.

Kohn, A. (2006). *Beyond discipline: From compliance to community.* Reston, VA: Association for Supervision and Curriculum Development.

Kounin, J. (1970). *Discipline and group management in classrooms.* New York: Holt, Rinehart & Winston.

Marks, L. (2003). Instructional management tips for teachers of students with autism-spectrum disorder. *Teaching Exceptional Children, 35*(4), 50-54.

Marsh, A., Elfenbein, H. & Ambady, N. (2003). Nonverbal "accents": cultural differences in facial expressions of emotion. *Psychological Science, 14*(3), 373-376.

Marzano, R. & Marzano, J. (2004). The key to classroom management. *Educational Leadership, 62,* pp. 2-7.

McCafferty, S., Jacobs, G., & Iddings, S. (Eds.). (2006). *Cooperative learning and second language teaching.* New York: Cambridge University Press.

Moritz, J. & Christie, A. (2005). It's elementary: Using elementary portfolios with young students. In C. Crawford (Ed.), *Proceedings of the Society for Information Technology and Teacher Education*

International Conference 2005 (pp. 144-151). Chesapeake, VA: Association for the Advancement of Computing in Education.

Nations, S. & Boyett, S. (2002). *So much stuff, so little space: Creating and managing the learner-centered classroom.* Gainesville, FL: Maupin House.

Reynolds, A. (1992). What is competent beginning teaching? *Review of Educational Research, 62*(1), 1-35.

Stevens, B. & Tollafield, A. (2003). Creating comfortable and productive parent/teacher conferences. *Phi Delta Kappan, 84*(7), 521-525.

Stiggins, R. & Chappuis, J. (2005). Using student-involved classroom assessment to close achievement gaps. *Theory into Practice 44*(1), 11-18.

Thorson, S. (2003). *Listening to students: Reflections on secondary classroom management.* Boston: Allyn & Bacon.

Turiel, E. (2006). The development of morality. In W. Damon, R. Lerner, & N. Eisenberg (Eds.), *Handbook of child psychology, vol. 3, pp. 789-857.* New York: Wiley.

Van Meerionboer, J., Kirschner, P., & Kester, L. (2003). Taking the cognitive load off a learner's mind: Instructional design for complex learning. *Educational Psychologist, 38*(1), 5-13.

White, C. (2005). Student portfolios: An alternative way of encouraging and evaluating student learning. In M. Achacoso & N. Svinicki (Eds.), *Alternative Strategies for Evaluating Student Learning* (pp. 37-42). San Francisco: Jossey-Bass.

Weinstein, C.,Tomlinson-Clarke, S., & Curran, M. (2004). Toward a conception of culturally responsive classroom management. *Journal of Teacher Education, 55*(1), 25-38.

8. The nature of classroom communication

"Be sincere; be brief; be seated."

(Franklin Delano Roosevelt)

Franklin Roosevelt was a former president of the United States, and he advised being brief and sincere when communicating. In advising to be seated, he was being somewhat more indirect; perhaps he was suggesting that conversation and dialog would be improved by reducing the power differences between individuals. If so, he was giving good advice, though perhaps it was also a bit misleading in its simplicity. As teachers, we face almost continual talk at school, supplemented by ample amounts of nonverbal communication—gestures, facial expressions, and other "body language". Often the talk involves many people at once, or even an entire class, and individuals have to take turns speaking while also listening to others having their turns, or sometimes ignoring the others if a conversation does not concern them. As the teacher, therefore, you find yourself playing an assortment of roles when communicating in classrooms: Master of Ceremonies, referee—and of course source of new knowledge. Your challenge is to sort the roles out so that you are playing the right ones in the right combinations at the right times. As you learn to do this, interestingly, much of your communication with students will indeed acquire the qualities recommended by Franklin Roosevelt. Often, you will indeed be more sincere and brief, and you will find that minimizing power differences between you and students is a good idea.

In this chapter we look at how you might begin to move toward these goals. We describe briefly several major features of classroom communication that distinguish it from communication in other familiar situations. Then we explain several techniques, both verbal and nonverbal, that contribute to effective communication, and describe how these manifest themselves in several common activity settings, which we call *structures of participation*. As you will see, how an activity is organized—its structure of participation—has a major effect on how students communicate with each other and with the teacher.

Communication in classrooms *vs* communication elsewhere

Classroom events are often so complex that just talking with students can become confusing. It helps to think of the challenge as a problem in **communication**—or as one expert put it, of "who says what to whom, and with what effect" (Lasswell, 1964). In classrooms, things often do not happen at an even pace or in a logical order, or with just the teacher and one student interacting while others listen or wait patiently. While such moments do occur, events may sometimes instead be more like a kaleidoscope of overlapping interactions, disruptions, and decision—even when activities are generally going *well*. One student finishes a task while another is still only half-way done. A third student looks like she is reading, but she may really be dreaming. You begin to bring her back on task by speaking to her, only to be interrupted by a fourth student with a question about an assignment. While you answer the fourth student, a fifth walks in with a message from the office requiring a response; so the bored (third) student is overlooked awhile longer. Meanwhile, the first student—the one who finished the current task—now begins telling a joke to a sixth student, just to pass the time. You wonder, "Should I speak now to the bored, quiet reader or to the joke-telling student? Or should I move on with the lesson?" While you are wondering this, a seventh student raises his hand with a question, and so on.

One way to manage situations like these is to understand and become comfortable with the key features of communication that are characteristic of classrooms. One set of features has to do with the functions or purposes of communication, especially the balance among talk related to content, to procedures, and to controlling behavior. Another feature has to do with the nature of nonverbal communication—how it supplements and sometimes even contradicts what is said verbally. A third feature has to do with the unwritten expectations held by students and teachers about *how* to participate in particular kinds of class activities—what we will later call the structure of participation.

Functions of talk: content, procedures, and behavior control

Classrooms are different from many other group situations in that communication serves a unique combination of three purposes at once: content, procedures, or behavior control (Wells, 2006). **Content talk** focuses on *what* is being learned; it happens when a teacher or student states or asks about an idea or concept, for example, or when someone explains or elaborates on some bit of new knowledge (Burns & Myhill, 2004). Usually content talk relates in some obvious way to the curriculum or to current learning objectives, as when a teacher tells a high school history class, "As the text explains, there were several major causes of the American Civil War." But content talk can also digress from the current learning objectives; a first-grade student might unexpectedly bring a caterpillar to school and ask about how it transforms into a butterfly.

Procedural talk, as its name implies, is about administrative rules or routines needed to accomplish tasks in a classroom. It happens, for example, when the teacher says, "When you are done with your spelling books, put them in the bins at the side of the room", or when a student asks, "Do you want us to print our names at the top of page?" Procedural talk provides information that students need to coordinate their activities in what can be a relatively crowded space—the classroom—and under conditions in which time may be relatively short or tightly scheduled. It generally keeps activities organized and flowing smoothly. Procedural talk is not primarily about removing or correcting unwanted behavior, although certain administrative procedures might sometimes annoy a particular student, or students might sometimes forget to follow a procedure. Instead it is intended to provide the guidance that students need to coordinate with each other and with the teacher.

Control talk is about preventing or correcting misbehaviors when they occur, particularly when the misbehaviors are not because of ignorance of procedures. It happens, for example, when a teacher says, "Jill, you were talking when you should have been listening", or "Jason, you need to work on your math instead of doodling." Most control talk originates with the teacher, but students sometimes engage in it with each other, if not with the teacher. One student may look at a nearby classmate who is whispering out of turn and quietly say, "Shhh!" in an attempt to silence the behavior. Or a student may respond to being teased by a classmate by saying simply, "Stop it!" Whether originating from the teacher or a student, control talk may not always be fully effective. But its purpose is, by definition, to influence or control inappropriate behavior. Since control talk is obviously important for managing class effectively, we discussed it at length in Chapter 7.

What can make classroom discourse confusing is that two of its functions—content and procedures—often become combined with the third, control talk, in the same remark or interaction. A teacher may ask a content-related question, for example, as a form of control talk. She may, for example, ask, "Jeremy, what did *you* think of the film we just saw?" The question is apparently about content, but the teacher may also be trying to end Jeremy's daydreaming and to get him back on task—an example of control talk. Or a teacher may state a rule: "When one person is talking, others need to be listening." The rule is procedural in that it helps to coordinate classroom dialogue, but it may also control inattentive behavior. Double functions like these can sometimes confuse students because of their ambiguity, and lead to misunderstandings between certain students and teachers. A student may hear only the content or procedural function of a teacher's comment, and miss an implied request or command to change inappropriate behavior (Collins & Michaels, 2006). But double functions can also help lessons to flow smoothly by minimizing the disruption of attending to a minor behavior problem and by allowing more continuous attention to content or procedures.

Verbal, nonverbal, and unintended communication

Another way to understand classroom communication is to distinguish verbal from nonverbal communication, and intended both *un*intended forms of communication. As the name suggests, **verbal communication** is a message or information expressed in words, either orally or in writing. Classrooms obviously have lots of verbal communication; it happens every time a teacher explains a bit of content, asks a question, or writes information or instructions on the chalkboard. **Non-verbal communications** are gestures or behaviors that convey information, often simultaneously with spoken words (Guerrero, 2006). It happens, for example, when a teacher looks directly at students to emphasize a point or to assert her authority, or when the teacher raises her eyebrows to convey disapproval or disagreement. Nonverbal behaviors are just as plentiful as verbal communications, and while they usually add to a current verbal message, they sometimes can also contradict it. A teacher can state verbally, "This math lesson will be fun", and a nonverbal twinkle in the eye can send the confirm message nonverbally. But a simultaneous nonverbal sigh or slouch may send the opposite message—that the lesson will not, in fact be fun, in spite of the teacher's verbal claim.

Whether verbal or nonverbal, however, classroom communications often convey more meaning than is intended. **Unintended communications** are the excess meanings of utterances; they are the messages received by students without the teacher's awareness or desire. A teacher may say, "This section of the text won't be on the test, but read it anyway for background." But a student may instead hear the message, "Do not read this section of the text." What is heard is not what the teacher intended to be heard.

Like many public settings that involve a diversity of people, classrooms tend to rely heavily on explicit, verbal communication, while at the same time recognizing and allowing nonverbal communications to occur (Neill, 1991). This priority accounts for the characteristically businesslike style of teacher talk—a style that we discuss in detail in the next chapter. A major reason for relying on an explicit, businesslike verbal style is that diversity among individuals increases the chances of their misinterpreting each other. Because of differences in background, the partners may differ in how they expect to structure conversation as well as other kinds of dialog. Misunderstandings may result—sometimes without the partners being able to pinpoint the cause. Later in this chapter we suggest how to minimize these problems.

Effective verbal communication

Communicating effectively requires using all forms of classroom talk in combinations appropriate for particular utterances and interactions. In various places earlier in this book, we have suggested ways of doing so, though in those places we usually did not frame the discussion around the term *communication* as such.

Effective content talk

In Chapter 8, for example, we suggested ways of talking about content so that it is most likely to be understood clearly, but in that chapter we described these as instructional strategies. In explaining ideas, for example, whether briefly or as a extended lecture, we pointed out that it helps to offer, in advance, organizing ideas, to relate new content to prior knowledge, and to organize and elaborate on new information. In the same chapter, we also suggested strategies about content talk intended for students, so that students understand their own thinking as well as possible. We especially highlighted two ways of learning: inquiry learning and cooperative learning. Table 18summarizes instructional strategies both for students and for teachers, and indicates how they contribute to effective verbal communication about content.

Table 18: Strategies for supporting content talk

Content talk by teachers		
Strategy	**Definition**	**How it helps communication**
Using advance organizers	Statements or ideas that give a concise overview of new material	Orients students' attention to new ideas about to be learned; assists in understanding and remembering new material
Relating new material to prior knowledge	Explicit connections of new ideas to students' existing knowledge	Facilitates discussion of new material by making it more meaningful to students
Elaborating and extending new information	Explanations of new ideas in full, complete terms	Avoids ambiguities and misunderstandings about new ideas or concepts
Organizing new information	Providing and following a clear structure when explaining new material	Assists in understanding and remembering new material
Content talk by students		
Inquiry learning	Students pursue problems that they help to formulate for themselves	To formulate and and investigate a problem, students need to express clearly what they wish to find out.
Cooperative learning	Students work in small groups to	To work together, students need

	solve a common problem or task	to explain ideas and questions to fellow students clearly.

Table 19: Major strategies of effective procedural and control talk

These strategies are also discussed in Chapter 7 as features of classroom management, rather than of communication. Note, too, that the difference between procedural and content talk is arbitrary to some extent; in many situations one kind of talk serves the needs of the other kind.

Strategy for procedural talk	Strategy for control talk
Creating and discussing procedures for daily routines	Creating and discussing classroom rules of appropriate behavior
Announcing transitions between activities	Clarifying problem ownership
Providing clear instructions and guidance for activities	Listening actively and empathetically
Reminding students periodically of procedures for completing a task	Using I-messages

Effective procedural and control talk

In addition to communicating about content, teachers need to communicate procedures and expectations about appropriate classroom behavior. In Chapter 7 we described quite a few ways to communicate with students about these matters, though, in that chapter we did not refer to them as methods of communication, but as methods of classroom management, of creating a positive learning environment, and of resolving conflicts in the class. Table 19 summarizes several of the major strategies described in that chapter.) By framing communication in these ways, we called attention to their importance as forms of communication. As we pointed out, procedural talk and control talk matter are used in teaching simply because clear procedures and appropriate classroom behavior are necessary students are to learn.

Effective nonverbal communication

In spite of their importance, words are not the only way that teachers and students communicate. Gestures and behaviors convey information as well, often supporting a teacher's words, but sometimes also contradicting them. Students and teachers express themselves nonverbally in all conversations, so freely and automatically in fact that this form of communication can easily be overlooked.

Eye contact

One important nonverbal behavior is **eye contact,** which is the extent and timing of when a speaker looks directly at the eyes of the listener. In conversations between friends of equal status, for example, most native speakers of English tend to look directly at the speaker when listening, but to avert their gaze when speaking (Kleinke, 1986). Re-engaging eye contact, in fact, often signals that a speaker is about to finish a turn and is inviting a response from the listener.

But conversations follow different rules if they involve someone of greater authority talking with someone of lesser authority, such as between a teacher and a student. In that case, the person in authority signals greater status by gazing directly at the listener almost continuously, whether listening *or* speaking. This alternate pattern can sometimes prove awkward if either party is not expecting it. For students unused to continuous eye contact, it can feel like the teacher is staring excessively, intrusively, or inappropriately; an ironic effect can be for the student to feel more self-conscious rather than more engaged, as intended. For similar reasons, inexperienced or first-time teachers can also feel uncomfortable with gazing at students continuously. Nevertheless research about the effects of eye contact suggests that it may help anyone, whether a student or teacher, to remember what they are seeing and hearing (Mason, Hood, & Macrae, 2004).

Communication problems result less from eye contact as such than from differences in expectations about eye contact. If students' expectations differ very much from the teacher's, one party may misinterpret the other party's motivations. Among some non-white ethnic groups, for example, eye contact follows a pattern that reverses the conventional white, English-language pattern: they tend to look more intently at a partner when *talking*, and avert gaze when *listening* (Razack, 1998). The alternative pattern works perfectly well as long as both parties expect it and use it. As you might imagine, though, there are problems if the two partners use opposite patterns of eye contact. In that case one person may interpret a direct gaze as an invitation to start talking, when really it is an invitation to stop talking. Eventually the conversational partner may find himself interrupting too much, or simply talking too long at a turn. The converse can also happen: if the first person looks away, the partner may take the gesture as inviting the partner to keep listening, when really the first person is inviting the partner to start talking. Awkward gaps between comments may result. In either case, if the conversational partners are a teacher and student, rapport may deteriorate gradually. In the first case, the teacher may even conclude, wrongly, that the student is socially inept because the student interrupts so much. In the second case, the teacher may conclude—also wrongly—that the student is very shy or even lacking in language skill.

To avoid such misunderstandings, a teacher needs to note and remember students' preferred gaze patterns at times when students are free to look wherever and at whomever they please. Traditional seats-in-a-row desk arrangements do not work well for this purpose; as you might suppose, and as research confirms, sitting in rows makes students more likely to look either at the teacher or to look at nothing in particular (Rosenfeld, Lambert, & Black, 1985; Razack, 1998). Almost any other seating arrangement, such as sitting in clusters or in a circle, encourages freer patterns of eye contact. More comfortable eye contact, in turn, makes for verbal communication that is more comfortable and productive.

Wait time

Another important nonverbal behavior is **wait time**, which is the pause between conversational turns. Wait time marks when a conversational turn begins or ends. If a teacher asks a question, for example, the wait time both allows and prompts students to formulate an appropriate response. Studies on classroom interaction generally show that wait times in most classes are remarkably short—less than one second (Good & Brophy, 2002). Unfortunately wait times this short can actually interfere with most students' thinking; in one second, most students either cannot decide what to say or can only recall a simple, automatic fact (Tobin, 1987). Increasing wait times to several seconds has several desirable effects: students give longer, more elaborate responses, they express more complex ideas, and a wider range of students participate in discussion. For many teachers, however, learning to increase wait time this much takes conscious effort, and may feel uncomfortable at first. (A trick, if you are trying to wait longer, is to count silently to five before calling on anyone.) After a few weeks of practice, discomfort with longer wait times usually subsides, and the academic benefits of waiting become more evident.

As with eye contact, preferred wait times vary both among individuals and among groups of students, and the differences in expected wait times can sometimes lead to awkward conversations. Though there are many exceptions, girls tend to prefer longer wait times than boys—perhaps contributing to an impression that girls are unnecessarily shy or that boys are self-centered or impulsive. Students from some ethnic and cultural groups tend to prefer a much longer wait time than is typically available in a classroom, especially when English is the student's second language (Toth, 2004). When a teacher converses with a member of such a group, therefore, what feels to the student like a respectful pause may seem like hesitation or resistance to the teacher. Yet other cultural groups actually prefer overlapping comments—a sort of negative wait time. In these situations, one conversational partner will begin at exactly the same instant as the previous speaker, or even *before* the speaker has finished (Chami-Sather & Kretschmer, 2005). The negative wait time is meant to signal lively interest in the conversation. A teacher who is used to a one-second gap between comments, however, may regard overlapping comments as rude interruptions, and may also have trouble getting chances to speak.

Even though longer wait times are often preferable, they do not always work well with certain individuals or groups. For teachers, the most widely useful advice is to match wait time to the students' preferences as closely as possible, regardless of whether these are slower or faster than what the teacher normally prefers. To the extent that a teacher and students can match each other's pace, they will communicate more comfortably and fully, and a larger proportion of students will participate in discussions and activities. As with eye contact, observing students' preferred wait times is easier in situations that give students some degree of freedom about when and how to participate, such as open-ended discussions or informal conversations throughout the day.

Social distance

When two people interact, the physical space or distance between them—their **social distance**—often indicates something about how intimate or personal their relationship is (Noller, 2006). Social distance also affects how people describe others and their actions; someone who habitually is more distant physically is apt to be described in more general, abstract terms than someone who often approaches more closely (Fujita, et al., 2006). In white American society, a distance of approximately half a meter to a meter is what most people prefer when talking face-to-face with a personal friend. The closer end of this range is more common if the individuals turn sideways to each other, as when riding on an elevator; but usually the closest distances are reserved for truly intimate friendships, such as between spouses. If the relationship is more businesslike, individuals are more likely to situate themselves in the range of approximately one meter to a three meters. This is a common distance, for example, for a teacher talking with a student or talking with a small group of students. For still more formal interactions, individuals tend to allow more than three meters; this distance is typical, for example, when a teacher speaks to an entire class.

Just as with eye contact and wait time, however, individuals differ in the distances they prefer for these different levels of intimacy, and complications happen if two people expect different distances for the same kind of relationship. A student who prefers a shorter social distance than her partner can seem pushy or overly familiar to the partner. The latter, in turn, can seem aloof or unfriendly—literally "distant". The sources of these effects are easy to overlook since by definition the partners never discuss social distance verbally, but they are real. The best remedy, again, is for teachers to observe students' naturally occurring preferences as closely as possible, and to respect them as much as possible: students who need to be closer should be allowed to be closer, at least within reasonable limits, and those who need to be more distant should be allowed to be more distant.

Structures of participation: effects on communication

Many class activities take on patterns that guide communication in ways that class members learn to expect, often without even being reminded. Each pattern is a **participation structure,** a set of rights and responsibilities expected from students and teacher during an activity. Sometimes the teacher announces or explains the rights and responsibilities explicitly, though often they are just implied by the actions of class members, and individual students learn them simply by watching others. A lecture, for example, has a particular participation structure: students are responsible for listening, for raising a hand to speak, and for keeping comments brief and relevant if called on. The teacher, on the other hand, has the right to talk at length, but also the responsibility to keep the talk relevant and comprehensible.

In principle, a host of participation structures are possible, but just a handful account for most class activities (Cazden, 2001). Here are some of the most common:

- Lecturing—the teacher talks and students listen. Maybe students take notes, but maybe not.

- Questions and answers—the teacher asks a series of questions, calling on one student at a time to answer each of them. Students raise their hands to be recognized and give answers that are brief and "correct". In earlier times this participation structure was sometimes called recitation.

- Discussion—the teacher briefly describes a topic or problem and invites students to comment on it. Students say something relevant about the topic, but also are supposed to respond to previous speakers if possible.

- Group work—the teacher assigns a general task, and a small group of students work out the details of implementing it. The teacher may check on the group's progress before they finish, but not necessarily.

Each of these structures influences how communication among teachers and students tends to occur; in fact each is itself sort of an implied message about how, when, and with whom to interact. To see how this influence works, look in the next sections at how the participation structures affected classroom communication for one of us authors (Kelvin Seifert) as he taught one particular topic—children's play—over a twenty-year period. The topic was part of a university-level course for future teachers. During this time, Kelvin's goals about the topic remained the same: to stimulate students' thinking about the nature and purposes of play. But over time he tried several different structures of participation, and students' ways of communicating changed as a result.

Lecture

The first time Kelvin taught about children's play, he lectured about it. He used this structure of participation not because he believed on principle that it was the best, but because it was convenient and used widely by his fellow university teachers. An excerpt from Kelvin's lecture notes is shown in Table 20, and gives a sense of what he covered at that time.

In some ways the lecture proved effective: Kelvin covered the material efficiently (in about 20 minutes), related the topic to other ones in the course, defined and explained all key terms clearly, and did his best to relate the material to what he thought were students' own interests. These were all marks of good lecturing (Christensen, 2006). Students were mostly quiet during the lecture, but since only about one-third of them took notes, Kelvin had to assume that the rest had committed the material to memory while listening. The students quietness bothered him a little, but as a newcomer to university teaching, Kelvin was relieved simply to get through the class without embarrassment or active resistance from the students.

But there were also some negative signs. In spite of their courtesy, few students lingered after class to talk about children's play or to ask questions. Worse yet, few students chose children's play as a term paper topic, even though it might have made a highly interesting and enjoyable one. On the final exam few seemed able to relate concepts about play to their own experiences as teachers or leaders of recreational activities.

There was an even more subtle problem. The lecture about play focused overtly on a topic (play) that praised action, intrinsic motivation, and self-choice. But by presenting these ideas as a lecture, Kelvin also implied an opposite message unintentionally: that learning is something done passively, and that it follows an intellectual path set only by the teacher. Even the physical layout of the classroom sent this message—desks faced forward, as if to remind students to look only at the person lecturing. These are features of lecturing, as Kelvin later discovered, that are widely criticized in educational research (McKeachie & Svinicki, 2005; Benedict & Hoag, 2004). To some students the lecture format might even have implied that learning is equivalent to daydreaming, since both activities require sitting quietly and showing little expression. An obvious solution might have been to invite students to comment from time to time during the lecture, relating the topic to experiences and knowledge of their own. But during Kelvin's first year of teaching about play, he did little of this. The lecture medium, ironically, contradicted the lecture message, or at least it assumed that students would think actively about the material without ever speaking.

Questions and answers

Because of these problems, Kelvin modified his approach after a few years of teaching to include more asking of questions which students were invited to answer. This turned the lecture on children's play into something more like a series of explanations of key ideas, interrupted by asking students to express their beliefs, knowledge, or experience about children's play. Kelvin's preparation notes changes in appearance as a result (see Table 21). Asking questions and inviting brief responses was reassuring because it gave indications of whether students were listening and understanding the material. Questions served both to motivate students to listen and to assess how much and how well they knew the material. In this regard Kelvin was using a form of communication that was and continues to be very popular with many teachers (Cazden, 2001).

But there were also new challenges and problems. For one thing the topic of children's play took longer to cover than before, since Kelvin now had to allow time for students to respond to questions. This fact forced him to leave out a few points that he used to include. More serious, though, was his impression that students often did not listen to each other's responses; they only listened carefully to Kelvin, the teacher. The interactions often become simply two-way exchanges between the teacher and one student at a time: Kelvin asked, one student responded, Kelvin acknowledged or (sometimes) evaluated. (Mehan, 1979; Richards, 2006). Some of the exchanges could in principle have happened just as easily without any classmates present.

In general students still had little control over the course of discussion. Kelvin wondered if he was controlling participation too much—in fact whether the question-and-answer strategy attempted the impossible task of controlling students' very thought processes. By asking most of the questions himself and allowing students only brief responses, was Kelvin trying to insure e that students thought about children's play in the "right" way, *his* way? To give students more influence in discussion, it seemed that Kelvin would have to become less concerned about precisely what ideas about children's play he covered.

Classroom discussion

After several more years of teaching, Kelvin quit lectures altogether, even ones interspersed with questions and answers. He began simply leading general discussions about children's play. The change again affected his planning for this topic. Instead of outlining detailed content, he now just made concise notes that listed issues about children's play that students needed to consider (some of the notes are shown in Table 23). The shift in participation structure led to several major changes in communication between teacher and students as well as among students. Since students spoke more freely than before, it became easier to see whether they cared about the topic. Now, too, more students seemed motivated to think and learn about children's play; quite a few selected this topic, for example, for their term projects. Needless to say, these changes were all to the good.

But there were also changes that limited the effectiveness of classroom communication, even though students were nominally freer to speak than ever. Kelvin found, for example, that certain students spoke more than their share of the time—almost too freely, in fact, in effect preventing more hesitant students from speaking. Sometimes, too, it seemed as if certain students did not listen to others' comments, but instead just passed the time waiting for their turn to speak, their hands propped permanently in the air. Meanwhile there were still others who passed the time apparently hoping *not* to speak; they were busy doodling or staring out the window. Since the precise focus of discussion was no longer under Kelvin's control, furthermore, discussions often did not cover all of the ideas about children's play that Kelvin considered important. On one occasion, for example, he meant for students to discuss whether play is always motivated intrinsically, but instead they ended up talking about whether play can really be used to teach every possible subject area. In itself the shift in focus was not bad, but it did make Kelvin wonder whether he was covering the material adequately. In having these misgivings, as it happened, he was supported by other educators who have studied the effects of class discussions on learning (McKeatchie & Svinciki, 2005).

Group work

By the time he had taught about children's play for twenty years, Kelvin had developed enough concerns about discussion as a communication strategy that he shifted approach again. This time he began using a form of **collaborative group work**: small teams of students carrying out projects on aspects of children's play that interested them, making observations of children at play, reporting on their results to the class, and writing a common report about their work. (Kelvin's work guidelines given to the groups are shown in Table 22.) Kelvin hoped that by giving students a common focus, communication among them would improve. Conversations would deal with the tasks at hand, students would necessarily listen to each other, and no one could afford either to dominate talk excessively or to fall silent.

In some ways these benefits did take place. With a bit of encouragement from Kelvin, students listened to each other more of the time than before. They also diversified their tasks and responsibilities within each group, and they seemed to learn from each other in the course of preparing projects. Participation in the unit about children's play reached an all-time high in Kelvin's twenty years of teaching at university. Yet even still there were problems. Some groups seemed much more productive than others, and observing them closely suggested that differences were related to ease of communication within groups. In some groups, one or two people dominated conversations unduly. If they listened to others at all, they seemed immediately to forget that they had done so and proceeded to implement their own ideas. In other groups, members all worked hard, but they did not often share ideas or news about each other's progress; essentially they worked independently in spite of belonging to the group. Here, too, Kelvin's experience corroborated other, more systematic observations of communication within classroom work groups (Slavin, 1995). When all groups were planning at the same time, furthermore, communication broke down for a very practical reason: the volume of sound in the classroom got so high that even simple conversation became difficult, let alone the expression of subtle or complex ideas.

Communication styles in the classroom

Teachers and students have identifiable styles of talking to each other that linguists call a *register*. A **register** is a pattern of vocabulary, grammar, and expressions or comments that people associate with a social role. A familiar example is the "baby-talk" register often used to speak to an infant. Its features—simple repeated words and nonsense syllables, and exaggerated changes in pitch—mark the speaker as an adult and mark the listener as an infant. The classroom language register works the same way; it helps indicate who the teacher is and who the student is. Teachers and students use the register more in some situations than in others, but its use is common enough that most people in our society have no trouble recognizing it when they hear it (Cazden, 2001). In the following scene, for example, the speakers are labeled only with letters of the alphabet; yet figuring out who is the teacher and who are the students is not difficult:

> A: All right now, I want your eyes up here. All eyes on me, please. B, are you ready to work? We are going to try a new kind of math problem today. It's called long division. Does anyone know what long division is? C, what do you think it is?

> C: Division with bigger numbers?

> A: Any other ideas? D?

> E (not D): Division by two digits.

> A: ...I only call on people who raise their hands. D, can you help with the answer?

> D: Division with remainders.

> A: Close. Actually you're both partly right.

In this scene Person A must surely be the teacher because he or she uses a lot of procedural and control talk, and because he or she introduces a new curriculum topic, long division. The other Persons (B, C, D, and E) must be students because they only respond to questions, and because they individually say relatively little compared to Person A.

In general, effective classroom communication depends on understanding how features of the classroom talk register like these operate during actual class times. In the following sections therefore we describe details of classroom talk, and then follow with suggestions about how to use the register as effectively as possible. In both of these sections we assume that the better the communication, the better the learning and thinking displayed by students. For convenience we divide classroom talk into two parts, teacher talk and student talk.

How teachers talk

Although teacher talk varies somewhat with the tasks or purposes at hand, it also has uniformities that occur across a range of situations. Using detailed observations of discourse in science activities, for example, Jay Lemke identified all of the following strategies from observations of teachers' classroom talk (1990). Each strategy simultaneously influences the course of discussion and focuses students' attention, and in these ways also helps indirectly to insure appropriate classroom behavior:

- *Nominating, terminating, and interrupting speakers:* Teachers often choose who gets to speak. ("Jose, what do you think about X?"). On the other hand, they often bring an end to a student's turn at speaking or even interrupt the student before he or she finishes. ("Thanks; we need to move on now.")

- *Marking importance or irrelevance:* Teachers sometimes indicate that an idea is important ("That's a good idea, Lyla."). On the other hand, they sometimes also indicate that an idea is not crucial or important ("Your right, but that's not quite the answer I was looking for."), or fully relevant ("We're talking about the book *Wuthering Heights,* not the movie that you may have seen."). Marking importance and relevance obviously helps a teacher to reinforce key content. But the strategy can also serve to improve relationships among students if the teacher deliberately marks or highlights an idea offered by a quiet or shy student (O'Connor & Michaels, 1996; Cohen, et al., 2004). In that case marking importance can build both a student's confidence and the student's status in the eyes of classmates.

- *Signaling boundaries between activities:* Teachers declare when an activity is over and a new one is starting—an example of the procedural talk that we discussed earlier. ("We need to move on. Put away your spelling and find your math books.") In addition to clarifying procedures, though, signaling boundaries can also insure appropriate classroom behavior. Ending an activity can sometimes help restore order among students who have become overly energetic, and shifting to a new activity can sometimes restore motivation to students who have become bored or tired.

- Asking "test" questions and evaluating students' responses: Teachers often ask test questions—questions to which they already know the answer. Then they evaluate the quality or correctness of the students' answers (Teacher: "How much is 6 x 7 ?" Student: "42." Teacher: "That's right."). Test questions obviously help teachers to assess students' learning, but they also mark the teacher as the expert in the classroom, and therefore as a person entitled to control the flow of discourse.

There are additional features of teacher-talk that are not unique to teachers. These primarily function to make teachers' comments more comprehensible, especially when spoken to a group, but they also help to mark a person who uses them as a teacher (Cazden, 2001; Black, 2004):

- *Exaggerated changes in pitch:* When busy teaching, teachers tend to exaggerate changes in the pitch of their voice—reminiscent of the "sing-song" style of adults when directing speech to infants. Exaggerated pitch changes are especially characteristic of teachers of young students, but they happen at all grade levels.

- *Careful enunciation:* In class teachers tend to speak more slowly, clearly, and carefully than when conversing with a friend. The style makes a speaker sound somewhat formal, especially when combined with formal vocabulary and grammar, mentioned next.

- *Formal vocabulary and grammar:* Teachers tend to use vocabulary and grammar that is more formally polite and correct, and that uses relatively few slang or casual expressions. (Instead of saying "Get out your stuff", they more likely say, "Please get out your materials.") The formality creates a businesslike distance between teachers and students—hopefully one conducive to getting work done, rather than one that seems simply cold or uncaring. The touch of formality also makes teachers sound a bit more intelligent or intellectual than in casual conversation, and in this way reinforces their authority in the classroom.

How students talk

Children and youth also use a characteristic speech register when they are in a classroom and playing the role of students in the presence of a teacher. Their register—student talk—differs somewhat from the teacher's because of their obvious differences in responsibilities, levels of knowledge, and relationships with each other and with the teacher. Student-talk and teacher-talk are similar in that both involve language strategies that guide content and procedures, and that sometimes seek to limit the inappropriate behavior of others. Compared to teachers', though, students' language strategies often pursue these goals a bit more indirectly.

- *Agenda enforcement:* Sometimes students interrupt a discussion to ask about or remind others, and especially the teacher, of an agreed-on agenda. If the teacher tells students to open their text to an incorrect page, for example, a student may raise her hand to correct the teacher—or even do so without raising a hand. This communication strategy is one of more public, direct ways that students influence activities in the classroom, but its power is limited, since it does not create new activities, but simply returns the class to activities agreed on previously.

- *Digression attempts:* During a discussion or activity, a student asks a question or makes a statement that is not relevant to the task at hand. While the teacher is leading students in a discussion of a story that they read, for example, a student raises his hand and asks, "Mr X, when does recess begin?"

- *Side talk:* One student talks to another student, either to be sociable ("Did you see that movie last week?") or to get information needed for the current assigned task ("What page are we on?"). Sometimes side talk also serves to control or limit fellow students' behavior, and in this way functions like control-talk by teachers (as when a student whispers, "Shhh! I'm trying to listen" or "Go ahead and ask her!"). The ability of such talk to influence classmates' behavior is real, but limited, since students generally do not have as much authority as teachers.

- *Calling out:* A student speaks out of turn without being recognized by the teacher. The student's comment may or may not be relevant to the ongoing task or topic, and the teacher may or may not acknowledge or respond to it. Whether ignored or not, however, calling out may change the direction of a discussion by influencing fellow students' thinking or behavior, or by triggering procedural and control talk by the teacher. ("Jason, it's not your turn; I only call on students who raise their hands.")

- *Answering a question with a question:* Instead of answering a teacher's "test" question directly, the student responds with a question of her own, either for clarification or as a stalling tactic ("Do you mean X?"). Either way, the effect is to shift the discussion or questioning to content or topics that are safer and more familiar.

- *Silence:* The student says nothing in response to a speaker's comments or to an invitation to speak. The speaker could be either the teacher or a fellow student. The silence makes the speaker less likely to continue the current topic, and more likely to seek a new one.

- *Eye contact, gaze aversion, and posture:* The student looks directly at the teacher while the teacher is speaking, or else deliberately averts gaze. The student may also adopt any variety of postures while sitting (sit up straight vs slouching). As we discussed earlier in this chapter, the timing of eye gaze depends partly on cultural expectations that the student brings to school. But it may also represent a deliberate choice by the student—a message to the teacher and to classmates. The same can be said about sitting posture. In classroom situations, listening is conventionally indicated by looking directly at the teacher, and either sitting up straight or leaning slightly forward. Although these behaviors can be faked, they tend to indicate, and to be taken as, a show of interest in and acceptance of what a speaker is saying. By engaging in or avoiding these behaviors, therefore, students can sometimes influence the length and direction of a discussion or activity.

Using classroom talk to stimulate students' thinking

The various features of classroom talk characterize the communication of most teachers and students, at least when they are in a classroom and "doing school". (Communication outside of school is a different matter: then teachers as well as students may speak, listen, and behave quite differently!) As you might suppose, the extent and balance among the features varies depending on grade level, curriculum area, and personalities of students or teachers. But failing to use a classroom register at all can easily create communication problems. Suppose, for example, that a teacher never asks informal test questions. In that case the teacher will learn much less than otherwise about her students' knowledge of the current material. Then also suppose that a student does not understand teachers' questions as test questions. That student may easily respond in ways that seem disrespectful (Teacher: "How much is 23 x 42?" Student: "I don't know; how much do *you* think it is?") (Bloome, et al., 2005).

The classroom talk register, then, constrains how communication between teachers and students can take place, but it also gives teachers and students a "language" for talking about teaching and learning. Given this double-edged reality, how can teachers use the classroom talk register to good advantage? How, in particular, can teachers communicate in ways that stimulate more and better thinking and discussion? In the next, final section of the chapter, we offer some suggestions for answering these questions. As you will see, the suggestions often reinforce each other. They are more like a network of ideas, not a list of priorities to be considered or followed in sequence.

Probing for learner understanding

How do you know whether a student understands what you are saying? One clue, of course, is by whether the student is looking at and concentrating on you and your comments. But this clue is not foolproof; we have all had moments of staring at a speaker while daydreaming, only to realize later that we have not heard anything that the speaker said. It is sometimes important, therefore, to probe more actively how much students are actually understanding during lessons or other activities.

Strategies for probing understanding generally involve mixing instruction with conversation (Renshaw, 2004). In explaining a new topic, for example, you can check for understanding by asking preliminary questions connecting the topic to students' prior experiences and knowledge about the topic. Note that this strategy combines qualities of both instruction and conversation, in the sense that it involves combining "test" questions, to which you already know the answer, with real questions, to which you do not. When introducing a science lesson about density to kindergarten children, for example, the teacher might reasonably ask both of the following:

Teacher: Which of these objects that I have do you expect will sink and which ones will float? (A test question—the teacher already will know the answer.)

Teacher: What other things have you seen that float? Or that sink? (A real question—the teacher is asking about their experience and does not know the answer.)

By asking both kinds of questions, the teacher scaffolds the children's learning, or creates a *zone of proximal development,* which we described in Chapter 2 as part of Vygotsky's theory of learning. Note that this zone has two important features, both of which contribute to children's thinking. One is that it stimulates students' thinking (by asking them questions), and the other is that it creates a supportive and caring atmosphere (by honoring their personal experiences with real questions). The resulting mix of warmth and challenge can be especially motivating (Goldstein, 1999).

When warmth and challenge are both present in a discussion, it sometimes even becomes possible to do what may at first seem risky: calling on individual students randomly without the students' volunteering to speak. In a study of "cold calling" as a technique in university class discussions, the researchers found that students did *not* find the practice especially stressful or punitive, as the teachers feared they might, and that spontaneous participation in discussion actually improved as a result (Dallimore, et al., 2006). The benefit was most likely to happen, however, when combined with gestures of respect for students, such as warning individuals ahead of class that they might be called on, or allowing students to formulate ideas in small groups before beginning to call on individuals.

Helping students to articulate their ideas and thinking

The classroom talk register is well designed to help students articulate ideas and thoughts, particularly when used in the context of discussion. In addition to the conversational probes, like the ones we described in the previous section, there are other ways to support students in expressing their ideas fully and clearly. One way is for the teacher to check repeatedly on her own understanding of students' contributions as a discussion unfolds. Consider this exchange:

Student (during a class discussion): It seems to me that we all need to learn more climate change.

Teacher: What do you mean by "learn more"? It's a big topic; what parts of it are you thinking about?

Still another strategy for helping students to articulate their ideas is to increase the *wait time* between when the teacher asks a question and when the teacher expects a student to answer. As we pointed out earlier, wait times that are longer than average—longer than one second, that is—give students more time to formulate ideas and therefore to express themselves more completely and precisely (Good & Brophy, 2002). In addition, longer wait times have the added advantage of indirection: instead of telling a student to say more, the teacher needs only to wait for the student to say more.

In general any communication strategy will help students become more articulate if it both allows and invites further comment and elaboration on their ideas. Taken together, the invitations closely resemble a description of class discussion, though they can actually be used singly at any time during teaching. Consider these possible conversational moves:

- The teacher asks the student to explain his initial idea more completely.

- The teacher rephrases a comment made by a student.

- The teacher compares the student's idea to another, related idea, and asks the student to comment.

- The teacher asks for evidence supporting the student's idea.

- The teacher asks the student how confident he is in his idea.

- The teacher asks another student to comment on the first student's idea.

Promoting academic risk-taking and problem-solving

In Chapter 8 we described major features of problem solving, as well as three techniques that assist in solving problems—problem analysis, working backwards from the beginning, and analogical thinking. While all of the techniques are helpful, they do not work if a student will not take the risk of attempting a solution to a problem in the first place. For various reasons students may sometimes avoid such risks, especially if he or she has sometimes failed at a task in the past, and is therefore concerned about negative evaluations again (Hope & Oliver, 2005).

What can a teacher say or do to counteract such hesitation? There are several strategies, all of which involve focusing attention on the process of doing an activity rather than on its outcome or evaluation.

- Where possible, *call attention to the intrinsic interest or satisfaction of an activity.* Consider, for example, an elementary-level activity of writing a Japanese *haiku*—a poem with exactly seventeen syllables. This activity can be satisfying in itself, regardless of how it is evaluated. Casually reminding individuals of this fact can contribute to students' sense of ease about writing the haiku and encourage them indirectly to do better work.

- *Minimize the importance of grades* where possible. This strategy supports the one above; by giving students less to worry about, they become freer to experience the intrinsic satisfactions of an activity. In writing that haiku mentioned above, for example, you can try saying something like: "Don't worry too much about your grade; just do the best you can and you will come out well enough in the end."

- *Make sure students know that they have ample time to complete an activity.* If students need to rush—or merely just thinks they do—then they are more likely to choose the safest, most familiar responses possible.

In writing an amusing story from their early childhood, for example, middle years students may need time to consider and choose among story possibilities. Then they may need additional time to experiment with ways of expressing the story in writing. In this case, to make sure students know that they have such time, try saying something like: "Writing a good story will take time, and you may have to return to it repeatedly. So we will start working on it today, but do not expect to finish today. We'll be coming back to it several times in the next couple of weeks."

- *Show that you value unusual ideas and elegant solutions to problems.* When a student does something out of the ordinary, show your enthusiasm for it. A visually appealing drawing, a well-crafted essay, a different solution to a math problem than the one you expected—all of these deserve an explicit compliment. Expressing your interest and respect does more than support the specific achievement. It also expresses a more general, underlying message that in your classroom, it is safe and rewarding to find and share the unusual and elegant.

Note that these communication strategies support problem-solving and the related skills of *creativity* that we discussed in Chapter 8. In describing creativity in that chapter, in particular, we called attention to the difference and importance of *divergent* (open-ended) thinking. As with problem-solving, though, divergent thinking may seem risky to some students unless they are encouraged to do so explicitly. The strategies for boosting academic risk-taking can help to communicate this encouragement—that process matters more than product, that there will be time enough to work, and that you, as teacher, indeed value their efforts.

Promoting a caring community

A **caring community** is one in which all members have a respected place, in which diversity among individuals is expected, and in which individuals assist each other with their work or activities wherever appropriate. Classrooms and even entire schools can be caring communities, though moving them in this direction takes work on the part of teachers and other school staff (Noddings, 1992, 2004). The key work in promoting a caring community involves arranging for students to work together on tasks, while at the same time communicating the teacher's commitment to mutual respect among students and between students and teachers. Many of the instructional strategies discussed earlier in this book, such as cooperative learning and inquiry learning (in Chapter 8), therefore contribute to community in the classroom.

More specifically, you can, as a teacher, encourage community by doing any or all of the following:

- Tell students that you value mutual respect, and describe some of the ways that students can show respect for each other and for school staff. Better yet, invite students themselves to describe how they might show respect.

- Look for ways to sustain relationships among students and teachers for extended times. These ways may be easier to find in elementary school, where a teacher and class normally remain together for an entire year, than in middle and secondary school, where students learn from many teachers and teachers teach many students. But still there are ways. Participating in extra-curricular activities (like sports teams or drama club), for example, can sometimes provide settings where relationships develop for relatively long periods of time—even more than a single school year.

- Ask for input from students about what they want to learn, how they want to learn it, and what kind of evaluation they consider fair. Although using their ideas may feel at first as if you are giving up your responsibility as the teacher, asking for students' input indicates respect for students. It is likely that many of their suggestions need clarification or revision to become workable, especially if the class must also cover a particular curriculum during a set time. But even just the asking for input shows respect, and can contribute to community in the classroom.

- If conflicts arise between students or between a student and teacher, encourage respectful communication as explicitly as you can. Some communication strategies about conflict resolution were described in Chapter 7 and are helpful in this regard: identifying true problem ownership, listening actively, assertive (not aggressive) I-messages, and negotiation.

- Find times and ways for the class to experience itself as a community. This suggestion may look a bit vague at first glance, but in practice it is actually quite concrete. Any action builds community if it is carried out by the group as a whole, especially if it is done regularly and repeatedly and if it truly includes every member of the class. Such actions become *rituals,* not in the negative sense of empty or mindless repetitions, but in the positive sense of confirmations by group members of their commitment to each other (Ehrenreich, 2007). In the elementary grades, an obvious example of a ritual is reciting the Pledge of Allegiance (or its equivalent in classrooms outside the United States). But there are many other examples of classroom routines that gradually acquire the (positive) qualities of ritual or community-affirmation, often without deliberate intention or effort. A daily, regular time to work through homework problems together in class, for example, may serve obvious academic purposes. But it may also gradually contribute to a classroom's identity as a class. With time and familiarity the group homework time may eventually come to represent "who we are" and of "what we do here" for that class.

The bottom line: messages sent, messages reconstructed

As we have explained in this chapter, teachers and students communicate in multiple, overlapping ways. Communications may often be expressed in words—but not necessarily and not completely. They may be organized into lectures, questions, discussions, or group projects. They tend to be expressed in particular language registers that we have called simply *teacher talk* and *student talk.* All things considered, communication obviously serves a wide range of teaching and learning tasks and activities, from stimulating students' thinking, to orchestrating classroom routines, to managing inappropriate behaviors. It is an intrinsic part of the parts of teaching that involve interaction among class members.

Note, though, that teaching consists of more than interaction among class members. There are times when teachers prepare lessons or activities, for example, without talking to students or anyone else. There are also times when they develop their own skills as teachers—for example, by reading and reflecting, or by attending professional development seminars or workshops—which may involve communication, but not in the sense discussed in this chapter. It is to these other parts of teaching that we turn in the next chapter.

Table 20: Year one: Kelvin's lecture notes

Nature and Purposes of Children's Play

1. Introduction to topic: What do we mean by play?

- excess energy

- seeking stimulation—relieve boredom

- escape from work

2. Six qualities defining play

- intrinsic motivation

- attention to the process, not the product

- non-literal behavior—make-believe

- no external rules

- self-governed

- active engagement

3. Implications for teaching

- devise activities with play-like qualities

- learn by watching children playing

Table 21: Year three: Kelvin's question-and-answer notes

Nature and Purposes of Children's Play

1. Introduction to topic: What do we mean by play? *[First ask 1-2 students for their own answers to question.]*

- excess energy *[Ask: What evidence is there for this?]*

- seeking stimulation—relieve boredom *[...or for this?]*

- escape from work

2. Six qualities of children's play *[Invite students' definitions, but keep them brief.]*

- intrinsic motivation

- attention to the process, not the product

- nonliteral behavior—make-believe

- no external rules

- self-governed

- active engagement

> [Can you think of examples and/or counterexamples of each quality?]
>
> 3. Implications for teaching
>
> - devise activities with playlike qualities *[What activities have you already seen as a student teacher?]*
>
> - learn by watching children playing *[How could you do this? Invite suggested strategies from students.]*

Table 22: Year eight: Kelvin's discussion notes

> **Nature and Purposes of Children's Play**
>
> - Discuss possible explanations for play—what do students think are its true purposes? (10 minutes?)
>
> - Can we define play? Brainstorm defining qualities, with examples. (30 minutes)
>
> - Important question for all defining qualities: Are there exceptions—examples of play that do not show certain defining qualities, but are still play? (15 minutes)
>
> - What is important about play for teaching? (10 minutes +)
>
> - ...for the welfare of children? (10 minutes +)
>
> - Etc. (anything else brought up by students)

Table 23: Year twenty: Kelvin's guidelines for group work

> **Nature and Purposes of Children's Play**
>
> - Make sure you listen to everyone, and not just to the people you agree with the most. Part of the challenge of this project is to include *all* team members.
>
> - You do not have to be best friends with someone in order to be partners. But you do have to get the work done.
>
> - Remember that it takes *many* skills and abilities to do this project well. Among other things, you need to:
>
>   1) find and understand research and other publications about children's play,
>
>   2) observe children skillfully when they are playing,
>
>   3) have confidence in describing what you learn to group mates,
>
>   4) write about what you learn, and 5) be tactful and respectful when listening and talking with partners.

Chapter summary

Because communication in classrooms is more complex and unpredictable than in many other situations, it is important for teachers to understand its unique features and functions. It is helpful to think of classroom communication as serving a mixture of three purposes at once: content talk, procedural talk, and behavior control talk. It is also helpful to recognize that classroom communication has elements that are not only verbal, but also nonverbal and unintended.

To be effective in using verbal communication, teachers need to use appropriate instructional strategies related to content, such as using advance organizers, relating new information to prior knowledge, and organizing new information on behalf of students. It includes strategies that assist students to communicate, such as inquiry learning and cooperative learning. To communicate well about procedures and about the behaviors expected of students, teachers need a variety of management techniques, such as those discussed in Chapter 7 and summarized again in Table 19. To be effective in using nonverbal communication, teachers need to use appropriate eye contact, allow ample wait time between speaking turns, and be aware of the effects of social distance on students.

Structures of participation influence communication by facilitating particular patterns of speaking and listening, while at the same time making other patterns less convenient or disapproved. Four common participation structures are lectures, questions-and-answers, classroom discussions, and group work.

Key terms

Caring community	Procedural talk
Class discussions	Questions-and-answer
Collaborative group work	Register
Communication	Social distance
Content talk	Student talk register
Control talk	Teacher talk register
Eye contact	Unintended communication
Lecture	Verbal communication
Nonverbal communication	Wait time
Participation structures	

On the Internet

<http://www.uu.edu/centers/faculty/resources/index.cfm?CatID=13> This URL offers tips for enhancing classroom communication. It is organized around ten basic topics (e.g. "Organizing Effective Discussions") and focuses primarily on verbal communication. It is part of the more general website for Union University of Jackson, Tennessee.

<http://www.idea.ksu.edu/index.html> This website contains over 40 short papers (1-4 pages each) on a variety of topics, including many related to enhancing communication, but also some related to classroom organization and management in general. Some of the papers refer to college or university teaching, but many are quite relevant to public school teaching.

<http://www.fhsu.edu/~zhrepic/Teaching/GenEducation/nonverbcom/nonverbcom.htm> This website contains a thorough discussion of nonverbal communication—more detailed than possible in this chapter, and with photos and drawings to illustrate key points.

<http://www.responsiveclassroom.org/index.html> This website contains many resources, among which are articles about classroom management and communication, including nonverbal communication. It is intended strictly for public school teachers. Once you get to the homepage, click on their "Newsletter" for the articles.

References

Benedict, M. & Hoag, J. (2004). Seating location in large lectures: Is location related to performance? *Journal of Economics Eduction, 35*(3), 215-231.

Black, L. (2004). Teacher-pupil talk in whole-class discussions and processes of social positioning in primary classrooms. *Language and Education, 18*(1), 347-360.

Bloome, D., Carter, S., Christian, B., Otto, S., & Shuart-Faris, N. (2005). *Discourse analysis and the study of classroom language.* Mahwah, NJ: Erlbaum.

Burns, C. & Myhill, D. (2004). Interactive or inactive? A consideration of the nature of interaction in whole-class instruction. *Cambridge Journal of Education, 34*(1), 35-49.

Cazden, C. (2001). *Classroom discourse: The language of teaching and learning, 2nd edition.* Westport, CT: Heinemann.

Chami-Sather, G. & Kretschmer, R. (2005). Lebanese/Arabic and American children's discourse in group-solving situations. *Language and Education, 19*(1), 10-22.

Christensen, N. (2006). The nuts and bolts of running a lecture course. In A. DeNeef & C. Goodwin (Eds.), *The academic's handbook, 3rd edition,* pp. 179-186. Durham, NC: Duke University Press.

Cohen, E., Brody, C., & Sapon-Shevin, M. (2004). *Teaching cooperative learning.* Albany, NY: State University of New York Press.

Collins, J. & Michaels, S. (2006). Speaking and writing: Discourse strategies and the acquisition of literacy. In J. Cook-Gumperz (Ed.), *The social construction of literacy, 2nd edition,*245-263. New York: Cambridge University Press.

Dallimore, E., Hertenstein, J., & Platt, M. (2006). Nonvoluntary class participation in graduate discussion courses: Effects of grading and cold calling. *Journal of Management Education, 30*(2), 354-377.

DePaulo, B., Lindsay, J., Malone, B., Muhlenbruck, L., Charlton, K., & Cooper, H. (2003). Cues to deception. *Psychological Bulletin, 129,* 74-118.

Ehrenreich, B. (2007). *Dancing in the streets.* New York: Henry Holt/Metropolitan Books.

Fujita, K., Henderson, M., Eng, J., Trope, Y., & Liberman, N. (2006). Spatial distance and mental construal of events. *Psychological Science, 17*(4), 278-282.

Global Deception Research Team. (2006). A world of lies. *Journal of Cross-cultural Psychology, 37*(6), 60-74.

Goldstein, L. (1999). The relational zone: The role of caring relationships in the co-construction of mind. *American Educational Research Journal, 36*(3), 647-673.

Good, T. & Brophy, J. (2002). *Looking in Classrooms, 9th edition.* Boston: Allyn & Bacon.

Guerrero, L. (2006). *Nonverbal communication in close relationships.* Mahwah, NJ: Erlbaum.

Hope, A. & Oliver, P. (2005). *Risk, education, and culture.* Burlington, VT: Ashgate Publishing Company.

Kleinke, C. (1986). Gaze and eye contact: A research review. *Psychological Bulletin, 100*(1), 78-100.

Lasswell, H. (1964). The structure and function of communication in society. In W. Schramm (Ed.), *Mass communications.* Urbana, IL: University of Illinois Press.

Lemke, J. (1990). *Talking science: Language, learning, and values.* Westport, CT: Greenwood Publishing Group.

Mason, M., Hood, B., & Macrae, C. (2004). Look into my eyes: Gaze direction and person memory. *Memory, 12*(5), 637-643.

McCarthy, A., Lee, K., Itakura, S., & Muir, D. (2006). Cultural display rules drive eye gaze during thinking. *Journal of Cross-cultural Psychology, 37*(6), 717-722.

McKeatchie, W. & Svinicki, M. (2005). *Teaching tips: Strategies, research, and theory for college teachers, 12th edition.* Boston: Houghton Mifflin.

Mehan, H. (1979). *Learning lessons: Social organization of the classroom.* Cambridge, MA: Harvard University Press.

Neill, S. (1991). *Classroom nonverbal communication.* New York: Routledge.

Noddings, N. (1992). *The challenge to care in schools: An alternative approach to education.* New York: Teachers College Press.

Noddings, N. (2004). *Happiness and education.* New York: Cambridge University Press.

Noller, P. (2006). Nonverbal communication in close relationships. In V. Mansunov & M. Patterson (Eds.), *Handbook of nonverbal communication,* pp. 403-420.

O'Connor, M. & Michael, S. (1996). Shifting participant frameworks: Orchestrating thinking practices in group discussion. In D. Hicks (Ed.), *Discourse, learning, and schooling* (pp. 63-103). New York: Cambridge University Press.

Razack, S. (1998). *Looking White people in the eye: Gender, race, and culture in courtrooms and classrooms.* Toronto, Ontario: University of Toronto Press.

Renshaw, P. (2004). Dialogic teaching, learning, and instruction: Theoretical roots and analytic perspectives. In J. van der Linden & P. Renshaw (Eds.), *Dialogic learning: Shifting perspectives to learning, instruction, and teaching.* Norwell, MA: Kluwer Academic.

Richards, K. (2006). 'Being the teacher': Identity and classroom discourse. *Applied Linguistics, 27*(1), 51-77.

Rosenfeld, P., Lambert, N., & Black, A. (1985). Desk arrangement effects on pupil classroom behavior. *Journal of Educational Psychology, 77* (1), 101-108.

Slavin, R. (1995). *Cooperative learning: Theory, research, and practice, 2nd edition.* Boston: Allyn & Bacon.

Tobin, K. (1987). The role of wait time in higher cognitive functions. *Review of Educational Research, 57*(1), 69-95.

8. The nature of classroom communication

Toth, P. (2004). When grammar instruction undermines cohesion in L2 Spanish classroom discourse. *The Modern Language Journal, 88*(1), 14-30.

Wells, G. (2006). The language experience of children at home and at school. In J. Cook-Gumperz (Ed.), *The social construction of literacy, 2ⁿᵈ edition*, 76-109. New York: Cambridge University Press.

9. Facilitating complex thinking

A few years ago one of us (Kelvin) had the privilege of co-teaching with an experienced first grade teacher, Carolyn Eaton. As part of a research project, Ms Eaton allowed some of her reading lessons to be observed. Here is what Kelvin saw when Ms Eaton was having a conference with Joey. They are reading a book "together", except that Ms Eaton wants Joey to do as much reading as possible himself. Joey's comments are capitalized, and Ms Eaton's are in lowercase.

JOEY: FIRST YOU READ—THEN ME. THIS IS WHAT YOU HAVE TO DO. I READ AFTER YOU, OK?

Ms Eaton: OK. [Ms Eaton begins.] "In the great green room there was a telephone, a red balloon, and a picture of..." Are you going to read, or what?

YES.

"In the great green room there was..." Are you ready yet? Ready to read?

OK. "IN THE GREAT GREEN ROOM..."

"...there was..."

"THERE WAS A..." [pauses, looking at Ms Eaton rather than at the words]

"...a telephone..."

YES, THAT'S IT, A TELEPHONE! "IN THE GREAT GREEN ROOM THERE WAS A TELEPHONE, A RED BALLOON..."

"and a picture of..."

"AND A PICTURE OF" [pauses, staring at the wall]...A COW JUMPING?"

"a cow jumping over the moon".

"OVER MOON" [smiles from both Joey and Ms Eaton].

Joey, what does this say? [She points to the word telephone.]

"THERE WAS A TELEPHONE".

How about here? [She points to next page, which reads "And there were three little bears, sitting on chairs".]

"THERE WERE BEARS, THREE BEARS, AND THEY SAT ON CHAIRS".

Can you read the whole book?

SURE!

OK, then you start this time.

[Joey looks at first page, alternately at the picture and at the words.]

"IN THE GREAT GREEN ROOM THERE WAS A TELEPHONE".

[Actual text: "In the great green room, there was a telephone",]

"AND THERE WAS A RED BALLOON",

[Actual text: "...and a red balloon",]

"AND A PICTURE OF THE COW JUMPING OVER THE MOON".

[Actual text: "...and a picture of the cow jumping over the moon".]

"AND THERE WERE..." THREE BEARS?... "LITTLE BEARS SITTING ON CHAIRS".

[Actual text: "And there were three little bears, sitting on chairs,..."]

Could you read this book with you eyes closed?

SURE; WANT TO SEE ME DO IT?!

Well, not right now; maybe another time. Could you read it without the pictures, just looking at the words? That's how I do best—when I see the words instead of the pictures.

[Joey pauses to consider this.] MAYBE, BUT NOT QUITE SO WELL.

Let's try it. [Ms Eaton proceeds to copy the words on a large sheet for Joey to "read" later.]

As Carolyn Eaton's behavior suggests, there are decisions to make "on the fly", even during the very act of teaching. Ms Eaton wonders when to challenge Joey, and when to support him. She also wonders when to pause and ask Joey to take stock of what he has read, and when to move him on ahead—when to consolidate a student's learning, and when to nudge the student forward. These are questions about instructional strategies which *facilitate complex learning*, either directly or indirectly. In this chapter we review as many strategies as space allows, in order to give a sense of the major instructional options and of their effects. We concentrate especially on two broad categories of instruction, which we call *direct instruction* and *student-centered instruction*. As we hope that you will see, each approach to teaching is useful for certain purposes. We begin, though, by looking at the ways students think, or at least how teachers would like students to think. What does it mean for students to think critically (astutely or logically)? Or to think creatively? Or to be skillful problem solvers? Forms of thinking lead to choices among instructional strategies.

Forms of thinking associated with classroom learning

Although instructional strategies differ in their details, they each encourage particular forms of learning and thinking. The forms have distinctive educational purposes, even though they sometimes overlap, in the sense that one form may contribute to success with another form. Consider three somewhat complex forms of thinking that are commonly pursued in classroom learning: (1) critical thinking, (2) creative thinking, and (3) problem-solving.

Critical thinking

Critical thinking requires skill at analyzing the reliability and validity of information, as well as the attitude or disposition to do so. The skill and attitude may be displayed with regard to a particular subject matter or topic, but in principle it can occur in any realm of knowledge (Halpern, 2003; Williams, Oliver, & Stockade, 2004). A critical thinker does not necessarily have a negative attitude in the everyday sense of constantly criticizing someone or something. Instead, he or she can be thought of as *astute*: the critical thinker asks key questions, evaluates the evidence for ideas, reasons for problems both logically and objectively, and expresses ideas and conclusions clearly and precisely. Last (but not least), the critical thinker can apply these habits of mind in more than one realm of life or knowledge.

With such a broad definition, it is not surprising that educators have suggested a variety of specific cognitive skills as contributing to critical thinking. In one study, for example, the researcher found how critical thinking can be reflected in regard to a published article was stimulated by **annotation**—writing questions and comments in the margins of the article (Liu, 2006). In this study, students were initially instructed in ways of annotating reading materials. Later, when the students completed additional readings for assignments, it was found that some students in fact used their annotation skills much more than others—some simply underlined passages, for example, with a highlighting pen. When essays written about the readings were later analyzed, the ones written by the annotators were found to be more well reasoned—more critically astute—than the essays written by the other students.

In another study, on the other hand, a researcher found that critical thinking can also involve oral discussion of personal issues or dilemmas (Hawkins, 2006). In this study, students were asked to verbally describe a recent, personal incident that disturbed them. Classmates then discussed the incident together in order to identify the precise reasons why the incident was disturbing, as well as the assumptions that the student made in describing the incident. The original student—the one who had first told the story—then used the results of the group discussion to frame a topic for a research essay. In one story of a troubling incident, a student told of a time when a store clerk has snubbed or rejected the student during a recent shopping errand. Through discussion, classmates decided that an assumption underlying the student's disturbance was her suspicion that she had been a victim of racial profiling based on her skin color. The student then used this idea as the basis for a research essay on the topic of "racial profiling in retail stores". The oral discussion thus stimulated critical thinking in the student and the classmates, but it also *relied* on their prior critical thinking skills at the same time.

Notice that in both of these research studies, as in others like them, what made the thinking "critical" was students' use of **metacognition**—strategies for thinking *about* thinking and for monitoring the success and quality of one's own thinking. This concept was discussed in Chapter 2 as a feature of constructivist views about learning. There we pointed out that when students acquire experience in building their own knowledge, they also become skilled both at knowing *how* they learn, and at knowing *whether* they have learned something well. These are two defining qualities of metacognition, but they are part of critical thinking as well. In fostering critical thinking, a teacher is really fostering a student's ability to construct or control his or her own thinking and to avoid being controlled by ideas unreflectively.

How best to teach critical thinking remains a matter of debate. One issue is whether to infuse critical skills into existing courses or to teach them through separate, free-standing units or courses. The first approach has the potential advantage of integrating critical thinking into students' entire educations. But it risks diluting students' understanding and use of critical thinking simply because critical thinking takes on a different form in each learning context. Its details and appearance vary among courses and teachers. The free-standing approach has the opposite qualities: it stands a better chance of being understood clearly and coherently, but at the cost of obscuring how it is related to other courses, tasks, and activities. This dilemma is the issue—again—of **transfer,** discussed in Chapter 2. Unfortunately, research to compare the different strategies for teaching critical thinking does not settle the matter. The research suggests simply that either infusion or free-standing approaches can work as long as it is implemented thoroughly and teachers are committed to the value of critical thinking (Halpern, 2003).

A related issue about teaching critical thinking is about deciding who needs to learn critical thinking skills the most. Should it be all students, or only some of them? Teaching all students seems the more democratic alternative and thus appropriate for educators. Surveys have found, however, that teachers sometimes favor teaching of critical thinking only to high-advantage students—the ones who already achieve well, who come from relatively high-income families, or (for high school students) who take courses intended for university entrance (Warburton & Torff, 2005). Presumably the rationale for this bias is that high-advantage students can benefit and/or understand and use critical thinking better than other students. Yet, there is little research evidence to support this idea, even if it were not ethically questionable. The study by Hawkins (2006) described above, for example, is that critical thinking was fostered even with students considered low-advantage.

Creative thinking

Creativity is the ability to make or do something new that is also useful or valued by others (Gardner, 1993). The "something" can be an object (like an essay or painting), a skill (like playing an instrument), or an action (like using a familiar tool in a new way). To be creative, the object, skill, or action cannot simply be bizarre or strange; it cannot be new without also being useful or valued, and not simply be the result of accident. If a person types letters at random that form a poem by chance, the result may be beautiful, but it would not be creative by the definition above. Viewed this way, creativity includes a wide range of human experience that many people, if not everyone, have had at some time or other (Kaufman & Baer, 2006). The experience is not restricted to a few geniuses, nor exclusive to specific fields or activities like art or the composing of music.

Especially important for teachers are two facts. The first is that an important form of creativity is **creative thinking,** the generation of ideas that are new as well as useful, productive, and appropriate. The second is that creative thinking can be stimulated by teachers' efforts. Teachers can, for example, encourage students' **divergent thinking**—ideas that are open-ended and that lead in many directions (Torrance, 1992; Kim, 2006). Divergent thinking is stimulated by open-ended questions—questions with many possible answers, such as the following:

- How many uses can you think of for a cup?

- Draw a picture that somehow incorporates all of these words: cat, fire engine, and banana.

- What is the most unusual use you can think of for a shoe?

Note that answering these questions creatively depends partly on having already acquired knowledge about the objects to which the questions refer. In this sense divergent thinking depends partly on its converse, **convergent thinking,** which is focused, logical reasoning about ideas and experiences that lead to specific answers. Up to a point, then, developing students' convergent thinking—as schoolwork often does by emphasizing mastery of content—facilitates students' divergent thinking indirectly, and hence also their creativity (Sternberg, 2003; Runco, 2004; Cropley, 2006). But carried to extremes, excessive emphasis on convergent thinking may discourage creativity.

Whether in school or out, creativity seems to flourish best when the creative activity is its own intrinsic reward, and a person is relatively unconcerned with what others think of the results. Whatever the activity—composing a song, writing an essay, organizing a party, or whatever—it is more likely to be creative if the creator focuses on and enjoys the activity in itself, and thinks relatively little about how others may evaluate the activity (Brophy, 2004). Unfortunately, encouraging students to ignore others' responses can sometimes pose a challenge for teachers. Not only is it the teachers' job to evaluate students' learning of particular ideas or skills, but also they have to do so within restricted time limits of a course or a school year. In spite of these constraints, though, creativity still can be encouraged in classrooms at least some of the time (Claxton, Edwards, & Scale-Constantinou, 2006). Suppose, for example, that students have to be assessed on their understanding and use of particular vocabulary. Testing their understanding may limit creative thinking; students will understandably focus their energies on learning "right" answers for the tests. But assessment does not have to happen constantly. There can also be times to encourage experimentation with vocabulary through writing poems, making word games, or in other thought-provoking ways. These activities are all potentially creative. To some extent, therefore, learning content and experimenting or playing with content can both find a place—in fact one of these activities can often support the other. We return to this point later in this chapter, when we discuss student-centered strategies of instruction, such as cooperative learning and play as a learning medium.

Problem-solving

Somewhat less open-ended than creative thinking is **problem solving,** the analysis and solution of tasks or situations that are complex or ambiguous and that pose difficulties or obstacles of some kind (Mayer & Wittrock, 2006). Problem solving is needed, for example, when a physician analyzes a chest X-ray: a photograph of the chest is far from clear and requires skill, experience, and resourcefulness to decide which foggy-looking blobs to ignore, and which to interpret as real physical structures (and therefore real medical concerns). Problem solving is also needed when a grocery store manager has to decide how to improve the sales of a product: should she put it on sale at a lower price, or increase publicity for it, or both? Will these actions actually increase sales enough to pay for their costs?

Problem solving in the classroom

Problem solving happens in classrooms when teachers present tasks or challenges that are deliberately complex and for which finding a solution is not straightforward or obvious. The responses of students to such problems, as well as the strategies for assisting them, show the key features of problem solving. Consider this example, and students' responses to it. We have numbered and named the paragraphs to make it easier to comment about them individually:

Scene #1: a problem to be solved

*A teacher gave these instructions: "Can you connect all of the dots below using only **four** straight lines?" She drew the following display on the chalkboard:*

● ● ●

● ● ●

● ● ●

Exhibit 10: The teacher gave these
instructions: "Can you connect these dots with
only four lines

The problem itself and the procedure for solving it seemed very clear: simply experiment with different arrangements of four lines. But two volunteers tried doing it at the board, but were unsuccessful. Several others worked at it at their seats, but also without success.

Scene #2: coaxing students to re-frame the problem

When no one seemed to be getting it, the teacher asked, "Think about how you've set up the problem in your mind—about what you believe the problem is about. For instance, have you made any assumptions about how long the lines ought to be? Don't stay stuck on one approach if it's not working!"

Scene #3: Alicia abandons a fixed response

After the teacher said this, Alicia indeed continued to think about how she saw the problem. "The lines need to be no longer than the distance across the square," she said to herself. So she tried several more solutions, but none of them worked either.

The teacher walked by Alicia's desk and saw what Alicia was doing. She repeated her earlier comment: "Have you assumed anything about how long the lines ought to be?"

*Alicia stared at the teacher blankly, but then smiled and said, "Hmm! You didn't actually **say** that the lines could be no longer than the matrix! Why not make them longer?" So she experimented again using oversized lines and soon discovered a solution:*

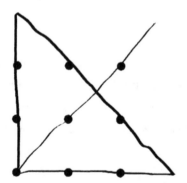

Exhibit 11: Alicia's solution

Scene #4: Willem's and Rachel's alternative strategies

*Meanwhile, Willem worked on the problem. As it happened, Willem loved puzzles of all kinds, and had ample experience with them. He had not, however, seen this particular problem. "It **must** be a trick," he said to himself, because he knew from experience that problems posed in this way often were not what they first appeared to be. He mused to himself: "Think outside the box, they always tell you..." And **that** was just the hint he needed: he drew lines outside the box by making them longer than the matrix and soon came up with this solution:*

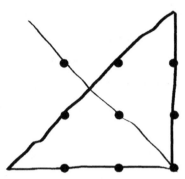

Exhibit 12: Willem's and
Rachel's solution

When Rachel went to work, she took one look at the problem and knew the answer immediately: she had seen this problem before, though she could not remember where. She had also seen other drawing-related puzzles, and knew that their solution always depended on making the lines longer, shorter, or differently angled than first expected. After staring at the dots briefly, she drew a solution faster than Alicia or even Willem. Her solution looked exactly like Willem's.

This story illustrates two common features of problem solving: the effect of degree of structure or constraint on problem solving, and the effect of mental obstacles to solving problems. The next sections discuss each of these features, and then looks at common techniques for solving problems.

The effect of constraints: well-structured versus ill-structured problems

Problems vary in how much information they provide for solving a problem, as well as in how many rules or procedures are needed for a solution. A **well-structured problem** provides much of the information needed and can in principle be solved using relatively few clearly understood rules. Classic examples are the word problems often taught in math lessons or classes: everything you need to know is contained within the stated problem and the solution procedures are relatively clear and precise. An **ill-structured problem** has the converse qualities: the information is *not* necessarily within the problem, solution procedures are potentially quite numerous, and a multiple solutions are likely (Voss, 2006). Extreme examples are problems like "How can the world achieve lasting peace?" or "How can teachers insure that students learn?"

By these definitions, the nine-dot problem is relatively well-structured—though not completely. Most of the information needed for a solution is provided in *Scene #1:* there are nine dots shown and instructions given to draw four lines. But not *all* necessary information was given: students needed to consider lines that were longer than implied in the original statement of the problem. Students had to "think outside the box", as Willem said—in this case, literally.

When a problem is well-structured, so are its solution procedures likely to be as well. A well-defined procedure for solving a particular kind of problem is often called an **algorithm;** examples are the procedures for multiplying or dividing two numbers or the instructions for using a computer (Leiserson, et al., 2001). Algorithms are only effective when a problem is very well-structured and there is no question about whether the algorithm is an appropriate choice for the problem. In that situation it pretty much guarantees a correct solution. They do not work well, however, with ill-structured problems, where they are ambiguities and questions about how to proceed or even about precisely *what* the problem is about. In those cases it is more effective to use **heuristics,** which are general strategies—"rules of thumb", so to speak—that do not always work, but often do, or that provide at least partial solutions. When beginning research for a term paper, for example, a useful heuristic is to scan the library catalogue for titles that look relevant. There is no guarantee that this strategy will yield the books most needed for the paper, but the strategy works enough of the time to make it worth trying.

In the nine-dot problem, most students began in Scene #1 with a simple algorithm that can be stated like this: "Draw one line, then draw another, and another, and another". Unfortunately this simple procedure did not produce a solution, so they had to find other strategies for a solution. Three alternatives are described in Scenes #3 (for Alicia) and 4 (for Willem and Rachel). Of these, Willem's response resembled a heuristic the most: he knew from experience that a good *general* strategy that *often* worked for such problems was to suspect a deception or trick in how the problem was originally stated. So he set out to question what the teacher had meant by the word *line,* and came up with an acceptable solution as a result.

Common obstacles to solving problems

The example also illustrates two common problems that sometimes happen during problem solving. One of these is **functional fixedness:** a tendency to regard the *functions* of objects and ideas as *fixed* (German & Barrett, 2005). Over time, we get so used to one particular purpose for an object that we overlook other uses. We may think of a dictionary, for example, as necessarily something to verify spellings and definitions, but it also can function as a gift, a doorstop, or a footstool. For students working on the nine-dot matrix described in the last section, the notion of "drawing" a line was also initially fixed; they assumed it to be connecting dots but not extending lines beyond the dots. Functional fixedness sometimes is also called **response set,** the tendency for a person to frame or think about each problem in a series in the same way as the previous problem, even when doing so is not appropriate to later problems. In the example of the nine-dot matrix described above, students often tried one solution after another, but each solution was constrained by a set response *not* to extend any line beyond the matrix.

Functional fixedness and the response set are obstacles in **problem representation,** the way that a person understands and organizes information provided in a problem. If information is misunderstood or used inappropriately, then mistakes are likely—if indeed the problem can be solved at all. With the nine-dot matrix problem, for example, construing the instruction to draw four lines as meaning "draw four lines entirely within the matrix" means that the problem simply could not be solved. For another, consider this problem: "The number of water lilies on a lake doubles each day. Each water lily covers exactly one square foot. If it takes 100 days for the lilies to cover the lake exactly, how many days does it take for the lilies to cover exactly *half* of the lake?" If you think that the size of the lilies affects the solution to this problem, you have not represented the problem correctly. Information about lily size is *not* relevant to the solution, and only serves to distract from the truly crucial information, the fact that the lilies *double* their coverage each day. (The answer, incidentally, is that the lake is half covered in 99 days; can you think why?)

Strategies to assist problem solving

Just as there are cognitive obstacles to problem solving, there are also general strategies that help the process be successful, regardless of the specific content of a problem (Thagard, 2005). One helpful strategy is **problem analysis**—identifying the parts of the problem and working on each part separately. Analysis is especially useful when a problem is ill-structured. Consider this problem, for example: "Devise a plan to improve bicycle transportation in the city." Solving this problem is easier if you identify its parts or component subproblems, such as (1) installing bicycle lanes on busy streets, (2) educating cyclists and motorists to ride safely, (3) fixing potholes on streets used by cyclists, and (4) revising traffic laws that interfere with cycling. Each separate subproblem is more manageable than the original, general problem. The solution of each subproblem contributes the solution of the whole, though of course is not equivalent to a whole solution.

Another helpful strategy is **working backward** *from* a final solution *to* the originally stated problem. This approach is especially helpful when a problem is well-structured but also has elements that are distracting or misleading when approached in a forward, normal direction. The water lily problem described above is a good example: starting with the day when *all* the lake is covered (Day 100), ask what day would it therefore be *half* covered (by the terms of the problem, it would have to be the day before, or Day 99). Working backward in this case encourages reframing the extra information in the problem (i. e. the size of each water lily) as merely distracting, not as crucial to a solution.

A third helpful strategy is **analogical thinking**—using knowledge or experiences with similar features or structures to help solve the problem at hand (Bassok, 2003). In devising a plan to improve bicycling in the city, for example, an analogy of cars with bicycles is helpful in thinking of solutions: improving conditions for both vehicles requires many of the same measures (improving the roadways, educating drivers). Even solving simpler, more basic problems is helped by considering analogies. A first grade student can partially decode unfamiliar printed words by analogy to words he or she has learned already. If the child cannot yet read the word *screen,* for example, he can note that part of this word looks similar to words he may already know, such as *seen* or *green,* and from this observation derive a clue about how to read the word *screen.* Teachers can assist this process, as you might expect, by suggesting reasonable, helpful analogies for students to consider.

Broad instructional strategies that stimulate complex thinking

Because the forms of thinking just described—critical thinking, creativity and problem solving—are broad and important educationally, it is not surprising that educators have identified strategies to encourage their development. Some of the possibilities are shown in Table 24 and group several instructional strategies along two dimensions: how much the strategy is student-centered and how much a strategy depends on group interaction. It should be emphasized that the two-way classification in Table 24 is not very precise, but it gives a useful framework for understanding the options available for planning and implementing instruction. The more important of the two dimensions in the table is the first one—the extent to which an instructional strategy is either directed by the teacher or initiated by students. We take a closer look at this dimension in the next part of this chapter, followed by discussion of group-oriented teaching strategies.

Table 24: Major instructional strategies grouped by level of teacher direction and student focus

Directed by student(s) more

	Cooperative learning	Self-reflection	
	Inquiry	Independent study	
	Discovery learning	Concept maps	
Emphasizes groups somewhat more	Lectures	Mastery learning	**Emphasizes individuals somewhat more**
	Direct instruction	Textbook readings	
	Madeline Hunter's "Effective Teaching"	Advance organizers	
		Outlining	
		Recalling, relating, and elaborating	

Directed by teacher more

Definitions of Terms in Table 8.1

Lecture	Telling or explaining previously organized information—usually to a group
Assigned reading	Reading, usually individually, of previously organized information
Advance organizers	Brief overview, either verbally or graphically, of material about to be covered in a lecture or text
Outlining	Writing important points of a lecture or reading, usually in a hierarchical format
Taking notes	Writing important points of a lecture or reading, often organized according to the learning needs of an individual student
Concept maps	Graphic depiction of relationships among a set of concepts, terms, or ideas; usually organized by the student, but not always
Madeline Hunter's "Effective Teaching"	A set of strategies that emphasizes clear presentation of goals, the explanation and modeling of tasks to students and careful monitoring of students' progress toward the goals

Teacher-directed instruction

As the name implies, teacher-directed instruction includes any strategies initiated and guided primarily by the teacher. A classic example is exposition or lecturing (simply telling or explaining important information to students) combined with assigning reading from texts. But teacher-directed instruction also includes strategies that involve more active response from students, such as encouraging students to elaborate on new knowledge or to explain how new information relates to prior knowledge. Whatever their form, teacher-directed instructional methods normally include the organizing of information on behalf of students, even if teachers also expect students to organize it further on their own. Sometimes, therefore, teacher-directed methods are thought of as transmitting knowledge from teacher to student as clearly and efficiently as possible, even if they also require mental work on the part of the student.

Lectures and readings

Lectures and readings are traditional staples of educators, particularly with older students (including university students). At their best, they pre-organize information so that (at least in theory) the student only has to remember what was said in the lecture or written in the text in order to begin understanding it (Exley & Dennick, 2004). Their limitation is the ambiguity of the responses they require: listening and reading are by nature quiet and stationary, and do not in themselves indicate whether a student is comprehending or even attending to the material. Educators sometimes complain that "students are too passive" during lectures or when reading. But physical quietness is intrinsic to these activities, not to the students who do them. A book just sits still, after all, unless a student makes an effort to read it, and a lecture may not be heard unless a student makes the effort to listen to it.

Advance organizers

In spite of these problems, there are strategies for making lectures and readings effective. A teacher can be especially careful about organizing information *for* students, and she can turn part of the mental work over to students themselves. An example of the first approach is the use of **advance organizers**—brief overviews or introductions to new material before the material itself is presented (Ausubel, 1978). Textbook authors (including ourselves) often try deliberately to insert periodic advance organizers to introduce new sections or chapters in the text. When used in a lecture, advance organizers are usually statements in the form of brief introductory remarks, though sometimes diagrams showing relationships among key ideas can also serve the same purpose (Robinson, et al., 2003). Whatever their form, advance organizers partially organize the material on behalf of the students, so that they know where to put it all, so to speak, as they learn them in more detail.

Recalling and relating prior knowledge

Another strategy for improving teacher-directed instruction is to encourage students to relate the new material to prior familiar knowledge. When one of us (Kelvin) first learned a foreign language (in his case French), for example, he often noticed similarities between French and English vocabulary. A French word for picture, for example, was *image,* spelled exactly as it is in English. The French word for *splendid* was *splendide,* spelled almost the same as in English, though not quite. Relating the French vocabulary to English vocabulary helped in learning and remembering the French.

As children and youth become more experienced in their academics, they tend to relate new information to previously learned information more frequently and automatically (Goodwin, 1999; Oakhill, Hartt, & Samols,

2005). But teachers can also facilitate students' use of this strategy. When presenting new concepts or ideas, the teacher can relate them to previously learned ideas deliberately—essentially modeling a memory strategy that students learn to use for themselves. In a science class, for example, she can say, "This is another example of…, which we studied before"; in social studies she can say, "Remember what we found out last time about the growth of the railroads? We saw that…"

If students are relatively young or are struggling academically, it is especially important to remind them of their prior knowledge. Teachers can periodically ask questions like "What do you already know about this topic?" or "How will your new knowledge about this topic change what you know already?" Whatever the age of students, connecting new with prior knowledge is easier with help from someone more knowledgeable, such as the teacher. When learning algorithms for multiplication, for example, students may not at first see how multiplication is related to addition processes which they probably learned previously (Burns, 2001). But if a teacher takes time to explain the relationship and to give students time to explore it, then the new skill of multiplication may be learned more easily.

Elaborating information

Elaborating new information means asking questions about the new material, inferring ideas and relationships among the new concepts. Such strategies are closely related to the strategy of recalling prior knowledge as discussed above: elaboration enriches the new information and connects it to other knowledge. In this sense elaboration makes the new learning more meaningful and less arbitrary.

A teacher can help students use elaboration by modeling this behavior. The teacher can interrupt his or her explanation of an idea, for example, by asking how it relates to other ideas, or by speculating about where the new concept or idea may lead. He or she can also encourage students to do the same, and even give students questions to guide their thinking. When giving examples of a concept, for example, a teacher can hold back from offering all of the examples, and instead ask students to think of additional examples themselves. The same tactic can work with assigned readings; if the reading includes examples, the teacher can instruct students to find or make up additional examples of their own.

Organizing new information

There are many ways to organize new information that are especially well-suited to teacher-directed instruction. A common way is simply to ask students to **outline information** read in a text or heard in a lecture. Outlining works especially well when the information is already organized somewhat hierarchically into a series of main topics, each with supporting subtopics or subpoints. Outlining is basically a form of the more general strategy of **taking notes**, or writing down key ideas and terms from a reading or lecture. Research studies find that that the precise style or content of notes is less important that the quantity of notes taken: more detail is usually better than less (Ward & Tatsukawa, 2003). Written notes insure that a student thinks about the material not only while writing it down, but also when reading the notes later. These benefits are especially helpful when students are relatively inexperienced at school learning in general (as in the earlier grade levels), or relatively inexperienced about a specific topic or content in particular. Not surprisingly, such students may also need more guidance than usual about *what* and *how* to write notes. It can be helpful for the teacher to provide a note-taking guide, like the ones shown in Exhibit 11.

Notes on Science Experiment	Guide to Notes About *Tale of Two Cities:*
1. Purpose of the experiment (in one sentence):	1. Main characters (list and describe in just a few words):
	a)
	b)
2. Equipment needed (list each item and define any special terms):	c)
	d)
1)	2. Setting of the story (time and place):
2)	
3)	3. Unfamiliar vocabulary in the story (list and define):
4)	a)
3. Procedure used (be specific!):	b)
4.	c)
4. Results (include each measurement, rounded to the nearest integer):	d)
	4. Plot (write down only the main events):
	a)
	b)
	c)
	d)
	5. Theme (or underlying "message") of the story:

Observation #1	
Observation #2	
Observation #3	
Observation #4	
Average measurement, #1-4:	

Exhibit 13: Two note taking guides

In learning expository material, another helpful strategy—one that is more visually oriented—is to make **concept maps**, or diagrams of the connections among concepts or ideas. Exhibit 10 shows concept maps made by two individuals that graphically depict how a key idea, *child development,* relates to learning and education. One of the maps was drawn by a classroom teacher and the other by a university professor of psychology (Seifert, 1991). They suggest possible differences in how the two individuals think about children and their development. Not surprisingly, the teacher gave more prominence to practical concerns (for example, classroom learning and child abuse), and the professor gave more prominence to theoretical ones (for example, Erik Erikson and Piaget). The differences suggest that these two people may have something different in mind when they use the same term, *child development*. The differences have the potential to create misunderstandings between them (Seifert, 1999; Super & Harkness, 2003). By the same token, the two maps also suggest what each person might need to learn in order to achieve better understanding of the other person's thinking and ideas.

Concept Map by a Teacher

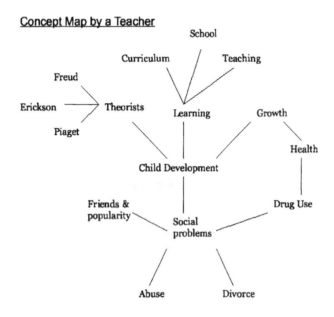

Concept Map by a University Professor

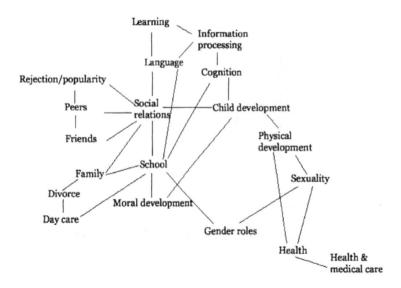

Exhibit 14: Maps of personal definitions of "child development"

Mastery learning

This term refers to an instructional approach in which all students learn material to an identically high level, even if some students require more time than others to do so (Gentile, 2004). In mastery learning, the teacher directs learning, though sometimes only in the sense of finding, writing, and orchestrating specific modules or units for students to learn. In one typical mastery learning program, the teacher introduces a few new concepts or topics through a brief lecture or teacher-led demonstration. Then she gives an ungraded assignment or test immediately in order to assess how well students have learned the material, and which ones still need help. The students who have already learned the unit are given enrichment activities. Those needing more help are provided individual tutoring or additional self-guiding materials that clarify the initial content; they work until they have in fact mastered the content (hence the name *mastery learning*). At that point students take another test or do another assignment to show that they have in fact learned the material to the expected high standard. When the system is working well, all students end up with high scores or grades, although usually some take longer to do so than others.

As you might suspect, mastery learning poses two challenges. The first is ethical: is it really fair to give enrichment only to faster students and remediation only to slower students? This practice could deteriorate into continually providing the fast with an interesting education, while continually providing the slow only with boring, repetitious material. In using the approach, therefore, it is important to make all materials interesting, whether enrichment or remedial. It is also important to make sure that the basic learning goals of each unit are truly important—even crucial—for everyone to learn, so that even slower individuals spend their time well.

The other challenge of mastery learning is more practical: the approach makes strong demands for detailed, highly organized curriculum. If the approach is to work, the teacher must either locate such a curriculum, write one herself, or assemble a suitable mixture of published and self-authored materials. However the curriculum is created, the end result has to be a program filled with small units of study as well as ample enrichment and remedial materials. Sometimes providing these practical requirements can be challenging. But not always: some subjects (like mathematics) lend themselves to detailed, sequential organization especially well. In many cases, too, commercial publishers have produced curricula already organized for use in mastery learning programs (Fox, 2004).

Direct instruction

Although the term *direct instruction* is sometimes a synonym for *teacher-directed instruction*, more often it refers to a version of mastery learning that is highly scripted, meaning that it not only organizes the curriculum into small modules or units as described above, but also dictates *how* teachers should teach and sometimes even the words they should speak (Adams & Engelmann, 1996; Magliaro, Lockee, & Burton, 2005). Direct instruction programs are usually based on a mix of ideas from behaviorism and cognitive theories of learning. In keeping with behaviorism, the teacher is supposed to praise students immediately and explicitly when they give a correct answer. In keeping with cognitive theory, she is supposed to state learning objectives in advance of teaching them (providing a sort of mini-advance organizer), provide frequent reviews of materials, and check deliberately on how well students are learning. Direct instruction usually also introduces material in small, logical steps, and calls for plenty of time for students to practice.

Direct instruction programs share one of the challenges of other mastery learning approaches: because they hold all students to the same high standard of achievement, they must deal with differences in how long students require to reach the standard. But direct instruction has an additional challenge, in that they often rely on small-group interaction more heavily than other mastery learning programs, and use self-guiding materials less. This difference has the benefit that direct instruction works especially well with younger students (especially kindergarten through third grade), who may have limited skills at working alone for extended periods. The challenge is that reliance on small-group interaction can make it impractical to use direct instruction with an entire class or for an entire school day. In spite of these limits, however, research has found direct instruction to be very effective in teaching basic skills such as early reading and arithmetic (Adams & Engelmann, 1996).

Madeline Hunter's effective teaching model

A number of direct instruction strategies have been combined by Madeline Hunter into a single, relatively comprehensive approach that she calls **mastery teaching** (not to be confused with the related term *mastery learning)* or the **effective teaching model** (M. Hunter, 1982; R. Hunter, 2004). Important features of the model are summarized in Table 25. As you can see, the features span all phases of contact with students—before, during, and after lessons.

Table 25: Madeline Hunter's "Effective Teaching Model"

Prepare students to learn.   • Make good use of time at the beginning of a lesson or activity, when attention is best   • Direct students' attention to what lies ahead in a lesson—for example, by offering "advance organizers"   • Explain lesson objectives explicitly
Present information clearly and explicitly.   • Set a basic structure to the lesson and stay with it throughout   • Use familiar terms and examples   • Be concise
Check for understanding and give guided practice.   • Ask questions that everyone responds to—for example, "Raise your hand if you think the answer is X"   • Invite choral responses—for example, "Is this a correct answer or not?"   • Sample individuals' understanding—for example, "Barry, what's your example of X?"
Provide for independent practice.   • Work through the first few exercises or problems together   • Keep independent practice periods brief and intersperse with discussions that offer feedback
Source: R. Hunter, 2004

What happens even before a lesson begins? Like many forms of teacher-directed instruction, the effective teaching model requires curricula and learning goals that are tightly organized and divisible into small parts, ideas, or skills. In teaching about photosynthesis, for example, the teacher (or at least her curriculum) needs to identify the basic elements that contribute to this process, and how they relate to each other. With photosynthesis, the elements include the sun, plants, animals, chlorophyll, oxygen produced by plants and consumed by animals, and carbon dioxide that produced by animals and consumed by plants. The roles of these elements need to be identified and expressed at a level appropriate for the students. With advanced science students, oxygen, chlorophyll, and carbon dioxide may be expressed as part of complex chemical reactions; with first-grade students, though, they may be expressed simply as parts of a process akin to breathing or respiration.

Once this analysis of the curriculum has been done, the Hunter's effective teaching model requires making the most of the lesson time by creating an **anticipatory set,** which is an activity that focuses or orients the attention of students to the upcoming content. Creating an anticipatory set may consist, for example, of posing one or more questions about students' everyday knowledge or knowledge of prior lessons. In teaching about differences between fruits and vegetables, the teacher could start by asking: "If you are making a salad strictly of fruit, which of these would be OK to use: apple, tomato, cucumber, or orange?" As the lesson proceeds, information needs to be offered in short, logical pieces, using language as familiar as possible to the students. Examples should be plentiful and varied: if the purpose is to define and distinguish fruits and vegetables, for example, then features defining each group should be presented singularly or at most just a few at a time, with clear-cut examples presented of each feature. Sometimes models or analogies also help to explain examples. A teacher can say: "Think of a fruit as a sort of 'decoration' on the plant, because if you pick it, the plant will go on living." But models can also mislead students if they are not used thoughtfully, since they may contain features that differ from the original concepts. In likening a fruit to a decoration, for example, students may overlook the essential role of fruit in plant reproduction, or think that lettuce qualifies as a fruit, since picking a few lettuce leaves does not usually kill a lettuce plant.

Throughout a lesson, the teacher repeatedly **checks for understanding** by asking questions that call for active thinking on the part of students. One way is to require all students to respond somehow, either with an actual choral response (speaking in unison together), another way with a non-verbal signal like raising hands to indicate answers to questions. In teaching about fruits and vegetables, for example, a teacher can ask, "Here's a list of fruits and vegetables. As I point to each one, raise your hand if it's a fruit, but not if it's a vegetable." Or she can ask: "Here's a list of fruits and vegetables. Say together what each on is as I point to it; you say 'fruit' or 'vegetable', whichever applies." Even though some students may hide their ignorance by letting more knowledgeable classmates do the responding, the general level or quality of response can still give a rough idea of how well students are understanding. These checks can be supplemented, of course, with questions addressed to individuals, or with questions to which individuals must respond briefly in writing. A teacher can ask everyone, "Give me an example of one fruit and one vegetable", and then call on individuals to answer. She can also say: "I want everyone to make a list with two columns, one listing all the fruits you can think of and the other listing all the vegetables you can think of."

As a lesson draws to a close, the teacher arranges for students to have further **independent practice**. The point of the practice is not to explore new material or ideas, but to consolidate or strengthen the recent learning. At the end of a lesson about long division, for example, the teacher can make a transition to independent practice by providing a set of additional problems similar to the ones she explained during the lesson. After working one or two with students, she can turn the rest of the task over to the students to practice on their own. But note that even though the practice is supposedly "independent", students' understanding still has be checked frequently. A long set of practice problems therefore needs to be broken up into small subsets of problems, and written or oral feedback offered periodically.

What are the limits of teacher-directed instruction?

Whatever the grade level, most subjects taught in schools have at least some features, skills, or topics that benefit from direct instruction. Even subjects usually considered "creative" can benefit from a direct approach at times: to draw, sing, or write a poem, for example, requires skills that may be easier to learn if presented sequentially in small units with frequent feedback from a teacher. Research supports the usefulness of teacher-directed instruction for a variety of educational contexts when it is designed well and implemented as intended (Rosenshine & Mesister,1995; Good & Brophy, 2004). Teachers themselves also tend to support the approach in principle (Demant & Yates, 2003).

But there are limits to its usefulness. Some are the practical ones are pointed out above. Teacher-directed instruction, whatever the form, requires well-organized units of instruction in advance of when students are to learn. Such units may not always be available, and it may not be realistic to expect busy teachers to devise their own. Other limits of direct instruction have more to do with the very nature of learning. Some critics argue that organizing material on behalf of the students encourages students to be passive—an ironic and undesirable result if true (Kohn, 2000, 2006). According to this criticism, the mere fact that a curriculum or unit of study is constructed by a teacher (or other authority) makes some students think that they should not bother seeking information actively on their own, but wait for it to arrive of its own accord. In support of this argument, critics point to the fact that direct instruction approaches sometimes contradict their own premises by requiring students to do a bit of cognitive organizational work of their own. This happens, for example, when a mastery learning program provides enrichment material to faster students to work on independently; in that case the teacher may be involved in the enrichment activities only minimally.

Criticisms like these have led to additional instructional approaches that rely more fully on students to seek and organize their own learning. In the next section we discuss some of these options. As you will see, student-centered models of learning do solve certain problems of teacher-directed instruction, but they also have problems of their own.

Student-centered models of learning

Student-centered models of learning shift some of the responsibility for directing and organizing learning from the teacher to the student. Being student-centered does not mean, however, that a teacher gives up organizational and leadership responsibilities completely. It only means a relative shift in the teacher's role, toward one with more emphasis on guiding students' self-chosen directions. As we explained earlier in this chapter, teacher-directed strategies do not take over responsibility for students' learning completely; no matter how much a teacher structures or directs learning, the students still have responsibility for working and expending effort to comprehend new material. By the same token, student-centered models of learning do not mean handing over all organizational work of instruction to students. The teacher is still the most knowledgeable member of the class, and still has both the opportunity and the responsibility to guide learning in directions that are productive.

As you might suspect, therefore, teacher-directed and student-centered approaches to instruction may overlap in practice. You can see the overlap clearly, for example, in two instructional strategies commonly thought of as student-centered, *independent study* and *self-reflection*. In **independent study,** as the name implies, a student works alone a good deal of the time, consulting with a teacher only occasionally. Independent study may be student-centered in the sense that the student may be learning a topic or skill—an exotic foreign language, for example—that is personally interesting. But the opposite may also be true: the student may be learning a topic or skill that a teacher or an official school curriculum has directed the student to learn—a basic subject for which the student is missing a credit, for example. Either way, though, the student will probably need guidance, support, and help from a teacher. In this sense even independent study always contain elements of teacher-direction.

Similarly, **self-reflection** refers to thinking about beliefs and experiences in order to clarify their personal meaning and importance. In school it can be practiced in a number of ways: for example by keeping diaries or logs of learning or reading, or by retelling stories of important experiences or incidents in a student's life, or by creating concept maps like the ones described earlier in this chapter. Whatever form it takes, self-reflection by definition happens inside a single student's mind, and in this sense is always directed by the student. Yet most research on self-reflection finds that self-reflection only works well when it involves and generates responses and interaction with other students or with a teacher (Seifert, 1999; Kuit, Reay, & Freeman, 2001). To be fully self-reflective, students need to have access to more than their existing base of knowledge and ideas—more than what they know already. In one study about students' self-reflections of cultural and racial prejudices (Gay & Kirkland, 2003), for example, the researchers found that students tended to reflect on these problems in relatively shallow ways if they worked on their own. It was not particularly effective to write about prejudice in a journal that no one read except themselves, or to describe beliefs in a class discussion in which neither the teacher nor classmates commented or challenged the beliefs. Much more effective in both cases was for the teacher to respond thoughtfully to students' reflective comments. In this sense the use of self-reflection, like independent study, required elements of teacher-direction to be successful.

How might a teacher emphasize students' responsibility for directing and organizing their own learning? The alternatives are numerous, as they are for teacher-directed strategies, so we can only sample some of them here. We concentrate on ones that are relatively well known and used most widely, and especially on two: inquiry learning and cooperative learning.

Inquiry learning

Inquiry learning stands the usual advice about expository (lecture-style) teaching on its head: instead of presenting well-organized knowledge to students, the teacher (or sometimes fellow students) pose thoughtful questions intended to stimulate discussion and investigation by students. The approach has been described, used, and discussed by educators literally for decades, though sometimes under other names, including *inquiry method* (Postman & Weingartner, 1969), *discovery learning* (Bruner, 1960/2006), or *progressive education* (Dewey, 1933; Martin, 2003). For convenience, we will stay with the term *inquiry learning*.

The questions that begin a cycle of inquiry learning may be posed either by the teacher or by students themselves. Their content depends not only on the general subject area being studied, but also on the interests which students themselves have expressed. In elementary-level science, for example, a question might be "Why do leaves fall off trees when winter comes?" In high school social studies classes, it might be "Why do nations get into conflict?" The teacher avoids answering such questions directly, even if asked to do so. Instead she encourages students to investigate the questions themselves, for example by elaborating on students' ideas and by asking further questions based on students' initial comments. Since students' comments can not be predicted precisely, the approach is by nature flexible. The initial questioning helps students to create and clarify questions which they consider worthy of further investigation. Discussing questions about leaves falling off trees, for example, can prompt students to observe trees in the autumn or to locate books and references that discuss or explain the biology of tress and leaves.

But inquiry is not limited to particular grade levels or topics. If initial questions in a high school social studies class have been about why nations get into conflict, for example, the resulting discussions can lead to investigating the history of past wars and the history of peace-keeping efforts around the world. Whether the topic is high school social studies or elementary school biology, the specific direction of investigations is influenced heavily by students, but with assistance from the teacher to insure that the students' initiatives are productive. When all goes well, the inquiry and resulting investigations benefit students in two ways. The first is that students (perhaps obviously) learn new knowledge from their investigations. The second is that students practice a constructive, motivating way of learning, one applicable to a variety of problems and tasks, both in school and out.

Cooperative learning

Even though inquiry-oriented discussion and investigation benefits when it involves the teacher, it can also be useful for students to work together somewhat independently, relying on a teacher's guidance only indirectly. Working with peers is a major feature of **cooperative learning** (sometimes also called *collaborative learning)*. In this approach, students work on a task in groups and often are rewarded either partially or completely for the success of the group as a whole. Aspects of cooperative learning have been part of education for a long time; some form of cooperation has always been necessary to participate on school sports teams, for example, or to produce a student-run school newspaper. What is a bit newer is using cooperative or collaborative activities systematically to facilitate the learning of a range of educational goals central to the academic curriculum (Prince, 2004).

Even though teachers usually value cooperation in students, circumstances at school can sometimes reduce students' incentives to show it. The traditional practice of assessing students individually, for example, can set the stage for competition over grades, and cultural and other forms of diversity can sometimes inhibit individuals from helping each other spontaneously. Strategies exist, however, for reducing such barriers so that students truly benefit from each other's presence, and are more likely to feel like sharing their skills and knowledge. Here, for example, are several key features that make cooperative learning work well (Johnson & Johnson, 1998; Smith, et al., 2005):

- *Students need time and a place to talk and work together.* This may sound obvious, but it can be overlooked if time in class becomes crowded with other tasks and activities, or with interruptions related to school (like assemblies) but not to the classroom. It is never enough simply to tell students to work together, only to leave them wondering how or when they are to do so.

- *Students need skills at working together.* As an adult, you may feel relatively able to work with a variety of partners on a group task. The same assumption cannot be made, however, about younger individuals, whether teenagers or children. Some students may get along with a variety of partners, but others may not. Many will benefit from advice and coaching about how to focus on the tasks at hand, rather than on the personalities of their partners.

- *Assessment of activities should hold both the group and the individuals accountable for success.* If a final mark for a project goes only to the group as a whole, then **freeloading** is possible: some members may not do their share of the work and may be rewarded more than they deserve. Others may be rewarded less than they deserve. If, on the other hand, a final grade for a group project goes only to each member's individual contribution to a group project, then **overspecialization** can occur: individuals have no real incentive to work together, and cooperative may deteriorate into a set of smaller individual projects (Slavin, 1994).

- *Students need to believe in the value and necessity of cooperation.* Collaboration will not occur if students privately assume that their partners have little to contribute to their personal success. Social prejudices from the wider society—like racial bias or gender sexism, for example—can creep into the operations of cooperative groups, causing some members to be ignored unfairly while others are overvalued. Teachers can help reduce these problems in two ways: first by pointing out and explaining that a diversity of talents is necessary for success on a group project, and second by pointing out to the group how undervalued individuals are contributing to the overall project (Cohen, Brody, & Sapon-Shevin, 2004).

As these comments imply, cooperative learning does not happen automatically, and requires monitoring and support by the teacher. Some activities may not lend themselves to cooperative work, particularly if every member of the group is doing essentially the same task. Giving everyone in a group the same set of arithmetic problems to work on collaboratively, for example, is a formula for cooperative failure: either the most skilled students do the work for others (freeloading) or else members simply divide up the problems among themselves in order to reduce their overall work (overspecialization). A better choice for a cooperative task is one that clearly requires a diversity of skills, what some educators call a *rich group work task* (Cohen, Brody, & Sapon-Shevin, 2004). Preparing a presentation about medieval castles, for example, might require (a) writing skill to create a report, (b) dramatic skill to put on a skit and (c) artistic talent to create a poster. Although a few students may have all of these skills, more are likely to have only one, and they are therefore likely to need and want their fellow group members' participation.

Examples of cooperative and collaborative learning

Although this description may make the requirements for cooperative learning sound somewhat precise, there are actually a variety of ways to implement it in practice. Error: Reference source not found summarizes several of them. As you can see, the strategies vary in the number of how many students they involve, the prior organization or planning provided by the teacher, and the amount of class time they normally require.

Table 26: Strategies for encouraging cooperative learning

9. Facilitating complex thinking

Strategy	Type of groups involved:	What the teacher does:	What the students do:
Think-pair-share (Lyman, 1981)	Pairs of students, sometimes linked to one other pair	Teacher poses initial problem or question.	First, students think individually of the answer; second, they share their thinking with partner; third, the partnership shares their thinking with another partnership.
Jigsaw classroom, version #1 (Aronson, et al., 2001)	5-6 students per group, and 5-6 groups overall	Teacher assigns students to groups and assigns one aspect of a complex problem to each group.	Students in each group work together to become experts in their particular aspect of the problem; later the expert groups disband, and form new groups containing one student from each of the former expert groups.
Jigsaw classroom, version #2 (Slavin, 1994)	4-5 students per group, and 4-5 groups overall	Teacher assigns students to groups and assigns each group to study or learn about the same *entire* complex problem.	Students initially work in groups to learn about the entire problem; later the groups disband and reform as expert groups, with each group focusing on a selected aspect of the general problem; still later the expert groups disband and the original general groups reform to learn what the expert students can now add to their general understanding.
STAD (Student-Teams-Achievement Divisions) (Slavin, 1994)	4-5 students per team (or group)	Teacher presents a lesson or unit to the entire class, and later tests them on it; grades individuals based partly on	Students work together to insure that team mates improve their performance as much as possible. Students take tests as

		individuals' and the team's improvement, not just on absolute level of performance.	individuals.
Project-Based Learning (Katz, 2000)	Various numbers of students, depending on the complexity of the project, up to and including the entire class	Teacher or students pose a question or problem of interest to other students; teacher assists students to clarify their interests and to make plans to investigate the question further.	Students work together for extended periods to investigate the original question or problem; project leads eventually to a presentation, written report, or other product.

Instructional strategies: an abundance of choices

Looking broadly at this chapter, you can see that choices among instructional strategies are numerous indeed, and that deciding among them depends on the forms of thinking that you want to encourage, the extent to which ideas or skills need to be organized by you to be understood by students, and the extent to which students need to take responsibility for directing their own learning. Although you may have personal preferences among possible instructional strategies, the choice will also be guided by the uniqueness of each situation of teaching—with its particular students, grade-level, content, and purposes. If you need to develop students' problem solving skills, for example, there are strategies that are especially well suited for this purpose; we described some (see, "Problem solving strategies" in this chapter). If you need to organize complex information so that students do not become confused by it, there are effective ways of doing so. If you want the students to take as much initiative as possible in organizing their own learning, this too can be done.

Yet having this knowledge is still not enough to teach well. What is still needed are ideas or principles for deciding *what* to teach. In this chapter we have still not addressed an obvious question: How do I find or devise goals for my teaching and for my students' learning? And assuming that I can determine the goals, where can I find resources that help students to meet them?

Chapter summary

Teaching involves numerous instructional strategies, which are decisions and actions designed to facilitate learning. The choice of strategies depends partly on the forms of thinking intended for students—whether the goal is for students to think critically, for example, or to think creatively, or to solve problems. A fundamental decision in choosing instructional strategies is how much to emphasize teacher-directed instruction, as compared to student-centered models of learning. Teacher-directed strategies of instruction include lectures and readings (expository teaching), mastery learning, scripted or direct instruction, and complex teacher-directed approaches such as Madeline Hunter's effective teaching model. Student-centered models of learning include independent study, student self-reflection, inquiry learning, and various forms of cooperative or collaborative learning. Although for some students, curriculum content and learning goals may lend themselves toward one particular type of instruction, teaching is often a matter of combining different strategies appropriately and creatively.

On the Internet

<**www.glossary.plasmalink.com/glossary.html**> This web page lists over 900 instructional strategies—about ten times as many as in this chapter! The strategies are arranged alphabetically and range from simple to complex. For many strategies there are links to other web pages with more complete explanations and advice for use. This is a good page if you have heard of a strategy but want to find out its definition quickly.

<**www.olc.spsd.sk.ca/DE/PD/instr/alpha.html**> Like the web page above, this one also describes instructional strategies. It includes fewer (about 200), but they are discussed in more detail and organized according to major categories or types of strategies—a good feature if you have a general idea of what sort of strategy you are looking for, but are not sure of precisely which one.

Key terms

Advance organizers

Algorithms

Analogical thinking

Collaborative learning

Concept map

Convergent thinking

Cooperative learning

Creative thinking

Critical thinking

Divergent thinking

Effective teaching model

Freeloading

Functional fixedness

Heuristics

Ill-structured problem

Independent study

Instructional strategies

Lectures

Mastery learning

Overspecialization

Problem analysis

Problem representation

Problem-solving

Response set

Self-reflection

Student-centered models of learning

Teacher-directed instruction

Transfer

Well-structured problem

Working backward

References

Aronson, E. (2001). *In the jigsaw classroom.* Beverly Hills, CA: Sage.

Benson, B. & Barnett, S. (2005). *Student-led conferencing using showcase portfolios.* Thousand Oaks, CA: Corwin Press.

Black, P., Harrison, C., Lee C., Marshall, B., & William, D. (2004). Working inside the black box: Assessment for learning in the classroom. *Phi Delta Kappan, 86*(1), 8-21.

Bothmer, S. (2003). *Creating the peaceable classroom.* Tuscon, AZ: Zephyr Press.

Britt, T. (2005). Effects of identity-relevance and task difficulty on task motivation, stress, and performance. *Motivation and Emotion, 29*(3), 189-202.

Brophy, J. (2004). *Motivating students to learn, 2nd edition.* Mahwah, NJ: Erlbaum.

Brown, D. (2004). Urban teachers' professed classroom management strategies: Reflections of culturally responsive teaching. *Urban Education, 39*(3), 266-289.

Brookfield, S. (2006). *The skillful teacher: On technique, trust, and responsiveness in the classroom, 2ⁿᵈ edition*. San Francisco: Jossey-Bass.

Chesebro, J. (2003). Effects of teacher clarity and nonverbal immediacy on student learning, receiver apprehension, and affect. *Communication Education, 52*(2), 135-147.

Cooper, P. & Simonds, C. (2003). *Communication for the classroom teacher, 7ᵗʰ edition*. Boston: Allyn & Bacon.

Cronbach, L. & Snow, R. (1977). *Aptitudes and instructional methods: A handbook for research on interaction*. New York: Irvington.

Crutsinger, C., Knight, D., & Kinley. (2005). Learning style preferences: Implications for Web-based instruction. *Clothing and Textiles Research Journal, 23*(4), 266-276.

Davidson, J. & Wood, C. (2004). A conflict resolution model. *Theory into Practice, 43*(1), 6-13.

Emmer, E. & Stough, L. (2001). Classroom management: A critical part of educational psychology, with implications for teacher education. *Educational Psychologist, 36*(2), 103-112.

Gibbs, J. (2003). *Moral development and reality: Beyond the theories of Kohlberg and Hoffman*. Thousand Oaks, CA: Sage.

Good, T. & Brophy, J. (2002). *Looking in classrooms, 9ᵗʰ edition*. Boston: Allyn & Bacon.

Gordon, T. (2003). *Teacher effectiveness training*. New York: Three Rivers Press.

Guerrero, L. & Floyd, K. (2005). *Nonverbal communication in close relationships*. Mahwah, NJ: Erlbaum.

Hawkins, J. (2006). Accessing multicultural issues through critical thinking, critical inquiry, and the student research process. *Urban Education, 41*(2), 169-141.

Heimann, M. Strid, K., Smith, L., Tjus, T., Ulvund, S. & Meltzoff, A. (2006). Exploring the relation between memory, gestural communication, and the emergence of language in infancy: a longitudinal study. *Infant and Child Development, 15*(3), 233-249.

Hunter, R. (2004). *Madeline Hunter's Mastery Teaching, Revised Edition*. Thousand Oaks, CA: Corwin Press.

Jones, T. (2004). Conflict resolution education: The field, the findings, and the future. *Conflict Resolution Quarterly, 22*(1-2), 233-267.

Jones, V. & Jones, L. (2006). *Comprehensive classroom management: Creating communities of support and solving problems, 6ᵗʰ edition*. Boston: Allyn & Bacon.

Katz, L. (2000). *Engaging children's minds: The project approach*. Norwood, NJ: Ablex Publishers.

Kohn, A. (2006). *Beyond discipline: From compliance to community*. Reston, VA: Association for Supervision and Curriculum Development.

Kounin, J. (1970). *Discipline and group management in classrooms*. New York: Holt, Rinehart & Winston.

Lyman, F. T. (1981). The responsive classroom discussion: The inclusion of all students. In A. Anderson (Ed.), *Mainstreaming Digest* (pp. 109-113). College Park: University of Maryland Press.

Marks, L. (2003). Instructional management tips for teachers of students with autism-spectrum disorder. *Teaching Exceptional Children, 35*(4), 50-54.

Marsh, A., Elfenbein, H. & Ambady, N. (2003). Nonverbal "accents": cultural differences in facial expressions of emotion. *Psychological Science, 14*(3), 373-376.

Marzano, R. & Marzano, J. (2004). The key to classroom management. *Educational Leadership, 62,* pp. 2-7.

McCafferty, S., Jacobs, G., & Iddings, S. (Eds.). (2006). *Cooperative learning and second language teaching.* New York: Cambridge University Press.

Moritz, J. & Christie, A. (2005). It's elementary: Using elementary portfolios with young students. In C. Crawford (Ed.), *Proceedings of the Society for Information Technology and Teacher Education International Conference 2005* (pp. 144-151). Chesapeake, VA: Association for the Advancement of Computing in Education.

Nations, S. & Boyett, S. (2002). *So much stuff, so little space: Creating and managing the learner-centered classroom.* Gainesville, FL: Maupin House.

Peterson, T. (2004). So you're thinking of trying problem-based learning?: Three critical success factors for implementation. *Journal of Management Education, 28*(5), 630-647.

Reynolds, A. (1992). What is competent beginning teaching? *Review of Educational Research, 62*(1), 1-35.

Slavin. R. (1994). *Cooperative learning, 2nd edition.* Boston: Allyn & Bacon.

Snow, R. (1989). Aptitude-treatment interaction as a framework for research on individual differences in learning. In P. Ackerman, R. Sternberg, & R. Glaser (Eds.), *Learning and individual differences,* pp. 13-60. New York: W. H. Freeman.

Sternberg, R. & Grigorenko, E. (2004). Successful intelligence in the classroom. *Theory into Practice, 43*(4), 274-280.

Stevens, B. & Tollafield, A. (2003). Creating comfortable and productive parent/teacher conferences. *Phi Delta Kappan, 84*(7), 521-525.

Stiggins, R. & Chappuis, J. (2005). Using student-involved classroom assessment to close achievement gaps. *Theory into Practice 44*(1), 11-18.

Thorson, S. (2003). *Listening to students: Reflections on secondary classroom management.* Boston: Allyn & Bacon.

Turiel, E. (2006). The development of morality. In W. Damon, R. Lerner, & N. Eisenberg (Eds.), *Handbook of child psychology, vol. 3, pp. 789-857.* New York: Wiley.

Van Meerionboer, J., Kirschner, P., & Kester, L. (2003). Taking the cognitive load off a learner's mind: Instructional design for complex learning. *Educational Psychologist, 38*(1), 5-13.

White, C. (2005). Student portfolios: An alternative way of encouraging and evaluating student learning. In M. Achacoso & N. Svinicki (Eds.), *Alternative Strategies for Evaluating Student Learning* (pp. 37-42). San Francisco: Jossey-Bass.

Weinstein, C.,Tomlinson-Clarke, S., & Curran, M. (2004). Toward a conception of culturally responsive classroom management. *Journal of Teacher Education, 55*(1), 25-38.

10. Planning instruction

"If you don't know where you're going, you could end up someplace else."

(Casey Stengel)

Casey Stengel, a much-admired baseball coach, was talking about baseball when he made this remark. But he could easily have been speaking of teaching as well. Almost by definition, education has purposes, goals, and objectives, and a central task of teaching is to know what these are and to transform the most general goals into specific objectives and tasks for students. Otherwise, as Casey Stengel said, students may end up "someplace else" that neither they, nor the teacher, nor anyone else intends. A lot of the clarification and specification of goals needs to happen before a cycle of instruction actually begins, but the benefits of planning happen throughout all phases of teaching. If students know precisely what they are supposed to learn, they can focus their attention and effort more effectively. If the teacher knows precisely what students are supposed to learn, then the teacher can make better use of class time and choose and design assessments of their learning that are more fair and valid. In the long run everyone benefits.

This chapter is therefore about **instructional planning,** the systematic selection of educational goals and objectives and their design for use in the classroom. We will divide this idea into four parts, and discuss them one at a time. First is the problem of selecting general goals to teach; where can a teacher find these, and what do they look like? Second is the problem of transforming goals into specific objectives, or statements concrete enough to guide daily activity in class; what will students actually *do* or *say* into order to learn what a teacher wants them to learn? Third is the problem of balancing and relating goals and objectives to each other; since we may want students to learn numerous goals, how can we combine or integrate them so that the overall classroom program does not become fragmented or biased? Fourth is the challenge of relating instructional goals to students' prior experiences and knowledge. We have discussed this challenge before from the perspective of learning theory (in Chapter 2), but in this chapter we look at it from the more practical perspective of curriculum planning.

Selecting general learning goals

At the most general or abstract level, the goals of education include important philosophical ideas like "developing individuals to their fullest potential" and "preparing students to be productive members of society". Few teachers would disagree with these ideas in principle, though they might disagree about their wording or about their relative importance. As a practical matter, however, teachers might have trouble translating such generalities into specific lesson plans or activities for the next day's class. What does it mean, concretely, to "develop an individual to his or her fullest potential"? Does it mean, for example, that a language arts teacher should ask students to write an essay about their personal interests, or does it mean that the teacher should help students learn to write as well as possible on *any* topic, even ones that are not of immediate interest? What exactly should a teacher do, from day to day, to "prepare students to be productive members of society" as well? Answers to questions like these are needed to plan instruction effectively. But the answers are not obvious simply by examining statements of general educational goals.

National and state learning standards

Some (but not all) of the work of transforming such general purposes into more precise teaching goals and even more precise objectives has been performed by broad US organizations that represent educators and other experts about particular subjects or types of teaching (Riley, 2002). The groups have proposed **national standards**, which are summaries of what students can reasonably be expected to learn at particular grade levels and in particular subjects areas. In the United States, in addition, all state governments create **state standards** that serve much the same purpose: they express what students in the state should (and hopefully can) learn at all grade levels and in all subjects. Examples of organizations that provide national standards are listed in Table 27, and examples of state standards are listed in Table 28 for one particular state, Ohio, in the area of language arts.

Table 27: Organizations with statements of US educational standards

Subject	Organization
English and Language Arts	Council of Teachers of English American Council on the Teaching of Foreign Languages
Mathematics	National Council of Teachers of Mathematics
Physical Education and Health	National Association for Sport and Physical Education American Cancer Society
Science	National Academies of Science American Association for the Advancement of Science
Social Studies	National Council for the Social Studies Center for Civic Education National Council on Economic Education National Geographic Society National Center for History in the Schools
Technology	International Society for Technology in Education
Other Specialized Standards Statements:	

American Indian Content Standards	Center for Educational Technology in Indian America
Ethical Standards for School Counselors	American School Counselors Association
Information Literacy Standards	American Association of School Librarians
Business Education	National Business Education Association
Parent Education and Involvement	Parent-Teacher Association (PTA)

Source: <http://www.education-world.com/standards>, accessed December 5, 2006. Summaries of all of these standards, as well as access to the relevant web pages of the corresponding organizations, can be found at this website. Because standards are revised continually, and because of the dynamic nature of websites, the information may differ slightly from the above when you actually access it.

Table 28: Examples of state curriculum standards about language arts

Grade-level:	Classroom example:
Kindergarten-Grade 3: Read accurately high-frequency sight words.	Play a game: "How many words can you see around the classroom that you can read already?"
Grade 4-7: Infer word meaning through identification and analysis of analogies and other word relationships.	Have students keep a journal of unfamiliar words which they encounter and of what they think the words mean.
Grade 8-10: Recognize the importance and function of figurative language.	Have students write a brief essay explaining the meaning of a common figure of speech, and speculating on why it became common usage.
Grade 11-12: Verify meanings of words by the author's use of definition, restatement, example, comparison, contrast and cause and effect.	Have students analyze an essay that includes unfamiliar terms using clues in the essay to determine their meaning.

Source for standards: Ohio Department of Education, 2003, p. 30-31

Because they focus on grade levels and subject areas, general statements of educational standards tend to be a bit more specific than the broader philosophical goals we discussed above. As a rule of thumb, too, state standards tend to be more comprehensive than national standards, both in coverage of grade levels and of subjects. The difference reflects the broad responsibility of states in the United States for all aspects of public education; national organizations, in contrast, usually assume responsibility only for a particular subject area or particular group of students. Either type of standards provides a first step, however, toward transforming the grandest purposes of schooling (like developing the individual or preparing for society) into practical classroom activities. But they provide a first step only. Most statements of standards do not make numerous or detailed suggestions of actual activities or tasks for students, though some might include brief classroom examples—enough to clarify the meaning of a standard, but not enough to plan an actual classroom program for extended periods of time. For these latter purposes, teachers rely on more the detailed documents, the ones often called *curriculum frameworks* and *curriculum guides*.

Curriculum frameworks and curriculum guides

The terms *curriculum framework* and *curriculum guide* sometimes are used almost interchangeably, but for convenience we will use them to refer to two distinct kinds of documents. The more general of the two is **curriculum framework**, which is a document that explains how content standards can or should be organized for a particular subject and at various grade levels. Sometimes this information is referred to as the **scope and sequence** for a curriculum. A curriculum framework document is like a standards statement in that it does not usually provide a lot of detailed suggestions for daily teaching. It differs from a standards statement, though, in that it analyzes each general standard in a curriculum into more specific skills that students need to learn, often a dozen or more per standard. The language or terminology of a framework statement also tends to be somewhat more concrete than a standards statement, in the sense that it is more likely to name behaviors of students—things that a teacher might see them do or hear them say. Sometimes, but not always, it may suggest ways for assessing whether students have in fact acquired each skill listed in the document. Table 29 shows a page from a curriculum framework published by the California State Board of Education (Curriculum Development and Supplemental Materials Committee, 1999). In this case the framework explains the state standards for learning to read, and the excerpt in   Table 29 illustrates how one particular standard, that "students speak and write with command of English conventions appropriate to this grade level", is broken into nine more specific skills. Note that the excerpt names observable behaviors of students (what they do or say); we will discuss this feature again, more fully, in the next part of this chapter, because it is helpful in classroom planning. In spite of this feature, though, the framework document does not lay out detailed activity plans that a teacher could use on a daily basis. (Though even so, it is over 300 pages long!)

Table 29: An excerpt from reading/language arts framework for California public schools

Comments:	**Written and oral English language conventions, third grade**
More general standards statement	Students write and speak with a command of standard English conventions appropriate to this grade level.
More specific or concrete framework statements → (stated as relatively specific skills or behaviors)	Sentence Structure 1.1 Understand and be able to use complete and correct declarative, interrogative, imperative, and exclamatory sentences in writing and speaking. Grammar

1.2 Identify subjects and verbs that are in agreement and identify and use pronouns, adjectives, compound words, and articles correctly in writing and speaking.

1.3 Identify and use past, present, and future verb tenses properly in writing and speaking.

1.4 Identify and use subjects and verbs correctly in speaking and writing simple sentences.

Punctuation

1.5 Punctuate dates, city and state, and titles of books correctly.

1.6 Use commas in dates, locations, and addresses and for items in a series.

Capitalization

1.7 Capitalize geographical names, holidays, historical periods, and special events correctly.

Spelling

1.8 Spell correctly one-syllable words that have blends, contractions, compounds, orthographic patters, and common homophones.

1.9 Arrange words in alphabetical order.

Teachers' need for detailed activity suggestions is more likely to be met by a **curriculum guide,** a document devoted to graphic descriptions of activities that foster or encourage the specific skills explained in a curriculum framework document. The descriptions may mention or list curriculum goals served by an activity, but they are also likely to specify materials that a teacher needs, time requirements, requirements for grouping students, drawings or diagrams of key equipment or materials, and sometimes even suggestions for what to say to students at different points during the activity. In these ways the descriptions may resemble lesson plans.

Since classroom activities often support more than one specific skill, activities in a curriculum guide may be organized differently than they might be in a framework document. Instead of highlighting only one standard at a time, as the framework document might, activities may be grouped more loosely—for example, according to the dominant purpose or goal of an activity ("Activities that encourage the practice of math facts") or according to a dominant piece of equipment or material ("Ten activities with tin cans"). Table 30 shows a description of a kindergarten-level activity about "autumn leaves" that might appear in a curriculum guide. Note that the activity meets several educational objectives at once—tracing shapes, knowledge of leaves and of colors, descriptive language skill. Each of these skills may reflect a different curriculum standard.

Table 30: Sample curriculum guide activity

Curriculum guides provide graphic descriptions of activities that can be used fairly directly in the classroom. Although they are relevant to standards and framework statements, they often are not organized around standards and objectives as such.

Activity: Autumn Leaves

Level: Kindergarten

Themes and Curriculum Connections: trees, autumn, color naming, color comparisons, size comparisons, functions of leaves, growth, the life cycle. See also Standards #xx-yy.

Best time to do it: Fall (October), or whenever leaves are available

Materials needed: (1) small paper (6 x 6 inches); (2) access to leaves; (3) white glue; (4) felt pens or colored pencils

What to do: Give one piece of the small paper to each child. Invite children to color the sheet so that the entire sheet is decorated. Invite children to choose one leaf. Place leaf under the colored (decorated) paper and trace the shape of the leaf lightly in pencil. Then invite children to cut out the colored paper in the shape that has been traced of the leaf.

Cautions: (1) Some children may need individual help with tracing or cutting. (2) Try to use leaves that are still somewhat pliable, because some very old leaves (dried out) may crumble when traced.

Things to talk about: Are some leaves bigger than others? Do they change shape as they grow, or only their size? How do leaves benefit trees? How many different colors can real leaves be?

Formulating learning objectives

Given curriculum frameworks and guides like the ones just described, how do you choose and formulate actual learning objectives? Basically there are two approaches: either start by selecting content or topics that what you want students to know (the cognitive approach) or start with what you want students to do (the behavioral approach). In effect the cognitive approach moves from the general to the specific, and the behavioral approach does the opposite. Each approach has advocates, as well as inherent strengths and problems. In practice, teachers often combine or alternate between them in order to give students some of the advantages of each.

From general to specific: selecting content topics

The cognitive approach assumes that teachers normally have a number of long-term, general goals for students, and it begins with those goals. It also assumes that each student work toward long-term, general goals along different pathways and using different styles of learning. Because of these assumptions, it is necessary to name **indicators,** which are examples of specific behaviors by which students might show success at reaching a general learning goal. But it is neither desirable nor possible for a list of indicators to be complete—only for it to be representative (Gronlund, 2004). Consider this example from teaching middle-school biology. For this subject you might have a general goal like the following, with accompanying indicators:

Goal:

The student will understand the nature and purpose of photosynthesis.

Indicators:

1. explains the purpose of photosynthesis and steps in the process

2. diagrams steps in the chemical process

3. describes how plant photosynthesis affects the animal world

4. writes a plan for how to test leaves for presence of photosynthesis

5. makes an oral presentation and explains how the experiment was conducted

Using a strictly cognitive approach to planning, therefore, a teacher's job has two parts. First she must identify, find, or choose a manageable number of general goals—perhaps just a half dozen or so. (Sometimes these can be taken or adapted from a curriculum framework document such as discussed earlier.) Then the teacher must think of a handful of specific examples or behavioral indicators for each goal—just a half dozen or so of these as well. The behavioral indicators clarify the meaning of the general goal, but are not meant to be the only way that students might show success at learning. Then, at last, thoughtful planning for individual lessons or activities can begin. This approach works especially well for learning goals that are relatively long-term—goals that take many lessons, days, or weeks to reach. During such long periods of teaching, it is impossible to specify the exact, detailed behaviors that every student can or should display to prove that he or she has reached a general goal. It is possible, however, to specify general directions toward which all students should focus their learning and to explain the nature of the goals with a sample of well-chosen indicators or examples (Popham, 2002).

The cognitive, general-to-specific approach is reasonable on the face of it, and in fact probably describes how many teachers think about their instructional planning. But critics have argued that indicators used as examples may not in fact clarify the general goal enough; students therefore end up unexpectedly—as Casey Stengel said at the start of this chapter—"someplace else". Given the general goal of understanding photosynthesis described above, for example, how are we to know whether the five indicators that are listed really allow a teacher to grasp the full meaning of the goal? Put differently, how *else* might a student show understanding of photosynthesis, and how is a teacher to know that a student's achievement is s a legitimate display of understanding? To some educators, grasping the meaning of goals from indicators is not as obvious as it should be, and in any case is prone to misunderstanding. The solution, they say, is not to start planning with general goals, but with specific behaviors that identify students' success.

From specific to general: behavioral objectives

Compared to the cognitive approach, the behavioral approach to instructional planning reverses the steps in planning. Instead of starting with general goal statements accompanied by indicator examples, it starts with the identification of specific behaviors—concrete actions or words—that students should perform or display as a result of instruction (Mager, 2005). Collectively, the specific behaviors may describe a more general educational goal, but unlike the indicators used in the cognitive approach, they are not a mere sampling of the possible specific outcomes. Instead they represent *all* the intended specific outcomes. Consider this sampling of behavioral objectives:

Objectives: Learning to use in-line roller blade skates (beginning level)

1. Student ties boots on correctly.

2. Student puts on safety gear correctly, including helmet, knee and elbow pads.

3. Student skates 15 meters on level ground without falling.

4. Student stops on demand within a three meter distance, without falling.

The objectives listed are not merely a representative sample of how students can demonstrate success with roller-blading. Instead they are behaviors that every student should acquire in order to meet the goal of using roller blades as a beginner. There simply are no other ways to display learning of this goal; getting 100 per cent on a written test about roller blading, for example, would not qualify as success with this goal, though it might show success at some other goal, such as verbal knowledge about roller blading. Even adding other skating behaviors (like "Student skates backwards" or "Student skates in circles") might not qualify as success with this particular goal, because it could reasonably be argued that the additional skating behaviors are about skating at an advanced level, not a beginning level.

In the most commonly used version of this approach, originated by Robert Mager (1962, 2005), a good behavioral objective should have three features. First, it should specify a behavior that can in fact be observed. In practice this usually means identifying something that a student does or says, not something a student thinks or feels. Compare the following examples; the one on the left names a behavior to be performed, but the one on the right names a thinking process that cannot, in principle, be seen:

Behavioral objective

The student will make a list of animal species that live in the water but breathe air and a separate list of species that live in the water but do not require air to breathe.

***Not* behavioral object**

The student will understand the difference between fish and mammals that live in the water.

The second feature of a good behavioral objective is that it describes conditions of performance of the behavior. What are the special circumstances to be provided when the student performs the objective? Consider these two examples:

Special condition of performance *is* specified

Given a list of 50 species, the student will circle those that live in water but breathe air and underline those

A special condition of performance is not specified

After three days of instruction, the student will

that live in water but do not breathe air.

identify species that live in water but breathe air, as well as species that live in water but do not breathe air.

The objective on the left names a special condition of performance—that the student will be given a particular kind of list to work from—which is not part of the instruction itself. The objective on the right appears to name a condition—"three days of instruction". But the condition really describes what the teacher will do (she will instruct), not something specific to students' performance.

The third feature of a good behavioral objective is that it specifies a minimum level or degree of acceptable performance. Consider these two examples:

Specifies minimum level

Given a list of 50 species, the student will circle all of those that live in water but breathe air and underline all of those that live in water but do not breathe air. The student will do so within fifteen minutes.

Does *not* specify minimum level

The student will circle names of species that live in water but breathe air and underline those that live in water but do not breathe air.

The objective on the left specifies a level of performance—100 per cent accuracy within 15 minutes. The objective on the right leaves this information out (and incidentally it also omits the condition of performance mentioned on the left).

Behavioral objectives have obvious advantages because of their clarity and precision. They seem especially well suited for learning that by their nature they can be spelled out explicitly and fully, such as when a student is learning to drive a car, to use safety equipment in a science laboratory, or install and run a particular computer program. Most of these goals, as it happens, also tend to have relatively short learning cycles, meaning that they can be learned as a result of just one lesson or activity, or of just a short series of them at most. Such goals tend not to include the larger, more abstract goals of education. In practice, both kinds of goals— the general and the specific— form a large part of education at all grade levels.

Finding the best in both approaches

When it comes to teaching and learning the large or major goals, then, behavioral objectives can seem unwieldy. How, a teacher might ask, can you spell out *all* of the behaviors involved in a general goal like *becoming a good citizen?* How could you name in advance the numerous conditions under which good citizenship might be displayed, or the minimum acceptable level of good citizenship expected in each condition? Specifying these features seems impractical at best, and at times even undesirable ethically or philosophically. (Would we really want any students to become "minimum citizens"?) Because of these considerations, many teachers find it sensible to compromise between the cognitive and behavioral approaches. Here are some features that are often part of a compromise:

- When planning, think about BOTH long-term, general goals AND short-term, immediate objectives. A thorough, balanced look at most school curricula shows that they are concerned with the general as well as the specific. In teaching elementary math, for example, you may want students to learn general problem solving strategies (a general goal), but you may also want them to learn specific math facts (a specific objective). In teaching Shakespeare's plays in high school, you may want students to be able to compare the plays critically (a general goal), but doing so may require that they learn details about the characters and plots of the major plays (a specific objective). Since general goals usually take longer to reach than specific objectives, instructional planning has to include both time frames.

- Plan for what students do, not what the teacher does. This idea may seem obvious, but it is easy to overlook it when devising lesson plans. Consider that example again about teaching Shakespeare. If you want students to learn the details about Shakespeare's plays, it is tempting to plan objectives like "Summarize the plot of each play to students", or "Write and hand out to students an outline of the plays". Unfortunately these objectives describe only what the teacher does, and makes the assumption (often unwarranted) that students will remember what the teacher says or puts in writing for them. A better version of the same objective should focus on the actions of students, not of teachers—for example, "Students will write a summary, from memory, of each of the major plays of Shakespeare". This version focuses on what students do instead of what the teacher does. (Of course you may still have to devise activities that help students to reach the objective, such as providing guided practice in writing summaries of plays.)

- To insure diversity of goals and objectives when planning, consider organizing goals and objectives by using a systematic classification scheme of educational objectives. At the beginning of this section we stated that there is a need, when devising goals and objectives, for both the specific and the general. Actually a more accurate statement is that there is a need for goals and objectives that refer to a variety of cognitive processes and that have varying degrees of specificity or generality. One widely used classification scheme that does so, for example, is one proposed 50 years ago by Benjamin Bloom (1956) and revised recently by his associates (Anderson & Krathwohl, 2001). We describe this system, called a taxonomy of objectives, in the next section.

Taxonomies of educational objectives

When educators have proposed taxonomies of educational objectives, they have tended to focus on one of three areas or domains of psychological functioning: either students' cognition (thought), students' feelings and emotions (affect), or students' physical skills (psychomotor abilities). Of these three areas, they have tended to focus the most attention on cognition. The taxonomy originated by Benjamin Bloom, for example, deals entirely with cognitive outcomes of instruction.

Bloom's Taxonomy:

In its original form, **Bloom's Taxonomy** of educational objectives referred to forms of cognition or thinking, which were divided into the six levels (Bloom, et al., 1956). Table 31 summarizes the levels, and offers two kinds of examples—simple ones based on the children's story, *Goldilocks and the Three Bears*, and complex ones more typical of goals and objectives used in classrooms. The levels form a loose hierarchy from simple to complex thinking, at least when applied to some subjects and topics. When planning for these subjects it can therefore be helpful not only for insuring diversity among learning objectives, but also for sequencing materials. In learning about geography, for example, it may sometimes make sense to begin with information about specific places or societies (knowledge and comprehension), and work gradually toward comparisons and assessments among the places or societies (analysis and synthesis).

Table 31: Bloom's Taxonomy of objectives: cognitive domain

Type or level of learning	Simple example	Classroom example
Knowledge: recall of information, whether it is simple or complex in nature	"Name three things that Goldilocks did in the house of the three bears."	"List all of the planets of the solar system." "State five key features of life in the middle ages."
Comprehension: grasping the meaning of information, by interpreting it or translating it from one form to another	"Explain why Goldilocks preferred the little bear's chair."	"Convert the following arithmetic word problem to a mathematical equation." "Describe how plants contribute to the welfare of animal life."
Application: using information in new, concrete situations	"Predict some of the things Goldilocks might have used if she had entered your house."	"Illustrate how positive reinforcement might affect the behavior of a pet dog." "Use examples from the plot to illustrate the theme of novel."
Analysis: breaking information into its components to understand its structure	"Select the part of *Goldilocks and the Three Bears* where you think Goldilocks felt most comfortable."	"Compare the behavior of domestic dogs with the behavior of wolves." "Diagram the effects of weather patterns on plant metabolism."
Synthesis: putting parts of information together into a coherent whole	"Tell how the story would have been different if it had been three fishes."	"Design an experiment to test the effects of gravity on root growth." "Write an account of how humans would be different if life had originated on Mars instead of Earth."
Evaluation: judging the value of information for a particular purpose	"Justify this statement: *Goldilocks was a bad girl.*"	"Appraise the relevance of the novel for modern life." "Assess the value of information processing theory for planning instruction."

Such a sequence does *not* work well, however, for all possible topics or subjects. To learn certain topics in mathematics, for example, students may sometimes need to start with general ideas (like "What does it mean to multiply?") than with specific facts (like "How much is 4 x 6?") (Egan, 2005). At other times, though, the reverse sequence may be preferable. Whatever the case, a taxonomy of cognitive objectives, like Bloom's, can help to remind teachers to set a variety of objectives and to avoid relying excessively on just one level, such as simple recall of factual knowledge (Notar, et al., 2004).

Bloom's Taxonomy revised

A few years ago two of Benjamin Bloom's original colleagues, Linda Anderson and David Krathwohl, revised his taxonomy so as to clarify its terms and to make it more complete (Anderson & Krathwohl, 2001; Marzano, 2006). The resulting categories are summarized and compared to the original categories in Table 32. As the chart shows, several categories of objectives have been renamed and a second dimension added that describes the kind of thinking or cognitive processing that may occur. The result is a much richer taxonomy than before, since every level of the objectives can now take four different forms. *Remembering,* for example, can refer to four different kinds of memory: memory for facts, for concepts, for procedures, or for metacognitive knowledge. Table 32 gives examples of each of these kinds of memory.

Table 32: Bloom's Taxonomy of cognitive objectives—revised

Original term from Bloom's Taxonomy (1956)	**Revised term emphasizing cognitive processing (2001)**	**A new dimension added: types of knowledge learned (2001)**	**Example of cognitive process *remembering* combined with possible *types* of knowledge**
Knowledge	Remembering	• factual knowledge	**Memory for facts:** *recalling the names of each part of a living cell*
Comprehension	Understanding	• conceptual knowledge	
Application	Applying		**Memory for concepts:** *recalling the functions of each part of a living cell*
Analysis	Analyzing	• procedural knowledge	
Evaluation	Evaluating		**Memory for procedures:** *recalling how to view a cell under a microscope*
Synthesis	Creating	• metacognitive knowledge	
			Memory for metacognition: recalling not the names of the parts, but a *technique* for remembering the names of

			the parts of a living cell

Caption: The revision to Bloom's Taxonomy distinguishes between cognitive processes (left-hand column in the table) and types of knowledge learned (right-hand column). The original version has terms similar to the cognitive processing terms in the revised version. According to the revised version, any type of knowledge (from the right-hand column) can, in principle, occur with any type of cognitive processing (left-hand column).

Taxonomies of affective objectives and psychomotor objectives

Although taxonomies related to *affect,* or the feelings and emotions of students, are used less commonly than cognitive taxonomies for planning instruction, various educators have constructed them. One of the most widely known was also published by colleagues of Benjamin Bloom and classifies affect according to how committed a student feels toward what he is learning (Krathwohl, Bloom, & Masia, 1964/1999). Table 33 summarizes the categories and gives brief examples. The lowest level, called *receiving,* simply involves willingness to experience new knowledge or activities. Higher levels involve embracing or adopting experiences in ways that are increasingly organized and that represent increasingly stable forms of commitment.

Table 33: Taxonomies of objectives: affective domain and psychomotor domain

Affective domain		Psychomotor domain	
Receiving	Willingness to attend to particular experience	Imitation	Repeating a simple action that has been demonstrated
Responding	Willingness to participate actively in an experience	Manipulation	Practice of an action that has been imitated but only learned partially
Valuing	Perception of experience as worthwhile	Precision	Quick, smooth execution of an action that has been practiced
Organization	Coordination of valued experiences into partially coherent wholes	Articulation	Execution of an action not only with precision, but also with modifications appropriate to new circumstances
Characterization by a	Coordination of valued	Naturalization	Incorporation of an

value complex	experiences and of organized sets of experiences into a single comprehensive value hierarchy		action into the motor repertoire, along with experimentation with new motor actions

Taxonomies related to abilities and skills that are physical, or psychomotor, have also been used less widely than affective taxonomies, with the notable exception of one area of teaching where they are obviously relevant: physical education. As you might expect, taxonomic categories of motor skills extend from simple, brief actions to complex, extended action sequences that combine simpler, previously learned skills smoothly and automatically (Harrow, 1972; Simpson, 1972). One such classification scheme is shown in Table 33. An example of a very basic psychomotor skill might be imitating the action of throwing a ball when modeled by someone else; an example of the latter might be performing a 10 minute gymnastics routine which the student has devised for himself or herself. Note, though, that many examples of psychomotor skills also exist outside the realm of physical education. In a science course, for example, a student might need to learn to operate laboratory equipment that requires using delicate, fine movements. In art classes, students might learn to draw, and in music they might learn to play an instrument (both are partly motor skills). Most first graders are challenged by the motor skills of learning to write. For students with certain physical disabilities, furthermore, motor skill development is an important priority for the student's entire education.

Students as a source of instructional goals

So far our discussion of instructional planning has described goals and objectives as if they are selected primarily by educators and teachers, and not by students themselves. The assumption may be correct in many cases, but there are problems with it. One problem is that choosing goals and objectives *for* students, rather than *by* students, places a major burden on everyone involved in education—curriculum writers, teachers, and students. The curriculum writers have to make sure that they specify standards, goals, and objectives that are truly important for students to learn (what if it really does *not* matter, for example, whether a science student learns about the periodic table of the elements?). Teachers have to make sure that students actually become motivated to learn the specified goals and objectives, even if the students are not motivated initially. Students have to master pre-set goals and objectives even if they might not have chosen them personally. Some critics of education have argued that these requirements can be serious impediments to learning (Kohn, 2004). The problems are widespread and especially noticeable in two forms of teaching. One is with the youngest students, who may especially lack patience with an educational agenda set by others (Kohn, 1999; Seitz, 2006). The other is with culturally diverse classrooms, where students and their families may hold a variety of legitimate, but unconventional expectations about what they should learn (J. Banks & C. Banks, 2005).

In response to concerns like these, some educators advocate planning instruction around goals set or expressed either by students themselves or by the cultures or communities with which students identify. Their suggestions vary in detail, but can be organized into two broad categories: (1) emergent curriculum and (2) multicultural and anti-bias curriculum.

Emergent curriculum

An **emergent curriculum** is one that explicitly builds on interests expressed by students, rather than goals set by curriculum writers, curriculum documents, or teachers. As you might suspect, therefore, instructional planning for an emergent curriculum does not have the same meaning that the term has had in the chapter up to now. Instead, since an emergent curriculum by definition unfolds spontaneously and flexibly, students' interests may be predictable, but usually not very far in advance (Peterson, 2002). Suppose, for example, that a first-grade teacher plans a unit around Halloween, and that as one of the activities for this unit she reads a book about Halloween. In listening to the book, however, the students turn out to be less interested in its Halloween content than in the fact that one of the illustrations in the book shows a picture of a full moon partially hidden by clouds. They begin asking about the moon: why it is full sometimes but not other times, why it rises in different places each month, and whether the moon really moves behind clouds or whether the clouds actually do the moving. The teacher encourages their questions and their interest in moon astronomy. Over the next days or weeks, she arranges further activities and experiences to encourage students' interest: she sets aside her original plans about Halloween and finds books about the moon and about how the solar system works. She invites a local amateur astronomer to visit the group and talk about his observations of the moon. Several children build models of the moon out of paper maché. Some find books describing trips of the space shuttles to the moon. Others make a large mural depicting a moonscape. And so on; the original goals about Halloween are not so much rejected, as set aside or forgotten in favor of something more immediately interesting and motivating.

While these activities could in principle happen because of recommendations from a curriculum document, the key point about emergent curriculum is that they happen for a very different reason: these activities happen and the goals emerge because the children *want* them. A teacher's challenge is therefore not planning activities that match predetermined curriculum goals or objectives, but to respond flexibly and sensitively as students' interests become known and explicit. Teachers' responsiveness is facilitated by two practices that are especially prominent when a teacher adopts an emergent approach to curriculum. The first is careful, continuous *observation of students*. The teacher watches and listens, and may keep informal written records of students' comments and activities. The information allows her to respond more effectively to the interests they express, and at the same time it provides a type of assessment of students' progress—information about what the students are actually learning.

A second strategy that facilitates teachers' success is *curriculum webbing,* a process of brainstorming connections among initiatives suggested by students and ideas suggested by the teacher. In some cases webs can be created jointly with students by brainstorming with them about where their current interests may lead. In other cases they can be created independently by the teacher's own reflections. In still others, when a classroom has more than one adult responsible for it, they can be created jointly with fellow teachers or teacher assistants. The latter approach works especially well in preschool, kindergartens, or special education classrooms, which often have more than one adult responsible for the class (Vartuli & Rohs, 2006).

To some, emergent curriculum may seem like a formula for curriculum and management disasters. But the approach has often proved quite successful, particularly in early childhood education and the earliest grade levels of elementary school (Seitz, 2006; Wurm, 2005). Something akin to emergent curriculum is quite possible, in principle, even with older students. In Chapter 8, for example, we described a high school program in which students began with problems and experiences that were personally relevant, and discussed the problems with classmates to formulate research problems which they then studied more formally and systematically (Hawkins, 2006). In essence this strategy created an emergent curriculum analogous to the ones described above for young children. What the high school students studied was not predetermined, but emerged from their own expressed interests.

Multicultural and anti-bias education

A *culture* is an all-encompassing set of values, beliefs, practices and customs of a group or community—its total way of life. Cultures may be shared widely, even by much if not all of an entire nation, or they may be shared by relatively few, such as a small community within a large city. Sometimes the term *culture* is even applied to the way of life of an individual family or of a specialized group in society; some might argue, for example, that there is a culture of schooling shared by teachers, though not necessarily by all students.

Because culture by definition touches on all aspects of living, it is likely to affect students' perspectives about school, their ways of learning and their motivations to learn. The differences go beyond obvious differences in holidays, language, or food preferences. In some cultures, for example, individuals keep good eye contact with someone to whom they are speaking, and expect the same from others. In other cultures, such behavior is considered intrusive or overly aggressive, and avoiding eye contact while speaking is considered more respectful. Or another example: in some cultures it is expected that individuals will be punctual (or on time), whereas in others punctuality is considered overly compulsive, and a more casual approach to time is the norm. Students regularly bring differences like these to school, where they combine with expectations from teachers and other school staff, and contribute indirectly to differences in achievement and satisfaction among students.

To be fully effective, therefore, instructional planning has to take into account the diversity in students' cultural backgrounds, whether the differences are observable or subtle. Planning also has to work deliberately to reduce the social biases and prejudices that sometimes develop about cultural differences. **Multicultural education** and **anti-bias education** are two terms referring to these purposes. Their meanings often overlap significantly, depending on the context or on who is using the terms. Generally, though, the first term—multicultural education—has somewhat more to do with understanding the differences among cultures. The latter term—anti-bias education—has more to do with overcoming social prejudices and biases resulting from cultural differences. For convenience in this chapter, we will use the single term *multicultural education* to refer to both understanding differences and overcoming prejudices.

Fully effective multicultural education has several features. The most obvious and familiar one is **content integration:** the curriculum uses examples and information from different cultures to illustrate various concepts or ideas already contained in the curriculum (Vavrus, 2002). In studying holidays, for example, an elementary-school teacher includes activities and information about Kwanzaa as well as Christmas, Hanukkah, or other holidays happening at about the same time. In studying the US Civil War, another example, a middle-years teacher includes material written from the perspective of African-American slaves and Southern landowners. In teaching language arts, students learn basic vocabulary of any non-English languages spoken by some members of the class.

But there is more to multicultural education than integrating content from diverse cultures. Among other features, it also requires an **equity pedagogy,** which is an effort to allow or even encourage, a variety of learning styles—styles at which students may have become skillful because of their cultural backgrounds (Crow, 2005; C. Banks & J. Banks, 1995). In elementary language arts, for example, there may be more than one "best" way to tell a story. Should a student necessarily have to tell it alone and standing in front of the whole class, or might the student tell it jointly with a friend or in a smaller group? In learning to write a story, is legitimate variety also possible there? Should a written story necessarily begin with a topic sentence that announces what the story is about, or can it save a statement of topic for the ending or even it leave it out altogether in order to stimulate readers to think? The best choice is related in part to the nature and purpose of the story, of course, but partly also to differences in cultural expectations about story telling. Choosing a story form also points toward another feature of multicultural education, **the knowledge construction process,** which is the unstated, unconscious process by which a cultural group creates knowledge or information. The popular media, for example, often portray Hispanic-Americans in ways that are stereotypical, either subtly or blatantly (Lester & Ross, 2003). A fully multicultural curriculum finds way to call these images to the attention of students and to engage them in thinking about how and why the images oversimplify reality.

Yet there is even more to a fully multicultural education. In addition to content integration, equity pedagogy, and knowledge construction, it fosters **prejudice reduction**, or activities, discussions and readings that identify students' negative evaluations of cultural groups (Jacobson, 2003; J. Banks & C. Banks, 2004). The activities and discussions can of course take a somewhat philosophical approach—examining how students feel in general, what experiences they remember having involving prejudice, and the like. But the activities and discussions can also take a more indirect and subtle form, as when a teacher periodically speaks in a student's native language as a public sign of respect for the student. Gestures and discussions like these are especially effective if they contribute to the fifth element of multicultural education, **empowering the school and social structure,** in which all teachers and staff members find ways to convey respect for cultural differences, including even during extra-curricular and sports activities. A sports team or a debate club should not be limited to students from one cultural background and exclude those from another—or more subtly, accept everyone but give the more desirable roles only to individuals with particular social backgrounds. To the extent that cultural respect and inclusion are school-wide, teaching and learning both become easier and more successful, and instructional planning in particular becomes more relevant to students' needs.

Enhancing student learning through a variety of resources

Whether instructional goals originate from curriculum documents, students' expressed interests, or a mixture of both, students are more likely to achieve the goals if teachers draw on a wide variety of resources. As a practical matter, this means looking for materials and experiences that supplement—or occasionally even replace—the most traditional forms of information, such as textbooks. Precisely what resources to use depend on factors unique to each class, school, or community, but they might include one or more of the following.

The Internet as a learning tool

The Internet has become a fixture of modern society, and it offers a huge variety of information on virtually any topic, including any school subject and any possible grade level from kindergarten through university. At the time of writing this book (2007), about two-thirds of all households in the United States and Canada have at least some sort of Internet access, and virtually 100 per cent of public and private schools have some access (Parsad & Jones, 2006). These circumstances make the Internet a potential major resource for teachers and students—a virtual library many times larger than even the largest physical (or "bricks and mortar") libraries in the world.

But the vastness of the Internet is not entirely a blessing. A major problem is that the sheer volume of information available, which can sometimes make searching for a specific topic, article, or document overwhelming and inefficient. The newer search engines (such as Google at <http://www.google.com>) can help with this problem, though they do not solve it completely. When searching the term *photosynthesis,* for example, Google and other similar search engines return over six *million* web pages that discuss or refer this topic in some way! If a teacher is planning a unit about photosynthesis, or if a student is writing an essay about it, which of these web pages will prove most helpful? Choosing among web pages is a new, somewhat specialized form of *computer literacy,* one that can be learned partially by trial-and-error online, but that also benefits from assistance by a teacher or by more experienced peers (Ragains, 2006).

Another problem with the Internet is inequity of access. Even though, as we mentioned above, virtually all schools now have access of some sort, the access is distributed quite unevenly across communities and income groups (Skinner, Biscope, & Poland, 2003; Parsad & Jones, 2005). For one thing, the large majority of Web pages are posted in English, and this fact naturally poses a challenge for any students who still learning to read or write English. For another, schools vary widely in how much Internet service they can provide. In general, well-to-do schools and those in cities provide more access than those located in less well-off areas or in rural areas—though there are many exceptions. A richly endowed school might have an Internet connection in every classroom as well as multiple connections in a school library or in specialized computer rooms. Students as well as faculty would be able to use these facilities, and one or more teachers might have special training in Internet research to help when problems arise. At the other extreme, a school might have only a few Internet connections for the entire school, or even just one, located in a central place like the library or the school office. Usage by students would consequently be limited, and teachers would essentially teach themselves how to search the Internet and how to troubleshoot technical problems when they occur.

In spite of these problems, the Internet has considerable potential for enhancing students' learning, precisely *because* of its flexibility and near universality. Some of the best recent successes involve the creation of a **learning commons** (sometimes also called an *information commons* or *teaching commons),* a combination of a website and an actual, physical place in a school or library that brings together information, students and teachers so that both (though perhaps especially students) can learn (Haas & Robertson, 2004; Beagle, 2006). A learning commons includes an online library catalogue and online Internet service, but it also offers other services: online information and advice about study skills, for example, as well as access to peer tutors and support groups, either online or in person, that can help with difficulties about writing or doing assignments. As you might suspect, using a learning commons effectively sometimes requires reorganizing certain features of teaching and learning, chiefly toward greater explicit collaboration among students and teachers.

Using local experts and field trips

Two other ways of enhancing learning include bringing local experts to the classroom and taking the class on field trips outside the classroom. Both of these strategies help to make learning more vivid, as well as more relevant to the particular community and lives that students lead.

Local experts

Classroom visits by persons with key experience can often add a lot to many curriculum subjects and topics. In one tenth grade science class studying environmental issues, for example, the teacher invited the city forester, the person responsible for the health of trees planted in city parks and along city boulevards. The forester had special knowledge of the stresses on trees in urban environments, and he was able to explain and give examples of particular problems that had occurred and their solutions. In a second grade class with many Hispanic students, on the other hand, a teacher aide was able to serve as an expert visitor by describing her memories of childhood in a Spanish-speaking community in New Mexico. Later she also recruited an older Hispanic friend and relative to the class to describe their experiences growing up in Central America. She also acted as their English-Spanish interpreter. In all of these examples, the experts made the learning more real and immediate. Their presence counteracted the tendency to equate school learning with book-based knowledge—a common hazard when basing instructional planning primarily on curriculum documents.

Field trips

In addition to bringing the world to the classroom by inviting visitors, teachers can do the converse, they can take the classroom to the world by leading students on field trips. Such trips are not confined to any particular grade level. In the early grades of elementary school, for example, one common goal of the curriculum is to learn about community helpers—the police, firefighters, store owners, and others who make a community safe and livable. As indicated already, representatives of these groups can visit the class and tell about their work. But the class can also visit the places which these people tell about: a police station, a fire hall, a local retail store, and the like. Such trips offer a more complete picture of the context in which community professionals work than is possible simply from hearing and reading about it. The benefits are possible for older students as well. In learning about water-borne diseases as part of a biology class, for example, one middle-school class took a field trip to the local water-treatment facility, where staff members explained where the town's water came from and how the water was cleaned to become drinkable at any tap.

From a teacher's point of view, of course, there are certain risks about arranging classroom visitors or field trips. One is that a visitor may turn out not to communicate well with children or young people—he or she may assume too much prior knowledge, for example, or veer off the chosen topic. Another problem is that field trips often require additional funds (for admission fees or to pay for a bus), and require support from additional adults—often parents—to supervise students outside of school. Some of these problems are by-passed by arranging "virtual" field trips and hearing from "virtual" visitors: using computer software or media to show students places and activities which they cannot visit in person (Clark, 2006). Generally, though, a computer-based experience cannot compare with a real trip or visitor in vividness, and the benefits of actual, in-person field trips or visitors often therefore outweigh the challenges of arranging them.

Service learning

Still another way to enhance learning is to incorporate **service learning,** which is activity that combines real community service with analysis and reflection on the significance of the service (Johnson & O'Grady, 2006; Thomsen, 2006). Picking up trash in an urban stream bed, for example, is a community service which students can perform. To transform this service into service *learning,* students also need to note and reflect on the trash that they find; talk and write about the ecological environment of the stream and of the community; and even make recommendations for improving the local environment. To accomplish these objectives, service learning activities should not be sporadic, nor used as a punishment—as when a teacher or principal assigns trash pick-up as an after-school detention activity.

Under good conditions, service learning enhances instructional plans both morally and intellectually. Morally, it places students in the role of *creating* good for the community, and counteracts students' perception that being "good" simply means complying with teachers' or parents' rules passively. Intellectually, service learning places social and community issues in a vivid, lived context. The environment, economic inequality, or race relations, for example, are no longer just ideas that people merely talk about, but problems that people actually act upon (Dicklitch, 2005).

As you might suspect, though, making service learning successful is not automatic. For one thing, service learning lends itself well only to certain curriculum areas (for example, community studies or social studies). For another, some students may initially resist service learning, wondering whether it benefits them personally as students (Jones, Gilbride-Brown, & Gasiorski, 2005). Also, some service projects may inadvertently be invented only to benefit students, without adequate consultation or advice from community members. Bringing food hampers to low-income families may seem like a good idea to middle-class students or instructors, but some families may perceive this action less as a benefit than as an act of charity which they therefore resent. But none of these problems are insurmountable. Evaluations generally find that service learning, when done well, increases students' sense of moral empowerment as well as their knowledge of social issues (Buchanan, Baldwin, & Rudisill, 2002). Like many other educational practices, insuring success with service learning requires doing it well.

Creating bridges among curriculum goals and students' prior experiences

To succeed, then, instructional plans do require a variety of resources, like the ones discussed in the previous section. But they also require more: they need to connect with students' prior experiences and knowledge. Sometimes the connections can develop as a result of using the Internet, taking field trips, or engaging in service learning, particularly if students are already familiar with these activities and places. More often than not, though, teachers need to find additional ways to connect curriculum with students' experiences—ways that fit more thoroughly and continuously into the daily work of a class. Fortunately, such techniques are readily at hand; they simply require the teacher to develop a habit of looking for opportunities to use them. Among the possibilities are four that deserve special mention: (1) *modeling* behavior and *modeling representations* of ideas, (2) *activating prior knowledge* already familiar to students, (3) *anticipating preconceptions* held by students, and (4) *providing guided and independent practice,* including its most traditional form, *homework.*

Modeling

The term *modeling* can mean either a demonstration of a desired behavior or a representation of an important theory, idea, or object. Each of these meanings can link curriculum goals with students' prior knowledge and experience.

Modeling as a demonstration

In the first meaning, **modeling** refers to performing or demonstrating a desired new behavior or skill, as when a teacher or classmate demonstrates polite behaviors or the correct solution to a math problem. In this case we say that the teacher or classmate *models* the desired behavior, either deliberately or in the course of other ongoing activity. Students observe the modeled behavior and (hopefully) imitate it themselves. Research repeatedly shows that modeling desired behaviors is an effective way to learn new behaviors, especially when the model is perceived as important (like the teacher), similar to the learner (like a student's best friend), or has a warm, positive relationship with the learner (like the teacher or the student's friend) (Bandura, 2002; Gibson, 2004). Modeling in this sense is sometimes also called *observational learning*. It has many of the same properties as the classic operant conditioning discussed in Chapter 2, except that reinforcement during observational learning is witnessed in others rather than experienced by the learner directly. Watching others being reinforced is sometimes called *vicarious reinforcement*. The idea is that if, for example, a student observes a classmate who behaves politely with the teacher and then sees that classmate receive praise for the behavior (vicarious reinforcement), the student is more likely to imitate the polite behavior that he saw. As in classic operant conditioning, furthermore, if the student observes that politeness by classmates is ignored (extinction or no reinforcement), then the student is much less likely to imitate the politeness. Worse yet, if the student observes that negative behaviors in others lead to positive consequences (like attention from peers), then the student may imitate the negative behaviors (Rebellon, 2006). Cursing and swearing, and even bullying or vandalism, can be reinforced vicariously, just as can more desired behaviors.

Modeling—in this first sense of a demonstration—connects instructional goals to students' experiences by presenting real, vivid examples of behaviors or skills in a way that a student can practice directly, rather than merely talk about. There is often little need, when imitating a model, to translate ideas or instructions from verbal form into action. For students struggling with language and literacy, in particular, this feature can be a real advantage.

Modeling—as simplified representation

In a second meaning of modeling, a **model** is a simplified representation of a phenomenon that incorporates the important properties of the phenomenon. Models in this sense may sometimes be quite tangible, direct copies of reality; when I was in fourth grade growing up in California, for example, we made scale models of the Spanish missions as part of our social studies lessons about California history. But models can also be imaginary, though still based on familiar elements. In a science curriculum, for example, the behavior of gas molecules under pressure can be modeled by imagining the molecules as ping pong balls flying about and colliding in an empty room. Reducing the space available to the gas by making the room smaller, causes the ping pong balls to collide more frequently and vigorously, and thereby increases the pressure on the walls of the room. Increasing the space has the opposite effect. Creating an actual room full of ping pong balls may be impractical, of course, but the model can still be imagined.

Modeling in this second sense is not about altering students' behavior, but about increasing their understanding of a newly learned idea, theory, or phenomenon. The model itself uses objects or events that are already familiar to students—simple balls and their behavior when colliding—and in this way supports students' learning of new, unfamiliar material. Not every new concept or idea lends itself to such modeling, but many do: students can create models of unfamiliar animals, for example, or of medieval castles, or of ecological systems. Two-dimensional models—essentially drawings—can also be helpful: students can illustrate literature or historical events, or make maps of their own neighborhoods. The choice of model depends largely on the specific curriculum goals which the teacher needs to accomplish at a particular time.

Activating prior knowledge

Another way to connect curriculum goals to students' experience is by **activating prior knowledge**, a term that refers to encouraging students to recall what they know already about new material being learned. Various formats for activating prior knowledge are possible. When introducing a unit about how biologists classify animal and plant species, for example, a teacher can invite students to discuss how they already classify different kinds of plants and animals. Having highlighted this informal knowledge, the teacher can then explore how the same species are classified by biological scientists, and compare the scientists' classification schemes to the students' own schemes. The activation does not have to happen orally, as in this example; a teacher can also ask students to write down as many distinct types of animals and plants that they can think of, and then ask students to diagram or map their relationships—essentially creating a *concept map* like the ones we described in Chapter 8 (Gurlitt, et al., 2006). Whatever the strategy used, activation helps by making students' prior knowledge or experience conscious and therefore easier to link to new concepts or information.

Anticipating preconceptions of students

Ironically, activating students' prior knowledge can be a mixed blessing if some of the prior knowledge is misleading or downright wrong. Misleading or erroneous knowledge is especially common among young students, but it can happen at any grade level. A kindergarten child may think that the sun literally "rises" in the morning, since she often hears adults use this expression, or that the earth is flat because it obviously *looks* flat. But a high school student may mistakenly believe that large objects (a boulder) fall faster than small ones (a pebble), or that a heavy object dropped (not thrown) from a moving car window will fall straight down instead of traveling laterally alongside the car while it falls.

Because misconceptions are quite common among students and even among adults, teachers are more effective if they can **anticipate preconceptions of students** wherever possible. The task is twofold. First the teacher must know or at least guess students' preconceptions as much as possible in advance, so that she can design learning activities to counteract and revise their thinking. Some preconceptions have been well-documented by educational research and therefore can in principle be anticipated easily—though they may still sometimes take a teacher by surprise during a busy activity or lesson (Tanner & Allen, 2005; Chiu & Lin, 2005). Exhibit 9.8 lists a few of these common preconceptions. Others may be unique to particular students, however, and a teacher may only by able to learn of them through experience—by listening carefully to what students say and write and by watching what they do. A few preconceptions may be so ingrained or tied to other, more deeply held beliefs that students may resist giving them up, either consciously or unconsciously. It may be hard, for example, for some students to give up the idea that girls are less talented at math or science than are boys, even though research generally finds this is not the case (Hyde & Linn, 2006).

Table 34: Several misconceptions about science

Misconception	What to do
Stars and constellations appear in the same place in the sky every night.	Ask students to observe carefully the locations of a bright star once a week for several weeks.
The world is flat, circular like a pancake.	Use a globe or ball to find countries located over the horizon; use computer software (e.g. Global Earth) to illustrate how a round Earth can look flat up close.
Dinosaurs disappeared at the same time that human beings appeared and because of human activity.	Construct a timeline of major periods of Darwinian evolution.
Rivers always flow from North to South.	Identify rivers that flow South to North (e.g. the Red River in North Dakota and Canada); talk about how Southern locations are not necessarily "lower".
Force is needed not only to start an object moving, but to keep it moving.	Explain the concept of *inertia;* demonstrate inertia using low-friction motion (e.g. with a hovercraft or dry-ice puck).
Volume, weight, and size are identical concepts.	Have students weigh objects of different sizes or volumes, and compare the results.
Seasons happen because the Earth changes distance from the sun.	Explain the tilt of Earth's axis using a globe and light as a model; demonstrate reduced heating of surfaces by placing similar surfaces outdoors at different angles to the sun's rays.

Sources: Chi, 2005; D. Clark, 2006; Slotta & Chi, 2006; Owens, 2003.

The second task when anticipating preconceptions is to treat students' existing knowledge and beliefs with respect even when they do include misconceptions or errors. This may seem obvious in principle, but it needs remembering when students persist with misconceptions in spite of a teacher's efforts to teach alternative ideas or concepts. Most of us—including most students—have reasons for holding our beliefs, even when the beliefs do not agree with teachers, textbooks, or other authorities, and we appreciate having our beliefs treated with respect. Students are no different from other people in this regard. In a high school biology class, for example, some students may have personal reasons for not agreeing with the theory of evolution associated with Charles Darwin. For religious reasons they may support explanations of the origins of life that give a more active, interventionist role to God (Brumfiel, 2005). If their beliefs disagree with the teacher's or the textbook, then the disagreement needs to be acknowledged, but acknowledged respectfully. For some students (and perhaps some teachers), expressing fundamental disagreement respectfully may feel awkward, but it needs to be done nonetheless.

Guided practice, independent practice, and homework

So far, we have focused on bridging the goals or content of a curriculum to events, beliefs, and ideas from students' lives. In studying human growth in a health class, for example, a teacher might ask students to bring photos of themselves as a much younger child. In this case a concept from the curriculum—human growth—then is related to a personal event, being photographed as a youngster, that the student finds meaningful.

But teachers can also create bridges between curriculum and students' experiences in another way, by relating the *process* of learning in school with the *process* of learning outside of school. Much of this task involves helping students to make the transition from supervised learning to self-regulated learning—or put differently, from practice that is relatively guided to practice that is relatively independent.

Guided practice

When students first learn a new skill or a new set of ideas, they are especially likely to encounter problems and make mistakes that interfere with the very process of learning. In figuring out how to use a new software program, for example, a student may unknowingly press a wrong button that prevents further functioning of the program. In translating sentences from Spanish into English in language class, for another example, a student might misinterpret one particular word or grammatical feature. This one mistake may cause many sentences to be translated incorrectly, and so on. So students initially need **guided practice**—opportunities to work somewhat independently, but with a teacher or other expert close at hand prevent or fix difficulties when they occur. In general, educational research has found that guided practice helps all learners, but especially those who are struggling (Bryan & Burstein, 2004: Woodward, 2004). A first-grade child has difficulty in decoding printed words, for example, benefits from guidance more than one who can decode easily. But both students benefit in the initial stages of learning, since both may make more mistakes then. Guided practice, by its nature, sends a dual message to students: it is important to learn new material well, but it is also important to become able to use learning *without* assistance, beyond the lesson where it is learned and even beyond the classroom.

Guided practice is much like the concepts of the *zone of proximal development* (or *ZPD*) and *instructional scaffolding* that we discussed in Chapter 2 in connection with Vygotsky's theory of learning. In essence, during guided practice the teacher creates a ZPD or scaffold (or framework) in which the student can accomplish more with partial knowledge or skill than the student could accomplish alone. But whatever its name—guided practice, a ZPD, or a scaffold—insuring success of guidance depends on several key elements: focusing on the task at hand, asking questions that break the task into manageable parts, reframing or restating the task so that it becomes more understandable, and giving frequent feedback about the student's progress (Rogoff, 2003). Combining the elements appropriately takes sensitivity and improvisational skill—even artfulness—but these very challenges are among the true joys of teaching.

Independent practice

As students gain facility with a new skill or new knowledge, they tend to need less guidance and more time to consolidate (or strengthen) their new knowledge with additional practice. Since they are less likely to encounter mistakes or problems at this point, they begin to benefit from **independent practice**—opportunities to review and repeat their knowledge at their own pace and with fewer interruptions. At this point, therefore, guided practice may feel less like help than like an interruption, even if it is well-intentioned. A student who already knows how to use a new computer program, for example, may be frustrated by waiting for the teacher to explain each step of the program individually. If a student is already skillful at translating Spanish sentences into English in a language class, it can be annoying for the teacher to "help" by pointing out minor errors that the student is likely to catch for herself.

By definition, the purpose of independent practice is to provide more self-regulation of learning than what comes from guided practice. It implies a different message for students than what is conveyed by guided practice, a message that goes beyond the earlier one: that it is now time to take more complete responsibility for own learning. When all goes well, independent practice is the eventual outcome of the zone of proximal development created during the earlier phase of guided practice described above: the student can now do on his or her own, what originally required assistance from someone else. Or stated differently, independent practice is a way of encouraging *self-determination* about learning, in the sense that we discussed this idea in Chapter 6. In order to work independently, a student must set his or her own direction and monitor his or her own success; by definition, no one can do this for the student.

Homework

The chances are that you already have experienced many forms of homework in your own educational career. The widespread practice of assigning review work to do outside of school is a way of supplementing scarce time in class and of providing independent practice for students. Homework has generated controversy throughout most of its history in public education, partly because it encroaches on students' personal and family-oriented time, and partly because research finds no consistent benefits of doing homework (Gill & Schlossman, 2004; Kohn, 2004). In spite of these criticisms, though, parents and teachers tend to favor homework when it is used for two main purposes. One purpose is to review and practice material that has already been introduced and practiced at school; a sheet of arithmetic problems might be a classic example. When used for this purpose, the amount of homework is usually minimal in the earliest grades, if any is assigned at all. One educational expert recommends only ten minutes per day in first grade at most, and only gradual increases in amount as students get older (Cooper & Valentine, 2001).

The second purpose for supporting homework is to convey the idea of schoolwork being the "job" of childhood and youth. Just as on an adult job, students must complete homework tasks with minimal supervision and sometimes even minimal training. Doing the tasks, furthermore, is a way to get ahead or further along in the work place (for an adult) or at school (for a child). One study in which researchers interviewed children about these ideas, in fact, found that children do indeed regard homework as work in the same way that adults think of a job (Cornu & Xu, 2004). In the children's minds, homework tasks were not "fun", in spite of teachers' frequent efforts to make them fun. Instead they were jobs that needed doing, much like household chores. When it came to homework, children regarded parents as the teachers' assistants—people merely carrying out the wishes of the teacher. Like any job, the job of doing homework varied in stressfulness; when required at an appropriate amount and level of difficulty, and when children reported having good "bosses" (parents and teachers), the job of homework could actually be satisfying in the way that many adults' jobs can be satisfying when well-done.

Planning for instruction *as well as* for learning

This chapter started with one premise but ended with another. It started with the idea that teachers need to locate curriculum goals, usually from a state department of education or a publisher of a curriculum document. In much of the chapter we described what these authorities provide for individual classroom teachers, and how their documents can be clarified and rendered specific enough for classroom use. In the middle of the chapter, however, the premise shifted. We began noting that instruction cannot be planned simply for students; teachers also need to consider involving students themselves in influencing or even choosing their own goals and ways of reaching the goals. Instructional planning, in other words, should not be just *for* students, but also *by* students, at least to some extent. In the final parts of the chapter we described a number of ways of achieving a reasonable balance between teachers' and students' influence on their learning. We suggested considering relatively strong measures, such as an emergent or an anti-bias curriculum, but we also considered more moderate ones, like the use of the Internet, of local experts and field trips, of service learning, and of guided and independent practice. All things considered, then, teachers' planning is not just about organizing teaching; it is also about facilitating learning. Its dual purpose is evident in many features of public education, including the one we discuss in the next two chapters, the assessment of learning.

Chapter summary

In the United States, broad educational goals for most subject areas are published by many national professional associations and by all state departments of education. Usually the state departments of education also publish curriculum framework or curriculum guides that offer somewhat more specific explanations of educational goals, and how they might be taught.

Transforming the goals into specific learning objectives, however, remains a responsibility of the teacher. The formulation can focus on curriculum topics that can analyzed into specific activities, or it can focus on specific behaviors expected of students and assembled into general types of outcomes. Taxonomies of educational objectives, such as the ones originated by Benjamin Bloom, are a useful tool with either approach to instructional planning.

In addition to planning instruction on students' behalf, many teachers organize instruction so that students themselves can influence the choice of goals. One way to do so is through emergent curriculum; another way is through multicultural and anti-bias curriculum.

Whatever planning strategies are used, learning is enhanced by using a wide variety of resources, including the Internet, local experts, field trips, and service learning, among others. It is also enhanced if the teacher can build bridges between curriculum goals and students' experiences through judicious use of modeling, activation of prior knowledge, anticipation of students' preconceptions, and an appropriate blend of guided and independent practice.

Key terms
Affective objectives
Anti-bias education
Bloom's taxonomy
Content integration
Curriculum framework
Curriculum guide

Educational goals

Emergent curriculum

Equity pedagogy

Guided practice

Independent practice

Indicators

Instructional planning

Learning commons

Learning objectives

Modeling as demonstration

Modeling as simplified representation

Multicultural education

National standards

Psychomotor objectives

Scope and sequence

Service learning

State standards

Taxonomy of educational objectives

On the Internet

<http://med.fsu.edu/education/FacultyDevelopment/objectives.asp>

<http://www.adprima.com/objectives.htm>

These are two of *many* websites that explains what behavioral objectives are, and how to write them. They give more detail than is possible in this chapter.

<http://www.adl.org/tools_teachers/tips_antibias_ed.asp> This page is part of the website for the Anti-Defamation League of America, an organization dedicated to eliminating racial and ethnic bias throughout society. This particular page explains the concept of anti-bias education, but it also has links to pages that contain tips for teachers dealing with racial and ethnic bias.

<http://education-world.com/standards> This website contains links to educational standards documents written by every major state department of education and a number of national and professional associations. It covers all of the major subjects commonly taught in public schools.

References

Anderson, L. & Krathwohl, D. (2001). *A taxonomy for learning, teaching, and assessing*. New York: Longman.

Bandura, A. (2002). Social cognitive theory in cultural context. *Journal of Applied Psychology: An International Review, 51,* 269-290.

Banks, C. & Banks, J. (1995). Equity pedagogy: An essential component of multicultural education. *Theory into Practice, 34*(3), 152-158.

Banks, J. & Banks, C. (2005). *Multicultural education: Issues and perspectives, 5ᵗʰ edition*. New York: Wiley.

Beagle, D. Bailey, R., & Tierney, B. (2004). *The information commons handbook*. New York: Neal-Shuman Publishers.

Bloom, B. (1956). *Taxonomy of educational objectives*. New York: David McKay Publishers.

Brumfiel, G. (2005). Intelligent design: Who has designs on your students' minds? *Nature, 434,* 1062-1065.

Bryan, T. & Burstein, K. (2004). Improving homework completion and academic performance: Lessons from special education. *Theory into Practice, 43*(3), 213-219.

Buchanan, A., Baldwin, S., & Rudisill, M. (2002). Service learning as scholarship in teacher education. *Educational Researcher 32*(8), 28-34.

Chi, M. (2005). Commonsense conceptions of emergent processes: Why some misconceptions are robust. *Journal of the Learning Sciences, 14*(2), 161-199.

Chiu, M. & Lin, J. (2005). Promoting 4th-graders' conceptual change of their understanding of electrical current via multiple analogies. *Journal of Research in Science Teaching, 42*(4), 429-464.

Clark, D. (2006). Longitudinal conceptual change in students' understanding of thermal equilibrium: An examination of the process of conceptual restructuring. *Cognition and Instruction, 24*(4), 467-563.

Clark, K. (2006). Computer Based Virtual Field Trips in the K-12 Classroom. In C. Crawford et al. (Eds.), *Proceedings of Society for Information Technology and Teacher Education International Conference 2006,* pp. 3974-3980. Chesapeake, VA: AACE.

Cooper, H. & Valentine, J. (2001). Using research to answer practical questions about homework. *Educational Psychology, 36*(3), 143-153.

Corno, L. & Xu, J. (2004). Homework as the job of childhood. *Theory into Practice, 43*(3), 227-233.

Crow, C. (2005). *Multicultural education: Equity pedagogy on perspectives and practices of secondary teachers.* Unpublished doctoral dissertation. Waco, TX: Baylor University.

Curriculum Development and Supplemental materials Commission. (1999).

Reading/Language Arts Framework for California Public Schools. Sacramento, CA:

California Department of Education.

Derman-Sparks, L. (1994). Empowering children to create a caring culture in a world of differences. *Childhood Education, 70,* 66-71.

Dicklitch, S. (2005). Human rights—human wrongs: Making political science real through service-learning. In D. Butin (Ed.), *Service-learning in higher education: Critical issues and directions, pp. xxx-yyy.* New York: Palgrave Macmillan.

Egan, K. (2005). *An imaginative approach to teaching.* San Francisco: Jossey-Bass.

Gibson, S. (2004). Social learning (cognitive) theory and implications for human resources development. *Advances in Developing Human Resources, 6*(2), 192-210.

Gill, B. & Schlossman, S. (2004). Villain or savior? The American discourse on homework, 1850-2003. *Theory into practice, 43*(3), 174-181.

Gronlund, N. (2004). *Writing instructional objectives for teaching and assessment, 6th edition.* Upper Saddle River, NJ: Pearson.

Gulitt, J., Renkl, A., Motes, M., & Hauser, S. (2006). How can we use concept maps for prior knowledge activation? *Proceedings of the 7th International Conference on Learning Sciences,* 217-220.

Haas, L. & Robertson, J. (Eds). (2004). *The information commons.* Washington, D.C.: Association of Research Libraries.

Harrow, A. (1972). *A taxonomy of the psychomotor domain.* New York: David McKay.

Hawkins, J. (2006). Accessing multicultural issues through critical thinking, critical inquiry, and the student research process. *Urban Education, 41*(2), 169-141.

Haywood, K. & Getchell, N. (2005). *Life span motor development, 4th edition.* Champaign, IL: Human Kinetics Press.

Hyde, J. & Lynn, M. (2006). Gender similarities in mathematics and science. *Science, 314*(5799), 599-600.

Jacobson, T. (2003). *Confronting out discomfort: Clearing the way for anti-bias in early childhood.* Portsmouth, NH: Heinemann.

Johnson, B. & O'Grady, C. (Eds.). (2006). *The spirit of service: Exploring faith, service, and social justice in higher education.* Bolton, MA: Anker Publishers.

Jones, S., Gilbride-Brown, J., & Gasiorski, A. (2005). Getting inside the "underside" of service-learning: Student resistance and possibilities. In D. Butin (Ed.), *Service-learning in higher education: Critical issues and directions, pp. xxx-yyy.* New York: Palgrave Macmillan.

Kohn, A. (1999). *The schools our children deserve.* Boston: Houghton Mifflin.

Kohn, A. (2004). Challenging students, and how to have more of them. *Phi Delta Kappan,86*(3), 184-194.

Lester, P. & Ross, S. (2003). *Images that injure: Pictorial stereotypes in the media.* Westport, CT: Praeger.

Mager, R. (2005). *Preparing instructional objectives, 3rd edition.* Atlanta, GA: Center for Effective Performance.

Marzano, R. (2006). *Designing a new taxonomy of educational objectives.* Thousand Oaks, CA: Corwin Books.

Notar, C., Wilson, J., Yunker, B., & Zuelke, D. (2004). The table of specifications: Insuring accountability in teacher-made tests. *Journal of Instructional Psychology, 31*(3).

Ohio Department of Education. (2003). *Academic Content Standards.* Columbus, Ohio: Author.

Owens, C. (2003). Nonsense, sense and science: Misconceptions and illustrated trade books. *Journal of children's literature, 29*(1), 55-62.

Parsad, B. & Jones, J. (2005). *Internet access in U.S. public schools and classrooms: 1994-2003.* Washington, D.C.: United States Department of Education, National Center for Education Statistics.

Perkins, D. & Mebert, C. (2005). Efficacy of multicultural education for preschool children. *Journal of Cross-Cultural Psychology, 36*(4), 497-512.

Peterson, E. (2002). *A practical guide to early childhood curriculum: Linking thematic, emergent, and skill-based planning to children's outcomes, 2nd edition.* Boston: Allyn & Bacon.

Popham, J. (2002). *What every teacher should know about educational assessment.* Upper Saddle River, NJ: Pearson.

Ragains, P. (2006). *Information literacy instruction that works.* New York: Neal-Schuman Publishers.

Rebellon, C. (2006). Do adolescents engage in delinquency to attract the social attention of peers? An extension and longitudinal test of the social reinforcement hypothesis. *Journal of Research in Crime and Delinquency, 43*(4), 387-411.

Riley, R. (2002). Education reform through standards and partnerships, 1993-2000. *Phi Delta Kappan, 83*(9), 700-707.

Rogoff, B. (2003). *Cultural nature of human development,* Chapter 7, "Thinking with the tools and institutions of culture," pp. 236-281.

Seitz, H. (2006). The plan: building on children's interests. *Young Children, 61*(2), 36-41.

Skinner, H., Biscope, S., & Poland, B. (2003). *Quality of Internet access: Barriers behind Internet use statistics, 57*(5), 875-880.

Slotta, J. & Chi, M. (2006). Helping students understand challenging topics in science through ontology training. *Cognition and Instruction, 24*(2), 261-289.

Tanner, K. & Allen, D. (2005). Approaches to biology teaching and learning—understanding the wrong answers: Teaching toward conceptual change. *Cell Biology Education, 4,* 112-117.

Thomsen, K. (2006). *Service-learning in grades K-8: Experiential learning that builds character and motivation.* Thousand Oaks, CA: Corwin.

Vartuli, S. & Rohs, J. (2006). Conceptual organizers of early childhood curriculum content. *Early Childhood Education Journal, 33*(4), 231-237.

Vavrus, M. (2002). *Transforming the multicultural education of teachers.* New York: Teachers' College Press.

Woodward, J. (2004). Mathematics education in the United States: Past to present *Journal of Learning Disabilities, 37,* pp. 16-31.

Wurm, J. (2005). *Working in the Reggio way.* St. Paul, MN: Redleaf Press.

11. Teacher-made assessment strategies

Kym teaches sixth grade students in an urban school where most of the families in the community live below the poverty line. Each year the majority of the students in her school fail the state-wide tests. Kym follows school district teaching guides and typically uses direct instruction in her Language Arts and Social Studies classes. The classroom assessments are designed to mirror those on the state-wide tests so the students become familiar with the assessment format. When Kym is in a graduate summer course on motivation she reads an article called, "Teaching strategies that honor and motivate inner-city African American students" (Teel, Debrin-Parecki, & Covington, 1998) and she decides to change her instruction and assessment in fall in four ways. First, she stresses an incremental approach to ability focusing on effort and allows students to revise their work several times until the criteria are met. Second, she gives students choices in performance assessments (e.g. oral presentation, art project, creative writing). Third, she encourages responsibility by asking students to assist in classroom tasks such as setting up video equipment, handing out papers etc. Fourth, she validates student' cultural heritage by encouraging them to read biographies and historical fiction from their own cultural backgrounds. Kym reports that the changes in her students' effort and demeanor in class are dramatic: students are more enthusiastic, work harder, and produce better products. At the end of the year twice as many of her students pass the State-wide test than the previous year.

Afterward. Kym still teaches sixth grade in the same school district and continues to modify the strategies described above. Even though the performance of the students she taught improved the school was closed because, on average, the students' performance was poor. Kym gained a Ph.D and teaches Educational Psychology to preservice and inservice teachers in evening classes.

Kym's story illustrates several themes related to assessment that we explore in this chapter on teacher-made assessment strategies and in the Chapter 12 on standardized testing. First, choosing effective classroom assessments is related to instructional practices, beliefs about motivation, and the presence of state-wide standardized testing. Second, some teacher-made classroom assessments enhance student learning and motivation —some do not. Third, teachers can improve their teaching through action research. This involves identifying a problem (e.g. low motivation and achievement), learning about alternative approaches (e.g. reading the literature), implementing the new approaches, observing the results (e.g. students' effort and test results), and continuing to modify the strategies based on their observations.

Best practices in assessing student learning have undergone dramatic changes in the last 20 years. When Rosemary was a mathematics teacher in the 1970s, she did not *assess* students' learning she *tested* them on the mathematics knowledge and skills she taught during the previous weeks. The tests varied little format and students always did them individually with pencil and paper. Many teachers, including mathematics teachers, now use a wide variety of methods to determine what their students have learned and also use this assessment information to modify their instruction. In this chapter the focus is on using classroom assessments to improve student learning and we begin with some basic concepts.

Basic concepts

Assessment is an integrated process of *gaining information* about students' learning and *making value judgments* about their progress (Linn & Miller, 2005). Information about students' progress can be obtained from a variety of sources including projects, portfolios, performances, observations, and tests. The information about students' learning is often assigned specific numbers or grades and this involves **measurement.** Measurement answers the question, "How much?" and is used most commonly when the teacher scores a test or product and assigns numbers (e.g. 28 /30 on the biology test; 90/100 on the science project). *Evaluation* is the process of making judgments about the assessment information (Airasian, 2005). These judgments may be about individual students (e.g. should Jacob's course grade take into account his significant improvement over the grading period?), the assessment method used (e.g. is the multiple choice test a useful way to obtain information about problem solving), or one's own teaching (e.g. most of the students this year did much better on the essay assignment than last year so my new teaching methods seem effective).

The primary focus in this chapter is on **assessment *for* learning,** where the priority is designing and using assessment strategies to enhance student learning and development. Assessment for learning is often **formative assessment,** i.e. it takes place during the course of instruction by providing information that teachers can use to revise their teaching and students can use to improve their learning (Black, Harrison, Lee, Marshall & Wiliam, 2004). Formative assessment includes both **informal assessment** involving spontaneous unsystematic observations of students' behaviors (e.g. during a question and answer session or while the students are working on an assignment) and **formal assessment** involving pre-planned, systematic gathering of data. **Assessment *of* learning** is formal assessment that involves assessing students in order to certify their competence and fulfill accountability mandates and is the primary focus of the next chapter on standardized tests but is also considered in this chapter. Assessment of learning is typically **summative,** that is, administered after the instruction is completed (e.g. a final examination in an educational psychology course). Summative assessments provide information about how well students mastered the material, whether students are ready for the next unit, and what grades should be given (Airasian, 2005).

Assessment for learning: an overview of the process

Using assessment to advance students' learning not just check on learning requires viewing assessment as a process that is integral to the all phases of teaching including planning, classroom interactions and instruction, communication with parents, and self-reflection (Stiggins, 2002). Essential steps in assessment for learning include:

Step 1: Having clear instructional goals and communicating them to students

In the previous chapter we documented the importance of teachers thinking carefully about the purposes of each lesson and unit. This may be hard for beginning teachers. For example, Vanessa, a middle school social studies teacher, might say that the goal of her next unit is: "Students will learn about the Cvil War." Clearer goals require that Vanessa decides what it is about the US Civil War she wants her students to learn, e.g. the dates and names of battles, the causes of the US Civil War, the differing perspectives of those living in the North and the South, or the day-to-day experiences of soldiers fighting in the war. Vanessa cannot devise appropriate assessments of her students' learning about the US Civil War until she is clear about her own purposes.

For effective teaching Vanessa also needs to communicate clearly the goals and objectives to her students so they know what is important for them to learn. No matter how thorough a teacher's planning has been, if students do not know what they are supposed to learn they will not learn as much. Because communication is so important to teachers a specific chapter is devoted to this topic (Chapter 8), and so communication is not considered in any detail in this chapter.

Step 2: Selecting appropriate assessment techniques

Selecting and administrating assessment techniques that are appropriate for the goals of instruction as well as the developmental level of the students are crucial components of effective assessment for learning. Teachers need to know the characteristics of a wide variety of classroom assessment techniques and how these techniques can be adapted for various content, skills, and student characteristics. They also should understand the role reliability, validity, and the absence of bias should play is choosing and using assessment techniques. Much of this chapter focuses on this information.

Step 3: Using assessment to enhance motivation and confidence

Students' motivation and confidence is influenced by the type of assessment used as well as the feedback given about the assessment results. Consider, Samantha a college student who takes a history class in which the professor's lectures and text book focus on really interesting major themes. However, the assessments are all multiple choice tests that ask about facts and Samantha, who initially enjoys the classes and readings, becomes angry, loses confidence she can do well, and begins to spend less time on the class material. In contrast, some instructors have observed that that many students in educational psychology classes like the one you are now taking will work harder on assessments that are case studies rather than more traditional exams or essays. The type of feedback provided to students is also important and we elaborate on these ideas later in this chapter.

Step 4: Adjusting instruction based on information

An essential component of assessment *for* learning is that the teacher uses the information gained from assessment to adjust instruction. These adjustments occur in the middle of a lesson when a teacher may decide that students' responses to questions indicate sufficient understanding to introduce a new topic, or that her observations of students' behavior indicates that they do not understand the assignment and so need further explanation. Adjustments also occur when the teacher reflects on the instruction after the lesson is over and is planning for the next day. We provide examples of adjusting instruction in this chapter and consider teacher reflection in more detail in Appendix C..

Step 5: Communicating with parents and guardians

Students' learning and development is enhanced when teachers communicate with parents regularly about their children's performance. Teachers communicate with parents in a variety of ways including newsletters, telephone conversations, email, school district websites and parent-teachers conferences. Effective communication requires that teachers can clearly explain the purpose and characteristics of the assessment as well as the meaning of students' performance. This requires a thorough knowledge of the types and purposes of teacher made and standardized assessments (this chapter and Chapter 12) and well as clear communication skills (Chapter 8).

We now consider each step in the process of assessment for learning in more detail. In order to be able to select and administer appropriate assessment techniques teachers need to know about the variety of techniques that can be used as well as what factors ensure that the assessment techniques are high quality. We begin by considering high quality assessments.

Selecting appropriate assessment techniques I: high quality assessments

For an assessment to be high quality it needs to have good validity and reliability as well as absence from bias.

Validity

Validity is the evaluation of the "adequacy and appropriateness of the interpretations and uses of assessment results" for a given group of individuals (Linn & Miller, 2005, p. 68). For example, is it appropriate to conclude that the results of a mathematics test on fractions given to recent immigrants accurately represents their understanding of fractions? Is it appropriate for the teacher to conclude, based on her observations, that a kindergarten student, Jasmine, has Attention Deficit Disorder because she does not follow the teachers oral instructions? Obviously in each situation other interpretations are possible that the immigrant students have poor English skills rather than mathematics skills, or that Jasmine may be hearing impaired.

It is important to understand that validity refers to the *interpretation and uses made of the results* of an assessment procedure not of the assessment procedure itself. For example, making judgments about the results of the same test on fractions may be valid if the students all understand English well. A teacher concluding from her observations that the kindergarten student has Attention Deficit Disorder (ADD) may be appropriate if the student has been screened for hearing and other disorders (although the classification of a disorder like ADD cannot be made by one teacher). Validity involves making an overall judgment of the degree to which the interpretations and uses of the assessment results are justified. Validity is a matter of degree (e.g. high, moderate, or low validity) rather than all-or none (e.g. totally valid vs invalid) (Linn & Miller, 2005).

Three sources of evidence are considered when assessing validity—content, construct and predictive. **Content validity** evidence is associated with the question: How well does the assessment include the content or tasks it is supposed to? For example, suppose your educational psychology instructor devises a mid-term test and tells you this includes chapters one to seven in the text book. Obviously, all the items in test should be based on the content from educational psychology, not your methods or cultural foundations classes. Also, the items in the test should cover content from all seven chapters and not just chapters three to seven—unless the instructor tells you that these chapters have priority.

Teachers' have to be clear about their purposes and priorities for instruction *before* they can begin to gather evidence related content validity. Content validation determines the degree that assessment tasks are relevant and representative of the tasks judged by the teacher (or test developer) to represent their goals and objectives (Linn & Miller, 2005). It is important for teachers to think about content validation when devising assessment tasks and one way to help do this is to devise a Table of Specifications. An example, based on Pennsylvania's State standards for grade 3 geography, is in . In the left hand column is the instructional content for a 20-item test the teacher has decided to construct with two kinds of instructional objectives: identification and uses or locates. The second and third columns identify the number of items for each content area and each instructional objective. Notice that the teacher has decided that six items should be devoted to the sub area of geographic representations- more than any other sub area. Devising a table of specifications helps teachers determine if some content areas or concepts are over-sampled (i.e. there are too many items) and some concepts are under-sampled (i.e. there are too few items).

Table 35: Example of Table of Specifications: grade 3 basic geography literacy

Content	Instructional objective		Total number of items	Per cent of items
	Identifies	Uses or locates		
Identify geography tools and their uses				
Geographic representations: e.g. maps, globe, diagrams and photographs	3	3	6	30%
Spatial information: sketch & thematic maps	1	1	2	10%
Mental maps	1	1	2	10%
Identify and locate places and regions				
Physical features (e.g. lakes, continents)	1	2	3	15%
Human features (countries, states, cities)	3	2	5	25%
Regions with unifying geographic characteristics e.g. river basins	1	1	2	10%
Number of items	10	10	20	
Percentage of items	50%	50%		100%

Construct validity evidence is more complex than content validity evidence. Often we are interested in making broader judgments about student's performances than specific skills such as doing fractions. The focus may be on constructs such as mathematical reasoning or reading comprehension. A construct is a characteristic of a person we assume exists to help explain behavior. For example, we use the concept of test anxiety to explain why some individuals when taking a test have difficulty concentrating, have physiological reactions such as sweating, and perform poorly on tests but not in class assignments. Similarly mathematics reasoning and reading comprehension are constructs as we use them to help explain performance on an assessment. Construct validation is the process of determining the extent to which performance on an assessment can be interpreted in terms of the intended constructs and is not influenced by factors irrelevant to the construct. For example, judgments about recent immigrants' performance on a mathematical reasoning test administered in English will have low construct validity if the results are influenced by English language skills that are irrelevant to mathematical problem solving. Similarly, construct validity of end-of-semester examinations is likely to be poor for those students who are highly anxious when taking major tests but not during regular class periods or when doing assignments. Teachers can help increase construct validity by trying to reduce factors that influence performance but are irrelevant to the construct being assessed. These factors include anxiety, English language skills, and reading speed (Linn & Miller 2005).

A third form of validity evidence is called **criterion-related validity.** Selective colleges in the USA use the ACT or SAT among other criteria to choose who will be admitted because these standardized tests help predict freshman grades, i.e. have high criterion-related validity. Some K-12 schools give students math or reading tests in the fall semester in order to predict which are likely to do well on the annual state tests administered in the spring semester and which students are unlikely to pass the tests and will need additional assistance. If the tests administered in fall do not predict students' performances accurately then the additional assistance may be given to the wrong students illustrating the importance of criterion-related validity.

Reliability

Reliability refers to the consistency of the measurement (Linn & Miller 2005). Suppose Mr Garcia is teaching a unit on food chemistry in his tenth grade class and gives an assessment at the end of the unit using test items from the teachers' guide. Reliability is related to questions such as: How similar would the scores of the students be if they had taken the assessment on a Friday or Monday? Would the scores have varied if Mr Garcia had selected different test items, or if a different teacher had graded the test? An assessment provides information about students by using a specific measure of performance at one particular time. Unless the results from the assessment are reasonably consistent over different occasions, different raters, or different tasks (in the same content domain) confidence in the results will be low and so cannot be useful in improving student learning.

Obviously we cannot expect perfect consistency. Students' memory, attention, fatigue, effort, and anxiety fluctuate and so influence performance. Even trained raters vary somewhat when grading assessment such as essays, a science project, or an oral presentation. Also, the wording and design of specific items influence students' performances. However, some assessments are more reliable than others and there are several strategies teachers can use to increase reliability

First, assessments with more tasks or items typically have higher reliability. To understand this, consider two tests one with five items and one with 50 items. Chance factors influence the shorter test more then the longer test. If a student does not understand one of the items in the first test the total score is very highly influenced (it would be reduced by 20 per cent). In contrast, if there was one item in the test with 50 items that were confusing, the total score would be influenced much less (by only 2 percent). Obviously this does not mean that assessments should be inordinately long, but, on average, enough tasks should be included to reduce the influence of chance variations. Second, clear directions and tasks help increase reliability. If the directions or wording of specific tasks or items are unclear, then students have to guess what they mean undermining the accuracy of their results. Third, clear scoring criteria are crucial in ensuring high reliability (Linn & Miller, 2005). Later in this chapter we describe strategies for developing scoring criteria for a variety of types of assessment.

Absence of bias

Bias occurs in assessment when there are components in the assessment method or administration of the assessment that distort the performance of the student because of their personal characteristics such as gender, ethnicity, or social class (Popham, 2005). Two types of assessment bias are important: *offensiveness* and *unfair penalization.* An assessment is most likely to be offensive to a subgroup of students when negative stereotypes are included in the test. For example, the assessment in a health class could include items in which all the doctors were men and all the nurses were women. Or, a series of questions in a social studies class could portray Latinos and Asians as immigrants rather than native born Americans. In these examples, some female, Latino or Asian students are likely to be offended by the stereotypes and this can distract them from performing well on the assessment.

Unfair penalization occurs when items disadvantage one group not because they may be offensive but because of differential background experiences. For example, an item for math assessment that assumes knowledge of a particular sport may disadvantage groups not as familiar with that sport (e.g. American football for recent immigrants). Or an assessment on team work that asks students to model their concept of a team on a symphony orchestra is likely to be easier for those students who have attended orchestra performances—probably students from affluent families. Unfair penalization does not occur just because some students do poorly in class. For example, asking questions about a specific sport in a physical education class when information on that sport had been discussed in class is not unfair penalization as long as the questions do not require knowledge beyond that taught in class that some groups are less likely to have.

It can be difficult for new teachers teaching in multi-ethnic classrooms to devise interesting assessments that do not penalize any groups of students. Teachers need to think seriously about the impact of students' differing backgrounds on the assessment they use in class. Listening carefully to what students say is important as is learning about the backgrounds of the students.

Selecting appropriate assessment techniques II: types of teacher-made assessments

One of the challenges for beginning teachers is to select and use appropriate assessment techniques. In this section we summarize the wide variety of types of assessments that classroom teachers use. First we discuss the informal techniques teachers use during instruction that typically require instantaneous decisions. Then we consider formal assessment techniques that teachers plan before instruction and allow for reflective decisions.

Teachers' observation, questioning, and record keeping

During teaching, teachers not only have to communicate the information they planned but also continuously monitor students' learning and motivation in order to determine whether modifications have to be made (Airasian, 2005). Beginning teachers find this more difficult than experienced teachers because of the complex cognitive skills required to improvise and be responsive to students needs while simultaneously keeping in mind the goals and plans of the lesson (Borko & Livingston, 1989). The informal assessment strategies teachers most often use during instruction are *observation* and *questioning.*

Observation

Effective teachers observe their students from the time they enter the classroom. Some teachers greet their students at the door not only to welcome them but also to observe their mood and motivation. Are Hannah and Naomi still not talking to each other? Does Ethan have his materials with him? Gaining information on such questions can help the teacher foster student learning more effectively (e.g. suggesting Ethan goes back to his locker to get his materials before the bell rings or avoiding assigning Hannah and Naomi to the same group).

During instruction, teachers observe students' behavior to gain information about students' level of interest and understanding of the material or activity. Observation includes looking at non-verbal behaviors as well as listening to what the students are saying. For example, a teacher may observe that a number of students are looking out of the window rather than watching the science demonstration, or a teacher may hear students making comments in their group indicating they do not understand what they are supposed to be doing. Observations also help teachers decide which student to call on next, whether to speed up or slow down the pace of the lesson, when more examples are needed, whether to begin or end an activity, how well students are performing a physical activity, and if there are potential behavior problems (Airasian, 2005). Many teachers find that moving around the classroom helps them observe more effectively because they can see more students from a variety of perspectives. However, the fast pace and complexity of most classrooms makes it difficult for teachers to gain as much information as they want.

Questioning

Teachers ask questions for many instructional reasons including keeping students' attention on the lesson, highlighting important points and ideas, promoting critical thinking, allowing students' to learn from each others answers, and providing information about students' learning. Devising good appropriate questions and using students' responses to make effective instantaneous instructional decisions is very difficult. Some strategies to improve questioning include planning and writing down the instructional questions that will be asked, allowing sufficient wait time for students to respond, listening carefully to what students say rather than listening for what is expected, varying the types of questions asked, making sure some of the questions are higher level, and asking follow-up questions.

While the informal assessment based on spontaneous observation and questioning is essential for teaching there are inherent problems with the validity, reliability and bias in this information (Airasian, 2005; Stiggins 2005). We summarize these issues and some ways to reduce the problems in Table 35.

Table 36: Validity and reliability of observation and questioning

Problem	Strategies to alleviate problem
Teachers lack of objectivity about overall class involvement and understanding	Try to make sure you are not only seeing what you want to see. Teachers typically want to feel good about their instruction so it is easy to look for positive student interactions. Occasionally, teachers want to see negative student reactions to confirm their beliefs about an individual student or class.
Tendency to focus on process rather than learning	Remember to concentrate on student learning not just involvement. Most of teachers' observations focus on process—student attention, facial expressions posture—rather than pupil learning. Students can be active and engaged but not developing new skills.
Limited information and selective sampling	Make sure you observe a variety of students—not just those who are typically very good or very bad.

	Walk around the room to observe more students "up close" and view the room from multiple perspectives. Call on a wide variety of students—not just those with their hands up, or those who are skilled as the subject, or those who sit in a particular place in the room. Keep records
Fast pace of classrooms inhibits corroborative evidence	If you want to know if you are missing important information ask a peer to visit your classroom and observe the students' behaviors. Classrooms are complex and fast paced and one teacher cannot see much of what is going on while trying to also teach.
Cultural and individual differences in the meaning of verbal and non verbal behaviors	Be cautious in the conclusions that you draw from your observations and questions. Remember that the meaning and expectations of certain types of questions, wait time, social distance, and role of "small talk" varies across cultures (Chapter 4). Some students are quiet because of their personalities not because they are uninvolved, nor keeping up with the lesson, nor depressed or tired.

Record keeping

Keeping records of observations improves reliability and can be used to enhance understanding of one student, a group, or the whole class' interactions. Sometimes this requires help from other teachers. For example, Alexis, a beginning science teacher is aware of the research documenting that longer wait time enhances students' learning (e.g. Rowe, 2003) but is unsure of her behaviors so she asks a colleague to observe and record her wait times during one class period. Alexis learns her wait times are very short for all students so she starts practicing silently counting to five whenever she asks students a question.

Teachers can keep *anecdotal records* about students without help from peers. These records contain descriptions of incidents of a student's behavior, the time and place the incident takes place, and a tentative interpretation of the incident. For example, the description of the incident might involve Joseph, a second grade student, who fell asleep during the mathematics class on a Monday morning. A tentative interpretation could be the student did not get enough sleep over the weekend, but alternative explanations could be the student is sick or is on medications that make him drowsy. Obviously additional information is needed and the teacher could ask Joseph why he is so sleepy and also observe him to see if he looks tired and sleepy over the next couple of weeks.

Anecdotal records often provide important information and are better than relying on one's memory but they take time to maintain and it is difficult for teachers to be objective. For example, after seeing Joseph fall asleep the teacher may now look for any signs of Joseph's sleepiness—ignoring the days he is not sleepy. Also, it is hard for teachers to sample a wide enough range of data for their observations to be highly reliable.

Teachers also conduct more *formal observations* especially for students with special needs who have IEP's. An example of the importance of informal and formal observations in a preschool follows:

The class of preschoolers in a suburban neighborhood of a large city has eight special needs students and four students—the peer models—who have been selected because of their well developed language and social skills. Some of the special needs students have been diagnosed with delayed language, some with behavior disorders, and several with autism. The students are sitting on the mat with the teacher who has a box with sets of three "cool" things of varying size (e.g. toy pandas) and the students are asked to put the things in order by size, big, medium and small. Students who are able are also requested to point to each item in turn and say "This is the big one", "This is the medium one" and "This is the little one". For some students, only two choices (big and little) are offered because that is appropriate for their developmental level. The teacher informally observes that one of the boys is having trouble keeping his legs still so she quietly asks the aid for a weighted pad that she places on the boy's legs to help him keep them still. The activity continues and the aide carefully observes students behaviors and records on IEP progress cards whether a child meets specific objectives such as: "When given two picture or object choices, Mark will point to the appropriate object in 80 per cent of the opportunities." The teacher and aides keep records of the relevant behavior of the special needs students during the half day they are in preschool. The daily records are summarized weekly. If there are not enough observations that have been recorded for a specific objective, the teacher and aide focus their observations more on that child, and if necessary, try to create specific situations that relate to that objective. At end of each month the teacher calculates whether the special needs children are meeting their IEP objectives.

Selected response items

Common formal assessment formats used by teachers are *multiple choice, matching,* and *true/false items.* In selected response items students have to select a response provided by the teacher or test developer rather than constructing a response in their own words or actions. Selected response items do not require that students *recall* the information but rather *recognize* the correct answer. Tests with these items are called *objective* because the results are not influenced by scorers' judgments or interpretations and so are often machine scored. Eliminating potential errors in scoring increases the reliability of tests but teachers who only use objective tests are liable to reduce the validity of their assessment because objective tests are not appropriate for all learning goals (Linn & Miller, 2005). Effective assessment *for* learning as well as assessment *of* learning must be based on aligning the assessment technique to the learning goals and outcomes.

For example, if the goal is for students to conduct an experiment then they should be asked to do that rather that than being asked *about* conducting an experiment.

Common problems

Selected response items are easy to score but are hard to devise. Teachers often do not spend enough time constructing items and common problems include:

1. Unclear wording in the items

    - *True or False:* Although George Washington was born into a wealthy family, his father died when he was only 11, he worked as a youth as a surveyor of rural lands, and later stood on the balcony of Federal Hall in New York when he took his oath of office in 1789.

2.   Cues that are not related the content being examined.

- A common clue is that all the true statements on a true/false test or the corrective alternatives on a multiple choice test are longer than the untrue statements or the incorrect alternatives.

3.   Using negatives (or double negatives) the items.

- A poor item. "True or False: None of the steps made by the student was unnecessary."

- A better item. True or False: "All of the steps were necessary."

Students often do not notice the negative terms or find them confusing so avoiding them is generally recommended (Linn & Miller 2005). However, since standardized tests often use negative items, teachers sometimes deliberately include some negative items to give students practice in responding to that format.

4.   Taking sentences directly from textbook or lecture notes.

Removing the words from their context often makes them ambiguous or can change the meaning. For example, a statement from Chapter 3 taken out of context suggests all children are clumsy. "Similarly with jumping, throwing and catching: the large majority of children can do these things, though often a bit clumsily." A fuller quotation makes it clearer that this sentence refers to 5-year-olds: For some fives, running still looks a bit like a hurried walk, but usually it becomes more coordinated within a year or two. Similarly with jumping, throwing and catching: the large majority of children can do these things, though often a bit clumsily, by the time they start school, and most improve their skills noticeably during the early elementary years." If the abbreviated form was used as the stem in a true/false item it would obviously be misleading.

5.   Avoid trivial questions

e.g. Jean Piaget was born in what year?

- a) 1896

- b) 1900

- c) 1880

- d) 1903

While it important to know approximately when Piaget made his seminal contributions to the understanding of child development, the exact year of his birth (1880) is not important.

Strengths and weaknesses

All types of selected response items have a number of strengths and weaknesses. *True/False* items are appropriate for measuring factual knowledge such as vocabulary, formulae, dates, proper names, and technical terms. They are very efficient as they use a simple structure that students can easily understand, and take little time to complete. They are also easier to construct than multiple choice and matching items. However, students have a 50 per cent probability of getting the answer correct through guessing so it can be difficult to interpret how much students know from their test scores. Examples of common problems that arise when devising true/false items are in Table 37.

11. Teacher-made assessment strategies

Table 37: Common errors in selected response items

Type of item	Common errors	Example
True False	The statement is not absolutely true—typically because it contains a broad generalization.	T F The President of the United States is elected to that office. This is usually true but the US Vice President can succeed the President.
	The item is opinion not fact .	T F Education for K-12 students is improved though policies that support charter schools. Some people believe this, some do not.
	Two ideas are included in item	T F George H Bush the 40th president of the US was defeated by William Jefferson Clinton in 1992. *The 1st idea is false; the 2nd is true making it difficult for students to decide whether to circle T or F.*
	Irrelevant cues	T F The President of the United States is usually elected to that office. True items contain the words such as usually generally; whereas false items contain the terms such as always, all, never.
Matching	Columns do not contain homogeneous information	Directions: On the line to the US Civil War Battle write the year or confederate general in Column B. Column A Column B Ft Sumter General Stonewall Jackson 2nd Battle of Bull Run General Johnson Ft Henry 1861 1862 Column B is a mixture of generals and dates.
	Too many items in each list	Lists should be relatively short (4 – 7) in each column. More than 10 are too confusing.
	Responses are not in logical order	In the example with Spanish and English words should be in a logical order (they are alphabetical). If the order is not logical, student spend too much time searching for the correct answer.

Multiple Choice	Problem (i.e. the stem) is not clearly stated problem	New Zealand a) Is the worlds' smallest continent b) Is home to the kangaroo c) Was settled mainly by colonists from Great Britain d) Is a dictatorship This is really a series of true-false items. Because the correct answer is c) a better version with the problem in the stem is Much of New Zealand was settled by colonists from a) Great Britain b) Spain c) France d) Holland
	Some of the alternatives are not plausible	Who is best known for their work on the development of the morality of justice. 1. Gerald Ford 2. Vygotsky 3. Maslow 4. Kohlberg Obviously Gerald Ford is not a plausible alternative.
	Irrelevant cues	1. Correct alternative is longer 2. Incorrect alternatives are not grammatically correct with the stem 3. Too many correct alternatives are in position "b" or "c" making it easier for students to guess. All the options (e.g. a, b, c, d) should be used in approximately equal frequently (not exact as that also provides clues).

11. Teacher-made assessment strategies

	Use of "All of above"	1. If all of the "above is used" then the other items must be correct. This means that a student may read the 1st response, mark it correct and move on. Alternatively, a student may read the 1st two items and seeing they are true does nor need to read the other alternatives to know to circle "all of the above". The teacher probably does not want either of these options.

In *matching items,* two parallel columns containing terms, phrases, symbols, or numbers are presented and the student is asked to match the items in the first column with those in the second column. Typically there are more items in the second column to make the task more difficult and to ensure that if a student makes one error they do not have to make another. Matching items most often are used to measure lower level knowledge such as persons and their achievements, dates and historical events, terms and definitions, symbols and concepts, plants or animals and classifications (Linn & Miller, 2005). An example with Spanish language words and their English equivalents is below:

Directions: On the line to the left of the Spanish word in Column A, write the letter of the English word in Column B that has the same meaning.

Column A   *Column B*

_____ 1. Casa   A. Aunt

_____ 2. Bebé   B. Baby

_____ 3. Gata   C. Brother

_____ 4. Perro   D. Cat

_____ 5. Hermano   E. Dog

     F. Father

     G. House

While matching items may seem easy to devise it is hard to create homogenous lists. Other problems with matching items and suggested remedies are in Table 37.

Multiple Choice items are the most commonly used type of objective test items because they have a number of advantages over other objective test items. Most importantly they can be adapted to assess higher levels thinking such as application as well as lower level factual knowledge. The first example below assesses knowledge of a specific fact whereas the second example assesses application of knowledge.

Who is best known for their work on the development of the morality of justice?

a) Erikson

b) Vygotsky

253

c) Maslow

d) Kohlberg

Which one of the following best illustrates the law of diminishing returns

a) A factory doubled its labor force and increased production by 50 per cent

b) The demand for an electronic product increased faster than the supply of the product

c) The population of a country increased faster than agricultural self sufficiency

d) A machine decreased in efficacy as its parts became worn out

(Adapted from Linn and Miller 2005, p, 193).

There are several other advantages of multiple choice items. Students have to recognize the correct answer not just know the incorrect answer as they do in true/false items. Also, the opportunity for guessing is reduced because four or five alternatives are usually provided whereas in true/false items students only have to choose between two choices. Also, multiple choice items do not need homogeneous material as matching items do.

However, creating good multiple choice test items is difficult and students (maybe including you) often become frustrated when taking a test with poor multiple choice items. Three steps have to be considered when constructing a multiple choice item: formulating a clearly stated problem, identifying plausible alternatives, and removing irrelevant clues to the answer. Common problems in each of these steps are summarized in Table 38

Constructed response items

Formal assessment also includes constructed response items in which students are asked to recall information and create an answer—not just recognize if the answer is correct—so guessing is reduced. Constructed response items can be used to assess a wide variety of kinds of knowledge and two major kinds are discussed: *completion or short answer* (also called short response) and *extended response.*

Completion and short answer

Completion and short answer items can be answered in a word, phrase, number, or symbol. These types of items are essentially the same only varying in whether the problem is presented as a statement or a question (Linn & Miller 2005). For example:

Completion: The first traffic light in the US was invented by................

Short Answer: Who invented the first traffic light in the US?

These items are often used in mathematics tests, e.g.

$3 + 10 = $ ....?

If $x = 6$, what does $x(x-1) =$ ....

Draw the line of symmetry on the following shape

A major advantage of these items is they that they are easy to construct. However, apart from their use in mathematics they are unsuitable for measuring complex learning outcomes and are often difficult to score. Completion and short answer tests are sometimes called objective tests as the intent is that there is only one correct answer and so there is no variability in scoring but unless the question is phrased very carefully, there are frequently a variety of correct answers. For example, consider the item

Where was President Lincoln born?....................

The teacher may expect the answer "in a log cabin" but other correct answers are also "on Sinking Spring Farm", "in Hardin County" or "in Kentucky". Common errors in these items are summarized in Table 38.

Table 38: Common errors in constructed response items

Type of item	Common errors	Example
Completion and short answer	There is more than one possible answer.	e.g. Where was US President Lincoln born? *The answer could be in a log cabin, in Kentucky etc.*
	Too many blanks are in the completion item so it is too difficult or doesn't make sense.	e.g. In ..... theory, the first stage, ... is when infants process through their .... and ....
	Clues are given by length of blanks in completion items.	e.g. Three states are contiguous to New Hampshire: . ....is to the West, ...is to the East and .... is to the South.
Extended Response	Ambiguous questions	e.g. Was the US Civil War avoidable? *Students could interpret this question in a wide variety of ways, perhaps even stating "yes" or "no". One student may discuss only political causes another moral, political and economic causes. There is no guidance in the question for students.*
	Poor reliability in grading	The teacher does not use a scoring rubric and so is inconsistent in how he scores answers especially unexpected responses, irrelevant information, and grammatical errors.
	Perception of student influences grading	By spring semester the teacher has developed expectations of each student's performance and this influences the grading (numbers can be used instead of names). The test consists of three constructed responses and the teacher grades the three answers on each students' paper before moving to the next paper. This means that the grading of questions 2 and 3 are influenced by the answers to question 1 (teachers should grade all the 1st question then the 2nd etc).
	Choices are given on	Testing experts recommend not giving choices in tests

	the test and some answers are easier than others.	because then students are not really taking the same test creating equity problems.

Extended response

Extended response items are used in many content areas and answers may vary in length from a paragraph to several pages. Questions that require longer responses are often called *essay* questions. Extended response items have several advantages and the most important is their adaptability for measuring complex learning outcomes—particularly integration and application. These items also require that students write and therefore provide teachers a way to assess writing skills. A commonly cited advantage to these items is their ease in construction; however, carefully worded items that are related to learning outcomes and assess complex learning are hard to devise (Linn & Miller, 2005). Well-constructed items phrase the question so the task of the student is clear. Often this involves providing hints or planning notes. In the first example below the actual question is clear not only because of the wording but because of the format (i.e. it is placed in a box). In the second and third examples planning notes are provided:

Example 1: Third grade mathematics:

The owner of a bookstore gave 14 books to the school. The principal will give an equal number of books to each of three classrooms and the remaining books to the school library. How many books could the principal give to each student and the school?

Show all your work on the space below and on the next page. Explain in words how you found the answer. Tell why you took the steps you did to solve the problem.

From Illinois Standards Achievement Test, 2006; (http://www.isbe.state.il.us/assessment/isat.htm)

Example 2: Fifth grade science: The grass is always greener

Jose and Maria noticed three different types of soil, black soil, sand, and clay, were found in their neighborhood. They decided to investigate the question, "How does the type of soil (black soil, sand, and clay) under grass sod affect the height of grass?"

Plan an investigation that could answer their new question.

In your plan, be sure to include:

- Prediction of the outcome of the investigation

- Materials needed to do the investigation

- Procedure that includes:

  - logical steps to do the investigation

  - one variable kept the same (controlled)

  - one variable changed (manipulated)

  - any variables being measure and recorded

11. Teacher-made assessment strategies

• how often measurements are taken and recorded

(From Washington State 2004 assessment of student learning)

http://www.k12.wa.us/assessment/WASL/default.aspx)

Example 3: Grades 9-11 English:

Writing prompt

Some people think that schools should teach students how to cook. Other people think that cooking is something that ought to be taught in the home. What do you think? Explain why you think as you do.

Planning notes

Choose One:

☐　I think schools should teach students how to cook

☐　I think cooking should l be taught in the home

I think cooking should be taught in ....because.........

(school) or (the home)

(From Illinois Measure of Annual Growth in English http://www.isbe.state.il.us/assessment/image.htm)

A major disadvantage of extended response items is the difficulty in reliable scoring. Not only do various teachers score the same response differently but also the same teacher may score the identical response differently on various occasions (Linn & Miller 2005). A variety of steps can be taken to improve the reliability and validity of scoring. First, teachers should begin by writing an outline of a model answer. This helps make it clear what students are expected to include. Second, a sample of the answers should be read. This assists in determining what the students can do and if there are any common misconceptions arising from the question. Third, teachers have to decide what to do about irrelevant information that is included (e.g. is it ignored or are students penalized) and how to evaluate mechanical errors such as grammar and spelling. Then, a *point scoring* or *a scoring rubric* should be used.

In point scoring components of the answer are assigned points. For example, if students were asked:

What are the nature, symptoms, and risk factors of hyperthermia?

Point Scoring Guide:

Definition (natures)	2 pts
Symptoms (1 pt for each)	5 pts
Risk Factors (1 point for each)	5 pts
Writing	3 pts

This provides some guidance for evaluation and helps consistency but point scoring systems often lead the teacher to focus on facts (e.g. naming risk factors) rather than higher level thinking that may undermine the validity of the assessment if the teachers' purposes include higher level thinking. A better approach is to use a scoring rubric that *describes* the quality of the answer or performance at each level.

Scoring rubrics

Scoring rubrics can be *holistic* or *analytical*. In holistic scoring rubrics, general descriptions of performance are made and a single overall score is obtained. An example from grade 2 language arts in Los Angeles Unified School District classifies responses into four levels: not proficient, partially proficient, proficient and advanced is on Table 39.

Table 39: Example of holistic scoring rubric: English language arts grade 2

Assignment. Write about an interesting, fun, or exciting story you have read in class this year. Some of the things you could write about are: • What happened in the story (the plot or events) • Where the events took place (the setting) • People, animals, or things in the story (the characters) In your writing make sure you use facts and details from the story to describe everything clearly. After you write about the story, explain what makes the story interesting, fun or exciting.	
Scoring rubric	
Advanced Score 4	The response demonstrates well-developed reading comprehension skills. Major story elements (plot, setting, or characters) are clearly and accurately described. Statements about the plot, setting, or characters are arranged in a manner that makes sense. Ideas or judgments (why the story is interesting, fun, or exciting) are clearly supported or explained with facts and details from the story.
Proficient Score 3	The response demonstrates solid reading comprehension skills. Most statements about the plot, setting, or characters are clearly described. Most statements about the plot, setting, or characters are arranged in a manner that makes sense. Ideas or judgments are supported with facts and details from the story.
Partially Proficient	The response demonstrates some reading comprehension skills

Score 1	There is an attempt to describe the plot, setting, or characters Some statements about the plot, setting, or characters are arranged in a manner that makes sense. Ideas or judgments may be supported with some facts and details from the story.
Not Proficient Score 1	The response demonstrates little or no skill in reading comprehension. The plot, setting, or characters are not described, or the description is unclear. Statements about the plot, setting, or characters are not arranged in a manner that makes sense. Ideas or judgments are not stated, and facts and details from the text are not used.
Source: Adapted from English Language Arts Grade 2 Los Angeles Unified School District, 2001 (http://www.cse.ucla.edu/resources/justforteachers_set.htm)	

Analytical rubrics provide descriptions of levels of student performance on a variety of characteristics. For example, six characteristics used for assessing writing developed by the Northwest Regional Education Laboratory (NWREL) are:

- ideas and content

- organization

- voice

- word choice

- sentence fluency

- conventions

Descriptions of high, medium, and low responses for each characteristic are available from:

http://www.nwrel.org/assessment/toolkit98/traits/index.html).

Holistic rubrics have the advantages that they can be developed more quickly than analytical rubrics. They are also faster to use as there is only one dimension to examine. However, they do not provide students feedback about which aspects of the response are strong and which aspects need improvement (Linn & Miller, 2005). This means they are less useful for assessment *for* learning. An important use of rubrics is to use them as teaching tools and provide them to students *before* the assessment so they know what knowledge and skills are expected.

Teachers can use scoring rubrics as part of instruction by giving students the rubric during instruction, providing several responses, and analyzing these responses in terms of the rubric. For example, use of accurate terminology is one dimension of the science rubric in Table 40. An elementary science teacher could discuss why it is important for scientists to use accurate terminology, give examples of inaccurate and accurate terminology, provide that component of the scoring rubric to students, distribute some examples of student responses (maybe from former students), and then discuss how these responses would be classified according to the rubric. This strategy of assessment for learning should be more effective if the teacher (a) emphasizes to students why using accurate terminology is important when learning science rather than how to get a good grade on the test (we provide more details about this in the section on motivation later in this chapter); (b) provides an exemplary response so students can see a model; and (c) emphasizes that the goal is student improvement on this skill not ranking students.

Table 40: Example of a scoring rubric, Science

*On the High School Assessment, the application of a concept to a practical problem or real-world situation will be scored when it is required in the response and requested in the item stem.

	Level of understanding	Use of accurate scientific terminology	Use of supporting details	Synthesis of information	Application of information*
4	There is evidence in the response that the student has a full and complete understanding.	The use of accurate scientific terminology enhances the response.	Pertinent and complete supporting details demonstrate an integration of ideas.	The response reflects a complete synthesis of information.	An effective application of the concept to a practical problem or real-world situation reveals an insight into scientific principles.
3	There is evidence in the response that the student has a good understanding.	The use of accurate scientific terminology strengthens the response.	The supporting details are generally complete.	The response reflects some synthesis of information.	The concept has been applied to a practical problem or real-world situation.
2	There is evidence in the response that the student has a basic understanding.	The use of accurate scientific terminology may be present in the response.	The supporting details are adequate.	The response provides little or no synthesis of information.	The application of the concept to a practical problem or real-world situation is inadequate.
1	There is evidence in the response that the student has some	The use of accurate scientific terminology is not present in the	The supporting details are only	The response addresses the question.	The application, if attempted, is

understanding.	response.	minimally effective.		irrelevant.
0	The student has **NO UNDERSTANDING** of the question or problem. The response is completely incorrect or irrelevant.			

Performance assessments

Typically in performance assessments students complete a specific task while teachers observe the process or procedure (e.g. data collection in an experiment) as well as the product (e.g. completed report) (Popham, 2005; Stiggens, 2005). The tasks that students complete in performance assessments are not simple—in contrast to selected response items—and include the following:

- playing a musical instrument

- athletic skills

- artistic creation

- conversing in a foreign language

- engaging in a debate about political issues

- conducting an experiment in science

- repairing a machine

- writing a term paper

- using interaction skills to play together

These examples all involve complex skills but illustrate that the term performance assessment is used in a variety of ways. For example, the teacher may not observe all of the process (e.g. she sees a draft paper but the final product is written during out-of-school hours) and essay tests are typically classified as performance assessments (Airasian, 2000). In addition, in some performance assessments there may be no clear product (e.g. the performance may be group interaction skills).

Two related terms, *alternative assessment* and *authentic assessment* are sometimes used instead of performance assessment but they have different meanings (Linn & Miller, 2005). Alternative assessment refers to tasks that are not pencil-and-paper and while many performance assessments are not pencil-and paper tasks some are (e.g. writing a term paper, essay tests). Authentic assessment is used to describe tasks that students do that are similar to those in the "real world". Classroom tasks vary in level of authenticity (Popham, 2005). For example, a Japanese language class taught in a high school in Chicago conversing in Japanese in Tokyo is highly authentic— but only possible in a study abroad program or trip to Japan. Conversing in Japanese with native Japanese speakers in Chicago is also highly authentic, and conversing with the teacher in Japanese during class is moderately authentic. Much less authentic is a matching test on English and Japanese words. In a language arts class, writing a letter (to an editor) or a memo to the principal is highly authentic as letters and memos are common work products.

However, writing a five-paragraph paper is not as authentic as such papers are not used in the world of work. However, a five paragraph paper is a complex task and would typically be classified as a performance assessment.

Advantages and disadvantages

There are several advantages of performance assessments (Linn & Miller 2005). First, the focus is on complex learning outcomes that often cannot be measured by other methods. Second, performance assessments typically assess process or procedure as well as the product. For example, the teacher can observe if the students are repairing the machine using the appropriate tools and procedures as well as whether the machine functions properly after the repairs. Third, well designed performance assessments communicate the instructional goals and meaningful learning clearly to students. For example, if the topic in a fifth grade art class is one-point perspective the performance assessment could be drawing a city scene that illustrates one point perspective. (http://www.sanford-artedventures.com). This assessment is meaningful and clearly communicates the learning goal. This performance assessment is a good instructional activity and has good content validity—common with well designed performance assessments (Linn & Miller 2005).

One major disadvantage with performance assessments is that they are typically very time consuming for students and teachers. This means that fewer assessments can be gathered so if they are not carefully devised fewer learning goals will be assessed—which can reduce content validity. State curriculum guidelines can be helpful in determining what should be included in a performance assessment. For example, Eric, a dance teacher in a high school in Tennessee learns that the state standards indicate that dance students at the highest level should be able to do demonstrate consistency and clarity in performing technical skills by:

- performing complex movement combinations to music in a variety of meters and styles

- performing combinations and variations in a broad dynamic range

- demonstrating improvement in performing movement combinations through self-evaluation

- critiquing a live or taped dance production based on given criteria

(http://www.tennessee.gov/education/ci/standards/music/dance912.shtml)

Eric devises the following performance task for his eleventh grade modern dance class.

In groups of 4-6 students will perform a dance at least 5 minutes in length. The dance selected should be multifaceted so that all the dancers can demonstrate technical skills, complex movements, and a dynamic range (Items 1-2). Students will videotape their rehearsals and document how they improved through self evaluation (Item 3). Each group will view and critique the final performance of one other group in class (Item 4). Eric would need to scaffold most steps in this performance assessment. The groups probably would need guidance in selecting a dance that allowed all the dancers to demonstrate the appropriate skills; critiquing their own performances constructively; working effectively as a team, and applying criteria to evaluate a dance.

Another disadvantage of performance assessments is they are hard to assess reliably which can lead to inaccuracy and unfair evaluation. As with any constructed response assessment, scoring rubrics are very important.

11. Teacher-made assessment strategies

An example of holistic and analytic scoring rubrics designed to assess a completed *product* are in Table 39 and Table 40. A rubric designed to assess the *process* of group interactions is in Table 41.

Table 41: Example of group interaction rubric

Score	Time management	Participation and performance in roles	Shared involvement
0	Group did not stay on task and so task was not completed.	Group did not assign or share roles.	Single individual did the task.
1	Group was off-task the majority of the time but task was completed.	Groups assigned roles but members did not use these roles.	Group totally disregarded comments and ideas from some members.
2	Group stayed on task most of the time.	Groups accepted and used some but not all roles.	Group accepted some ideas but did not give others adequate consideration.
3	Group stayed on task throughout the activity and managed time well.	Group accepted and used roles and actively participated.	Groups gave equal consideration to all ideas.
4	Group defined their own approach in a way that more effectively managed the activity.	Group defined and used roles not mentioned to them. Role changes took place that maximized individuals' expertise.	Groups made specific efforts to involve all group members including the reticent members.

Source: Adapted from Group Interaction (GI) SETUP (2003). Issues, Evidence and You. Ronkonkomo, NY Lab-Aids. (http://cse.edc.org/products/assessment/middleschool/scorerub.asp))

This rubric was devised for middle grade science but could be used in other subject areas when assessing group process. In some performance assessments several scoring rubrics should be used. In the dance performance example above Eric should have scoring rubrics for the performance skills, the improvement based on self evaluation, the team work, and the critique of the other group. Obviously, devising a good performance assessment is complex and Linn and Miller (2005) recommend that teachers should:

- Create performance assessments that require students to use complex cognitive skills. Sometimes teachers devise assessments that are interesting and that the students enjoy but do not require students to use higher level cognitive skills that lead to significant learning. Focusing on high level skills and learning outcomes is particularly important because performance assessments are typically so time consuming.

- Ensure that the task is clear to the students. Performance assessments typically require multiple steps so students need to have the necessary prerequisite skills and knowledge as well as clear directions. Careful scaffolding is important for successful performance assessments.

- Specify expectations of the performance clearly by providing students scoring rubrics during the instruction. This not only helps students understand what it expected but it also guarantees that teachers are clear about what they expect. Thinking this through while planning the performance assessment can be difficult for teachers but is crucial as it typically leads to revisions of the actual assessment and directions provided to students.

- Reduce the importance of unessential skills in completing the task. What skills are essential depends on the purpose of the task. For example, for a science report, is the use of publishing software essential? If the purpose of the assessment is for students to demonstrate the process of the scientific method including writing a report, then the format of the report may not be significant. However, if the purpose includes integrating two subject areas, science and technology, then the use of publishing software is important. Because performance assessments take time it is tempting to include multiple skills without carefully considering if all the skills are essential to the learning goals.

Portfolios

"A portfolio is a meaningful collection of student work that tells the story of student achievement or growth" (Arter, Spandel, & Culham, 1995, p. 2). Portfolios are a *purposeful* collection of student work not just folders of all the work a student does. Portfolios are used for a variety of purposes and developing a portfolio system can be confusing and stressful unless the teachers are clear on their purpose. The varied purposes can be illustrated as four dimensions (Linn & Miller 2005):

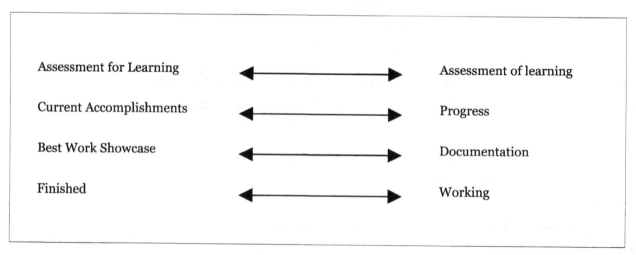

When the primary purpose is assessment *for* learning, the emphasis is on student self-reflection and responsibility for learning. Students not only select samples of their work they wish to include, but also reflect and interpret their own work. Portfolios containing this information can be used to aid communication as students can present and explain their work to their teachers and parents (Stiggins, 2005). Portfolios focusing on assessment *of* learning contain students' work samples that certify accomplishments for a classroom grade, graduation, state requirements etc. Typically, students have less choice in the work contained in such portfolios as some consistency is needed for this type of assessment. For example, the writing portfolios that fourth and seventh graders are required to submit in Kentucky must contain a self-reflective statement and an example of three pieces of writing (reflective, personal experience or literary, and transactive). Students do choose which of their pieces of writing in each type to include in the portfolio.

(http://www.kde.state.ky.us/KDE/Instructional+Resources/Curriculum+Documents+and+Resources/Student +Performance+Standards/).

Portfolios can be designed to focus on student progress or current accomplishments. For example, audio tapes of English language learners speaking could be collected over one year to demonstrate growth in learning. Student progress portfolios may also contain multiple versions of a single piece of work. For example, a writing project may contain notes on the original idea, outline, first draft, comments on the first draft by peers or teacher, second draft, and the final finished product (Linn & Miller 2005). If the focus is on current accomplishments, only recent completed work samples are included.

Portfolios can focus on documenting student activities or highlighting important accomplishments. Documentation portfolios are inclusive containing all the work samples rather than focusing on one special strength, best work, or progress. In contrast, showcase portfolios focus on best work. The best work is typically identified by students. One aim of such portfolios is that students learn how to identify products that demonstrate what they know and can do. Students are not expected to identify their best work in isolation but also use the feedback from their teachers and peers.

A final distinction can be made between a finished portfolio—maybe used to for a job application—versus a working portfolio that typically includes day-to-day work samples. Working portfolios evolve over time and are not intended to be used for assessment *of* learning. The focus in a working portfolio is on developing ideas and skills so students should be allowed to make mistakes, freely comment on their own work, and respond to teacher feedback (Linn & Miller, 2005). Finished portfolios are designed for use with a particular audience and the products selected may be drawn from a working portfolio. For example, in a teacher education program, the working portfolio may contain work samples from all the courses taken. A student may develop one finished portfolio to demonstrate she has mastered the required competencies in the teacher education program and a second finished portfolio for her job application.

Advantages and disadvantages

Portfolios used well in classrooms have several advantages. They provide a way of documenting and evaluating growth in a much more nuanced way than selected response tests can. Also, portfolios can be integrated easily into instruction, i.e. used for assessment *for* learning. Portfolios also encourage student self-evaluation and reflection, as well as ownership for learning (Popham, 2005). Using classroom assessment to promote student motivation is an important component of assessment for learning which is considered in the next section.

However, there are some major disadvantages of portfolio use. First, good portfolio assessment takes an enormous amount of teacher time and organization. The time is needed to help students understand the purpose and structure of the portfolio, decide which work samples to collect, and to self reflect. Some of this time needs to be conducted in one-to-one conferences. Reviewing and evaluating the portfolios out of class time is also enormously time consuming. Teachers have to weigh if the time spent is worth the benefits of the portfolio use.

Second, evaluating portfolios reliability and eliminating bias can be even more difficult than in a constructed response assessment because the products are more varied. The experience of the state-wide use of portfolios for assessment in writing and mathematics for fourth and eighth graders in Vermont is sobering. Teachers used the same analytic scoring rubric when evaluating the portfolio. In the first two years of implementation samples from schools were collected and scored by an external panel of teachers. In the first year the agreement among raters (i.e. inter-rater reliability) was poor for mathematics and reading; in the second year the agreement among raters improved for mathematics but not for reading. However, even with the improvement in mathematics the reliability was too low to use the portfolios for individual student accountability (Koretz, Stecher, Klein & McCaffrey, 1994). When reliability is low, validity is also compromised because unstable results cannot be interpreted meaningfully.

If teachers do use portfolios in their classroom, the series of steps needed for implementation are outlined in Table 36. If the school or district has an existing portfolio system these steps may have to be modified.

Table 42: Steps in implementing a classroom portfolio program

1. Make sure students own their portfolios.	Talk to your students about your ideas of the portfolio, the different purposes, and the variety of work samples. If possible, have them help make decisions about the kind of portfolio you implement.
2. Decide on the purpose.	Will the focus be on growth or current accomplishments? Best work showcase or documentation? Good portfolios can have multiple purposes but the teacher and students need to be clear about the purpose.
3. Decide what work samples to collect,	For example, in writing, is every writing assignment included? Are early drafts as well as final products included?
4. Collect and store work samples,	Decide where the work sample will be stored. For example, will each student have a file folder in a file cabinet, or a small plastic tub on a shelf in the classroom?
5. Select criteria to evaluate samples,	If possible, work with students to develop scoring rubrics. This may take considerable time as different rubrics may be needed for the variety of work samples. If you are using existing scoring rubrics, discuss with students possible modifications after the rubrics have been used at least once.
6. Teach and require students conduct self evaluations of their own work,	Help students learn to evaluate their own work using agreed upon criteria. For younger students, the self evaluations may be simple (strengths, weaknesses, and ways to improve); for older students a more analytic approach is desirable including using the same scoring rubrics that the teachers will use.
7. Schedule and conduct portfolio conferences ,	Teacher-student conferences are time consuming but conferences are essential for the portfolio process to significantly enhance learning. These conferences should aid students' self evaluation and should take place frequently.

8. Involve parents.	Parents need to understand the portfolio process. Encourage parents to review the work samples. You may wish to schedule parent, teacher-students conferences in which students talk about their work samples.

Source: Adapted from Popham (2005)

Assessment that enhances motivation and student confidence

Studies on *testing* and learning conducted more than 20 years ago demonstrated that tests promote learning and that more frequent tests are more effective than less frequent tests (Dempster & Perkins, 1993). Frequent smaller tests encourage continuous effort rather than last minute cramming and may also reduce test anxiety because the consequences of errors are reduced. College students report preferring more frequent testing than infrequent testing (Bangert-Downs, Kulik, Kulik, 1991). More recent research indicates that teachers' assessment *purpose and beliefs*, the *type* of assessment selected, and the *feedback* given contributes to the assessment climate in the classroom which influences students' confidence and motivation. The use of self-assessment is also important in establishing a positive assessment climate.

Teachers' purposes and beliefs

Student motivation can be enhanced when the purpose of assessment is promoting student learning and this is clearly communicated to students by what teachers say and do (Harlen, 2006). This approach to assessment is associated with what the psychologist, Carol Dweck, (2000) calls an incremental view of ability or intelligence. An incremental view assumes that ability increases whenever an individual learns more. This means that effort is valued because effort leads to knowing more and therefore having more ability. Individuals with an incremental view also ask for help when needed and respond well to constructive feedback as the primary goal is increased learning and mastery. In contrast, a fixed view of ability assumes that some people have more ability than others and nothing much can be done to change that. Individuals with a fixed view of ability often view effort in opposition to ability ("Smart people don't have to study") and so do not try as hard, and are less likely to ask for help as that indicates that they are not smart. While there are individual differences in students' beliefs about their views of intelligence, teachers' beliefs and classroom practices influence students' perceptions and behaviors.

Teachers with an incremental view of intelligence communicate to students that the goal of learning is mastering the material and figuring things out. Assessment is used by these teachers to understand what students know so they can decide whether to move to the next topic, re-teach the entire class, or provide remediation for a few students. Assessment also helps students' understand their own learning and demonstrate their competence. Teachers with these views say things like, "We are going to practice over and over again. That's how you get good. And you're going to make mistakes. That's how you learn." (Patrick, Anderman, Ryan, Edelin, Midgley, 2001, p. 45).

In contrast, teachers with a fixed view of ability are more likely to believe that the goal of learning is doing well on tests especially outperforming others. These teachers are more likely to say things that imply fixed abilities e.g. "This test will determine what your math abilities are", or stress the importance of interpersonal competition, "We will have speech competition and the top person will compete against all the other district schools and last year the winner got a big award and their photo in the paper." When teachers stress interpersonal competition some students may be motivated but there can only a few winners so there are many more students who know they have no chance of winning. Another problem with interpersonal competition in assessment is that the focus can become winning rather than understanding the material.

Teachers who communicate to their students that ability is incremental and that the goal of assessment is promoting learning rather that ranking students, or awarding prizes to those who did very well, or catching those who did not pay attention, are likely to enhance students' motivation.

Choosing assessments

The choice of assessment task also influences students' motivation and confidence. First, assessments that have clear criteria that students understand and can meet rather than assessments that pit students against each other in interpersonal competition enhances motivation (Black, Harrison, Lee, Marshall, Wiliam, 2004). This is consistent with the point we made in the previous section about the importance of focusing on enhancing learning for all students rather than ranking students. Second, meaningful assessment tasks enhance student motivation. Students often want to know why they have to do something and teachers need to provide meaningful answers. For example, a teacher might say, "You need to be able to calculate the area of a rectangle because if you want new carpet you need to know how much carpet is needed and how much it would cost." Well designed performance tasks are often more meaningful to students than selected response tests so students will work harder to prepare for them.

Third, providing choices of assessment tasks can enhance student sense of autonomy and motivation according to self determination theory (see Chapter 6). Kym, the sixth grade teacher whose story began this chapter, reports that giving students choices was very helpful. Another middle school social studies teacher Aaron, gives his students a choice of performance tasks at the end of the unit on the US Bill of Rights. Students have to demonstrate specified key ideas but can do that by making up a board game, presenting a brief play, composing a rap song etc. Aaron reports that students work much harder on this performance assessment which allows them to use their strengths than previously when he did not provide any choices and gave a more traditional assignment. Measurement experts caution that a danger of giving choices is that the assessment tasks are no longer equivalent and so the reliability of scoring is reduced so it is particularly important to use well designed scoring rubrics. Fourth, assessment tasks should be challenging but achievable with reasonable effort (Elliott, McGregor & Thrash, 2004). This is often hard for beginning teachers to do, who may give assessment tasks that are too easy or too hard, because they have to learn to match their assessment to the skills of their students.

Providing feedback

When the goal is assessment *for* learning, providing constructive feedback that helps students know what they do and do not understand as well as encouraging them to learn from their errors is fundamental. Effective feedback should be given as soon as possible as the longer the delay between students' work and feedback the longer students will continue to have some misconceptions. Also, delays reduce the relationship between students' performance and the feedback as students can forget what they were thinking during the assessment. Effective feedback should also inform students clearly what they did well and what needs modification. General comments just as "good work, A", or "needs improvement" do not help students understand how to improve their learning. Giving feedback to students using well designed scoring rubrics helps clearly communicate strengths and weaknesses. Obviously grades are often needed but teachers can minimize the focus by placing the grade after the comments or on the last page of a paper. It can also be helpful to allow students to keep their grades private making sure when returning assignments that the grade is not prominent (e.g. not using red ink on the top page) and never asking students to read their scores aloud in class. Some students choose to share their grades—but that should be their decision not their teachers.

When grading, teachers often become angry at the mistakes that student make. It is easy for teachers to think something like: "With all the effort I put into teaching, this student could not even be bothered to follow the directions or spell check!" Many experienced teachers believe that communicating their *anger* is not helpful, so rather than saying: "How dare you turn in such shoddy work", they rephrase it as, "I am disappointed that your work on this assignment does not meet the standards set" (Sutton, 2003). Research evidence also suggests that comments such as "You are so smart" for a high quality performance can be counterproductive. This is surprising to many teachers but if students are told they are smart when they produce a good product, then if they do poorly on the next assignment the conclusion must be they are "not smart" (Dweck, 2000). More effective feedback focuses on positive aspects of the task (not the person), as well as strategies, and effort. The focus of the feedback should relate to the criteria set by the teacher and how improvements can be made.

When the teacher and student are from different racial/ethnic backgrounds providing feedback that enhances motivation and confidence but also includes criticism can be particularly challenging because the students of color have historical reasons to distrust negative comments from a white teacher. Research by Cohen Steele, Ross (1999) indicates that "wise" feedback from teachers needs three components: positive comments, criticisms, and an assurance that the teacher believes the student can reach higher standards. We describe this research is more detail in "Deciding for yourself about the research" found in Appendix #2.

Self and peer assessment

In order to reach a learning goal, students need to understand the meaning of the goal, the steps necessary to achieve a goal, and if they are making satisfactory progress towards that goal (Sadler, 1989). This involves self assessment and recent research has demonstrated that well designed self assessment can enhance student learning and motivation (Black & Wiliam, 2006). For self assessment to be effective, students need explicit criteria such as those in an analytical scoring rubric. These criteria are either provided by the teacher or developed by the teacher in collaboration with students. Because students seem to find it easier to understand criteria for assessment tasks if they can examine other students' work along side their own, self assessment often involves peer assessment. An example of a strategy used by teachers involves asking students to use "traffic lights" to indicate of their confidence in their assignment or homework. Red indicates that they were unsure of their success, orange that they were partially unsure, and green that they were confident of their success. The students who labeled their own work as orange and green worked in mixed groups to evaluate their own work while the teacher worked with the students who had chosen red (Black & Wiliam, 2006).

If self and peer assessment is used, it is particularly important that the teachers establish a classroom culture for assessment that is based on incremental views of ability and learning goals. If the classroom atmosphere focuses on interpersonal competition, students have incentives in self and peer assessment to inflate their own evaluations (and perhaps those of their friends) because there are limited rewards for good work.

Adjusting instruction based on assessment

Using assessment information to adjust instruction is fundamental to the concept of assessment *for* learning. Teachers make these adjustments "in the moment" during classroom instruction as well as during reflection and planning periods. Teachers use the information they gain from questioning and observation to adjust their teaching during classroom instruction. If students cannot answer a question, the teacher may need to rephrase the question, probe understanding of prior knowledge, or change the way the current idea is being considered. It is important for teachers to learn to identify when only one or two students need individual help because they are struggling with the concept, and when a large proportion of the class is struggling so whole group intervention is needed.

After the class is over, effective teachers spend time analyzing how well the lessons went, what students did and did not seem to understand, and what needs to be done the next day. Evaluation of student work also provides important information for teachers. If many students are confused about a similar concept the teacher needs to re-teach it and consider new ways of helping students understand the topic. If the majority of students complete the tasks very quickly and well, the teacher might decide that the assessment was not challenging enough. Sometimes teachers become dissatisfied with the kinds of assessments they have assigned when they are grading—perhaps because they realize there was too much emphasis on lower level learning, that the directions were not clear enough, or the scoring rubric needed modification. Teachers who believe that assessment data provides information about their own teaching and that they can find ways to influence student learning have high teacher efficacy or beliefs that they can make a difference in students' lives. In contrast, teachers who think that student performance is mostly due to fixed student characteristics or the homes they come from (e.g. "no wonder she did so poorly considering what her home life is like") have low teacher efficacy (Tschannen-Moran, Woolfolk Hoy, & Hoy, 1998).

Communication with parents and guardians

Clear communication with parents about classroom assessment is important—but often difficult for beginning teachers. The same skills that are needed to communicate effectively with students are also needed when communicating with parents and guardians. Teachers need to be able to explain to parents the purpose of the assessment, why they selected this assessment technique, and what the criteria for success are. Some teachers send home newsletters monthly or at the beginning of a major assessment task explaining the purpose and nature of the task, any additional support that is needed (e.g. materials, library visits), and due dates. Some parents will not be familiar with performance assessments or the use of self and peer assessment so teachers need to take time to explain these approaches carefully.

Many school districts now communicate though websites that have mixtures of public information available to all parents in the class (e.g. curriculum and assessment details) as well information restricted to the parents or guardians of specific students (e.g. the attendance and grades). Teachers report this is helpful as parents have access to their child's performance immediately and when necessary, can talk to their child and teacher quickly.

The recommendations we provided above on the type of feedback that should be given to students also apply when talking to parents. That is, the focus should be on students' performance on the task, what was done well and what needs work, rather than general comments about how "smart" or "weak" the child is. If possible, comments should focus on strategies that the child uses well or needs to improve (e.g. reading test questions carefully, organization in a large project). When the teacher is white and the student or parents are minority, trust can be an issue so using "wise" feedback when talking to parents may help.

Action research: studying yourself and your students

Assessment *for* learning emphasizes devising and conducting assessment data in order to improve teaching and learning and so is related to action research (also called teacher research). In Chapter 1, we described action research as studies conducted by teachers of their own students or their own work. Action research can lead to decisions that improve a teacher's own teaching or the teaching of colleagues. Kym, the teacher we described at the beginning of this chapter, conducted action research in her own classroom as she identified a problem of poor student motivation and achievement, investigated solutions during the course on motivation, tried new approaches, and observed the resulting actions.

Cycles of planning, acting and reflecting

Action research is usually described as a cyclical process with the following stages (Mertler, 2006).

- *Planning Stage.* Planning has three components. First, planning involves identifying and defining a problem. Problems sometimes start with some ill defined unease or feeling that something is wrong and it can take time to identify the problem clearly so that it becomes a researchable question. The next step, is reviewing the related literature and this may occur within a class or workshop that the teachers are attending. Teachers may also explore the literature on their own or in teacher study groups. The third step is developing a research plan. The research plan includes what kind of data will be collected (e.g. student test scores, observation of one or more students, as well as how and when it will be collected (e.g. from files, in collaboration with colleagues, in spring or fall semester).

- *Acting sage.* During this stage the teacher is collecting and analyzing data. The data collected and the analyses do not need to be complex because action research, to be effective, has to be manageable.

- *Developing an action plan.* In this stage the teacher develops a plan to make changes and implements these changes. This is the action component of action research and it is important that teachers document their actions carefully so that they can communicate them to others.

- *Communicating and reflection.* An important component of all research is communicating information. Results can be shared with colleagues in the school or district, in an action research class at the local college, at conferences, or in journals for teachers. Action research can also involve students as active participants and if this is the case, communication may include students and parents. Communicating with others helps refine ideas and so typically aids in reflection. During reflection teachers/researchers ask such questions as: "What did I learn?" "What should I have done differently?" "What should I do next?" Questions such as these often lead to a new cycle of action research beginning with planning and then moving to the other steps.

Ethical issues—privacy, voluntary consent

Teachers are accustomed to collecting students' test scores, data about performances, and descriptions of behaviors as an essential component of teaching. However, if teachers are conducting action research and they plan to collect data that will be shared outside the school community then permission from parents (or guardians) and students must be obtained in order to protect the privacy of students and their families. Typically permission is obtained by an informed consent form that summarizes the research, describes the data that will be collected, indicates that participation is voluntary, and provides a guarantee of confidentiality or anonymity (Hubbard & Power, 2005). Many large school districts have procedures for establishing informed consent as well as person in the central office who is responsible for the district guidelines and specific application process. If the action research is supported in some way by a college of university (e.g. through a class) then informed consent procedures of that institution must be followed.

One common area of confusion for teachers is the voluntary nature of student participation in research. If the data being collected are for a research study, students can choose not to participate. This is contrary to much regular classroom instruction where teachers tell students they have to do the work or complete the tasks.

Grading and reporting

Assigning students grades is an important component of teaching and many school districts issue progress reports, interim reports, or mid term grades as well as final semester grades. Traditionally these reports were printed on paper and sent home with students or mailed to students' homes. Increasingly, school districts are using web-based grade management systems that allow parents to access their child's grades on each individual assessment as well as the progress reports and final grades.

Grading can be frustrating for teachers as there are many factors to consider. In addition, report cards typically summarize in brief format a variety of assessments and so cannot provide much information about students' strengths and weaknesses. This means that report cards focus more on assessment *of* learning than assessment *for* learning. There are a number of decisions that have to be made when assigning students' grades and schools often have detailed policies that teachers have to follow. In the next section, we consider the major questions associated with grading.

How are various assignments and assessments weighted?

Students typically complete a variety of assignments during a grading period such as homework, quizzes, performance assessments, etc. Teachers have to decide—preferably before the grading period begins—how each assignment will be weighted. For example, a sixth grade math teacher may decide to weight the grades in the following manner:

Weekly quizzes	35 per cent
Homework	15 per cent
Performance Assessment	30 per cent
Class participation	20 per cent

Deciding how to weight assignments should be done carefully as it communicates to students and parents what teachers believe is important, and also may be used to decide how much effort students will exert (e.g. "If homework is only worth 5 per cent, it is not worth completing twice a week").

Should social skills or effort be included? Elementary school teachers are more likely than middle or high school teachers to include some social skills into report cards (Popham, 2005). These may be included as separate criteria in the report card or weighted into the grade for that subject. For example, the grade for mathematics may include an assessment of group cooperation or self regulation during mathematics lessons. Some schools and teachers endorse including social skills arguing that developing such skills is important for young students and that students need to learn to work with others and manage their own behaviors in order to be successful. Others believe that grades in subject areas should be based on the cognitive performances—and that if assessments of social skills are made they should be clearly separated from the subject grade on the report card. Obviously, clear criteria such as those contained in analytical scoring rubrics should be used if social skills are graded.

Teachers often find it difficult to decide whether effort and improvement should be included as a component of grades. One approach is for teachers to ask students to submit drafts of an assignment and make improvements based on the feedback they received. The grade for the assignment may include some combination of the score for the drafts, the final version, and the amount of improvement the students made based on the feedback provided. A more controversial approach is basing grades on effort when students try really hard day after day but still cannot complete their assignments well. These students could have identified special needs or be recent immigrants that have limited English skills. Some school districts have guidelines for handling such cases. One disadvantage of using improvement as a component of grades is that the most competent students in class may do very well initially and have little room for improvement—unless teachers are skilled at providing additional assignments that will help challenge these students.

Teachers often use "hodgepodge grading", i.e. a combination of achievement, effort, growth, attitude or class conduct, homework, and class participation. A survey of over 8,500 middle and high school students in the US state of Virginia supported the hodgepodge practices commonly used by their teachers (Cross & Frary, 1999).

How should grades be calculated?

Two options are commonly used: absolute grading and relative grading. In *absolute grading* grades are assigned based on criteria the teacher has devised. If an English teacher has established a level of proficiency needed to obtain an A and no student meets that level then no A's will be given. Alternatively if every student meets the established level then all the students will get A's (Popham, 2005). Absolute grading systems may use letter grades or pass/fail.

In *relative grading* the teacher ranks the performances of students from worst to best (or best to worst) and those at the top get high grades, those in the middle moderate grades, and those at the bottom low grades. This is often described as "grading on the curve" and can be useful to compensate for an examination or assignment that students find much easier or harder than the teacher expected. However, relative grading can be unfair to students because the comparisons are typically within one class, so an A in one class may not represent the level of performance of an A in another class. Relative grading systems may discourage students from helping each other improve as students are in competition for limited rewards. In fact, Bishop (1999) argues that grading on the curve gives students a personal interest in persuading each other not to study as a serious student makes it more difficult for others to get good grades.

What kinds of grade descriptions should be used?

Traditionally a letter *grade system* is used (e.g. A, B, C, D, F) for each subject. The advantages of these grade descriptions are they are convenient, simple, and can be averaged easily. However, they do not indicate what objectives the student has or has not met nor students' specific strengths and weaknesses (Linn & Miller 2005). Elementary schools often use a *pass-fail* (or satisfactory-unsatisfactory) system and some high schools and colleges do as well. Pass-fail systems in high school and college allow students to explore new areas and take risks on subjects that they may have limited preparation for, or is not part of their major (Linn & Miller 2005). While a pass-fail system is easy to use, it offers even less information about students' level of learning.

A pass-fail system is also used in classes that are taught under a mastery-learning approach in which students are expected to demonstrate mastery on all the objectives in order to receive course credit. Under these conditions, it is clear that a pass means that the student has demonstrated mastery of all the objectives.

Some schools have implemented a *checklist of the objectives* in subject areas to replace the traditional letter grade system, and students are rated on each objective using descriptors such as Proficient, Partially Proficient, and Needs Improvement. For example, the checklist for students in a fourth grade class in California may include the four types of writing that are required by the English language state content standards (http://www.cde.ca.gov/be/st/ss/enggrade4.asp)

- writing narratives

- writing responses to literature

- writing information reports

- writing summaries

The advantages of this approach are that it communicates students' strengths and weaknesses clearly, and it reminds the students and parents the objectives of the school. However, if too many objectives are included then the lists can become so long that they are difficult to understand.

Chapter summary

The purpose of classroom assessment can be assessment for learning or assessment of learning. Essential steps of assessment for learning include communicating instructional goals clearly to students; selecting appropriate high quality assessments that match the instructional goals and students' backgrounds; using assessments that enhance student motivation and confidence, adjusting instruction based on assessment, and communicating assessment results with parents and guardians. Action research can help teachers understand and improve their teaching. A number of questions are important to consider when devising grading systems.

Key terms

Absence of bias	Authentic assessment
Action research	Constructed response items
Alternative assessment	Evaluation
Assessment	Formative assessment
Assessment for learning	Formal assessment measurement
Assessment of learning	Informal assessment

Performance assessment   Selected response items

Portfolios   Summative assessment

Reliability   Validity

References

Airasian, P. W. (2000). *Classroom Assessment: A concise approach 2nd ed.* Boston: McGraw Hill.

Airasian, P. W. (2004). *Classroom Assessment: Concepts and Applications 3rd ed.* Boston: McGraw Hill.

Bangert-Downs, R. L.,Kulik, J. A., & Kulik, C-L, C. (1991). Effects of frequent classroom testing. *Journal of Educational Research, 85* (2), 89-99.

Black, P., Harrison, C., Lee, C., Marshall, B. & Wiliam, D. (2004). Working inside the black box.: Assessment for learning in the classroom. *Phi Delta Kappan, 86* (1) 9-21.

Black, P., & Wiliam,D. (2006). Assessment for learning in the classroom. In J. Gardner (Ed.). *Assessment and learning* (pp. 9-25). Thousand Oaks, CA:Sage.

Bishop, J. H. (1999). Nerd harassment, incentives, school priorities, and learning.In S. E. Mayer & P. E. Peterson (Eds.) *Earning and learning: How school matters* (pp. 231-280). Washington, DC: Brookings Institution Press.

Borko, H. & Livingston, C. (1989) Cognition and Improvisation: Differences in Mathematics Instruction by Expert and Novice Teachers. *American Educational Research Journal, 26,* 473-98.

Cross, L. H., & Frary, R. B. (1999). Hodgepodge grading: Endorsed by students and teachers alike. *Applied Measurement in Education, 21*(1) 53-72.

Dempster, F. N. & Perkins, P. G. (1993). Revitalizing classroom assessment: Using tests to promote learning. *Journal of Instructional Psychology, 20* (3) 197-203.

Dweck, C. S. (2000) Self-theories: *Their role in motivation, personality, and development.* Philadelphia, PA: Psychology Press.

Elliott, A., McGregor, H., & Thrash, T. (2004). The need for competence. In E. Deci & R. Ryan (Eds.), *Handbook of self-determination research* (pp. 361-388). Rochester, NY: University of Rochester Press.

Harlen, W. The role of assessment in developing motivation for learning. In J. Gardner (Ed.). *Assessment and learning* (pp. 61-80). Thousand Oaks, CA: Sage.

Hubbard, R. S., & Power, B. M. (2003). The art of classroom inquiry, *A handbook for teachers-researchers* (2nd ed.). Portsmith, NH: Heinemann.

Koretz, D. Stecher, B. Klein, S. & McCaffrey, D. (1994). *The evolution of a portfolio program: The impact and quality of the Vermont program in its second year (1992-3).* (CSE Technical report 385) Los Angeles: University of California, Center for Research on Evaluation Standards and student Testing. Accessed January 25, 2006 from http://www.csr.ucla.edu.

Linn, R. L., & Miller, M. D. (2005). *Measurement and Assessment in Teaching* 9th ed. Upper Saddle River, NJ: Pearson .

Mertler, C. A. (2006). *Action research: Teachers as researchers in the classroom*. Thousand Oaks, CA: Sage.

Popham, W. J. (2005). *Classroom Assessment: What teachers need to know*. Boston, MA: Pearson.

Rowe, M. B. (2003). Wait-time and rewards as instructional variables, their influence on language, logic and fate control: Part one-wait time. *Journal of Research in science Teaching, 40* Supplement, S19-32.

Stiggins, R. J. (2002). *Assessment crisis: The absence of assessment FOR learning*. Phi Delta Kappan, 83 (10), 758-765.

Sutton, R. E. (2004). Emotional regulation goals and strategies of teachers. *Social Psychology of Education, 7*(4), 379-398.Teel, K. M., Debrin-Parecki, A., & Covington, M. V. (1998). Teaching strategies that honor and motivate inner-city African American students: A school/university collaboration. *Teaching and Teacher Education, 14*(5), 479-495.

Tschannen-Moran, M., Woolfolk-Hoy, A., & Hoy, W. K. (1998). Teacher efficacy: Its meaning and measure. *Review of Educational Research, 68*, 202-248.

12. Standardized and other formal assessments

Understanding standardized testing is very important for beginning teachers as K-12 teaching is increasingly influenced by the administration and results of standardized tests. Teachers also need to be able to help parents and students understand test results. Consider the following scenarios.

- *Vanessa, a newly licensed physical education teacher, is applying for a job at a middle school. During the job interview the principal asks how she would incorporate key sixth grade math skills into her PE and health classes as the sixth grade students in the previous year did not attain Adequate Yearly Progress in mathematics.*

- *Danielle, a first year science teacher in Ohio, is asked by Mr Volderwell, a recent immigrant from Turkey and the parent of a tenth grade son Marius, to help him understand test results. When Marius first arrived at school he took the Test of Cognitive Skills and scored on the eighty-fifth percentile whereas on the state Science Graduation test he took later in the school year he was classified as "proficient".*

- *James, a third year elementary school teacher, attends a class in gifted education over summer as standardized tests from the previous year indicated that while overall his class did well in reading the top 20 per cent of his students did not learn as much as expected.*

- *Miguel, a 1st grade student, takes two tests in fall and the results indicate that his grade equivalent scores are 3.3 for reading and 3.0 for math. William's parents want him immediately promoted into the second grade arguing that the test results indicate that he already can read and do math at the 3rd grade level. Greg, a first grade teacher explains to William's parents that a grade equivalent score of 3.3 does not mean William can do third grade work.*

Understanding standardized testing is difficult as there are numerous terms and concepts to master and recent changes in accountability under the *No Child Left Behind Act of 2001* (NCLB) have increased the complexity of the concepts and issues. In this chapter we focus on the information that beginning teachers need to know and start with some basic concepts.

Basic concepts

Standardized tests are created by a team—usually test experts from a commercial testing company who consult classroom teachers and university faculty—and are administered in standardized ways. Students not only respond to the same questions they also receive the same directions and have the same time limits. Explicit scoring criteria are used. Standardized tests are designed to be taken by many students within a state, province, or nation, and sometimes across nations. Teachers help administer some standardized tests and test manuals are provided that contain explicit details about the administration and scoring. For example, teachers may have to remove all the posters and charts from the classroom walls, read directions out loud to students using a script, and respond to student questions in a specific manner.

Criterion referenced standardized tests measure student performance against a specific standard or criterion. For example, newly hired firefighters in the Commonwealth of Massachusetts in the United States have to meet physical fitness standards by successfully completing a standardized physical fitness test that includes stair climbing, using a ladder, advancing a hose, and simulating a rescue through a doorway (Human Resources Division, n.d.). Criterion referenced tests currently used in US schools are often tied to state content standards and provide information about what students can and cannot do. For example, one of the content standards for fourth grade reading in Kentucky is "Students will identify and describe the characteristics of fiction, nonfiction, poetry or plays" (Combined Curriculum Document Reading 4.1, 2006) and so a report on an individual student would indicate if the child can accomplish this skill. The report may state that number or percentage of items that were successfully completed (e.g. 15 out of 20, i.e. 75 per cent) or include descriptions such as basic, proficient, or advanced which are based on decisions made about the percent of mastery necessary to be classified into these categories.

Norm referenced standardized tests report students' performance relative to others. For example, if a student scores on the seventy-second percentile in reading it means she outperforms 72 percent of the students who were included in the test's norm group. A norm group is a representative sample of students who completed the standardized test while it was being developed. For state tests the norm group is drawn from the state whereas for national tests the sample is drawn from the nation. Information about the norm groups is provided in a technical test manual that is not typically supplied to teachers but should be available from the person in charge of testing in the school district.

Reports from criterion and norm referenced tests provide different information. Imagine a nationalized mathematics test designed to basic test skills in second grade. If this test is norm referenced, and Alisha receives a report indicating that she scored in the eighty-fifth percentile this indicates that she scored better than 85 per cent of the students in the norm group who took the test previously. If this test is criterion-referenced Alisha's report may state that she mastered 65 per cent of the problems designed for her grade level. The relative percentage reported from the norm-referenced test provides information about Alisha's performance compared to other students whereas the criterion referenced test attempts to describe what Alisha or any student can or cannot do with respect to whatever the test is designed to measure. When planning instruction classroom teachers need to know what students can and cannot do so criterion referenced tests are typically more useful (Popham, 2004). The current standard-based accountability and NCLB rely predominantly on criterion based tests to assess attainment of content-based standards. Consequently the use of standardized norm referenced tests in schools has diminished and is largely limited to diagnosis and placement of children with specific cognitive disabilities or exceptional abilities (Haertel & Herman, 2005).

Some recent standardized tests can incorporate both criterion-referenced and norm referenced elements in to the same test (Linn & Miller, 2005). That is, the test results not only provide information on mastery of a content standard but also the percentage of students who attained that level of mastery.

Standardized tests can be high stakes i.e. performance on the test has important consequences. These consequences can be for students, e.g. passing a high school graduation test is required in order to obtain a diploma or passing PRAXIS II is a prerequisite to gain a teacher license. These consequences can be for schools, e.g. under NCLB an increasing percentage of students in every school must reach proficiency in math and reading each year. Consequences for schools who fail to achieve these gains include reduced funding and restructuring of the school building. Under NCLB, the consequences are designed to be for the schools not individual students (Popham, 2005) and their test results may not accurately reflect what they know because students may not try hard when the tests have low stakes for them (Wise & DeMars, 2005).

Uses of standardized tests

Standardized tests are used for a variety of reasons and the same test is sometimes used for multiple purposes.

Assessing students' progress in a wider context

Well-designed teacher assessments provide crucial information about each student's achievement in the classroom. However, teachers vary in the types of assessment they use so teacher assessments do not usually provide information on how students' achievement compares to externally established criteria. Consider two eighth grade students, Brian and Joshua, who received As in their middle school math classes. However, on the standardized norm referenced math test Brian scored in the fiftieth percentile whereas Joshua scored in the ninetieth percentile. This information is important to Brian and Joshua, their parents, and the school personnel. Likewise, two third grade students could both receive Cs on their report card in reading but one may pass 25 per cent and the other 65 per cent of the items on the Criterion Referenced State Test.

There are many reasons that students' performance on teacher assessments and standardized assessments may differ. Students may perform lower on the standardized assessment because their teachers have easy grading criteria, or there is poor alignment between the content they were taught and that on the standardized test, or they are unfamiliar with the type of items on the standardized tests, or they have test anxiety, or they were sick on the day of the test. Students may perform higher on the standardized test than on classroom assessments because their teachers have hard grading criteria, or the student does not work consistently in class (e.g. does not turn in homework) but will focus on a standardized test, or the student is adept at the multiple choice items on the standardized tests but not at the variety of constructed response and performance items the teacher uses. We should always be very cautious about drawing inferences from one kind of assessment.

In some states, standardized achievement tests are required for home-schooled students in order to provide parents and state officials information about the students' achievement in a wider context. For example, in New York home-schooled students must take an approved standardized test every other year in grades four through eight and every year in grades nine through twelve. These tests must be administered in a standardized manner and the results filed with the Superintendent of the local school district. If a student does not take the tests or scores below the thirty-third percentile the home schooling program may be placed on probation (New York State Education Department, 2005).

Diagnosing student's strengths and weaknesses

Standardized tests, along with interviews, classroom observations, medical examinations, and school records are used to help diagnose students' strengths and weaknesses. Often the standardized tests used for this purpose are administered individually to determine if the child has a disability. For example, if a kindergarten child is having trouble with oral communication, a standardized language development test could be administered to determine if there are difficulties with understanding the meaning of words or sentence structures, noticing sound differences in similar words, or articulating words correctly (Peirangelo & Guiliani, 2002). It would also be important to determine if the child was a recent immigrant, had a hearing impairment or mental retardation. The diagnosis of learning disabilities typically involves the administration of at least two types of standardized tests—an aptitude test to assess general cognitive functioning and an achievement test to assess knowledge of specific content areas (Peirangelo & Guiliani, 2006). We discuss the difference between aptitude and achievement tests later in this chapter.

Selecting students for specific programs

Standardized tests are often used to select students for specific programs. For example, the SAT (Scholastic Assessment Test) and ACT (American College Test) are norm referenced tests used to help determine if high school students are admitted to selective colleges. Norm referenced standardized tests are also used, among other criteria, to determine if students are eligible for special education or gifted and talented programs. Criterion referenced tests are used to determine which students are eligible for promotion to the next grade or graduation from high school. Schools that place students in ability groups including high school college preparation, academic, or vocational programs may also use norm referenced or criterion referenced standardized tests. When standardized tests are used as an essential criteria for placement they are obviously high stakes for students.

Assisting teachers' planning

Norm referenced and criterion referenced standardized tests, among other sources of information about students, can help teachers make decisions about their instruction. For example, if a social studies teacher learns that most of the students did very well on a norm referenced reading test administered early in the school year he may adapt his instruction and use additional primary sources. A reading teacher after reviewing the poor end-of-the-year criterion referenced standardized reading test results may decide that next year she will modify the techniques she uses. A biology teacher may decide that she needs to spend more time on genetics as her students scored poorly on that section of the standardized criterion referenced science test. These are examples of assessment for learning which involves data-based decision making. It can be difficult for beginning teachers to learn to use standardized test information appropriately, understanding that test scores are important information but also remembering that there are multiple reasons for students' performance on a test.

Accountability

Standardized tests results are increasingly used to hold teachers and administrators accountable for students' learning. Prior to 2002, many States required public dissemination of students' progress but under NCLB school districts in all states are required to send report cards to parents and the public that include results of standardized tests for each school. Providing information about students' standardized tests is not new as newspapers began printing summaries of students' test results within school districts in the 1970s and 1980s (Popham, 2005). However, public accountability of schools and teachers has been increasing in the US and many other countries and this increased accountability impacts the public perception and work of all teachers including those teaching in subjects or grade levels not being tested.

For example, Erin, a middle school social studies teacher, said:

"As a teacher in a 'non-testing' subject area, I spend substantial instructional time suporting the standardized testing requirements. For example, our school has instituted 'word of the day', which encourages teachers to use, define, and incorporate terminology often used in the tests (e.g. "compare", "oxymoron" etc.). I use the terms in my class as often as possible and incorporate them into written assignments. I also often use test questions of similar formats to the standardized tests in my own subject assessments (e.g. multiple choice questions with double negatives, short answer and extended response questions) as I believe that practice in the test question formats will help students be more successful in those subjects that are being assessed."

Accountability and standardized testing are two components of Standards Based Reform in Education that was initiated in the USA in 1980s. The two other components are academic content standards which are described later in this chapter and teacher quality which was discussed in Chapter 1.

Types of standardized tests

Achievement tests

Summarizing the past: K-12 achievement tests are designed to assess what students have learned in a specific content area. These tests include those specifically designed by states to access mastery of state academic content standards (see more details below) as well as general tests such as the California Achievement Tests, The Comprehensive Tests of Basic Skills, Iowa Tests of Basic Skills, Metropolitan Achievement Tests, and the Stanford Achievement Tests. These general tests are designed to be used across the nation and so will not be as closely aligned with state content standards as specifically designed tests. Some states and Canadian Provinces use specifically designed tests to assess attainment of content standards and also a general achievement test to provide normative information.

Standardized achievement tests are designed to be used for students in kindergarten though high school. For young children questions are presented orally, and students may respond by pointing to pictures, and the subtests are often not timed. For example, on the Iowa Test of Basic Skills (<u>http://www.riverpub.com/</u>) designed for students are young as kindergarten the vocabulary test assesses listening vocabulary. The teacher reads a word and may also read a sentence containing the word. Students are then asked to choose one of three pictorial response options.

Achievement tests are used as one criterion for obtaining a license in a variety of professions including nursing, physical therapy, and social work, accounting, and law. Their use in teacher education is recent and is part of the increased accountability of public education and most States require that teacher education students take achievement tests in order to obtain a teaching license. For those seeking middle school and high school licensure these are tests are in the content area of the major or minor (e.g. mathematics, social studies); for those seeking licenses in early childhood and elementary the tests focus on knowledge needed to teach students of specific grade levels. The most commonly used tests, the PRAXIS series, tests I and II, developed by Educational Testing Service, include three types of tests (<u>www.ets.org</u>):

- Subject Assessments, these test on general and subject-specific teaching skills and knowledge. They include both multiple-choice and constructed-response test items.

- Principles of Learning and Teaching (PLT) Tests assess general pedagogical knowledge at four grade levels: Early Childhood, K-6, 5-9, and 7-12. These tests are based on case studies and include constructed-response and multiple-choice items. Much of the content in this textbook is relevant to the PLT tests.

- Teaching Foundations Tests assess pedagogy in five areas: multi-subject (elementary), English, Language Arts, Mathematics, Science, and Social Science.

These tests include constructed-response and multiple-choice items which tests teacher education students. The scores needed in order to pass each test vary and are determined by each state.

Diagnostic tests

Profiling skills and abilities: Some standardized tests are designed to diagnose strengths and weaknesses in skills, typically reading or mathematics skills. For example, an elementary school child may have difficult in reading and one or more diagnostic tests would provide detailed information about three components: (1) word recognition, which includes phonological awareness (pronunciation), decoding, and spelling; (2) comprehension which includes vocabulary as well as reading and listening comprehension, and (3) fluency (Joshi 2003). Diagnostic tests are often administered individually by school psychologists, following standardized procedures. The examiner typically records not only the results on each question but also observations of the child's behavior such as distractibility or frustration. The results from the diagnostic standardized tests are used in conjunction with classroom observations, school and medical records, as well as interviews with teachers, parents and students to produce a profile of the student's skills and abilities, and where appropriate diagnose a learning disability.

Aptitude tests

Predicting the future: Aptitude tests, like achievement tests, measure what students have learned, but rather than focusing on specific subject matter learned in school (e.g. math, science, English or social studies), the test items focus on verbal, quantitative, problem solving abilities that are learned in school or in the general culture (Linn & Miller, 2005). These tests are typically shorter than achievement tests and can be useful in predicting general school achievement. If the purpose of using a test is to predict success in a specific subject (e.g. language arts) the best prediction is past achievement in language arts and so scores on a language arts achievement test would be useful. However when the predictions are more general (e.g. success in college) aptitude tests are often used. According to the test developers, both the ACT and SAT Reasoning tests, used to predict success in college, assess general educational development and reasoning, analysis and problem solving as well as questions on mathematics, reading and writing (http://www.collegeboard.com; http://www.act.org/). The SAT Subject Tests that focus on mastery of specific subjects like English, history, mathematics, science, and language are used by some colleges as entrance criteria and are more appropriately classified as achievement tests than aptitude tests even though they are used to predict the future.

Tests designed to assess general learning ability have traditionally been called Intelligence Tests but are now often called learning ability tests, cognitive ability tests, scholastic aptitude tests, or school ability tests. The shift in terminology reflects the extensive controversy over the meaning of the term intelligence and that its traditional use was associated with inherited capacity (Linn & Miller 2005). The more current terms emphasize that tests measure developed ability in learning not innate capacity. The Cognitive Abilities Test assesses K-12 students' abilities to reason with words, quantitative concepts, and nonverbal (spatial) pictures. The Woodcock Johnson III contains cognitive abilities tests as well as achievement tests for ages 2 to 90 years (<u>http://www.riverpub.com</u>).

High-stakes testing by states

While many States had standardized testing programs prior to 2000, the number of state-wide tests has grown enormously since then because NCLB required that all states test students in reading and mathematics annually in grades third through eighth and at least once in high school by 2005-6. Twenty-three states expanded their testing programs during 2005-6 and additional tests are being added as testing in science is required by 2007-8. Students with disabilities and English language learners must be included in the testing and provided a variety of accommodations so the majority of staff in school districts are involved in testing in some way (Olson, 2005). In this section we focus on these tests and their implications for teachers and students.

Standards based assessment

Academic content standards

NCLB mandates that states must develop academic content standards that specify what students are expected to know or be able to do at each grade level. These content standards used to be called goals and objectives and it is not clear why the labels have changed (Popham, 2004). Content standards are not easy to develop—if they are too broad and not related to grade level, teachers cannot hope to prepare students to meet the standards.

An example, a broad standard in reading is:

"Students should be able to construct meaning through experiences with literature, cultural events and philosophical discussion" (no grade level indicated). (American Federation of Teachers, 2006, p. 6).

Standards that are too narrow can result in a restricted curriculum. An example of a narrow standard might be:

Students can define, compare and contrast, and provide a variety of examples of synonyms and antonyms.

A stronger standard is:

"Students should apply knowledge of word origins, derivations, synonyms, antonyms, and idioms to determine the meaning of words (grade 4) (American Federation of Teachers, 2006, p. 6).

The American Federation of Teachers conducted a study in 2005-6 and reported that some of the standards in reading, math and science were weak in 32 states. States set the strongest standards in science followed by mathematics. Standards in reading were particularly problematic and with one-fifth of all reading standards redundant across the grade levels, i.e. word-by-word repetition across grade levels at least 50 per cent of the time (American Federation of Teachers, 2006).

Even if the standards are strong, there are often so many of them that it is hard for teachers to address them all in a school year. Content standards are developed by curriculum specialists who believe in the importance of their subject area so they tend to develop large numbers of standards for each subject area and grade level. At first glance, it may appear that there are only several broad standards, but under each standard there are subcategories called goals, benchmarks, indicators or objectives (Popham, 2004). For example, Idaho's first grade mathematics standard, judged to be of high quality (AFT 2000) contains five broad standards, including 10 goals and a total of 29 objectives (Idaho Department of Education, 2005-6).

Alignment of standards, testing and classroom curriculum

The state tests must be aligned with strong content standards in order to provide useful feedback about student learning. If there is a mismatch between the academic content standards and the content that is assessed then the test results cannot provide information about students' proficiency on the academic standards. A mismatch not only frustrates the students taking the test, teachers, and administrators it undermines the concept of accountability and the "theory of action" (See box "Deciding for yourself about the research") that underlies the NCLB. Unfortunately, the 2006 Federation of Teachers study indicated that in only 11 states were all the tests aligned with state standards (American Federation of Teachers, 2006).

State standards and their alignment with state assessments should be widely available—preferably posted on the states websites so they can be accessed by school personnel and the public. A number of states have been slow to do this.Table 43 summarizes which states had strong content standards, tests that were aligned with state standards, and adequate documents on online. Only 11 states were judged to meet all three criteria in 2006.

Table 43: Strong content standards, alignment, and transparency: evaluation for each state in 2006 (Adapted from American Federation of Teachers, 2006).

	Standards are strong	**Test documents match standards**	**Testing documents online**
Alabama			+
Alaska		+	+
Arizona		+	+
Arkansas		+	
California	+	+	+
Colorado			+
Connecticut			
Delaware		+	
District of Columbia	+	+	
Florida		+	+
Georgia	+		+
Hawaii		+	
Idaho	+		+
Illinois			+

Indiana		+	+
Iowa		+	
Kansas		+	+
Kentucky		+	+
Louisiana	+	+	+
Maine		+	
Maryland		+	
Massachusetts	+	+	
Michigan	+	+	
Minnesota		+	+
Mississippi			+
Missouri			
Montana			
Nebraska			
Nevada	+	+	+
New Hampshire		+	+
New Jersey	+		
New Mexico	+	+	+
New York	+	+	+
North Carolina	+		
North Dakota	+	+	
Ohio	+	+	+
Oklahoma		+	+
Oregon		+	+
Pennsylvania			+
Rhode Island		+	+
South Carolina			

South Dakota	+		+
Tennessee	+	+	+
Texas		+	+
Utah			+

Sampling content

When numerous standards have been developed it is impossible for tests to assess all of the standards every year, so the tests *sample* the content, i.e. measure some but not all the standards every year. Content standards cannot be reliably assessed with only one or two items so the decision to assess one content standard often requires not assessing another. This means if there are too many content standards a significant proportion of them are not measured each year. In this situation, teachers try to guess which content standards will be assessed that year and align their teaching on those specific standards. Of course if these guesses are incorrect students will have studied content not on the test and not studied content that is on the test. Some argue that this is a very serious problem with current state testing and Popham (2004) an expert on testing even said: "What a muddleheaded way to run a testing program." (p. 79)

Adequate Yearly Progress (AYP)

Under NCLB three levels of achievement, basic, proficient and advanced, must be specified for each grade level in each content area by each state. States were required to set a time table from 2002 that insured an increasing percentage of students would reach the proficient levels such that by 2013-14, so*every* child is performing at or the proficient level. Schools and school districts who meet this timetable are said to meet adequate yearly progress (AYP).

Because every child must reach proficiency by 2013-14 greater increases are required for those schools that had larger percentages of initially lower performing students.

Exhibit 16 illustrates the progress needed in three hypothetical schools. School A, initially the lowest performing school, has to increase the number of students reaching proficiency by an average of 6 per cent each year, the increase is 3 per cent for School B, and the increase is only 1 per cent for School C. Also, the checkpoint targets in the timetables are determined by the lower performing schools. This is illustrated on the figure by the arrow—it is obvious that School A has to make significant improvements by 2007-8 but School C does not have to improve at all by 2007-8. This means that schools that are initially lower performing are much more likely to fail to make AYP during the initial implementation years of NCLB.

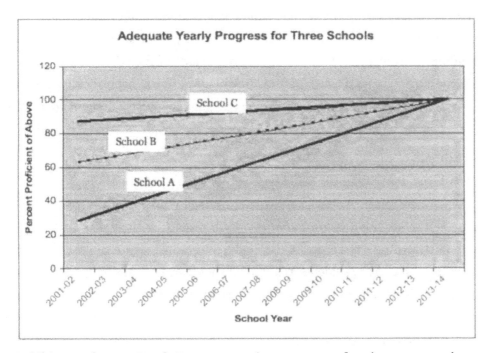

Exhibit 15: Adequate Yearly Progress requires greater student improvement in schools with lower levels of initial proficiency

Schools A, B and C all must reach 10 per cent student proficiency by 2013-4. However the school that initially has the lowest level of performance (A) has to increase the percentage of students proficient at a greater rate than schools with middle (B) or high (C) levels of initial proficiency rates.

Subgroups

For a school to achieve AYP not only must overall percentages of the students reach proficiency but subgroups must also reach proficiency in a process called desegregation. Prior to NCLB state accountability systems typically focused on overall student performance but this did not provide incentives for schools to focus on the neediest students, e.g. those children living below the poverty line (Hess & Petrilli, 2006). Under NCLB the percentages for each racial/ethnic group in the school (white, African American, Latino, Native American etc.), low income students, students with limited English proficiency, and students with disabilities are all calculated if there are enough students in the subgroup. A school may fail AYP if one group, e.g. English language learners do not make adequate progress. This means that it is more difficult for large diverse schools (typically urban schools) that have many subgroups to meet the demands of AYP than smaller schools with homogeneous student body (Novak & Fuller, 2003). Schools can also fail to make AYP if too few students take the exam. The drafters of the law were concerned that some schools might encourage low-performing students to stay home on the days of testing in order to artificially inflate the scores. So on average at least 95 per cent of any subgroup must take the exams each year or the school may fail to make AYP (Hess & Petrilli, 2006).

Sanctions

Schools failing to meet AYP for consecutive years, experience a series of increasing sanctions. If a school fails to make AYP for two years in row it is labeled "in need of improvement" and school personnel must come up with a school improvement plan that is based on "scientifically based research". In addition, students must be offered the option of transferring to a better performing public school within the district. If the school fails for three consecutive years, free tutoring must be provided to needy students. A fourth year of failure requires "corrective actions" which may include staffing changes, curriculum reforms or extensions of the school day or year. If the school fails to meet AYP for five consecutive years the district must "restructure" which involves major actions such as replacing the majority of the staff, hiring an educational management company, turning the school over to the state.

Growth or value added models

One concern with how AYP is calculated is that it is based on an absolute level of student performance at one point in time and does not measure how much students improve during each year. To illustrate this, Exhibit 16 shows six students whose science test scores improved from fourth to fifth grade. The circle represents a student's score in fourth grade and the tip of the arrow the test score in fifth grade. Note that students 1, 2, and 3 all reach the level of proficiency (the horizontal dotted line) but students 4, 5 and 6 do not. However, also notice that students 2, 5 and 6 improved much more than students 1, 3, and 4. The current system of AYP rewards students reaching the proficiency level rather than students' growth. This is a particular problem for low performing schools who may be doing an excellent job of improving achievement (students 5 and 6) but do not make the proficiency level. The US Department of Education in 2006 allowed some states to include growth measures into their calculations of AYP. While growth models traditionally tracked the progress of individual students, the term is sometimes used to refer to growth of classes or entire schools (Shaul, 2006).

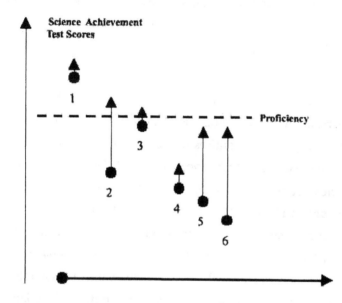

Exhibit 16: An illustration of value added vs proficiency approach to assessment. Each arrow represents the mathematics achievement results of one student who was tested in the fourth grade (shown by the dot) and also the fifth grade (shown by the tip of the arrow).

Some states include growth information on their report cards. For example, Tennessee (http://www.k-12.state.tn.us/rptcrd05/) provides details on which schools meet the AYP but also whether the students' scores on tests represent average growth, above average, or below average growth within the state. Exhibit 17 illustrates in a simple way the kind of information that is provided. Students in schools A, B, and C all reached proficiency and AYP but in Schools D, E, and F did not. However, students in schools A and D had low growth, in schools B and E average growth, in schools C and F high growth. Researchers have found that in some schools students have high levels of achievement but do not grow as much as expected (School A), and also that in some schools, the achievement test scores are not high but the students are growing or learning a lot (School F). These are called "school effects" and represent the effect of the school on the learning of the students.

	Low growth	Average growth	High growth	
Achievement	School A	School B	School C	
	School D	School E	School F	Proficiency

Exhibit 17: Proficiency and growth information

Growth over one year

Schools can vary on overall school achievement (proficiency) as well as the amount of growth in student learning, For example schools A, B, and C all have high achievement levels but only in School C do students have, on average, high growth. Schools D, C, and F all have low levels of proficiency but only in school D do students, on average, have low growth.

Growth models have intuitive appeal to teachers as they focus on how much a student learned during the school year—not what the student knew at the start of the school year. The current research evidence suggests that teachers matter a lot—i.e. students learn much more with some teachers than others. For example, in one study low-achieving fourth grade students in Dallas, Texas were followed for three years and 90 per cent of those who had effective teachers passed the seventh grade math test whereas only 42 per cent of those with ineffective teachers passed (cited in Bracey, 2004). Unfortunately, the same study reported that low achieving students were more likely to be assigned to ineffective teachers for three years in a row than high achieving students. Some policy makers believe that teachers who are highly effective should receive rewards including higher salaries or bonuses and that a primary criterion of effectiveness is assessed by growth models, i.e. how much students learn during a year (Hershberg, 2004). However, using growth data to make decisions about teachers is controversial as there is much more statistical uncertainty when using growth measures for a small group or students (e.g. one teacher's students) than larger groups (e.g. all fourth graders in a school district).

Growth models are also used to provide information about the patterns of growth among subgroups of students that may arise from the instructional focus of the teachers. For example, it may be that highest performing students in the classroom gain the most and the lowest performing students gain the least. This suggests that the teacher is focusing on the high achieving students and giving less attention to low achieving students. In contrast, it may be the highest performing students gain the least and the low performing students grow the most suggesting the teacher focuses on the low performing students and paying little attention to the high performing students. If the teacher focuses on the students "in the middle" they may grow the most and the highest and lowest performing students grow the least. Proponents of the value-added or growth models argue that teachers can use this information to help them make informed decisions about their teaching (Hershberg, 2004).

Differing state standards

Under NCLB each state devises their own academic content standards, assessments, and levels of proficiency. Some researchers have suggested that the rules of NCLB have encouraged states to set low levels of proficiency so it is easier to meet AYP each year (Hoff, 2002). Stringency of state levels of proficiency can be examined by comparing state test scores to scores on a national achievement test called the National Assessment of Educational Progress (NAEP). NCLB requires that states administer reading and math NAEP tests to a sample of fourth and eighth grade students every other year. The NAEP is designed to assess the progress of students at the state-wide or national level not individual schools or students and is widely respected as a well designed test that uses current best practices in testing. A large percentage of each test includes constructed-response questions and questions that require the use of calculators and other materials (http://nces.ed.gov/nationsreportcard).

Exhibit 18 illustrates that two states, Colorado and Missouri had very different state performance standards for the fourth grade reading/language arts tests in 2003. On the state assessment 67 per cent of the students in Colorado but only 21 per cent of the students in Missouri were classified as proficient. However, on the NAEP tests 34 per cent of Colorado students and 28 per cent of Missouri students were classified as proficient (Linn 2005). These differences demonstrate that there is no common meaning in current definitions of "proficient achievement" established by the states.

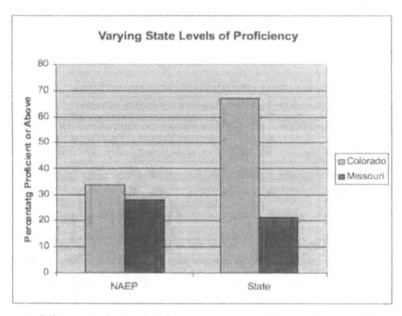

Exhibit 18: Relationship between state proficiency levels and scores on NAEP (Adapted from Linn 2005)

Implications for beginning teachers:

Dr Mucci is the principal of a suburban fourth through sixth grade school in Ohio that continues to meet AYP. We asked her what beginning teachers should know about high stakes testing by the states. "I want beginning teachers to be familiar with the content standards in Ohio because they clearly define what all students should know and be able to do. Not only does teaching revolve around the standards, I only approve requests for materials or professional development if these are related to the standards. I want beginning teachers to understand the concept of data-based decision making. Every year I meet with all the teachers in each grade level (e.g. fourth grade) to look for trends in the previous year's test results and consider remedies based on these trends. I also meet with each teacher in the content areas that are tested and discuss every student's achievement in his or her class so we can develop an instructional plan for every student. All interventions with students are research based. Every teacher in the school is responsible for helping to implement these instructional plans, for example the music or art teachers must incorporate some reading and math into their classes. I also ask all teachers to teach test taking skills, by using similar formats to the state tests, enforcing time limits, making sure students learn to distinguish between questions that required an extended response using complete sentences versus those that only requires one or two words, and ensuring that students answer what is actually being asked. We begin this early in the school year and continue to work on these skills, so by spring, students are familiar with the format, and therefore less anxious about the state test. We do everything possible to set each student up for success."

The impact of testing on classroom teachers does not just occur in Dr Mucci's middle school. A national survey of over 4,000 teachers indicated that the majority of teachers reported that the state mandated tests were compatible with their daily instruction and were based on curriculum frameworks that all teachers should follow. The majority of teachers also reported teaching test taking skills and encouraging students to work hard and prepare. Elementary school teachers reported greater impact of the high stakes tests: 56 per cent reported the tests influenced their teaching daily or a few times a week compared to 46 per cent of middle school teacher and 28 per cent of high school teachers. Even though the teachers had adapted their instruction because of the standardized tests they were skeptical about them with 40 per cent reporting that teachers had found ways to raise test scores without improving student learning and over 70 per cent reporting that the test scores were not an accurate measure of what minority students know and can do (Pedulla, Abrams, Madaus, Russell, Ramos, & Miao; 2003).

International testing
Testing in the Canadian provinces

Canada has developed a system of testing in the provinces as well as national testing. Each province undertakes its own curriculum based assessments. At the elementary school level provinces assess reading and writing (language arts) as well as mathematics (also called numeracy). In the middle grades science and social studies is often assessed in addition to language arts and mathematics. Summary results of these tests are published but there are no specific consequences for poor performance for schools. In addition, these tests are not high stakes for students. At the secondary school level high stakes curriculum based exit tests are common (http://edudata.educ.ubc.ca/Data_Pages/PanCan.htm).

Canada has developed pan-Canada assessment in mathematics, reading and writing, and science that are administered to a random sample of schools across the country. These assessments are intended to determine whether, on average, students across Canada reach similar levels of performance at about the same age (http://www.cmec.ca/pcap/indexe.stm). They are not intended to provide individual feedback to students are similar in purpose to the NAEP tests administered in the United States.

International comparisons

Along with the increasing globalization has come an interest with international comparisons in educational achievement and practices and more than 40 countries participate in two major testing initiatives. The Trends in International Mathematics and Science Study (TIMSS) have assessed students in fourth and eighth grades four times through 2007. The Programme for International Assessment (PISA) have assessed 15-year-olds in reading, mathematical and science literacy in more than forty countries on three times since 2000. The items on both series of tests include multiple choice, short answer and constructed response formats and are translated into more than 30 languages.

Policy makers are often interested in the comparison of average students' scores across countries. For example, in eighth grade science on the 2003 TIMMS students from Canada, United States, Hong Kong, and Australia scored significantly higher than the international average whereas students from Egypt, Indonesia, and the Philippines scored significantly below the international average (TIMMS 2003). On the mathematics test in the 2003 PISA, 15-year-old students from Hong Kong, China and Finland scored higher than students from Canada and New Zealand who in turn scored higher than the students from United States and Spain, who in turn scored higher than the student from Mexico and Brazil (OECD, 2004).

Both series of tests also collect survey data from students, teachers or school principals allowing for information about instructional practices and student characteristics. For example, teachers from the Philippines report spending almost twice as much time teaching science to fourth graders than in the United States (Martin, Mullis, Gonzalez, & Chrostowski, (2004). Student reports from PISA indicate that there is considerable cross-country variation in how much students feel anxiety when doing mathematics. Students in France, Italy, Japan, Korea report feeling the most anxious whereas students in Denmark, Finland and Netherlands and Sweden feel the least anxious (OECD 2004).

Understanding test results

In order to understand test results from standardized tests it is important to be familiar with a variety of terms and concepts that are fundamental to "measurement theory", the academic study of measurement and assessment. Two major areas in measurement theory, reliability and validity, were discussed in the previous chapter; in this chapter we focus on concepts and terms associated with test scores.

The basics

Frequency distributions

A frequency distribution is a listing of the number of students who obtained each score on a test. If 31 students take a test, and the scores range from 11 to 30 then the frequency distribution might look like Table 44. We also show the same set of scores on a histogram or bar graph inExhibit 20. The horizontal (or x axis) represents the score on the test and the vertical axis (y axis) represents the number or frequency of students. Plotting a frequency distribution helps us see what scores are typical and how much variability there are in the scores. We describe more precise ways of determining typical scores and variability next.

Table 44: Frequency distribution for 30 scores

Score on test	Frequency	Central tendency measures
17	1	
18	1	
19	0	
20	3	
21	2	
22	6	Mode
23	3	Median
24	2	Mean
25	0	
26	2	
27	6	Mode
28	2	
29	2	
30	1	
TOTAL	31	

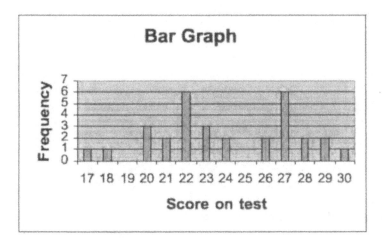

Exhibit 19: Tests scores from Table 44represented as a bar graph

Central tendency and variability

There are three common ways of measuring central tendency or which score(s) are typical. The *mean* is calculated by adding up all the scores and dividing by the number of scores. In the example in Table 44, the mean is 24. The *median* is the "middle" score of the distribution—that is half of the scores are above the median and half are below. The median on the distribution is 23 because 15 scores are above 23 and 15 are below. The *mode* is the score that occurs most often. In Table 44 there are actually two modes 22 and 27 and so this distribution is described as bimodal. Calculating the mean, median and mode are important as each provides different information for teachers. The median represents the score of the "middle" students, with half scoring above and below, but does not tell us about the scores on the test that occurred most often. The mean is important for some statistical calculations but is highly influenced by a few extreme scores (called outliers) but the median is not. To illustrate this, imagine a test out of 20 points taken by 10 students, and most do very well but one student does very poorly. The scores might be 4, 18, 18, 19, 19, 19, 19, 19, 20, 20. The mean is 17.5 (170/10) but if the lowest score (4) is eliminated the mean is now is 1.5 points higher at 19 (171/9). However, in this example the median remains at 19 whether the lowest score is included. When there are some extreme scores the median is often more useful for teachers in indicating the central tendency of the frequency distribution.

The measures of central tendency help us summarize scores that are representative, but they do not tell us anything about how variable or how spread out are the scores. Exhibit 20 illustrates sets of scores from two different schools on the same test for fourth graders. Note that the mean for each is 40 but in School A the scores are much less spread out. A simple way to summarize variability is the **range**, which is the lowest score subtracted from the lowest score. In School A with low variability the range is (45—35) = 10; in the school B the range is (55-22 = 33).

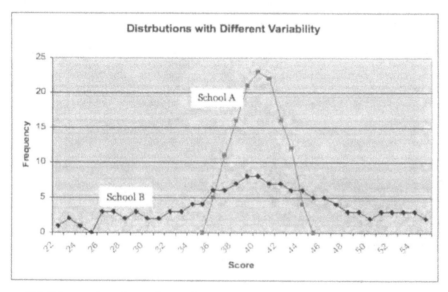

Exhibit 20: Fourth grade math scores in two different schools with the same mean but different variability

However, the range is only based on two scores in the distribution, the highest and lowest scores, and so does not represent variability in all the scores. The **standard deviation** is based on how much, on average, all the

294

scores deviate from the mean. In the example in Exhibit 17 the standard deviations are 7.73 for School A and 2.01 for School B. In the exercise below we demonstrate how to calculate the standard deviation.

Calculating a standard deviation

Example: The scores from 11 students on a quiz are 4, 7, 6, 3, 10, 7, 3, 7, 5, 5, and 9

5. Order scores.

6. Calculate the mean score.

7. Calculate the deviations from the mean.

8. Square the deviations from the mean.

9. Calculate the mean of the squared deviations from the mean (i.e. sum the squared deviations from the mean then divide by the number of scores). This number is called the variance.

10. Take the square root and you have calculated the standard deviation.

Score (Step 1, order)	Deviation from the mean	Squared deviation from the mean	
3	-3	9	
3	-3	9	
4	-2	4	(Step 4-5, complete the calculations)
5	-1	1	Formula:
5	-1	1	$Standard\ deviation = \dfrac{\sqrt{\sum (Score - Mean)^2}}{N}$
6	0	0	N = Number of scores
7	1	1	
7	1	1	
7	1	1	
9	3	9	
10	4	4	
TOTAL = 66		40	
(Step 2, calculate mean) MEAN 66/11 = 6		(Step 3, calculate deviations) Mean = 40/11 = 3.64	(Step 6, find the standard deviation) $Standard\ deviation = \sqrt{3.64} = 1.91$

Exhibit 21: Calculating a standard deviation

The normal distribution

Knowing the standard deviation is particularly important when the distribution of the scores falls on a normal distribution. When a standardized test is administered to a very large number of students the distribution of scores is typically similar, with many students scoring close to the mean, and fewer scoring much higher or lower than the mean. When the distribution of scores looks like the bell shape shown in Exhibit 19 it is called a normal distribution. In the diagram we did not draw in the scores of individual students as we did in Exhibit 20, because distributions typically only fall on a normal curve when there are a large number of students; too many to show individually. A normal distribution is symmetric, and the mean, median and mode are all the same.

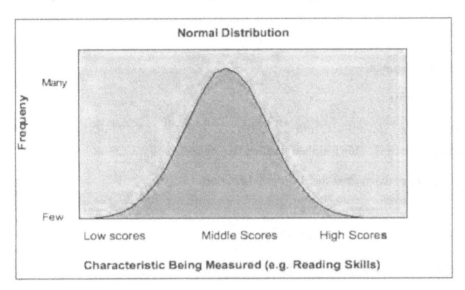

Exhibit 22: Bell shaped curve of normal distribution

Normal curve distributions are very important in education and psychology because of the relationship between the mean, standard deviation, and percentiles. In all normal distributions 34 per cent of the scores fall between the mean and one standard deviation of the mean. Intelligence tests often are constructed to have a mean of 100 and standard deviation of 15 and we illustrate that in Exhibit 15.

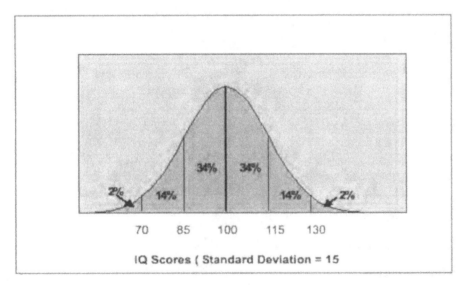

Exhibit 23: Normal distribution for an IQ test with mean 100 and standard deviation 15

In this example, 34 per cent of the scores are between 100 and 115 and as well, 34 per cent of the scores lie between 85 and 100. This means that 68 per cent of the scores are between -1 and +1 standard deviations of the mean (i.e. 85 and 115). Note than only 14 per cent of the scores are between +1 and +2 standard deviations of the mean and only 2 per cent fall above +2 standard deviations of the mean.

In a normal distribution a student who scores the mean value is always in the fiftieth percentile because the mean and median are the same. A score of +1 standard deviation above the mean (e.g. 115 in the example above) is the 84 per cent tile (50 per cent and 34 per cent of the scores were below 115). In Exhibit 10 we represent the percentile equivalents to the normal curve and we also show standard scores. [1]

Kinds of test scores

A **standard score** expresses performance on a test in terms of standard deviation units above of below the mean (Linn & Miller, 2005). There are a variety of standard scores:

Z-score: One type of standard score is a **z-score,** in which the mean is 0 and the standard deviation is 1. This means that a z-score tells us directly how many standard deviations the score is above or below the mean. For example, if a student receives a z score of 2 her score is two standard deviations above the mean or the eighty-fourth percentile. A student receiving a z score of -1.5 scored one and one half deviations below the mean. Any score from a normal distribution can be converted to a z score if the mean and standard deviation is known. The formula is:

$$Z-score = \frac{Score - mean\ score}{Standard\ deviation}$$

So, if the score is 130 and the mean is 100 and the standard deviation is 15 then the calculation is:

$$Z = \frac{130 - 100}{15} = 2$$

If you look at Exhibit 15 you can see that this is correct—a score of 130 is 2 standard deviations above the mean and so the z score is 2.

T-score: A **T-score** has a mean of 50 and a standard deviation of 10. This means that a T-score of 70 is two standard deviations above the mean and so is equivalent to a z-score of 2.

Stanines: Stanines (pronounced staynines) are often used for reporting students' scores and are based on a standard nine point scale and with a mean of 5 and a standard deviation of 2. They are only reported as whole numbers and Figure 11-10 shows their relation to the normal curve.

Grade equivalent sores

A grade equivalent score provides an estimate of test performance based on grade level and months of the school year (Popham, 2005, p. 288). A grade equivalent score of 3.7 means the performance is at that expected of a third grade student in the seventh month of the school year. Grade equivalents provide a continuing range of grade levels and so can be considered developmental scores. Grade equivalent scores are popular and seem easy to understand however they are typically misunderstood. If, James, a fourth grade student, takes a reading test and the grade equivalent score is 6.0; *this does not mean that James can do sixth grade work*. It means that James performed on

---

1 Exhibit 11.10 must be re-drawn. Please contact the Associate Editor for the original.

the *fourth grade test* as a sixth grade student is expected to perform. Testing companies calculate grade equivalents by giving one test to several grade levels. For example a test designed for fourth graders would also be given to third and fifth graders. The raw scores are plotted and a trend line is established and this is used to establish the grade equivalents. Note that in Error: Reference source not found the trend line extends beyond the grades levels actually tested so a grade equivalent above 5.0 or below 3.0 is based solely on the estimated trend lines.

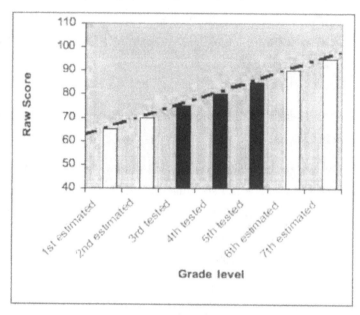

Exhibit 24: Using trend lines to estimate grade equivalent scores

Grade equivalent scores also assume that the subject matter that is being tested is emphasized at each grade level to the same amount and that mastery of the content accumulates at a mostly constant rate (Popham, 2005). Many testing experts warn that grade equivalent scores should be interpreted with considerable skepticism and that parents often have serious misconceptions about grade equivalent scores. Parents of high achieving students may have an inflated sense of what their child's levels of achievement.

Issues with standardized tests

Many people have very strong views about the role of standardized tests in education. Some believe they provide an unbiased way to determine an individual's cognitive skills as well as the quality of a school or district. Others believe that scores from standardized tests are capricious, do not represent what students know, and are misleading when used for accountability purposes. Many educational psychologists and testing experts have nuanced views and make distinctions between the information standardized tests can provide about students' performances and how the tests results are interpreted and used. In this nuanced view, many of the problems associated with standardized tests arise from their high stakes use such as using the performance on one test to determine selection into a program, graduation, or licensure, or judging a school as high vs low performing.

Are standardized tests biased?

In a multicultural society one crucial question is: Are standardized tests biased against certain social class, racial, or ethnic groups? This question is much more complicated than it seems because bias has a variety of meanings. An everyday meaning of bias often involves the fairness of using standardized test results to predict potential performance of disadvantaged students who have previously had few educational resources. For example, should Dwayne, a high school student who worked hard but had limited educational opportunities because of the poor schools in his neighborhood and few educational resources in his home, be denied graduation from high school because of his score on one test. It was not his fault that he did not have the educational resources and if given a chance with a change his environment (e.g. by going to college) his performance may blossom. In this view, test scores reflect societal inequalities and can punish students who are less privileged, and are often erroneously interpreted as a reflection of a fixed inherited capacity. Researchers typically consider bias in more technical ways and three issues will be discussed: item content and format; accuracy of predictions, and stereotype threat.

Item content and format. Test items may be harder for some groups than others. An example of social class bias in a multiple choice item asked students the meaning of the term *field*. The students were asked to read the initial sentence in italics and then select the response that had the same meaning of field (Popham 2004, p. 24):

> *My dad's <u>field</u> is computer graphics.*
>
> > *a. The pitcher could field his position*
> >
> > *b. We prepared the field by plowing it*
> >
> > *c. The doctor examined my field of vision*
> >
> > *d. What field will you enter after college?*

Children of professionals are more likely to understand this meaning of field as doctors, journalists and lawyers have "fields", whereas cashiers and maintenance workers have jobs so their children are less likely to know this meaning of field. (The correct answer is D).

Testing companies try to minimize these kinds of content problems by having test developers from a variety of backgrounds review items and by examining statistically if certain groups find some items easier or harder. However, problems do exist and a recent analyses of the verbal SAT tests indicated that whites tend to scores better on *easy* items whereas African Americans, Hispanic Americans and Asian Americans score better on *hard* items (Freedle, 2002). While these differences are not large, they can influence test scores. Researchers think that the easy items involving words that are used in every day conversation may have subtly different meanings in different subcultures whereas the hard words (e.g. vehemence, sycophant) are not used in every conversation and so do not have these variations in meaning. Test formast can also influence test performance. Females typically score better at essay questions and when the SAT recently added an essay component, the females overall SAT verbal scores improved relative to males (Hoover, 2006).

Accuracy of predictions

Standardized tests are used among other criteria to determine who will be admitted to selective colleges. This practice is justified by predictive validity evidence—i.e. that scores on the ACT or SAT are used to predict first year college grades. Recent studies have demonstrated that the predictions for black and Latino students are less accurate than for white students and that predictors for female students are less accurate than male students (Young, 2004). However, perhaps surprisingly the test scores tend to slightly over predict success in college for black and Latino students, i.e. these students are likely to attain *lower* freshman grade point averages than predicted by their test scores. In contrast, test scores tend to slightly under predict success in college for female students, i.e. these students are likely to attain higher freshman grade point averages than predicted by their test scores. Researchers are not sure why there are differences in how accurately the SAT and ACT test predict freshman grades.

Stereotype threat

Groups that are negatively stereotyped in some area, such as women's performance in mathematics, are in danger of stereotype threat, i.e. concerns that others will view them through the negative or stereotyped lens (Aronson & Steele, 2005). Studies have shown that test performance of stereotyped groups (e.g. African Americans, Latinos, women) declines when it is emphasized to those taking the test that (a) the test is high stakes, measures intelligence or math and (b) they are reminded of their ethnicity, race or gender (e.g. by asking them before the test to complete a brief demographic questionnaire). Even if individuals believe they are competent, stereotype threat can reduce working memory capacity because individuals are trying to suppress the negative stereotypes. Stereotype threat seems particularly strong for those individuals who desire to perform well. Standardized test scores of individuals from stereotyped groups may significantly underestimate actual their competence in low-stakes testing situations.

Do teachers teach to the tests?

There is evidence that schools and teachers adjust the curriculum so it reflects what is on the tests and also prepares students for the format and types of items on the test. Several surveys of elementary school teachers indicated that more time was spent on mathematics and reading and less on social studies and sciences in 2004 than 1990 (Jerald, 2006). Principals in high minority enrollment schools in four states reported in 2003 they had reduced time spent on the arts. Recent research in cognitive science suggests that reading comprehension in a subject (e.g. science or social studies) requires that students understand a lot of vocabulary and background knowledge in that subject (Recht & Leslie, 1988). This means that even if students gain good reading skills they will find learning science and social studies difficult if little time has been spent on these subjects.

Taking a test with an unfamiliar format can be difficult so teachers help students prepare for specific test formats and items (e.g. double negatives in multiple choice items; constructed response). Earlier in this chapter a middle school teacher, Erin, and Principal Dr Mucci described the test preparation emphasis in their schools. There is growing concern that the amount of test preparation that is now occurring in schools is excessive and students are not being educated but trained to do tests (Popham, 2004).

Do students and educators cheat?

It is difficult to obtain good data on how widespread cheating is but we know that students taking tests cheat and others, including test administrators, help them cheat (Cizek, 2003; Popham 2006). Steps to prevent cheating by students include protecting the security of tests, making sure students understand the administration procedures, preventing students from bringing in their notes or unapproved electronic devices as well as looking at each others answers. Some teachers and principals have been caught using unethical test preparation practices such as giving actual test items to students just before the tests, giving students more time than is allowed, answering students' questions about the test items, and actually changing students' answers (Popham, 2006). Concerns in Texas about cheating led to the creation of an independent task force in August 2006 with 15 staff members from the Texas

Education Agency assigned investigate test improprieties. (Jacobson, 2006). While the pressure on schools and teachers to have their student perform well is large these practices are clearly unethical and have lead to school personnel being fired from their jobs (Cizek, 2003).

Chapter summary

Standardized tests are developed by a team of experts and are administered in standard ways. They are used for a variety of educational purposes including accountability. Most elementary and middle school teachers are likely to be responsible for helping their students attain state content standards and achieve proficiency on criterion-referenced achievement tests. In order for teachers to interpret test scores and communicate that information to students and parents they have to understand basic information about measures of central tendency and variability, the normal distribution, and several kinds of test scores. Current evidence suggests that standardized tests can be biased against certain groups and that many teachers tailor their curriculum and classroom tests to match the standardized tests. In addition, some educators have been caught cheating.

Key terms

Achievement tests	Mean
Aptitude tests	Median
AYP (Annual Yearly Progress)	Mode
Criterion referenced tests	Norm referenced tests
Diagnostic tests	Range
Frequency distribution	Standard deviation
Grade equivalent scores	Stanine
High stakes tests	Z-score

On the Internet

<**http://www.cse.ucla.edu/**> The National Center for Research on Evaluation, Standards, and Student Testing (CRESST) at UCLA focuses on research and development that improves assessment and accountability systems. It has resources for researchers, K-12 teachers, and policy makers on the implications of NCLB as well as classroom assessment.

<**www.ets.org**> This is the home page of Educational Testing services which administers the PRAXIS II series of tests and has links to the testing requirements for teachers seeking licensure in each state District of Columbia and the US Virgin Islands.

<**http://www.ed.gov/nclb/landing.jhtml**> This is US Department of Education website devoted to promoting information and supporting and NCLB. Links for teachers and the summaries of the impact of NCLB in each state are provided.

References

American Federation of Teachers (2006, July) *Smart Testing: Let's get it right*. AFT Policy Brief. Retrieved August 8th 2006 from http://www.aft.org/presscenter/releases/2006/smarttesting/Testingbrief.pdf

Aronson, J., & Steele, C. M. (2005). Stereotypes and the Fragility of Academic Competence, Motivation, and Self-Concept. In A. J. Elliott & C. S. Dweck (Eds.). *Handbook of competence and motivation*. (pp.436-456) Guilford Publications, New York.

12. Standardized and other formal assessments

Bracey, G. W. (2004). Value added assessment findings: Poor kids get poor teachers. *Phi Delta Kappan, 86,* 331- 333

Cizek, G. J. (2003). Detecting and preventing classroom cheating: Promoting integrity in assessment. Corwin Press, Thousand Oaks, CA.

Combined Curriculum Document Reading 4.1 (2006). Accessed November 19, 2006 from http://www.education.ky.gov/KDE/Instructional+Resources/Curriculum+Documents+and+Resources/ Teaching+Tools/Combined+Curriculum+Documents/default.htm

Freedle, R. O. (2003). Correcting the SAT's ethnic and social–class bias: A method for reestimating SAT scores. *Harvard Educational Review, 73* (1), 1-42.

Fuhrman, S. H. (2004). Introduction, In S. H. Fuhrman & R. F. Elmore (Eds). *Redesigning accountability systems for education.* (pp. 3-14). New York: Teachers College Press.

Haertel, E. & Herman, J. (2005) A historical perspective on validity arguments for accountability testing. In J. L.Herman & E. H. Haertel (Eds.) Uses and misuses of data for educational accountability and improvement. *104th Yearbook of the National Society for the Study of Education.* Malden, MA: Blackwell

Hershberg, T. (2004). *Value added assessment: Powerful diagnostics to improve instruction and promote student achievement.* American Association of School Administrators, Conference Proceedings. Retrieved August 21 2006 from www.cgp.upenn.edu/ope_news.html

Hess, F. H. Petrilli, M. J. (2006). *No Child Left Behind Primer.* New York: Peter Lang.

Hoff, D. J. (2002) States revise meaning of proficient. *Educational Week, 22,*(6) 1,24-25.

Hoover, E. (2006, October 21). SAT scores see largest dip in 31 years. *Chronicle of Higher Education,* 53(10), A1.

Human Resources Division (n. d.). Firefighter Commonwealth of Massachusetts Physical Abilities Test (PAT) Accessed November, 19, 2006 from http://www.mass.gov/? pageID=hrdtopic&L=2&L0=Home&L1=Civil+Service&sid=Ehrd

Idaho Department of Education (2005-6). *Mathematics Content standards and assessment by grade level.* Accessed November 22 2006 from http://www.sde.idaho.gov/instruct/standards/

Jacobson, L. (2006). Probing Test irregularities: Texas launches inquiry into cheating on exams. *Education Week, 28(1),* 28

Jerald, C. D (2006,August).*The Hidden costs of curriculum narrowing.* Issue Brief, Washington DC: The Center for Comprehensive School Reform and Improvement. Accessed November 21, 2006 from www.centerforcsri.org/

Joshi, R. M. (2003). Misconceptions about the assessment and diagnosis of reading disability. *Reading Psychology, 24,* 247-266.

Linn, R. L., & Miller, M. D. (2005). *Measurement and Assessment in Teaching* 9th ed. Upper Saddle River, NJ: Pearson .

Linn, R. L. (2005). *Fixing the NCLB Accountability System*. CRESST Policy Brief 8. Accessed September 21, 2006 from http://www.cse.ucla.edu/products/policybriefs_set.htm

New York State Education Department (2005). Home Instruction in New York State. Accessed on November 19, 2006 from http://www.emsc.nysed.gov/nonpub/part10010.htm

Martin, M.O., Mullis, I.V.S., Gonzalez, E.J., & Chrostowski, S.J. (2004). *Findings From IEA's Trends in International Mathematics and Science Study at the Fourth and Eighth Grades* Chestnut Hill, MA: TIMSS & PIRLS International Study Center, Boston College. Accessed September 23, 2006 from http://timss.bc.edu/timss2003i/scienceD.html

Novak, J. R. & Fuller, B (2003, December), *Penalizing diverse schools? Similar test scores, but different students bring federal sanctions. Policy analysis for policy education.* University of California, Berkeley School of Education: Berkeley CA. Accessed on September 21, 2006 from http://pace.berkeley.edu/pace_index.html

(OECD 2004). Learning for Tomorrow's World—First Results from PISA 2003. Accessed on September 23, 2006 from http://www.pisa.oecd.org/document/

Olson, L. (2005, November 30th). State test program mushroom as NCLB kicks in. *Education Week 25(13)* 10-12.

Pedulla, J Abrams, L. M. Madaus, G. F., Russell, M. K., Ramos, M. A., & Miao, J. (2003). *Perceived effects of state-mandated testing programs on teaching and learning: Findings from a national survey of teachers.* Boston College, Boston MA National Board on Educational Testing and Public Policy. Accessed September 21 2006 from http://escholarship.bc.edu/lynch_facp/51/

Popham, W. J. (2004). *America's "failing" schools. How parents and teachers can copy with No Child Left Behind.* New York: Routledge Falmer.

Popham, W. J. (2005). *Classroom Assessment: What teachers need to know.* Boston:, MA: Pearson.

Popham, W. J. (2006). Educator cheating on No Child Left Behind Tests. *Educational Week, 25* (32) 32-33.

Recht, D. R. & Leslie, L. (1988). Effect of prior knowledge on good and poor readers' memory of text. *Journal of Educational Psychology 80*, 16-20.

Shaul, M. S. (2006). *No Child Left Behind Act: States face challenges measuring academic growth.* Testimony before the House Committee on Education and the Workforce Government Accounting Office. Accessed September 25, 2006 from www.gao.gov/cgi-bin/getrpt?GAO-06-948T

Stiggins, R (2004). New Assessment Beliefs for a New School Mission, *Phi Delta Kappan, 86* (1) 22 -27.

Wise, S. L. & DeMars, C. W. (2005). Low examinee effort in low-stakes assessment: Problems and potential solutions. *Educational Assessment 10*(1), 1-17.

Young, J. W. (2004). Differential validity and prediction: Race and sex differences in college admissions testing. In R. Zwick (Ed). *Rethinking the SAT: The future of standardized testing in university admissions.* New York (pp. 289-301). Routledge Falmer.

Appendix A: Preparing for licensure

If you live in the United States or another country that certifies or licenses teachers with some form of test or assessment of knowledge of teaching, you will find the following case studies helpful in preparing for at least the test. The cases each deal with a realistic teaching problem or dilemma. They are followed by a few questions that can, in principle, be answered in short (half-page) essay format. (This style parallels the style of the PRAXIS II examination taken by many future teachers in the United States.) The content or topic of the cases parallel major topics of the chapters of *Educational Psychology*—one case per chapter.

Readers who are planning to take the PRAXIS II test, especially the version called "Principles of Learning and Teaching", will know that the test also includes a number of structured, multiple-choice items. We have not included any examples of multiple-choice test items here, but they are widely available in various published study guides for the PRAXIS II. Perhaps the most authoritative is the one published by the administrators of the PRAXIS itself, the Educational Testing Service:

Educational Testing Service. (2004). *Study guide for* Principles of Learning and Teaching, *2nd edition*. Princeton, NJ, USA: Author.

Preparing for licensure : the decline and fall of Jane Gladstone

See also Chapter 2, The learning process; Chapter 7, Classroom management and the learning environment.

Jane Gladstone was student teaching in a sixth-grade classroom. She had been there for several weeks, helping with activities and occasionally leading specific activities that she had devised herself. She liked the students and felt that she had been developing good relationships with them.

One morning Ms Wilson, her supervising teacher, had to leave unexpectedly. "Something's come up, Jane, and the principal needs me to come to a meeting right away. It could be awhile before I'm back, so you'll need to take care of things. But you know the routines now, don't you?"

Jane was surprised and a bit worried, but also excited by the challenge. She did indeed know the routines, so she smiled cheerfully as Ms Wilson went out the door. "OK, everyone", she said. "We'll start with language arts. Turn to where we left off yesterday, page 46."

"But Ms Gladstone", said Paul, "We actually left off on page 32."

"No, dummy!" chimed in Katherine, "You were absent yesterday, and the day before we had an assembly. Remember?" Suddenly three or four students were discussing where in fact the class had left off in the book, and therefore where Jane ought to begin. Jane was wondering that herself.

"Page 46!" she said firmly—actually more firmly than she had intended. But the students agreed, and the lesson began. The lesson turned out to be a short story about an athlete who trained hard as a runner for a local competition. Students took turns reading selections from the story, and in this way got about half way through it. Then Joe raised his hand.

"Ms Gladstone", he asked. "Do you think athletes should be arrested for taking steroids?" Jane was taken off guard by this. She had been determined to finish the lesson smoothly. All she could think to say was, "Well I don't know. That's a hard question."

"My dad says they *should* be arrested, and that no one should have any doubts about that."

In seconds the language arts lesson was forgotten and students were arguing about whether athletes should take drugs. For the moment Jane was on the sidelines.

"My uncle took steroids at university", said Frank, "and it never hurt him."

"Gross!" called out Jill from across the room. "I suppose *you* take them too, then?"

"What's that supposed to mean?" asked Frank, obviously annoyed.

"She's saying your too fat, Frank", said Joe. "That's what steroids do, you know."

Jane was getting worried. How could she get the discussion back on track? Students were just getting more worked up.

"I've never taken any drugs!"

"Not real drugs—steroids—you weren't listening."

"I bet you have, though..."

On it went, with some students getting annoyed and others clearly tuning out. What if Ms Wilson came back now?

"BE QUIET!" Jane shouted, surprised at hearing herself be so loud. Everyone got still instantly, stunned and surprised. But not for long.

"Be quiet!" someone mimicked softly from the back of the room. A few snickers. Then someone else said it, with sarcasm dripping from the words. "Be quiet!" Jane glowered at the class, wondering what to do next.

Questions

> ➤ What did Jane do wrong?

> ➤ (a) How could the students' inappropriate behaviors be considered examples of operant behaviors being reinforced?

> ➤ (b) In what way did Jane's "clamping down" on the students reinforce Jane?

> ➤ Describe briefly a way for Jane and Ms Wilson to prevent behavior problems from occurring when and if Jane has to take over the class unexpectedly.

Preparing for licensure : Joey's individual educational plan

See also Chapter 5, Students with special educational needs; Chapter 10, Planning instruction.

> The following are excerpts from two parts of the Individual Educational Plan (IEP) for a fourth-grade student named Joey who has an intellectual disability. The excerpts list various performance objectives and actions, but only some of these are complete. For others—marked with question marks (??)—relevant information or plans have been deliberately left blank. Read the excerpts and then respond to the questions that follow:

Part 1: domain—communication

Performance Objectives	Methods, Materials, or Strategies	Roles and Responsibilities	Assessment
1. Joey will increase his vocabulary in all areas—people, things, and actions.	- Joey will use pictures to learn new words - TA will prompt active responses—e.g. "Show me ___." - Conversation book with pictures of Joey doing things	Teacher: -monitor -plan daily activities TA (i.e. "Teacher Assistant"): -modeling -direct instruction	-informal observation -checklists re whether desired vocabulary is being learned
2. Joey will begin using 2- or 3-word sentences more often.	-Joey will be provided with model phrases such as: " ___ ?? ___ " -Joey will be given an entire sentence and then ___ ?? ___	Teacher: -modeling TA: -modeling -facilitating	-informal observations -checklists of particular sentences used

Part 2: domain—academic/cognitive

Performance Objectives	Methods, Materials, or Strategies	Roles and Responsibilities	Assessment
3. Joey will recognize and print his name.	-Cards with one student's name per card. Joey will ___??___ -Make name using ___??___ -___??___	Teacher: -monitor TA: -facilitate -model	- ___??___
4. ___??___	-___??___ -___??___	Teacher: -monitor TA: -facilitate -model	-___??___ -___??___

Questions

> For Performance Objectives #2 and #3, the sample phrases and model sentences are missing in the "Methods, Materials, and Strategies" column. Suggest two reasonable sample phrases and two model sentences to fill in these blanks. Then suggest how each of the teaching strategies illustrate principles of learning.

> For Performance Objective #3, what is missing in the "Assessment" column? Suggest a reasonable method of assessment and then explain (1) why the method would be both valid and practical, and (2) any cautions the teacher should be aware of in using the method of assessment.

> Performance Objective #4 is missing both "Methods, Materials, and Strategies" and "Assessment." Fill in both boxes—i.e. suggest two ways of implementing the objective and two ways of assessing it. Then explain how your suggestions reflect the nature of Performance Objective #4.

Preparing for licensure: Rosemary's instructional decision

See also Chapter 8, Nature of classroom communication; Chapter 9, Facilitating complex thinking.

Rosemary had planned a lesson for her second grade class about personal and social management, but she was not satisfied with it. She had taken the general goal directly from the state's official curriculum guide for health education: "Students will identify positive communication skills", it said. But the guide said nothing about how to translate this goal into practice.

She was thinking that she would use puppets to demonstrate how to communicate in positive ways. The puppets would engage in dialogue, during which they would nod their heads appropriately, focus on the speaker, not interrupt, and keep still while listening. Maybe she would include a few communication mistakes as well—times when a puppet might interrupt in appropriately, for example—and challenge students to identify those moments.

Her plan seemed fine as far as it went, but she felt unsure about two things. One concern was how to make sure that students got the point of the activity, and did not regard it simply as entertainment. How should she introduce the activity? What should she say about it, either beforehand, during, or afterwards? What exactly should she tell students she is expecting from them?

The other concern was with the very format of the activity. She did not want students just to know about good communication skills; she wanted them to *use* them as well. The puppets did not seem to help with this latter purpose. How, she wondered, could she get students to take responsibility for practicing good communication? Was there a way to modify or extend the puppet activity that would do this? Or perhaps additional activities that students could do?

Think of the range of instructional strategies available to Rosemary. Then answer each of the following questions.

Questions

> ➤ Choose *two* strategies that would help her with the first of her concerns—with making sure that students understood the purpose of the puppets lesson. Compose an imaginary script of what she might say before, during, and after using the puppets in the way described.

> ➤ Devise one way to *modify* the puppet activity so that it focused less on students' knowledge of communication and more on students' skills with communication.

> ➤ Devise one *additional* activity to develop students' skills with communication and their sense of responsibility for doing so. Outline each activity in point (or summary) form.

> ➤ Comment briefly on how each of your answers above (to Questions #1-3) draws on principles and methods of major instructional strategies.

Preparing for licensure: *Mr Cullen teaches about houses*

See also Chapter 10, Planning instruction; Chapter 4, Student diversity.

Mr Cullen teaches fifth grade at an urban elementary school, where one of the normal curriculum topics is about "where people live". The general goal of the unit, as expressed in the curriculum framework document from the State Department of Education, is for students "to understand the nature and purposes of houses and how they are affected by the circumstances of their society". To get started in planning the unit, Mr Cullen brainstormed the conceptual web of ideas and topics shown below as "Document 1" below. He also introduced students to making conceptual webs about houses, one of which is shown below as "Document 2". Part way through the unit, in addition, he took the class on a simple field trip to look at the houses in the residential neighborhood near the school. His notes about that field trip are shown as "Document 3".

Document 1: Mr Cullen's conceptual map about houses

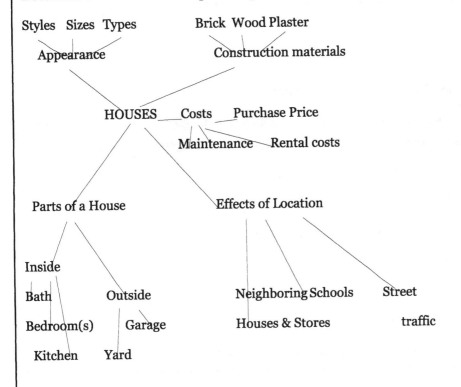

311

Document 2: Jill's conceptual map about houses

Document 3: Notes on Field Trip Looking at Neighborhood Houses

20 students walked about ½ mile around the neighborhood (30 minutes) and viewed approximately 100 houses in the process. Behavior during the walk was generally good.

Several questions asked by students (no particular order of importance):

(a) "Who lives in these houses?"

(b) "Why are some houses painted nicely but others are not?"

(c) "Why are some houses bigger than others?"

(d) "Where are some really BIG houses?"

(e) "Do children play on these yards and streets?"

Question to myself: How to address these questions back in class?

Questions

> Compare the concept webs of Mr Cullen and of the two students. Identify one topic or goal that appears to be a priority for all three individuals. Then devise a strategy or activity appropriate for teaching about this topic or goal. Use principles of instructional planning such as described in this chapter.

> ➤ Identify a topic or goal that appears to be a priority only for Mr Cullen (i.e. that does not appear on either student's concept web). Devise a strategy or activity appropriate for teaching about this topic or goal, taking into account the possibility that the students have less prior knowledge or motivation about this topic than about the one identified in Question #1.

> ➤ Identify a topic or goal that appears to be a priority only for one of the students (i.e. that appears only on that student's concept web). Devise a strategy or activity appropriate for supporting the student in pursuing this topic, and for connecting it to at least one other topic in Mr Cullen's concept web.

> ➤ Choose any two of the questions cited in Mr Cullen's field trip notes. Discuss how these questions might be addressed in the context of one of the other activities described in Questions #1-#3 "Deciding for yourself about research".

Preparing for licensure: facilitating students' communication through group work

See also Chapter 7, Classroom management and the learning environment; Chapter 8, The nature of classroom communication.

Scene 1: Barbara Fuller makes plans

It is late August.

Barbara Fuller, a third grade teacher, peers about her classroom, wondering how she will organize her program for the coming year. She wants to try some sort of collaborative group work because she has heard good things about it—especially that it gets students talking to each other in ways that are productive rather than mere chit-chat. Ms Fuller is thinking of trying a group project for social studies that she is calling "How many people does it take to raise a child?" Students are supposed to explore how people outside the family contribute to the welfare of infants and children. If they do collaborate successfully, then students can pool their research, share ideas and interpretations, and present their results to class more effectively.

Ms Fuller has read some very specific literature about how to get started with collaborative group work. One book recommends, for example, that she assign the members of each group rather than letting students select their own groups; this procedure is supposed to avoid cliques and ensure that everyone is included. But it also means that some group mates may not be each other's first choice. Ms Fuller considers this trade-off carefully, and finally decides to go ahead and assign the group members herself. To minimize possible complaints, she also decides to give each group an immediate task: choose a leader as well as a name for the group.

Scene 2: Collaborate groups that *don't* collaborate

Two weeks into the term, Ms Fuller begins the collaborative project about community helpers. She describes the purposes and advantages of group work: students can help each other, cover more reading material, and enjoy each other's company. They will also be challenged to explain what they learn to each other and to justify to each other their ideas for the final report and presentation.

Once the work begins, she begins noticing a variety of reactions from groups and the individuals within them. In one group (Ms Fuller dubs it "Group 1"), for example, Tom complains to her that he is the only boy in the group. "You'll be fine," she says to Tom. "If you look around, you'll see that most people are with other people they don't know terribly well." Tom looks uncomfortable with her response, but continues working.

In Group 2, Jasmine takes over almost immediately; everyone seems to agree that she should have this job. Unfortunately Jasmine is not pleased to be in charge: she issues orders reluctantly ("Kyla, you look up about nurses"), to which her group happily agree.

In Group 3, Ken and Serge confer about the project, but ignore the girls in the group. The girls soon are chatting about activities outside school, doodling in their notebooks, and apparently daydreaming.

In Group 4, Ms Fuller can hear voices periodically rising in anger. She can't make out who is saying what, but it seems to involve Jennifer, Sean, and possibly Lavar. The other two group members are sitting quietly, simply observing the argument and presumably waiting for it to be over.

Questions

➤ If you could speak to Ms Fuller right now (at the end of Scene 2), what advice could you give her to assist in continuing the activity? For this question, take the situation as it has in fact evolved so far; avoid giving advice, that is like "You should never have done X in the first place." Focus your advice on developing effective strategies of communication, either for Ms Fuller, for the students, or for both.

➤ Now imagine that you can, miraculously, turn the clock back to the beginning of Scene 1, when Ms Fuller was planning the collaborative activity in the first place. What advice could you give her at that initial point in time? Again, focus your advice on developing effective strategies of communication, either for Ms Fuller, for the students, or for both.

➤ Consider how nonverbal communication among the students might be affecting students' experience in particular. Describe a way in which one or more features of nonverbal communication might cause a collaborate group to fall apart or become unproductive. Then suggest ways that Ms Fuller might be able to help so that members of the group remained mutually supportive and productive.

Preparing for licensure: Ms Scanton teaches second grade

See also Chapter 10 Planning instruction; Appendix C: The reflective practitioner.

When Ms Scanton taught second grade, she kept a journal about her experiences. Sometimes she simply recorded interesting facts or information individuals, but other times she commented and reflected on individuals at more length. Here are three of her journal entries.

Document 1: **Ms Scanton's observation of Ashley's writing**

October 4: Ashley procrastinated a lot again today during journal-writing time—stared at the ceiling, at the kids near her, etc. etc. I reminded everyone that they were supposed to write about "this week at *school,*" but it didn't seem to sink in with Ashley. After sitting a long time, she drew a picture of her family—Mom, Dad, cat.

I know she especially loves her cat, but I also thought she should follow directions more closely. I ask her, "Is that all you've done?" She frowns. I smile—a sincere one.

"It's hard," she says cautiously—referring to the writing itself.

"But that's why it's important to work at it—to actually *write,*" say I.

A pause. Then, "How do you spell 'Mom'?" she asks.

I tell her to sound it out; ask what is the first sound, etc. /m/.../ah/.../m/... She says these sounds slowly, maybe to please me.

"/m/," she repeats, and then write down one letter: **M.** I have to leave to check on others. From a distance I see her write down **K,** then erase and switch it to **C.** Was she sounding out "cat"?

Document 2: **Later that year: Ms Scanton's log of Ashley's misspellings**

Ashley, November 21: Ashley is still misspelling so many words in her writing that I'm getting exasperated, to put it nicely. Here's a list of her misspellings from the past two weeks—mostly from her journal:

techrs   (teachers)

milmen(mailmen)

peliec   (police)

fier pepel (fire people)

pepl   (people)

librein (librarian)

lectrisudie (electricity)

doctrs   (doctors)

nrsis   (nurses)

loyors   (lawyers)

* What to do for her? *

Document #3: **Still later: Ms Scanton journal reflections**

April 21: Just finished a cool book, *GNYS AT WRK,* by Glenda Bissex, that made me think about Ashley and her misspellings. The author described her son's invented spellings and how they became more plentiful and complicated at first, but eventually became more "adultlike" or conventional. Fascinating! The mom was in no hurry to cure her child of his spelling problems, but he seemed to outgrow them on his own. The chief point seemed to be that invented spellings may be good because they show active efforts by the child to figure out the rules of spelling.

So maybe Ashley will outgrow her misspellings too? I do note that her misspellings—her inventions —have become more complicated across the year. Here's from her journal last week:

TDA W WT T JM NAD W PLY TWLIT TAG

With a little help from Ashley, I figured this out as "Today we went to gym and we played toilet tag."

Here's from the week before:

TIZ WK W MAD PTY MAX.

Translation: "This week we made party masks."

Quite a difference from the start of the year, when she would only write down a couple of letters during journal-writing time! Maybe I need to support her efforts more and worry about them less. But how to do that and still make sure she really is learning how to spell?

P.S. If you are interested, the book about invented spellings that Ms Scanton mentioned in Document #3 is listed in the bibliography.

Questions

> In these excerpts from her journal, Ms Scanton has observed and reflected on Ashley's learning to spell. Considered her activities as a whole, how much do they qualify as action research in the sense described in this chapter? What should be added or changed to make her activities a full-fledged example of action research?

> Consider the list of misspellings (or invented spellings) in Document #2. Suggest how, if at all, Ms Scanton might address those misspellings with Ashley. In particular, comment on whether she should make time to work with Ashley in the same way that she did in

Document #1. Assuming that she does make time, how she might set priorities about which word(s) to focus on if she does not have time to deal with them all?

➢ Suppose that Ms Scanton does not have time to review every misspelled word with Ashley. How else could she address Ashley's spelling problems? Consider briefly how she might use each of the following: (1) peer tutor, (2) classroom computer, (3) homework. Comment on how Ms Scanton might collect information about each of these strategies.

Appendix B: Deciding for yourself about the research

In most of this book, educational research is used to establish ideas and advice about teaching. Except in Chapter 13 ("The reflective practitioner"), however, we do not analyze research studies in depth. In this appendix therefore we look at examples or cases of research studies in detail. We describe how they were conducted, reflect on their significance and meaning, and pose a few questions to consider about each study. There is approximately one case per chapter, and their topics roughly parallel one or more of the major themes of each chapter. The references for the books cited are listed at the end of each case study, as well as in the bibliographies of the chapter related to each case. Looking at the research studies in detail gives a different perspective on the research than simply *using* the results: "up close" the implications of a study are often not as clear as when seen from a distance.

Deciding for yourself about the research

Chapter 1, The changing teaching profession and you: *effects of high-stakes testing on learning educational psychology*

As indicated in this chapter, the trend toward high-stakes testing has affected even the preparation of teachers themselves. Many American states now require new teachers to pass a standardized test of subject matter knowledge, and many also require them to pass a test about educational psychology—the sort of content that is the focus of this textbook (Cochran-Smith, 2003; Educational Testing Service [ETS], 2004). These changes highlight make the issues about testing very vivid—and at times anxiety-provoking—for many new teachers.

Rosemary Sutton studied the effects of high-stakes testing on her own teaching of educational psychology as well as on her undergraduate students' responses to studying this subject (Sutton, 2004). In her state of Ohio, new teachers must all take a test called the "PRAXIS II: Principles of Learning and Teaching" (ETS, 2004). She reported experiencing a number of new instructional dilemmas as a result of this test being introduced as a requirement for teacher licensing and certification, and she described how she resolved them. The effects of the dilemmas and of her solutions to them were not uniform, but depended on the particular feature of the course.

One negative effect was that Professor Sutton felt more pressure to cover as much of the content of the PRAXIS in her course as possible, so that students could be prepared as well as possible for the test. Doing so, however, meant covering more material and therefore reducing depth of coverage of certain topics. This was a serious problem, she feared, because some parts of the course became more shallow or fragmented. She also had less time for open-ended discussions that truly followed interests expressed by the students.

On the other hand, Professor Sutton also reported diversifying her teaching methods—for example by using more group work and less lecturing—as a way to make class sessions more interesting and motivating, and therefore insuring that students learned the increased material as well as possible. She also began using more assignments that resembled the PRAXIS test itself. In this case imitating the PRAXIS meant giving "case study quizzes" throughout the semester, which were featured prominently on the PRAXIS. The quizzes consisted of short anecdotes or stories followed by open-ended questions which students answered the space of a few sentences or brief paragraph. Since the students knew that the quizzes were a type of preparation for licensing, they tolerated them well, and even welcomed them. She and the students felt as if they were "on the same side", working together to help the students pass their exam. The relationship was therefore more positive and less "conflicted" compared to earlier times when Professor Sutton was expected not only to teach the students, but also to evaluate them.

With the introduction of the licensing exam, finally, some students seemed to regard educational psychology as more important than in the past—even using university break weeks for additional study of the textbook! On the other hand, some students seemed to worry about their performance on the test, and their anxiety may have interfered with learning about educational psychology itself. Their worries created a dilemma that Professor never truly resolved: how to get students to prepare for the test seriously without arousing undue worry or anxiety in them?

Questions

> How well do you feel that Professor Sutton's dilemmas about high-stakes testing reflect the dilemmas that public school teachers might face in preparing their own students for high-stakes tests?

> On balance, and taking into account Professor Sutton's experience, do you think that high-stakes tests are desirable?

References

Cochran-Smith, M. (2003). Assessing assessment in teacher education. Journal of Teacher Education, 54(3), 187-191.

Educational Testing Service. (2004). Study guide for Principles of Learning and Teaching, 2nd edition. Princeton, NJ: Author.

Deciding for yourself about the research

Chapter 2, The learning process: *behaviorist and constructivist teaching compared*

Numerous educators have planned and implemented activities and curriculum units that use either behaviorist or constructivist principles in one way or another. Often the demonstrated activities or units are hard to compare directly simply because behaviorism and constructivism address different aspects of learning, and therefore call upon teachers to perform somewhat different roles. To see what I mean, look at these two examples of instructional research. The first is grounded in behaviorism and the second is grounded in constructivism.

Behaviorism in action: a remedy for stuttering Mark Onslow and his colleagues have described a way to help young children overcome stuttering, a problem in which sounds and words are repeated or stretched unduly, so that fluent conversation is difficult (2001). Onslow's research strategy was simple, at least in principle: he trained parents of children who stuttered to praise their child more strongly is the child spoke fluently (without any stutter), and to correct the child quietly, but non-punitively whenever the child did stutter. A fluent sentence therefore produced praise, or even a gold star, from parents. A stuttered sentence produced an immediate sentence like "I think that was a stutter", stated factually and quietly. Value judgments and criticisms were not allowed.

Onslow's program contradicted the conventional advice to parents about stuttering, which was to ignore it wherever possible. Nonetheless the program produced very positive results. All of the stuttering children reduced or even eliminated their stuttering after a few weeks of the differential reinforcement by their parents, and the stuttering did not return when they were tested even one year after the program finished.

Constructivism in action: project-based learning Juliette Goldman, an educator working in Australia, demonstrated how this can be done with health education for middle years students (Goldman, 2006). She designed a project for seventh-grade students in which they had to publish a training manual for fellow-students on the topic of "good food handling", advice for restaurant workers about how they can keep for contaminating either themselves or the food that they serve. The writers of the manual worked in groups of three, researching information on a range of topics related to food handling. Then they used computer self-publishing software to prepare and print copies of their information. They also made oral presentations about their manuals to a school assembly to which local food-industry representatives were invited, and they arranged to display the finished manuals at the local public library.

The initiative used constructivist principles in a number of ways. For example, it challenged learners to make decisions about what their particular manual should "teach". The decision-making required learners constantly to monitor their own knowledge and learning—engage in metacognition—in order to insure that the content was complete, accurate, and important to learn. It also grouped students into teams, so that they could, to some extent, teach each other whatever they needed to learn, including helping each other to sense whether they actually were learning from their research.

Questions

> Obviously these two studies are about different educational problems or issues. What if the learning theories underlying them were switched? Could a stuttering program be built around constructivist principles of learning, and a health education program be built around behaviorist principles? What would each program look like?

> Be a skeptic for a moment. What do you suspect might be the *hardest* part of implementing behavioral conditioning for stuttering described by Onslow? And what might be *hardest* part of implementing the constructivist program about health education?

References

Onslow, M., Menzies, R., & Packman, A. (2001). An operant intervention for early stuttering. *Behavior modification 25*(1), 116-139.

Goldman, J. (2006). Web-based designed activities for young people in health education: A constructivist approach. *Health Education Journal 65*(1), 14-27.

Deciding for yourself about the research

Chapter 3, Student development: *schools and the obesity epidemic*

Childhood obesity leads not just to teasing by peers, but eventually also to a variety of serious medical problems, ranging from back pain to heart disease and diabetes. That is why medical experts are quite concerned that obesity in children has increased markedly since the 1950s, to the point of being considered a genuine health "epidemic" (Ogden, et al., 2002). Recent projections suggest that fully one-third of all children born in 2000 will eventually develop diabetes as a side-effect of being overweight (Narayan, et al., 2003).

Why have these changes happened? One factor is probably the vast increase in individuals' consumption of sugar especially "disguised" forms like corn syrup (Bawa, 2005). Another is a more sedentary, "stay-inside" lifestyle than in the past. The latter has happened, among other reasons, because of population shifts: cities and towns have increased in population and size, while rural areas have decreased in population, causing more people to rely on car travel more than ever before. The changes have also led residents in many areas of many cities to consider their neighborhoods less safe than in the past, causing them to respond with inactivity: either they stay inside more or they rely even more on cars to get around.

Even schools have contributed to the trend toward obesity. "Junk food" drinks and snacks are widely available in many schools through commercial vending machines—each one giving a student an extra 150 and 300 unneeded calories per day. More insidiously, perhaps, is the effect of the trend toward high-stakes testing: because of them, many schools tend to strengthen courses and special programs that prepare students in the "basic" subjects that they know will be tested, and to trim programs (like physical education, but also the arts) that will not be tested.

These considerations led a group of physicians at the University of Georgia to organize an after-school program of physical activity for elementary school students (Yin, et al., 2005), and to assess whether the program actually helped prevent weight gain in students. Students volunteered for a program that had three components: 30 minutes of physical activity, a healthy snack, and assistance with the students' homework. (The researchers explain that assistance with homework had nothing to do with weight loss, but was very important in getting students to attend and getting parents to support the program!) Staff for the program included a mix of regular teachers from the school (not necessarily physical education specialists) and other individuals hired specifically for the project. Physical activities were chosen in part by the students, and were generally non-competitive and cooperative in nature.

Initial results of the program have been very encouraging; students and parents support the program strongly, and teachers have been successful in making sure that students are actually active enough during the program sessions. Since the program is still ongoing, however, it will be a few more years before there will be definitive results about weight gain, or lack thereof.

Questions

> It is hard to disagree with the purposes of this study—reducing the prevalence of obesity. But does it really show what it claims? Be a deliberate skeptic for a moment and ask yourself these questions:

> If the students were volunteers, how typical do you think they are of all students?

> And if the teachers are receiving a large research grant to implement the program, might they be working harder to do a good job than most of us ordinarily work?

> An important ambiguity about the program was the fact that it included *both* physical activity and homework assistance. Think about this ambiguity.

> If the researchers split up these two elements—offering only one or the other at any one school—how might the split affect the outcomes?

> Would different sorts of students volunteer as a result of the split, and how if at all would their selection matter?

References

Ogden, C., Flega, K., Carroll, M. & Johnson, C. (2002). Prevalence and trends in overweight among U.S. children and adolescents, 1999-2000. *Journal of the American Medical Assocation, 288*(14), 1728-1732.

Narayan, K., Boyle, J., Thompson, T., Sorensen, S., & Williamson, D. (2003). Lifetime risk for diabetes mellitus in the United States. *Journal of the American Medical Association, 290*(14), 1884-1890.

Bawa, S. (2005). The role of the consumption of beverages in the obesity epidemic. *Journal of the Royal Society for the Promotion of Health, 125*(3), 124-128.Yin, Z., Hanes, J., Moore, J., Humbles, P., Barbeau, & Gutin, B. (2005). An after-school physical activity   program for obesity prevention in children. Evaluation and the Health Professions, 28(1), 67-89.

Deciding for yourself about the research

Chapter 4, Student diversity: using African-American English to enrich classroom discourse

In addition to speaking a language other than English at home, many students learn another version or dialect of English. A dialect is a version of a language with somewhat unique vocabulary, grammar, and pronunciation. The most prominent dialect of English in North America is African-American English, sometimes also called Ebonics. Intellectually and emotionally, Ebonics is just as rich and capable of expressiveness as "Standard English," the dialect usually used, for example, by radio and television news broadcasters. It is used by many African Americans in the United States, though not by all and often not in every possible situation.

But Ebonics has distinctive features not shared with Standard English. In grammar, for example, the verb to be is used differently than in Standard English. Instead of simply indicating existence or non-existence, to be can also distinguish between a one-time event and an ongoing, continuous state. Consider these two sentences and their meanings:

(1) He tired. ("He is tired right now.)

(2) He be tired. ("He is often or always tired.")

Ebonics also has features of language use or communication, just like a "foreign" language, which are different from Standard English. One is the use of repetitive, rhythmic phrases for emphasis—not unlike the style of an enthusiastic "preacher" in church. Another is the use of call-and-response, in which an individual asks a question or makes a statement to which the group expects to respond in unison.

What is interesting and important about the features of language use is that teachers can use them to communicate more effectively with students, often even if they themselves have not personally learned to speak African-American dialect. Anita Bohn (2003) illustrated this principle by carefully observing the teaching styles of two teachers who regularly incorporated the dialect into conversations with students and who used these conversations as a bridge for students to learn Standard English.

In one observation, for example, the class was beginning a writing activity and the teacher said, "This morning we are going to practice some sentences, and when we do that I want you to listen. Can you say that?" The class responded in chorus, "Listen!" The teacher said, "Do what?" The class replied even louder, "Listen!" The teacher repeated the work a few times together with the students: "Listen...listen..." Then she began clapping in between words: "Listen... [clap]...listen... [clap]...listen... [clap]..." Suddenly she stopped, leaned forward and asked the class, "How you gonna listen? With your feet?" All responded loudly: "Nooo!" After a pause, she asked again, "You gonna listen with your nose?" All responded again: "Nooo!" She asked, "How?" Everyone responded loudly together, "With our ears!"

The teacher's approach used both repetitive, rhythmic language and a call-and-response style with which, as it happened, many of her students were already familiar. By using these features of African-American communication, she gained students' attention effectively, but also used the style of communication to support an activity embedded in Standard English, writing sentences. In addition to being a familiar style of interaction, however, the technique worked for another reason: it implied respect for the language and communication skills that students had acquired already. Such respect has been shown to be important for success not only when students are learning two dialects, but also when they are learning two languages, such as Spanish and English (Marinez-Roldan & Malave, 2004).

Questions

> Most teachers agree that part of teachers' goals should be to encourage students in learning Standard English, both spoken and written. But an issue that we may disagree about, and that is raised by Bohn's study, is whether teachers should do so by using non-standard dialect in class. You could think about it this way: by "speaking Ebonics", is a teacher modeling inappropriate English or is he/she providing students with a bridge from Ebonics to standard English? What do you think about this?

> There is also a related question that is more practical. Is using non-standard dialect really practical for every teacher? Presumably using it is easier for those with prior experience speaking the dialect, than for those without experience. But could other teachers learn it well enough to be effective with students? If not, then how else, if at all, could such teachers communicate with students effectively?

References

Bohn, A. (2003). Familiar voices: Using Ebonics communication techniques in the primary classroom. *Urban Education, 38*(6), 688-707.

Martinez-Roldan, C. & Malave, G. (2004). Language ideologies mediating literacy and identity in bilingual contexts. *Journal of early childhood literacy, 4*(2), 155-180.

Deciding for yourself about the research

Chapter 5, Students with special educational needs: *How well does inclusion occur in high schools?*

The Individuals with Disabilities Education Act applies to all levels of schooling, from kindergarten through twelfth grade, and one of its revisions (Public Law 101-336, 104 Stat. 327, 1990) further addressed the needs of secondary schools by including provisions for school-to-work transitions for students with disabilities. Yet progress at including such students has generally been more rapid and complete in elementary schools—especially at the youngest grade levels—than in secondary schools. The reasons for the difference do not necessarily have to do high school teachers' attitudes about disabilities as compared to elementary teachers' attitudes. Much of it stems from differences in how the two levels of schooling are structured, with secondary schools being much larger and organized by a complex timetable of classes that tends to sort students—and even teachers themselves!—by academic background (Kelly, 2004; Oakes, 2005). One effect of this organization is to make it harder for special education and general education teachers to collaborate, and therefore to integrate learning experiences for students with disabilities into high school as a whole.

Yet some teachers and schools manage to collaborate anyway. A research study by Joseph Stowitschek and his colleagues explored the factors that account for comparative success at including students with disabilities in secondary school (Stowitschek, Lovitt, & Rodriguez, 2001). The researchers were interested, first, in how much teachers actually *do* collaborate to design and carry out programs for youth with disabilities, and second, in what specific circumstances or practices were associated with collaborating successfully. They chose three contrasting high schools to study in detail: a large urban public high school, a rural public high school in a small town, and a private urban high school. For each school they collected information from a wide range of staff—special education teachers, general education teachers, administrators, parents, and students with disabilities themselves. The information came from surveys, interviews, reviews of official school documents, and observations of classrooms.

What did they find? Among other things, they found that special education teachers at all of the schools strongly supported inclusion of students with disabilities to the fullest possible extent; they did not, that is, seek to strengthen or increase the schools' reliance on segregated special education classes. They also found significant interest and support from parents of the students with disabilities in the educational programs of their children. These factors suggested that change toward fuller inclusion may continue in the years ahead.

But they also found limitations on how much the teachers could collaborate at any of the schools. A major problem was the teachers' dependency on informal communication with general education teachers. Instead of regularly announced meetings to discuss inclusion initiatives, teachers had to "catch" each other in the hallway or during lunch hours, for example, in order to have conversations about students and ways of including them in class or school activities. At these moments the teachers tended already to be busy. A partial result was that the general education teachers ended up with limited knowledge both about the special education program at their school, and about why particular students might be placed successfully in their particular classrooms. All of the students with disabilities had IEPs, but the general teachers had little or no knowledge of their contents—or even of their existence. Not surprisingly, under these conditions there were few major collaborative activities, such as the co-teaching of a course by a special education teacher and a general teacher or jointly operated activities or programs.

Yet for each school there were also individual teachers and activities that boosted collaboration in the school, and that could in principle be tried elsewhere as well. The private high school, for example, had an especially effective, vital program for involving parents: there were regular advisory group meetings to assess the current needs of the special education program and to develop and sustain support for it among the parents. Another especially effective collaboration involved peer tutoring—using high school students to tutor the students with disabilities on a regular basis, often with course credit given as "payment" to the tutors. Peer tutoring proved a good way to communicate the nature and extent of the special education program to the student population as a whole. A third effective form of collaboration involved using a teacher as a "community coordinator", someone who developed linkages to agencies and potential employers in the community. The linkages proved especially helpful in students' transitions to work and life after high school.

All in all, there were limitations on inclusion in the secondary schools, but also grounds for optimism because of the collaborative successes and the dedication of the teachers. Although Stowitschek and his colleagues focused on only three schools, their findings suggested three key points: (1) that the motivation for inclusion and collaboration definitely exists among secondary teachers, (2) that it is possible to work around the organizational constraints of high schools, and (3) that changes in those constraints in the future should further increase levels of inclusion and collaboration.

Questions

> If you were a teacher in a high school (as many readers of this book plan to become), how would you prepare your students to receive a student with a disability into one of your classes? Consider actions that you would take both before and after the student actually arrives.

> ➤ Sometimes teachers at every grade level express concern about receiving students with disabilities into their classes, even if it can be arranged easily. Why do you think that the teachers feel this way? Think of three possible *objections* to inclusion, and then think of how an *advocate* for inclusion might respond to each of them.

References

Public Law 101-336, 104 Stat. 327 (July 26, 1990). Americans with Disabilities Act of 1990. Washington, D.C.: United States Government Printing Office.

Stowitschek, J., Lovitt, T., & Rodriguez, J. (2001). Patterns of collaboration in secondary education for youth with special needs: Profiles of three high schools. Urban Education, 36(1), 93-128.

Kelly, S. (2004). Are teachers tracked? On what basis and with what consequences. Social psychology in education, 7(1), 55-72.

Oakes, J. (2005). Keeping track: How schools structure inequality, 2nd edition. New Haven, CT: Yale University Press.

Deciding for yourself about the research

Chapter 6, Student motivation: *Is self-efficacy culturally biased?*

As we explain in this chapter, self-efficacy beliefs are based heavily on experiences—mastery, vicarious (or observed) mastery, and social persuasion. Research has found that these experiences are effective in a wide variety of situations, such as making decisions about careers, performing tasks at work, choosing courses at school, deciding whether to join after-school sports teams, and planning effective instruction as a teacher (Allison, Dwyer, & Makin, 1999; Bandura, 1997; Goddard, Hoy, & Hoy, 2004). Because it has proved valid in so many situations, self-efficacy seems relatively universal cognitive process—as if it "works" everywhere, for everyone.

But does it? The very fact that self-efficacy is based on *experience* should make us suspicious of its limits, since there are few experiences that are literally shared by all people in all places or societies. And the wide diversity among students in most schools should lead to similar skepticism. Maybe it is true that self-efficacy promotes motivation for many students, or even for most, but does it do so for *all* students? And if it does not, then what are the reasons?

These questions prompted a psychologist named Lori Lindley to investigate whether self-efficacy has in fact proved useful and valid for understanding motivation in unusually diverse populations (Lindley, 2006). She searched the research literature for studies about self-efficacy in each of the following groups:

(a) women with careers

(b) ethnic minorities living in the United States

(c) societies and cultures outside the United States

(d) self-identified gay, lesbian, and bisexual individuals

(e) people with disabilities

What has research shown about the self-efficacy of members of these groups? Compared to the "classic" research about this concept, is self-efficacy higher, lower, confined to just limited areas of activity, or not even a meaningful idea?

What Lindley found was that self-efficacy beliefs were (like the people she studied) complex and varied. Women, for example, were just as likely to express high self-efficacy and low motivation about using computers, as to express low self-efficacy and high motivation to use them. Among ethnic minority students (Hispanics, Asian-Americans, and African Americans), some studies found lower self-efficacy about choosing careers than among white students. But other studies found no differences.

Among societies outside the United States, however, high self-efficacy seemed to predict motivation, much as it does in the "classic" research with white American populations—though again with some differences. Among Italian high school students, for example, self-efficacy beliefs about career choice are strongly associated with the students' interest in and choice of career (Lent, et al., 2003). Yet the connection between self-efficacy and motivation was found to have a different character for students from Taiwan (Mau, 2000): for them high self-efficacy was associated not with being highly motivated, but with relying heavily on others to assist with making decisions and with being highly rational or logical in making them. Self-efficacy, under these conditions, was not so much a belief in yourself as a belief in your community.

Among the remaining groups—the gay/lesbian/bisexual individuals and the people with disabilities—research was especially scarce and conclusions were therefore hard to reach. The publications that did exist emphasized a belief in the potential value of self-efficacy for these groups, but they did not report research studies describing whether in fact self-efficacy in fact motivated the individuals, or even existed consistently and meaningfully as a concept or belief.

What does the diversity of these findings suggest (beyond Grandmother's rule that "sometimes one thing happens, and sometimes another")? Lindley noted two points, both of which were hinted at by some of the studies that she reviewed. The first point is that self-efficacy may be a belief about personal capacity only for *some* individuals in *some* situations. For others, efficacy may really be a belief in the group or community, such as your family, classroom, or workplace. Self-efficacy may really be **collective self-efficacy**—a belief that your group can accomplish its goals. Believing primarily in the group may be quite motivating, but also be quite a different experience from believing primarily in yourself. In recent years some psychologists and educators have acknowledged this possibility and begun studying the dynamics of collective self-efficacy (Bandura, 1997; Gordon, Hoy, & Hoy, 2004).

Lindley's second point is that for some groups, the main barriers to success are not *beliefs* in personal capacity, but real, external obstacles independent of personal beliefs. Imagine, for example, that a person encounters daily, real social prejudice because he or she is non-white, homosexual, or has a disability. For that person, self-confidence may only go part of the way to insuring success, and removing the real social barriers may be needed to go the rest of the way.

For teachers, three implications of this research seem clear. First, individual self-efficacy beliefs do often motivate students, and teachers should therefore encourage them in these students. Second, some students may see their personal capacity in terms of the capacity of groups to which they belong. Teachers can motivate these students by strengthening the capacity of their groups—perhaps using strategies like the ones described in this chapter and the next. Third, some students rightly perceive genuine injustices in their world which limit their chances of success; teachers should not deny the importance of these injustices, but recognize them and do what they can to reduce them.

Questions

> ➤ Think about your own belief in your capacity to teach well, as well as your doubts and worries about your capacity. You might call this your **teaching self-efficacy.** What is that belief primarily based on, and what would it take to raise that belief even higher?

> ➤ Suppose your students consisted of about equal numbers who believed in individual self-efficacy and in collective self-efficacy. Imagine and describe one *advantage* of having such a mix in your class, as well as one potential source of *conflict* that you might have to deal with between the two groups.

References

Allison, K., Dwyer, J., & Makin, S. (1999). Self-efficacy and participation in vigorous physical activity by high school students. Health Education and Behavior, 26(1), 12-24.

Bandura, A. (1997). Self-efficacy: The exercise of control. New York: Freeman.

Goddard, R., Hoy, W., & Hoy, A. (2004). Collective efficacy beliefs: Theoretical developments, empirical evidence, and future directions. Educational Researcher, 33(3), 3-13.

Rochester, NY: University of Rochester Press.

Lent, R., Brown, S., Nota, L., & Soresi, S. (2003). Teaching social cognitive interest and choice hypotheses across Holland types in Italian high school students. Journal of Vocational Behavior, 62, 101-118.

Mau, W.-C. (2003). Factors that influence persistence in science and engineering career aspirations. Career Development Quarterly, 51, 234-243

Deciding for yourself about the research:

Chapter 7, Classroom management and the learning environment: *Culturally responsive classroom management*

Even though teachers might believe that consistency is a mark of good classroom management, it is not always true that "one size fits all" when it comes to matching particular management strategies to specific students. A lot of research suggests, on the contrary, that success in classroom management needs to be adjusted to the cultural background and expectations of students. Educators sometimes call this approach **culturally responsive classroom management.**

Support for culturally responsive management comes a number of research studies. In one study, for example, David Brown interviewed 13 teachers who taught in classrooms from 1st through 12th grade in urban, inner-city schools in several different cities (Brown, 2004). A few of the teachers were themselves culturally diverse—one was from Sri Lanka, one was African American, two were Hispanic American—but most were white. Although the interviews were lengthy and detailed, they centered on just three underlying questions:

(1) How do you interact with students?

(2) How would you describe your management style?

(3) What works well for you in communicating with students?

The teachers' views could be summarized in several points. First, the teachers considered it important to show students that the teachers cared and respected them: this attitude was significantly more important, they felt, when teaching urban students than when teaching suburban students. The teachers therefore made more effort than usual to be friendly with all students and to get to know them as individuals. To do so, though, the teachers also had to know how the students themselves preferred to be publicly known or acknowledged. In some classrooms with Hispanic American students, for example, the teachers found it wise not to call on individuals during class, because some of the students preferred to be recognized for their relationships with classmates—for their membership in the class as a group—rather than for their distinctiveness from the group.

Interestingly, "caring" involved more than simple warmth and nurturance. It also meant teachers' asserting their authority to make clear demands on students both for high quality work and for appropriate classroom behavior. Asserting authority indirectly in order to sound polite (like saying "Would you like to sit down now?") was less effective and was often interpreted by students as a sign of a teacher's indifference. Direct, specific commands (like "Take your seat") were more effective, provided they did not also express hostility.

The teachers' caring had to be consistent in every way: not only did they have to say friendly things to students, but also they had to look friendly with eye contact and smiles. What made such consistency initially challenging for some teachers was recognizing students' own signs of friendliness for what they were. In some classrooms with African American students, for example, students engaged in a "call response" pattern of interaction: as the teacher gave instructions or explained an idea, some students would say or speak their own feelings or mention their own ideas. The pattern was not meant to interrupt the teacher, however, so much as to show involvement in the lesson or activity, and the teacher needed to acknowledge it as such.

Other educational researchers besides David Brown have found similar results, though some point out that actually practicing culturally responsive management can be harder than simply knowing what it involves (Weinstein, Tomlinson-Clarke, & Curran, 2004). To become skillful with the strategies described by Brown and others, for example, teachers also need to look honestly at their own preconceptions about ethnic, cultural and racial differences, so that they do not misconstrue culturally ambiguous behaviors of students just because students have a background different from the teacher's own. Teachers also need to be aware of how much society-wide prejudice on students' sense of efficacy, since pervasive prejudice and discrimination can stimulate some students to withdraw in ways that may be mistaken for laziness.

Perhaps the most challenging aspect of culturally responsive management, however, is for teachers to accommodate to students' cultural differences while also helping them learn how to function well in the somewhat bureaucratic, middle-class oriented "culture" of school. This challenge is full of dilemmas. How much, for example, should a teacher sacrifice conventional "politeness" behaviors (like using indirect questions) simply because students understand and respect directness more easily? How much should a teacher encourage students to critique each other's or the teacher's ideas even if students' families give higher priority to cooperation and compliance with authorities? And what if a particular class is itself culturally diverse, containing students from many cultural backgrounds in one room? What should a teacher do then?

Questions

> Think about the issue of politeness versus directness mention in the final paragraph above. Presumably teachers and students need some sort of mutual accommodation about this issue. If you were the teacher, what would the accommodation look like? Obviously it might depend on the particular students and on the precise the behavior at hand. But go beyond this generality. Imagine—and describe—what you might actually say to students to show respect for their preferred styles of talking while still encouraging them to respect or even adopt styles of speech that lead to more success in school?

> ➤ Culturally responsive classroom management has sometimes been criticized on the grounds that it encourages teachers to "profile" or stereotype students according to their ethnic, racial, or cultural backgrounds. Being culturally responsive, it is said, makes teachers overlook the individual differences among students. Others argue that treating students strictly as individuals makes teachers overlook students' obvious cultural heritages. How might you resolve this issue in your own mind? Again, go beyond the obvious: imagine an actual conversation that you might have with your own students about this issue.

References

Brown, D. (2004). Urban teachers' professed classroom management strategies: Reflections of culturally responsive teaching. *Urban Education, 39*(3), 266-289.

Weinstein, C.,Tomlinson-Clarke, S., & Curran, M. (2004). Toward a conception of culturally responsive classroom management. *Journal of Teacher Education, 55*(1), 25-38.

Chapter 8, Nature of classroom communication: *When is a student lying?*

Although we might wish that it were not true, students do occasionally tell a deliberate lie to the teacher. In explaining why an assignment is late, for example, a student might claim to have been sick when the student was not in fact sick. Worse yet, a student might turn in an assignment that the student claims to have written when in fact it was "borrowed" from another student or (especially among older students) even from Internet.

In situations like these, is there any way to discern when a person actually is lying? Many of the signs would have to be nonverbal, since by definition a liar's verbal statements may not indicate that falsehood is occurring. A large body of research has studied this question—looking for nonverbal signs by which deception might be detected. The research can be summarized like this: people generally believe that they can tell when someone is lying, but they can not in fact do so very accurately. In a survey of 75 countries around the world, for example, individuals from every nation expressed the belief that liars avoid eye contact (Global Deception Research Team, 2006). (This is an unusually strong trend compared to most in educational and psychological research!) Individuals also named additional behaviors: liars shift on the feet, for example, they touch and scratch themselves nervously, and their speech is hesitant or flawed. But the most important belief is about eye contact: a liar, it is thought, cannot "look you in the eye".

Unfortunately these beliefs seem to be simply stereotypes that have little basis in fact. Experiments in which one person deliberately lies to another person find little relationship between averting eye contact and lying, as well as little relationship between other nonverbal behaviors and lying (DePaulo et al., 2003). A person who is lying is just as likely to look directly at you as someone telling the truth—and on the other hand, also just as likely to look away. In fact gaze aversion can indicate a number of things, depending on the context. In another study of eye contact, for example, Anjanie McCarthy and her colleagues observed eye contact when one person asks another person a question. They found that when answering a question to which a person already knew the answer (like "What is your birthday?"), the person was likely to look the questioner directly in the eye (McCarthy, et al., 2006). When answering a question which required some thought, however, the person tended to avert direct gaze. The researchers studied individuals from three societies and found differences in where the individuals look in order to avoid eye contact: people from Canada and Trinidad looked up, but people from Japan looked down. All of their answers, remember, were truthful and none were lies.

If gaze aversion does not really indicate lying, then why do people believe that it does anyway? The research team that studied this belief suggested that the belief does not actually reflect our experiences with liars, but instead function as a deterrent to lying behavior (Global Deception

Research Team, 2006). Since nearly everyone disapproves of lying, and since detecting it is often difficult, the next best strategy is to persuade potential liars that they might in fact be detected. Furthermore, if we believe that liars should feel ashamed of their behavior, it is reasonable to suppose that they would show signs of shame—i.e. gaze aversion, shifting on their feet, hesitation, and the like. The irony is that if we begin to doubt a person's truthfulness, a truthful person is more likely to feel uncomfortable, so the person is likely to begin averting gaze and showing other signs of nervousness anyway. The end result is to reinforce the stereotype of gaze aversion, but not to identify an actual liar.

For teachers, the implications of this research are twofold. First, it suggests that we should be very careful before deciding whether or not a particular student is lying on a particular occasion. We should encourage students to be equally careful with each other; it is too easy, it seems, to jump to conclusions about this sort of judgment. Second, it implies that a better way to reduce lying by students is to develop high-quality relationships with them, so that students will not feel a need to lie. Obviously, developing high-quality relationships is a big job and it may be easier with some students than with others. But it appears to be more effective than falsely accusing truthful students while overlooking actual deceptions.

Questions

> Classrooms are like any other social setting in that they can only function well if their members' are truthful with each other. How could you communicate this message to students so that they endorse it themselves? One way, of course, is to discuss the problem with students. But another way might be to stage "simulated lying" between students, and have students see how well they can discern true liars. Would a simulation be a good idea, or would it be undesirable by giving students practice at lying effectively? Explain your views about this question.

> Recall the study above in which thought-questions caused individuals to avert direct gaze. Why do you suppose that people from Trinidad and Canada averted gaze by looking up, while people from Japan averted by looking down? What sort of cultural significance does this difference have, if any? In answering this question, think as well about how you could find out if the answer is valid.

References

Global Deception Research Team. (2006). A world of lies. *Journal of Cross-cultural Psychology, 37*(6), 60-74.

DePaulo, B., Lindsay, J., Malone, B., Muhlenbruck, L., Charlton, K., & Cooper, H. (2003). Cues to deception. *Psychological Bulletin, 129,* 74-118.

McCarthy, A., Lee, K., Itakura, S., & Muir, D. (2006). Cultural display rules drive eye gaze during thinking. *Journal of Cross-cultural Psychology, 37*(6), 717-722.

.

Deciding for yourself about research

Chapter 9, Facilitating complex thinking: *identifying attitude-treatment interactions*

As we have stated in various places in this chapter, and as many teachers will confirm from experience, there seems to be no instructional strategy that is best for all students. Instead a more guarded comment may be more accurate: there seem to be strategies that are especially good for certain students under certain conditions. Educational psychologists have long studied this idea and call it **aptitude-treatment interaction** (abbreviated **ATI**) (Cronbach & Snow, 1977; Snow, 1989). The *aptitude* in this term is the unique quality, talent, or skill of a student; the *treatment* is the instructional strategy or approach being used; and the *interaction* is the combination of the two.

The idea seems intuitively appealing, but it has proved surprisingly difficult to identify particular ATIs scientifically. Part of the problem is the ambiguity of the term *aptitude*. Numerous qualities, talents, and skills of students have been identified and studied, including memory for verbal material, memory for visual material, memory for sequences of ideas, ability to analyze a problem into its parts, and creativity .

The situation is just as ambiguous in defining *treatment*. Is it a specific teacher-directed strategy such as the use of advance organizers described in this chapter? Or does *treatment* mean a broad approach such as Madeline Hunter's effective teaching model that we describe in this chapter, or like student-centered inquiry learning that we also describe? Since both key terms have multiple possible meanings, it is not surprising that research studies of their combinations have also yielded ambiguous results. Sometimes a particular combination of aptitude and treatment help learning, but other times it makes little difference.

In spite of these problems with the research as a whole, the specific studies of ATIs have clearly been helpful to teachers. In one, for example, the researchers investigated human ecology students' preferred styles of learning—their *aptitudes* (Crutsinger, Knight, & Kinley, 2005). Did they prefer, for example, to learn from visual information (pictures, diagrams) or from verbal information (text and oral explanations)? Did they prefer to scan new information in sequence, or to skip around in it and piece it together at the end? The researchers found that this particular group of students tended to prefer new information to be visual and sequential. As a result, they were able to improve students' learning by adding to the course more computer-based instruction, which was relatively visual and sequential in its organization.

In another study, the researcher who initially was studying cooperative learning groups in university students discovered—and wondered why—some of the groups were more productive than others (Peterson, 2004). On closer investigation of the groups he found an ATI-related problem. Students in this particular university course were choosing their own group partners.

They therefore tended to choose their own friends, a practice that inadvertently *reduced* the talents and resources available in some groups. Friends, it seemed, tended to duplicate each other's styles of problem solving and of performing academic tasks, rendering the group as a whole less rich in talents and therefore less productive or successful.

To remedy this problem, the instructor undertook to identify students' strong points in different aspects of problem solving. He identified which students were inclined to take action, which were good at decision-making, which at identifying problems, and which at brainstorming. Then he assigned students to groups so that each group had one person strong in each of these areas. The results were a striking increase in the productivity of all groups. But there was a catch: although the students were indeed more productive, they did not like being assigned partners as well as choosing their own! Maintaining this particular ATI may therefore prove difficult over the long term—perhaps another reason by ATI research has not always found consistent results.

Questions

> Think about the fact that results of ATI have been inconsistent, even though it seems reasonable given the obvious diversity among students in every classroom. Assuming that you support the idea of ATIs, explain how you would justify it to two kinds of people: (1) a fellow teacher in your school, and (2) a professor of educational psychology.

> Given the results of Peterson's research study, what is the best advice you could give to teachers (or to yourself) about how to set up cooperative learning groups? Should students choose their own partners, or should the teacher choose them? Keep in mind the proviso mentioned at the end—that the students preferred to choose their own partners, even though it meant learning less.

References

Cronbach, L. & Snow, R. (1977). *Aptitudes and instructional methods: A handbook for research on interaction.* New York: Irvington.

Crutsinger, C., Knight, D., & Kinley. (2005). Learning style preferences: Implications for Web-based instruction. *Clothing and Textiles Research Journal, 23*(4), 266-276.

Snow, R. (1989). Aptitude-treatment interaction as a framework for research on individual differences in learning. In P. Ackerman, R. Sternberg, & R. Glaser (Eds.), *Learning and individual differences,* pp. 13-60. New York: W. H. Freeman.

Peterson, T. (2004). So you're thinking of trying problem-based learning?: Three critical success factors for implementation. *Journal of Management Education, 28*(5), 630-647.

Deciding for yourself about the research

Chapter 10, Planning instruction: *How does multicultural curriculum affect racial knowledge and biases?*

Multicultural and anti-racist curricula work partly by portraying and discussing individuals of diverse racial or ethnic background in ways that counteract stereotypes. Students read stories, watch videos, and talk about respected citizens—doctors, political leaders, celebrities, and the like —who happen to be African-American, Hispanic, or of some other non-Caucasian origin. In some cases, especially at the early childhood level, students' interests and concerns are used to guide the selection and integration of diversity-related activities (Derman-Sparks, 1994).

One way of thinking about such a curriculum is that it tries to make students into "experts," even at relatively young ages, about racial and ethnic differences. Instead of thinking about diversity in superficial terms—as based merely on skin color, for example—students learn to see diversity as complex and multi-faceted. An African-American child and a White child do not simply differ in color, for example; they are both similar and different in many ways. Hopefully the greater subtlety of their expert knowledge also reduces negative biases felt about race.

To test these possibilities, Donna Perkins and Carolyn Mebert interviewed 79 children at six preschool and after-school child care centers (2005). Some of the centers emphasized multicultural education, some emphasized multicultural education as well as an emergent curriculum, and some emphasized neither. Perkins and Mebert assessed children's knowledge and attitudes about race in several ways. For example, they displayed pictures of other children over various races on a felt board, and asked the participating children to arrange the pictures so that children were closer together if more similar and farther apart if more different. They also asked participating children to evaluate simple stories or anecdotes about three pictures, one of a white child, one of an African-American child, and one of an Asian-American child. In one of the anecdotes, for example, the researcher asked, "Some children are naughty because they draw with crayons on the walls. Which of these children (in the pictures) might do that?" The participating child could then choose any or all of the pictured children—or choose none at all.

What did Perkins and Mebert find from this study? Four ideas stood out especially clearly:

(1) Children indeed showed more "expertise" about race if they attended a child care center that emphasized multicultural education—but only if they center *also* emphasized emergent curriculum. To be effective, in other words, information about human diversity had to grow out of children's personal concerns and interests. It was not enough simply to tell them about human diversity.

(2) Although a multicultural/emergent program was effective in sensitizing children to differences *between* races, it was not especially effective for sensitizing them to differences *within* races. When it came to differences among African-Americans, for example, the multicultural/emergent children were no more subtle or "expert" in their judgments than any other children.

(3) Children in the multicultural programs tended to view all children, regardless of race, in a relatively more positive light, and this tendency increased as they got older (i.e. from age 4 to 6).

(4) Most important of all, the program orientation *did* affect the children's knowledge and attitudes, even at (or perhaps because of) their young age.

Questions

> Why do you suppose that multicultural education worked *only* in conjunction with an emergent curriculum? Imagine that you writing a brief summary of this study for a school newsletter, and that you need to comment on this question. What would you say about it?

> Skeptics might say that the study assessed only what children say about race, not how children might act in racially related situations. In an interview, in other words, a child might express positive sentiments about every race or ethnic group, but still behave in prejudiced ways during play or other activities at school. Is this a legitimate criticism of the Perkins and Mebert study? How could you devise another study to test whether there is truth to the criticism?

References

Perkins, D. & Mebert, C. (2005). Efficacy of multicultural education for preschool children. *Journal of Cross-Cultural Psychology, 36*(4), 497-512.

Derman-Sparks, L. (1994). Empowering children to create a caring culture in a world of differences. *Childhood Education, 70,* 66-71.

Deciding for yourself about the research

Chapter 11, Teacher-made assessment strategies: *the importance of establishing trust when giving critical feedback across the racial divide*

Providing accurate but constructive feedback to students is difficult for teachers. Identifying problems in student work and pointing out areas for improvement can undermine students' confidence and motivation. However, students cannot make significant improvements in their work if they do not get accurate information about their strengths and weaknesses. Cohen, Steele and Ross (2002) argue that trust is crucial to this dilemma: students are more likely to respond well to accurate feedback if they trust the teacher and believe that the feedback is not biased. However, if the student distrusts the teacher feedback that points out weaknesses is likely to lower motivation and confidence.

The dilemma of providing trust and accurate feedback that enhances motivation is particularly acute when the students come from a group that has been stereotyped as less competent (e.g. African American, Latino) and the teacher is white. Several studies suggest that feedback that is "wise" can help establish trust and foster motivation even though the feedback includes information about weaknesses. In one study, 45 African American and 48 White College students were asked by a White experimenter to write a letter of commendation for their favorite teacher (Cohen Steele, Ross, 1999). The students were told that the best letters would be published in a journal and that the skills needed were similar to those needed to write an effective college paper. A photo of each student was attached to their draft letter. A week later the students returned for the second session of the study and were given one of three types of feedback:

(1) Unbuffered criticism: Spelling and grammatical errors were marked as well as some shortcomings in the writing (e.g. stylistic concerns). Also two check marks *acknowledging good points were included.*

(2) Criticism and positive buffer: In addition to the criticism described for the unbuffered group, students were told that they did a good job and made a number of good points.

(3) Wise feedback: Criticism, positive buffer, and assurance. In addition to the criticism and positive buffer described above, students were also told that the person critiquing the letter believed that the student could meet the high standards needed for publication.

The researchers assessed how biased the students believed the reviewer was, how motivated students were to revise the letter, and how much students identified with writing skills. All students were less motivated and identified less with writing if they received unbuffered criticism. However, for White students the distinction between criticism with positive buffer *vs* the wise feedback was not as important as it was for African American students. The group of African American students who received wise feedback was more motivated, identified more with writing, and was significantly less likely to believe the reviewer was biased than the groups that received the other forms of criticism.

This study suggests that the kind of feedback given is important: unbuffered criticism is associated with lower motivation for all students. However, for African American students who grow up amidst negative stereotypes about their competence, feedback that promotes motivation, needs to include three components: some positive comments, criticism that identifies specific weaknesses, and comments that make it clear the teacher believes the student can do well.

Questions

> This study was conducted using College students—do you think the findings would also apply to elementary, middle, and high school students?

> This study focused on African American students. Do you think the findings might also apply to Latino and Native American students who are also often stereotyped as less competent?

> How important is trust in classroom interactions?

> Have you received the kinds of feedback described here? Did it influence your motivation?

References

Cohen, G., Steele, C., & Ross, L. (1999). The mentor's dilemma: Providing critical feedback across the racial divide. *Personality and social psychology bulletin, 25(10), 1302-1318.*

Cohen, G., Steele, C., & Ross, L. (2002). A barrier of mistrust: How negative stereotypes affect cross-race mentoring. In Aronson, J. M. & Aronson, J. (Eds.), Improving academic achievement: Impact of psychological factors in education, 305-331. Emerald Group Publishing.

Deciding for yourself about the research

Chapter 12, Standardized assessment strategies: *Why are standardized tests so important to NCLB?*

The use of standardized testing in NCLB arises from reforms that were initiated in the 1980s. These reforms were heavily influenced by business leaders who were concerned with the rising productivity of international competitors and believed that improving education would aid USA competitiveness. Corporate leaders who had orchestrated company turnarounds stressed the importance of setting explicit goals, performance or outputs, use of benchmarks or standards, and organizational restructuring. Policy makers needed support from the business leaders for the additional financial resources needed for widespread education reforms they wished so it is not surprising they adopted these business ideas as they devised ways to make teachers and students more accountable.

According to Susan Fuhrman (2004) a "theory of action" underlies these new accountability systems that contains the following assumptions:

(a) Schools' primary focus should be student achievement in the key areas of math, reading and science. *Clear content standards* developed by each State for each subject area and grade level help schools in this focus. If rewards and sanctions are based on the basis of students' meeting the content standards in that school then the teachers and administrators will devote energy and resources to improving student achievement.

(b) *Standardized tests* that are aligned with the content standards can accurately and authentically measure student performance. Well designed tests are reliable and valid and so other measures such as classroom observations are not needed to determine if teachers and schools are doing a good job.

(c) Meaningful *consequences* will not only motivate teachers, students, and administrators but also improve instruction. Positive consequences include bonuses for teachers and administrators and negative consequences include denial of graduation or promotion for students, or school take over and restructuring. Because these consequences are real, teachers will work harder to teach and be more likely to additional professional development to improve their skills. Students will also work harder to learn so teacher-student interactions around content will improve. Frequent assessment will provide meaningful feedback on student performance which in turn will promote improved teaching.

(d) There will be *minimal unintended consequences* if the systems work as intended. For example, instruction will improve rather then becoming narrowly focused on test taking skills, and high school graduation tests will promote learning not increase drop out rates.

Questions

Our questions focus on part of each assumption.

> - How much emphasis should schools place on reading, mathematics and science? What role should art, physical education, social studies, and music play in school classrooms?
>
> - Do standardized tests measure students' performance on content standards adequately? Should schools be judged on students' scores on standardized tests? Is it important that classroom observations of students (by teachers or others) are not included.
>
> - Will students and teachers be motivated by the tests. Stiggins (2004) argued that while high achieving students may be motivated by tests many students who find the tests difficult will give up and so be less motivated. Do you agree with Stiggins or the assumption underlying NCLB?
>
> - Are the unintended consequences minimal? Is classroom instruction improving or becoming narrowly focused on test taking skills and content?

References

Fuhrman, S. H. (2004). Introduction, In S. H. Fuhrman & R. F. Elmore (Eds). *Redesigning accountability systems for education.* (pp. 3-14). New York: Teachers College Press.

Deciding for yourself about research

Appendix C, The reflective practitioner: *action research as a way to deal with the isolation of teaching*

Observers of education have sometimes noted that classroom teachers tend to be isolated from each other by the very nature of their work (Lortie, 1975; Zeichner, 2007). A teacher may be constantly surrounded by students, but chances are that no colleague will be there to witness what the teacher does in class. Conversation about classroom experiences do happen, but they tend to happen outside of class time—perhaps over lunch, or before or after school. This circumstance does not prevent teachers' from sharing experiences or concerns related to teaching altogether, but delaying conversations probably makes them less frequent or likely. Fewer collegial conversations, in turn, can limit teachers by reducing their opportunities to learn from each other—or even to realize many of the instructional options open to them.

Action research addresses teachers' isolation because it promotes not only reflection on practice, but also collaboration and sharing (Hayes, 2006). The benefits of sharing may be the most obvious when an action research project is actually published for a wider audience. Over the past 20 years, numerous teachers and other educators have published studies of their own teaching or their own students' learning. There are now entire books compiling such accounts (for example, Samaras & Freese, 2006; Tidwell & Fitzgerald, 2006), a comprehensive handbook discussing aspects of teachers' studies of their own teaching (Loughran, et al., 2004), several journals whose purpose is largely or solely to publish examples of action research (one, for example, is called simply Action Research), and a variety of blogs and websites that post action research projects. Collectively these publications are a rich source of practical wisdom from which individual teachers can learn and think about their own teaching.

But an action research project does not have to published formally in order to promote collaboration or sharing. The benefits can happen locally—even within a single school building—whenever a teacher plans, carries out, and talks about a research initiative. A teacher named Betty Ragland, for example, described how this happened in her highly unusual teaching situation, a juvenile correctional facility (Ragland, 2006). The facility functioned somewhat like a prison for youth convicted of various crimes. As you might suppose, Ms Ragland's students experienced behavior problems and conflicts more often than usual in schools, to the extent that teachers sometimes felt physically vulnerable themselves, as well as isolated from help if serious conflicts developed during class. To deal with these stresses, Ms Ragland initiated a self-study of her practice in which she wrote and thought about her experiences and her reactions to the experiences. She shared the results, both in writing and through meetings, with fellow teachers. In the course of doing so, she developed a number of insights which colleagues found helpful in formulating their own thinking:

As Ms Ragland reflected on her work as a teacher, she realized that teaching in a correctional facility had made her more cautious about her safety even *outside* of teaching hours. For example, she had become more careful about locking her car door, where she walked at night, and even where she sat in restaurants (she preferred to sit with her back to the wall).

Ms Ragland found it impossible to describe her work in a fully detached or objective way, and finally decided that being detached was not even desirable. Her feelings and interpretations of students' behavior were essential to understanding experiences with them, so she decided that it was better to include these in whatever she wrote about them.

As she wrote, talked, and reflected on her experiences, she found herself governed by two incompatible perspectives about her work, which she called the *educational perspective* (try to help students and turn their lives around) and the *correctional perspective* (remember that the students had committed serious crimes and often could not be trusted).

More importantly, she discovered, through conversations with fellow staff, that they too felt torn between these same two perspectives.

By talking with each other about the dilemmas in how to interpret students' needs and (mis)behaviors, she and the other staff were able to develop a common perspective about their purposes, about appropriate ways of helping students, and about appropriate ways of dealing with conflicts when they arose.

In the end, a study initiated by one teacher, Ms Ragland, benefited all the teachers. What began as a self-study eventually became a group study, and teachers' mutual isolation at work decreased.

Not many teachers, of course, find themselves teaching in a correctional facility. But many—perhaps most—do experience serious dilemmas and stresses either about students' behavior or about their learning. Depending on circumstances, for example, a teacher may wonder how to respond to students who treat the teacher or other students disrespectfully. Or a teacher may feel lost about helping certain students who are struggling or wonder where the teacher's responsibility ends if a student persists in not learning even after receiving special help. Such uncertainties may not lead to physical threats, as actually happened to Betty Ragland occasionally, but they can create a lot of stress nonetheless. But action research can help—systematically studying and reflecting on how to solve them, reading and listening to how others have done the same, and sharing what teachers therefore learn. Because of these activities, questions about teaching can be resolved, or at least clarified, and classroom practice can be enhanced. Most important, the benefits can be shared not only with the teacher as researcher, but with a teacher's colleagues as well.

Questions

➤ Consider the three ways discussed in this chapter that research articles can differ: (1) by how much they seek universal truths, (2) by the response the author expects from the reader, and (3) by the assumptions the author makes about the reader's prior experiences. Where is Ms Ragland's action research situated on each of these dimensions of difference?

➢ Consider the ethical issues about action research discussed at the end of this chapter—insuring privacy of students, gaining informed consent, and insuring freedom to participate. Given the nature and focus of Ms Ragland's particular action research, how might she honor these ethical considerations? Does the fact that her students were (literally) captives make any difference?

➢ Suppose that instead of an inside staff member like Ms Ragland studying youthful offenders, an outsider unfamiliar with youth correctional facilities wanted to do so. How would outsider status affect what could be learned about life in a juvenile correctional facility?

References

Lortie, D. (1975). *Schoolteacher*. Chicago: University of Chicago Press.

Zeichner, K. (2007). Accumulating knowledge across self-studies in teacher education. *Journal of Teacher Education, 58*(1), 36-46.

Hayes, D. (2006). Telling stories: Sustaining improvement in schools operating under adverse conditions. *Improving Schools, 9*(3), 203-213.

Samaras, A. & Freese, A. (Eds.). (2006). *Self-study of teaching practices*. New York: Peter Lang.

Tidwell, D. & Fitzgerald, L. (Eds.). (2006). *Self-study and diversity*. Rotterdam, The Netherlands: Sense Publishers.

Ragland, B. (2007). Positioning the practitioner-researcher: Five ways of looking at practice. *Action Research, 4*(2), 165-182.

Appendix C: The reflective practitioner

The experience in reflective teaching is that you must plunge into the doing, and try to educate yourself before you know what it is you're trying to learn.

(Donald Schön, 1987)

Donald Schön, a philosopher and educational researcher, makes an important observation: learning about teaching often means making choices and taking actions without knowing in advance quite what the consequences will be. The problem, as we have pointed out more than once, is that classroom events are often ambiguous and ambivalent, in that they usually serve more than one purpose. A teacher compliments a student's contribution to a discussion: at that moment she may be motivating the student, but also focusing classmates' thinking on key ideas. Her comment functions simultaneously as behavioral reinforcement, information, and expression of caring. At that moment complimenting the student may be exactly the right thing to do. Or not: perhaps the praise causes the teacher to neglect the contributions of others, or focuses attention on factors that students cannot control, like their ability instead of their effort. In teaching, it seems, everything cuts more than one way, signifies more than one thing. The complications can make it difficult to prepare for teaching in advance, though they also make teaching itself interesting and challenging.

The complications also mean that teachers need to learn from their own teaching by reflecting (or thinking about the significance of) their experiences. In the classrooms, students are not the only people who need to learn. So do teachers, though what teachers need to learn is less about curriculum and more about students' behavior and motivation, about how to assess their learning well, and about how to shape the class into a mutually supportive community.

Thinking about these matters helps to make a teacher a reflective practitioner (Schön, 1983), a professional who learns both from experience and about experience. Becoming thoughtful helps you in all the areas discussed in this text: it helps in understanding better how students' learning occurs, what motivates students, how you might differentiate your instruction more fully, and how you can make assessments of learning more valid and fair.

Learning to reflect on practice is so important, in fact, that we have referred to and illustrated its value throughout this book. In addition we devote this entire chapter to how you, like other professional teachers, can develop habits of reflective practice in yourself. In most of this chapter we describe what reflective practice feels like as an experience, and offer examples of places, people, and activities that can support your own reflection on practice. We finish by discussing how teachers can also learn simply by observing and reflecting on their own teaching systematically, and by sharing the results with other teachers and professionals. We call this activity teacher research or action research. As you will see, reflective practice not only contributes to teachers' ability to make wise decisions, but also allows them to serve as effective, principled advocates on behalf of students.

Types of resources for professional development and learning

At some level reflection on practice is something you must do for yourself, since only you have had your particular teaching experiences, and only you can choose how to interpret and make use of them. But this rather individual activity also benefits from the stimulus and challenge offered by fellow professionals. Others' ideas may differ from your own, and they can therefore help in working out your own thoughts and in alerting you to ideas that you may otherwise take for granted. These benefits of reflection can happen in any number of ways, but most fall into one of four general categories:

- talking and collaborating with colleagues

- participating in professional associations

- attending professional development workshops and conferences

- reading professional literature

In the next sections we explore what each of these activities has to offer.

Colleagues as a resource

Perhaps the simplest way to stimulate reflections about your own teaching is to engage fellow teachers or other colleagues in dialogue (or thoughtful conversation) about teaching and learning: What do you think of this kind of experience? Have you ever had one like it yourself, and what did you make of it? Note that to be helpful in stimulating reflection, these conversations need to be largely about educational matters, not about personal ones ("What movie did you see last night?"). Dialogues with individual colleagues have certain advantages to more complex or formal professional experiences. Talking with an individual generally allows more participation for both of you, since only two people may need to express their views. It also can provide a measure of safety or confidentiality if your conversation partner is a trusted colleague; sometimes, therefore, you can share ideas of which you are not sure, or that may be controversial.

A somewhat more complex way of stimulating reflection is group study. Several teachers at a school gather regularly to bring themselves up to date on a new curriculum, for example, or to plan activities or policies related to a school-wide theme (e.g. "the environment"). Group meetings often result in considerable dialog among the members about the best ways to teach and to manage classrooms, as well as stories about students' behavior and learning experiences. For a beginning teacher, group study can be a particularly good way to learn from experienced, veteran teachers.

Sharing of ideas becomes even more intense if teachers collaborate with each other about their work on an extended basis. Collaboration can take many forms; in one form it might be "team teaching" by two or more teachers working with one group of students, and in another form it might be two or more teachers consulting regularly to coordinate the content of their courses. Collaborations work best when each member of the team brings responsibilities and expertise that are unique, but also related to the other members' responsibilities. Imagine, for example, a collaboration between Sharon, who is a middle-years classroom teacher, and Pat, who is a resource teacher—one whose job is to assist classroom teachers in working with students with educational disabilities or special needs. If Pat spends time in Sharon's classroom, then not only will the students benefit, but they both may learn from each other's presence. Potentially, Pat can learn the details of the middle-years curriculum and learn more about the full range of students' skills—not just those of students having difficulties. Sharon can get ideas about how to help individuals who, in a classroom context, seem especially difficult to help. Achieving these benefits, of course, comes at a cost: the two teachers may need to take time not only for the students, but also to talk with each other. Sometimes the time-cost can be reduced somewhat if their school administrators can arrange for a bit of extra planning and sharing time. But even if this does not happen, the benefits of collaboration will be very real, and often make the investment of time worthwhile.

Professional associations and professional development activities

Another way to stimulate reflection about teaching is by joining and participating in professional associations—organizations focused on supporting the work of teachers and on upholding high standards of teaching practice. Table 45 lists several major professional associations related to education and their Internet addresses. Most of them are composed of local branches or chapters serving the needs of a particular city, state, or region.

Table 45: A selection of professional associations related to education

- American Association for the Mentally Retarded (AAMR) [www.aamr.org]

- Association for Health, Physical Education, Recreation, & Dance (AAHPERD) [www.aahperd.org]

- Association for Experiential Education (AEE) [www.princeton.edu/~rcurtis/aee.html]

- Association for Retarded Citizens (ARC) [www.thearc.org/welcome.html]

- ENC Online Resources for Math and Science Education [www.enc.org/stan.htm]

- National Association for Bilingual Education (NABE) [www.nabe.org/]

- National Association for the Education of Young Children (NAEYC) [www.naeyc.org/]

- National Council for Teachers of Mathematics (NCTM) [[www.nctm.org/]

- National Council for the Social Studies (NCSS) [www.socialstudies.org/]

- National Council for Teachers of English (NCTE) [www.ncte.org]

- National Science Teachers Association [www.nsta.org/]

- Organization of American Historians (OAH) [www.oah.org]

To achieve their purposes, a professional association provides a mixture of publications, meetings, and conferences intended for the professional development of educators, including classroom teachers. Typically the publications include either a relatively frequent newsletter or a less frequent journal focused on issues of practice or research. Very large associations often publish more than one newsletter or journal, each of which is focused on a particular topic or type of news (for example, the National Education Association in the United States publishes eight separate periodicals). Some also publish online journals (there are several listed as part of Table 46 or online versions of print journals. Whatever format they take, professionally sponsored publications stimulate thinking by discussing issues and dilemmas faced by professional educators, and sometimes also by presenting recent educational research and the recommendations for teaching that flow from that research. We discuss ways of using these publications further in the next section of this chapter.

Table 46: A sampling of journals related to professional education

- Annotated Bibliography of Education Journals - annotations of over 426 education related journals and extensive links to educational organizations and institutions that sponsor them.

- CSS Journal - Computers in the Social Studies - dedicated to the encouragement of the use of computers and related technology in K-12 social studies classrooms.

- Education Policy and Analysis - published by the College of Education at Arizona State University

- Educational Theory - publishes work in the philosophy of education and other disciplines.

- Effective Teaching - electronic journal devoted to the exchange of ideas and information relevant to college and university teaching in North Carolina.

- Harvard Educational Review - quarterly journal that provides an inter-disciplinary forum for innovative thinking and research in education.

- Interact - European platform for interactive learning and new media.

- Journal of Computing in Higher Education - publishes articles that contribute to our understanding of the issues, problems, and research associated with instructional technology

- New jour - electronic journal and newsletter archive.

- Revista Iberoamericana de Educacion - Revista de la OEI.

- Scholarly Electronic Journals - Trends and Attitudes: A Research Proposal

- WORLDSPEAKER online - an international academic journal written by and for international scholars, university administrators, and researchers.

Meetings and conferences sponsored by a professional association also take a variety of forms. Depending on the size of the association and on the importance of the topic, a meeting could be as short as a one half-day workshop or as long as a full week with many sessions occurring simultaneously. Sometimes, too, an association might sponsor a more extended course—a series of meetings focused on one topic or problem of concern to teachers, such as classroom management or curriculum planning. In some cases, the course might carry university credit, though not always.

As you might expect, the size of a professional association makes a difference in kinds of professional development experiences it can provide. In general, the smaller the association, the more exclusively it focuses on local news and educational needs, both in its publications and in its meetings or other activities. At a professional development workshop sponsored by a local teachers' association, for example, you are relatively likely to see colleagues and acquaintances not only from your own school, but from other neighboring schools. Locally sponsored events are also more likely to focus on local issues, such as implementing a new system for assessing students' learning within the local schools. In general, too, local events tend to cost less to attend, in both time and money.

By the same token, the larger the association, the more its professional development opportunities are likely to focus on large-scale trends in education, such as the impact of the *No Child Left Behind* legislation we discussed in Chapter 1 or the latest trends in using computer technology for teaching. Conferences or other professional development events are more likely to span several days and to be located outside the immediate town or region whether you live and work. You may therefore see fewer of your everyday colleagues and acquaintances, but you may also have a greater incentive to make new acquaintances whose interests or concerns are similar to your own. The event is more likely to feature educators who are well-known nationally or internationally, and to call attention to educational trends or issues that are new or unfamiliar.

Whether large or small, the activities of professional associations can stimulate thinking and reflecting about teaching. By meeting and talking with others at a meeting of an association, teachers learn new ideas for teaching, become aware of emerging trends and issues about education, and confront assumptions that they may have made about their own practices with students. Professional meetings, conferences, and workshops can provide these benefits because they draw on the expertise and experience of a wide range of professionals—usually wider than is possible within a single school building. But compared simply to talking with your immediate colleagues, they have a distinct disadvantage: they take effort and a bit of money to attend, and sometimes they are available at convenient times. Well-balanced professional development should therefore also include activities that are available frequently, but that also draw on a wide range of expertise. Fortunately, an activity with these features is often easily at hand: the reading of professional publications about educational research and practice.

Reading and understanding professional articles

Although publications about educational issues and research can take many forms, they tend to serve three major purposes in some sort of combination. A publication could either (1) provide a framework for understanding teaching and learning, (2) offer advice about how to teach, or (3) advocate particular ideas or practices about education. Benefiting from a professional publication depends partly on understanding which of these purposes a particular article or book is emphasizing.

Three purposes of educational publications

Consider the first purpose, to provide a framework for understanding teaching and learning (Hittleman and Simon, 2005). A "framework" in this context means a perspective or general viewpoint for understanding specific events and actions. They are much like the theories described earlier in this book, though not always as formal or broad. A published article might propose, for example, a way of understanding why certain students are disrespectful in spite of teachers' efforts to prevent such behavior (perhaps they are reinforced by peers for being disrespectful). It might offer evidence supporting this perspective. In doing so, the author provides a sort of "theory of disrespectful behavior", though he or she may not call it a theory explicitly.

A second purpose is to offer advice about appropriate teaching practices. An article intended for this purpose, for example, might suggest how to introduce reading instruction to first graders, or how to use fiction to teach high school history, or how to organize a class to include a student with a disability. Often giving such advice overlaps with the first purpose, providing a framework for understanding, since thinking about an educational issue in a particular way may imply certain ways of dealing with it in practice.

A third purpose of a published article is to advocate ideas and persuade others to take actions benefiting students and society. It might take a position about important issues in education: Is it a good idea or not to retain (or hold back) a student in grade level for another year if the student fails the curriculum the first time? Should schools teach about sexuality? Should girls learn science in classrooms separate from boys? In advocating for ideas or policies about such matters, the article may express concern about what is good, ethical or desirable in education, not just about what is factually true or practical. The author may seek explicitly to persuade readers of the author's point of view. These features do not mean, however, that you need to give up thinking for yourself. On the contrary, when reading an advocacy-oriented article, reflection may be especially important.

Whatever its purpose—understanding, advice, or advocacy—an article or book about a professional issue can stimulate thinking about what you know and believe about teaching and learning. It should therefore create, rather than undermine, your individuality as a teacher. Think of professional reading as a dialogue or conversation about education: some of the comments in the conversation will probably be more helpful than others, but each participant contributes somehow, even if none can give a final answer or everlasting truth. It is the same with publications; some may be more helpful than others, but none will be so perfect that you can afford to cease further reading or further thinking. If you are about to begin a teaching career, for example, you may be especially interested in anything published about classroom management, but less interested in the problems of administering schools or in the political issues that usually accompany educational systems. Yet some publications may discuss these latter issues anyway, and eventually you may find yourself more concerned about them than at the start of a career. Your job, as a reflective teacher, will be sort out the currently useful articles (or parts of articles) from ones you cannot use immediately.

To experience educational publications in this way, however, you must think of the authors as your collaborators as well as general authorities. As a reader, you need to assume that you are entitled to consider an author's ideas, but not obligated to accept it without journals related to professional education question. There are several strategies for developing this attitude, but to keep the discussion focused, we will look at just two. We have already discussed the first strategy, which is to understand the purposes of any particular piece of research which you encounter, in order to assess its current usefulness to your daily work and your long-term professional goals. We have already indicated several general purposes of educational research publications, but we will go into more detail about this in the next section. The second strategy for relating to authors as collaborators is to think about how you yourself might contribute to professional knowledge by engaging in research of your own, even as a classroom teacher—an activity often called action research (Mills, 2006; Stringer, 2007). At the end of this chapter we discuss what action research involves, and how you might consider using it.

Authors' assumptions about readers

Authors of professional articles and books also make assumptions about their readers, and it helps to be aware of these while you read. The assumptions affect the style, content, and significance of the author's ideas in ways that are both obvious and subtle.

One assumption is about the response which an author expects from you, the reader: does he or she expect you actually to do something new, or simply to consider doing something new? Or does the author just want you to be aware of a new idea? Consider, for example, an article reviewing best practices about inclusion of students with special needs. The author may imply, or even urge you to take a moral position: you should include these students, the author may seem to say. But in a different article—one recommending particular teaching practices—the author may merely ask you to think about alternatives to your normal ways of teaching. Certain strategies worked under certain teaching conditions, the author says, so simply consider whether they might work for you as well.

A second, less obvious difference among professional publications is in their un-stated assumptions about prior experiences and attitudes of readers. This assumption may be either helpful or frustrating, depending on you actual prior background. A piece intended as a "framework for understanding" may assume, for example, that you are familiar with basic theories of learning already. If you have read and understood what we outlined in Chapter 2 of this book, the article may turn out to be relatively accessible or understandable to you even if you have relatively little experience in actual classroom teaching, and even if you have never studied learning theories in detail. The article might seem more accessible than you expect because, for example, it focuses primarily on how teacher's praise affects students' learning, an idea with which you may be somewhat familiar already.

On the other hand, a professional publication may assume that you have taught school for a number of years already, or that you are at least familiar with classroom life from the point of view not of students, but of a teacher. An author writing about "withitness" (discussed in Chapter 7), for example, may make this assumption, since the concept originated by observing teachers managing large group classroom activities. If you yourself are experienced at actual teaching, reading about withitness may trigger a lot of questions about just how withit teachers are able to be in practice, and about whether in fact they always need to be withit. You can also ask yourself these questions even if you have not yet been a teacher yourself, of course, but they may seem less immediate or urgent.

A professional article intended to advocate for a particular educational policy or practice may make very different assumptions about you as a reader. It may assume, for example, that you do in fact enjoy persuading others of your point of view, even when others initially disagree or react indifferently. This sort of assumption may show up as much in what the writing omits, as in what it includes: if the term cooperative learning activity is used without explanation, for example, the researcher may be assuming not only that you are the sort of person— perhaps a teacher—who knows what that term means already, but also that you already believe in the value of cooperative learning and are motivated to explain its value to others.

In making these distinctions among published articles, keep in mind a point we made at the outset: that an individual article usually serves more than one purpose at a time and makes more than one assumption about your prior knowledge and about how you are supposed to respond to the article. The differences are only about emphasis. To illustrate these ideas about the purposes and effects of research, look in the next section at three examples of actual published articles relevant to education. The studies are not a full cross-section of educational research or publications, but they do suggest some of the variety possible (and necessary) among them. Each example serves a mixture of purposes, but also emphasizes one purpose in particular (perspective-taking, teaching recommendations, or advocacy) described earlier. The authors of each example also make particular assumptions about you, the reader—about the intellectual work which the authors expect you to do and about the motivations which they assume you have or hope that you will acquire. For each example, we describe the reactions of one of us (Kelvin Seifert) as he read the article.

Example #1: How do children acquire moral commitments?

In 1997, Herbert Saltzstein and several colleagues published a research-oriented article about how children acquire moral beliefs (Saltzstein, et al., 1997). The group of researchers were all graduate students and professors of psychology, working mostly at the City University of New York. When Kelvin read of their affiliation with psychology, he suspected that they would talk about moral beliefs in general, and not necessarily about moral issues in classrooms, such as cheating or treating classmates with care and respect. Still, the article interested Kelvin as a former teacher and current university professor, because he had long been concerned with fostering qualities like integrity, honesty, cooperation, and loyalty in students. If Kelvin could find out about the mechanism or process by which children acquire mature moral beliefs, he reasoned, maybe he could modify his teaching to take advantage of that knowledge.

So Kelvin began reading the article. He discovered some parts were challenging and required careful reflection, whereas others were easier to read. One of the most challenging passages came almost immediately, in the second and third paragraphs; these paragraphs, it seemed, required a bit of prior knowledge about theories of moral development. But Kelvin was willing to concentrate more fully on these paragraphs, because he expected that they might clarify the rest of the study. Here are the paragraphs, and some of Kelvin's thoughts as he read them:

Initial problem: We began by re-examining the phenomenon of heteronomy, Piaget's assertion (1932/1965) following Kant (1785/1959) that young children equate moral obligation with deference to authority when justifying their moral judgments. The concept is important because it is central to the organismic account of moral development as a series of differentiations and integrations.... [p. 37]	This was one of the difficult paragraphs, perhaps especially because Kelvin had never read the specific book by Piaget or by the philosopher Kant. But Kelvin did recall reading, at various times over the years, *about* Piaget's views on moral development. Piaget believed that at first, children define morality in terms of what adults think: an action is "good" if and only if adults (e.g. parents) consider it good, and "bad" if and only if adults consider it bad. This is the idea of "heteronomy" to which Saltzstein is referring. Children, in this view, take quite awhile to develop or "grow" into truly autonomous moral beliefs. Autonomous beliefs form slowly out of earlier beliefs, in the way that a young plant or animal might grow. This is the "organismic account of moral development" that Saltzstein is talking about.
...This account has been challenged by Turiel's domain theory (Turiel, 1983). According to Turiel and his colleagues, even young children intuitively distinguish moral from conventional rules. [p. 37]	Here was an idea that was intriguing! Saltzstein and his colleagues were pointing to research (by the person cited, named Turiel) that suggests that even preschoolers know the difference between truly moral

rules and merely conventional rules. Apparently they believe, for example, that it would be wrong to steal toys or to hit someone, even if adults gave you permission to do so. But apparently they also know that it would be OK for traffic lights to use different colors—for red to mean "go" and green to mean "stop"—provided that everyone agreed on changing the rule. That is what the researcher named Turiel apparently meant by distinguishing convention from morality.

The introduction continued in this challenging style for about two pages, requiring Kelvin to read slowly and carefully in order to understand its points. Kelvin was not discouraged from continuing, though, because he wanted to find out more about how, in general, children acquire moral beliefs. Did moral beliefs take time to develop—did they "grow" on children slowly after initially being borrowed from parents or other adults? In this case, then maybe Kelvin owed it to his students to adopt and express desirable moral attitudes myself, so as to provide a good model for their developing beliefs. Or were students' key moral beliefs already in place when they entered school—almost as if "hard wired" in their minds, or at least already learned during infancy and the preschool years? In this second case, it might still be desirable for Kelvin to adopt positive moral attitudes, but not for the purpose of modeling them for students. Students already "hard wired" for key moral beliefs might not need a model so much as an enforcer of desirable moral behaviors. Concerning the issue of cheating, for example, the students might already understand the undesirable nature and implications of this behavior. As a result they might not need demonstrations of honest integrity from their teacher as much as affirmations from the teacher of the importance of honesty and integrity, along with consistent enforcement of appropriate sanctions against cheating when it did occur.

For Kelvin, therefore, the outcomes of research on moral development—including Saltzstein's that he was currently reading—posed issues of classroom management, both in university classrooms and in public school classrooms. So Kelvin read on. Saltzstein proposed resolving the issues about the origins of moral development by distinguishing between moral conflicts and moral dilemmas:

Moral conflicts are conflicts between moral duty or right and a non-moral desire. An example might be the conflict between whether to return a wallet to its rightful owner or keep the coveted wallet with its extra cash. In contrast, moral dilemmas are conflicts involving two moral rights or duties. For example, [a person might feel a dilemma between] whether to steal a drug to save a spouse's life. [p. 38]	The distinction between conflicts and dilemmas looked promising to Kelvin. Moral conflicts looked fairly simple in cognitive terms, even if they were sometimes difficult emotionally. The "right" action was obvious. Moral dilemmas were more complex cognitively as well as emotionally, because two "goods" were being weighed against each other. The moral alternatives might both be right and wrong at the same time, and their relative "rightness" might not be immediately obvious.

Saltzstein and his colleagues proposed that when young children show awareness of moral rules, they may be doing so in the simpler context of moral conflicts. A young child might believe that you should return a dollar to its owner, even if the child has trouble in practice overcoming a selfish impulse to keep the dollar. The same child might have trouble deciding, however, whether it is "right" to inform his teacher if a best friend has cheated on a test. In that case two moral principles compete for attention—honesty and loyalty to a friend. To sort out the implications of choosing between these principles, a young child might need to rely on older, wiser minds, such as parents or other adults. The minute that he or she does so, the child is showing the moral heteronomy that Piaget used to write about and that Saltzstein referred to early in the article.

Understanding these ideas took effort, but once Kelvin began figuring them out, the rest of the article was easier to follow. In reading the remaining pages, he noted in passing that the researchers used several techniques common in educational research. For example, they interviewed participants, a common way of gathering systematic information about individuals' thinking. They also imposed controls on their procedures and on the selection of participants. Procedures were controlled, for example, by posing the same three moral dilemmas and to all participants, so that individuals' responses could be compared meaningfully. The selection of participants was controlled by selecting two age groups for deliberate comparison with each other—one that was seven years old and the other that was eleven. Since the researchers wanted to generalize about moral development as much as possible, but they obviously could not interview every child in the world, they sampled participants: they selected a manageable number (sixty-five, to be exact) from the larger student population of one particular school. In a second part of the investigation, they also selected a comparable number of children of the same two ages (7 and 11) from the city of Recife, located in Brazil. The Brazilian group's responses were compared deliberately with the American group's responses, in order to allow for the impact of cultural beliefs on moral development in general. Kelvin recognized this research strategy as an example of using control groups. In research terms, the Brazilian group "controlled for" the impact of American culture on children's moral beliefs, and vice versa, the American group controlled for the impact of Brazilian culture on children's moral beliefs. Altogether, these techniques helped insure that the interviews of children's moral beliefs really illustrated what they were supposed to illustrate—that they were reliable and valid, in the senses that we discussed in earlier chapters. As Kelvin noticed Saltzstein's attention to good research techniques, he gained confidence in Saltzstein's observations and in the interpretations that the authors made from them.

What did Saltzstein and his colleagues find out—or more to the point, what did Kelvin Seifert learn from what Saltzstein and his colleagues wrote about? There were three ideas that occurred to Kelvin. One was that in everyday life, children probably deal with moral beliefs of all levels of cognitive complexity, and not just "simple" moral conflicts and "complex" moral dilemmas. Saltzstein found that children's solutions to moral dilemmas depended a lot on the content of the dilemma. Children advocated strongly for truthfulness in some situations (for example, in deciding whether to tell the teacher about a friend's cheating), but not in other situations (like in deciding whether to back up a friend who is being teased and who has lied in an effort to stop the teasing). But it was rare for all children to support any one moral principle completely; they usually supported a mix.

Another idea that Kelvin learned from Saltzstein's research was about how children expressed moral heteronomy versus moral autonomy. Age, it seemed, did not affect the beliefs that children stated; younger and older children took similar positions on all dilemmas initially. But age did affect how steadfastly children held to initial beliefs. Younger children were more easily influenced to switch opinions when an adult "cross-examined" with probing questions; older children were more likely to keep to their initial position. Moral heteronomy was revealed not by a child's views as such, but by the kind of dialogue a child has with adults.

A third idea that Kelvin learned was about children's perceptions of adults' moral beliefs. Saltzstein found that even though older children (the 11-year-olds) showed more moral autonomy (were more steadfast) than younger children, they tended to believe that adults thought about moral issues in ways similar to children who were younger. In the "teasing" dilemma mentioned above, for example, the 11-year-olds opted much more often than 7-year-olds for remaining loyal to a friend, even though doing so meant further untruthfulness with peers. Yet the 11-year-olds also more often stated a belief that adults would resolve the same dilemma in a way characteristic of 7-year-olds—that is, by telling the truth to peers and thus betraying loyalty to a friend. This finding puzzled Kelvin. Why should older, and presumably more insightful, children think that adults are more like younger children than like themselves? Saltzstein suggested an interpretation, however, that helped him make sense of the apparent inconsistency:

...Consistent with our past research, children attributed the kinds of moral choices made by younger children to adults. In our view, this finding tends to support a constructivist rather than a [social modeling] view of morality, which would predict that the child's judgments mirror (or develop toward) their representation of adult judgments. [p. 41]	In other words, thought Kelvin, if children learned moral beliefs by imitating (or modeling themselves after) parents or other adults, then they ought to see themselves as resembling adults more and more as they get older. Instead, they see themselves as resembling adults less, at least during middle childhood. This would happen only if they were preoccupied with "constructing" their own beliefs on the basis of their experiences, and therefore failed to notice that adults might also have constructed beliefs similar to their own.

Relevance: a framework for understanding moral development

The article by Saltzstein offered a way to understand how children develop moral beliefs, and especially to understand the change from moral heteronomy to moral autonomy. By imposing controls on the procedures (uniform interviews) and on the selection of participants (particular ages, particular societies or cultures), the researchers eliminated certain sources of ambiguity or variability in children's responses. By framing their project in terms of previous theories of moral development (Piaget's, Turiel's), furthermore, they made it easier to interpret their new results in the general terms of these theories as well. In these ways the investigation aspired to provide a general perspective about children's moral development. Providing a framework for understanding, you recall, is one of the major purposes of many professional publications.

But note that the authors paid a price for emphasizing this purpose. By organizing their work around existing general theory and research, they had to assume that readers already had some knowledge of that theory and research. This is not an unreasonable assumption if the readers are expected to be fellow researchers; after all, many of them make a living by "knowing the literature" of psychology. But assuming such knowledge can be an obstacle if the authors intend to communicate with non-psychologists: in that case, either the authors must make more of an effort to explain the relevant background research, or readers must educate themselves about the research. The latter activity is not necessarily difficult (the background knowledge for Saltzstein's work, for example, took me only a few paragraphs to explain in writing), but it must be done to make full sense of research that tries to provide a universal framework of psychological knowledge.

The reader's role: interested observer of children

In conducting and reporting their research, Saltzstein and his colleagues were not presenting themselves as school teachers, nor were they expecting readers necessarily to respond as teachers. As they put it in the first paragraph of the article, they sought to offer "a more contextualized perspective for understanding the development of moral judgments" [p. 37]. Unlike most teachers, they seemed indifferent to recommending how children's moral judgements ought to be fostered. Observation of children was their purpose, not intervention. The meaning of the term "contextualized perspective" was not obvious to Kelvin when he first read it, but eventually it became clearer: they were talking about the importance of distinguishing among types of moral decisions and moral beliefs. They did sometimes note information relevant to teaching—for example, they pointed out that for cultural reasons, teachers in Brazil do not command high respect and therefore compared to American children, Brazilian children may feel less compelled to tell the truth to their teachers. But this comment was not the primary focus of their research, nor did the authors discuss what (if anything) it might imply about teaching in the United States.

Yet the non-teaching perspective of the article did not keep Kelvin, a long-time school teacher and current university teacher, from reflecting on the article in terms of its educational relevance. As we mentioned already, Kelvin was attracted to the article because of his own concerns about character development in students—how do they acquire moral beliefs and commitments, and how should he help them in doing so? Kelvin did not really expect to find an answer to the second of these questions, given the "observation" orientation of the authors. He did hope to find an answer to the first, although even here he also expected that to make allowances for the fact that research interviews are not usually identical to classroom situations. Children might respond differently when interviewed individually by a researcher, compared to how they might respond to a teacher in class. Or perhaps not. So in reflecting on the article, Kelvin had to note the context and purposes of Saltzstein's study, and to remind himself that once a teacher went beyond simply observing children to intervening on their behalf, the teacher might be led to different conclusions about children's moral development. But in spite of these cautions—or maybe because of them—Kelvin found much food for thought in the article related to teaching.

Example #2: Learning disability as a misleading label

In 2006, Ray McDermott, Shelley Goldman, and Hervé Varenne published an article that discussed the use of disability categories in education. The article attracted Kelvin's attention because he had been concerned for a long time about the ambiguities of disability categories (see Chapter 5 of this book) as well as about their potential for stigmatizing individuals. He expected the article to document additional problems with labeling when a student is from a non-white ethnic group. Kelvin's expectation was fulfilled partially, but he was surprised also to encounter an additional and tougher message in the article. Here is how the study began:

Since about 1850...classifying human beings by mental ability, accurately or not, has been a politically	Kelvin had a mixed reaction to this opening. In one way it seemed to say something familiar—that

rewarded activity. Those with power have placed others, usually the downtrodden, into ability and disposition groups that they cannot escape... People who live together in a culture must struggle constantly with the constraints...of systems of classification and interpretation used in the culture.	classification systems (such as categories for disabilities) may create problems for individuals. But the tone of the paragraph sounded more severely critical than Kelvin had expected: it was saying that power governed all classifications, implying that misclassifications may be widespread or even universal.

Kelvin's initial hunch was therefore that the article would express a radically critical view of disability classifications—particularly as they affect the "downtrodden", which presumably included children from minority ethnic groups. His expectation proved correct as the authors explained their point of view, which they called a *cultural approach* to understanding disability. Using learning disabilities (LD) as an example, here is how they explained their position:

We are not as interested in LD behavior as in the preoccupations—as seen from the level of classroom organization—of all those adults who are professionally poised to discover LD behavior. We are less interested in the characteristics of LD children than in the cultural arrangements that make an LD label relevant.	At this point Kelvin was not sure if he wanted to continue reading the article because it seemed like it might not be relevant to classroom life specifically. It also implied a severe criticism of professional educators—implied that they are too eager to find examples of LD and for this reason may misclassify students. On the other hand, Kelvin was already aware that LD are an especially ambiguous category of disability; maybe the article would help to show why. So he kept reading.

The authors continued by outlining the history of LD as a category of disability, describing this category as an outgrowth of the general intelligence testing movement during the twentieth century. By the 1970s, they argued, the concept of LD offered a way to classify children with academic difficulties without having to call the children mentally disabled. Because of this fact, the LD category was needed—literally—by well-off parents who did not want their children treated or educated as children with mental disabilities. LD as a concept and category came to be applied primarily to children from the white middle-class, and mental disability became, by default, the equivalent category for the non-white and poor.

To support this assertion, the authors reported a classroom observation of three non-white boys—Hector, Ricardo, and Boomer—while they worked together to design an imaginary research station in Antarctica. Citing actual transcripts of conversation while the boys worked, the authors concluded that all three boys showed intelligence and insight about the assignment, but that the teacher was only aware of the contributions of one of the boys. Hector systematically hid his knowledge from the teacher's view by getting Boomer to speak for their group; Ricardo participated well in the group work but was rarely acknowledged by the other two boys. Boomer received considerable praise from the teacher, thanks to his speaking for the group. Yet the teacher was never aware of these subtleties. The authors blamed her oversight not on the teacher herself, but on an educational and cultural system that leads educators to classify or typify students too quickly or easily. Here is how they put it:

The American classroom is well organized for the production of display of failure, one child at a time if possible, but group by group if necessary...Even if the teacher manages to treat every child as capable, the children can hammer each other into negative status; and even if both...resist dropping everyone into predefined categories, the children's parents can take over, demanding more and more boxes with which to specify kinds of kids doing better than other kinds of kids. In such a classroom, if there were no LD categories, someone would have to invent them.

When Kelvin read this conclusion, he did not really disagree, but he did feel that it was beside the point for most teachers. Maybe children do get classified too easily, he thought, but a teacher's job is not just to lament this possibility, as the authors seemed to be doing. Instead their job is to help the real, live children for whom they have daily responsibility. What teachers need are therefore suggestions to avoid misclassifying students by overlooking key information about them. Kelvin wished, at the end, that the authors had made some of these suggestions.

Relevance: a critical framework

In this study the authors offered a sort of backhanded framework of thinking about categories of disability; or more precisely they offered a framework for understanding what the categories are *not*. In essence they said that disability categories describe qualities "in" students only in the sense that educators and others happen to think of disability categories in this way. An equally reasonable way to think about disabilities, they argued, is that modern society is organized so that its citizens have to be classified for many different reasons. Educators are simply helping to implement this society-wide expectation. A frequent result in classrooms is that teachers classify students too easily and that key evidence of students' capacity is overlooked.

In making this argument, the authors implied an indirect recommendation about how to teach, though the recommendation actually focused on what teachers should *not* do. Instead of (mis)identifying children with learning difficulties, the authors implied, teachers and other educators should stop concerning themselves with classifying children, and seek to reorganize classrooms and schools so that classification is less important. "Change the school", they wrote, "and LD becomes less relevant". This conclusion may be an important reminder, but it is not especially helpful as a recommendation to practicing teachers, who usually need to know about more than what to avoid.

The readers' role: concerned advocate for social justice

It is not surprising that the article lacked concrete recommendations for teaching, given that the authors seemed to speak to readers not as classroom teachers, but as general critics of society who are concerned about fairness or social justice. Their comments made two assumptions: first, that readers will want to minimize unfair stereotypes of students, and second, that readers will seek greater fairness in how teachers treat students. For readers who happen to be teachers themselves, the first of these assumptions is a reasonable one; most of us would indeed like to minimize unfair stereotyping of students. The second is also reasonable, but perhaps not in a way that the authors intended. Teachers probably do try their best to treat students fairly and respectfully. Their responsibilities usually mean, however, that they can only do this conveniently with their own students; the time available to work toward general social justice is often limited. (As you might suspect, Kelvin was not fully satisfied after he finished reading this article!)

Example #3: The impact of bilingualism on reading

In 1995, three education professors—Robert Jiménez, Georgia García, and David Pearson—published a study about the impact of bilingualism on children's ability to read English (1995). The three specialized in curriculum studies, literacy acquisition, and bilingual language development, and were therefore motivated by a concern for the academic success of bilingual children and especially by concern for identifying why bilingual children sometimes have difficulty learning to read English. Too much research on bilingualism, they argued, was based on what they called a "deficit" framework: it focused on what bilingual children lacked compared to monolinguals. They sought an alternative framework, one focused on bilingual students' competence, and especially on their competence to read a second language.

To search for this alternative, the researchers mounted a large research program, and the article published in 1995 was one of the studies resulting from this research. It caught Kelvin's interest not only because of its topic, but because of its approach. Instead of surveying dozens of students with a questionnaire, as researchers sometimes do, these investigators relied on just three students studied intensively. Each student became a case study and included detailed, lengthy observations and interviews of that particular student. Each student was chosen deliberately for a particular purpose. One was a highly proficient reader who was also bilingual (Spanish and English); a second was a marginally proficient reader who was bilingual (Spanish and English); and a third was a highly proficient reader who was monolingual in English. To qualify for the study, furthermore, each student had to be comfortable reflecting on and talking about their own reading processes, so that the authors could interview them at length on this topic. The researchers asked each student to read six one-page passages in English and (where relevant) in Spanish. They invited all three to think aloud about their reading as they went along, commenting on how they figured out particular words or passages. The oral readings and think-aloud commentaries were taped and transcribed, and became the information on which the authors based their conclusions and recommendations.

Using these procedures, Jiménez, García, and Pearson discovered important differences among the three girls. The proficient bilingual, Pamela, used her growing knowledge of each language to help in learning vocabulary from the other language. When she encountered the English word "species" , for example, she guessed correctly that it meant the same as the similar Spanish word "especies"; and when she encountered the Spanish "liquído", she guessed correctly that it meant the English "liquid". Her focus on learning vocabulary was stronger than for the proficient monolingual, Michelle, who commented less on specific words than how the overall reading passages related to her prior general knowledge. The difference presumably stemmed from Michelle's greater familiarity with English vocabulary—so much greater, in fact, that Michelle did not need to think about individual words deliberately. Both Michelle and Pamela differed, however, from the less-proficient bilingual reader, Christine. Like Pamela, Christine focused on vocabulary, but she did not think of her native Spanish as a resource for this task. When reading a Spanish word, she was sometimes reminded of English equivalents ("cognates," as language teachers call them), but she did not use her much greater knowledge of Spanish to assist with her more limited English. She did not search for equivalent words deliberately, as Pamela did.

Relevance: recommendations for teaching english as an additional language

The authors of this article focused more directly on particular learning behaviors than did the authors of the two articles described earlier. Jimenez and his colleagues emphasized the importance of regarding a child's native language as a strength in the process, not a liability, and they then pointed out the importance of facilitating vocabulary development. But they did not claim this recommendation to be appropriate for all children or for all forms of bilingualism. They only focused on a particular pair of languages (Spanish and English in the USA), and on three combinations of skill level in these two languages. These are common bilingual experiences in the United States, but they are not the only ones, either in the United States or elsewhere in the world.

For other bilingual situations, their conclusions might not hold true. For some students (e.g. Chinese-Americans), the native language and the second language are much more different in vocabulary, pronunciation, and grammar than Spanish is to English, and therefore may provide less of a resource to a child learning to read. In some settings, relationships between languages are more equal than in the United States. In Canada, for example, both the numbers and the overall social status of English speakers and French speakers are more equal than in the United States. In both of these situations, if a child fails to learn to read the second language, it may not be for the reasons suggested by Robert Jiménez, but for other reasons, ranging from difficulties with reading per se to cultural differences in how a child expects to be taught (Johnson, 2004).

The reader's role: both teacher and researcher

In the published article describing their research, Jiménez, García, and Pearson assumed that readers have some familiarity with bilingual students and with issues related to teaching reading. They began their article by describing previous research studies in these areas—more than a dozen of them, in fact. In the middle they described numerous responses of the three bilingual students to the passages they were asked to read. At the end of the article they made specific suggestions for teaching, such as "focus more on vocabulary development". When Kelvin read these various sections, he found that his prior knowledge of and reflections about teaching helped to make sense of them. But he also found that did not need to be an expert in bilingualism order to understand the authors' messages—he had never, in fact, taught English as a Second Language, nor had he ever conducted research on reading or bilingual language development.

Action research: hearing from teachers about improving practice

Each of the professional articles just described offers ideas and recommendations that can stimulate reflection about teaching and learning. But they all suffer from a particular limitation: Although they often relate to teachers and classrooms, teachers' role in influencing in designing and interpreting a study is minimal. In the world of educational research, persons other than teachers—typically professors, educational administrators, or other professional researchers—tend to speak on behalf of teachers. All three of the articles described earlier in this chapter had this feature. Persons other than teachers chose the research topics.

The information that emerges from this arrangement often still relates to teaching and learning, and may contain useful insights for classroom work. But by definition, it is framed by people whose interests and fundamental commitments may not be identical with classroom teachers. As a result, the studies are somewhat more likely to attend to problems posed by academic disciplines or by educational administrators. Two of the studies which we described earlier—the ones about moral development and about labels for disabilities—showed this quality. Classroom teachers are concerned, of course, about both moral development and categorizing of students. But if teachers had designed the two projects themselves, they might have re-framed both of them to focus more explicitly on the challenges of classroom teaching. In studying moral beliefs, for example, teachers might have focused more squarely on how to foster moral beliefs in their students. In studying inclusive education, they might have focused more fully on the practical difficulties faced by teachers in assessing students' learning disabilities with validity.

The nature of action research

In view of these issues, a particularly important kind of investigation for teachers is action research (sometimes also teacher research), an activity referring to systematic, intentional inquiry by teachers for the purpose of improving their own practice (Stenhouse, 1985; Brydon-Miller, Greenwood, & Maguire, 2003; Russell, T. & Loughran, J. 2005). Action research is not to be confused with research about teaching and learning, which are investigations by professional researchers on topics of teachers, teaching, or learning.

Action research has several defining characteristics, in addition to being planned and conducted by teachers. First, it originates in the problems and dilemmas of classroom practice, or in chronic problems with certain students, materials, or activities. Second, its outcomes offer information focused on particular teachers and classrooms, rather than about teachers in general or students in general. Although this feature might make action research seem less useful as a source of advice or knowledge that is truly general, supporters argue that focusing on specific learning contexts makes action research more credible or valid as a source of practical information and ideas. It is, they argue, simply more attuned to the context of real classrooms (St. Clair, 2005). Third, while the audience for action research can certainly include professors and educational administrators, the audience tends to be other teachers (Fenstermacher, 1994; Ackerman & MacKenzie, 2007). Action research is therefore in an especially strong position to provide "insider" perspectives on educational problems.

Action research in practice

Action research makes a number of assumptions as a result of its nature and purposes (Richardson, 1994; Schmuck, 2006). To varying degrees, most such studies support some combination of these ideas:

- that teaching is itself really a form of research

- that action research, like teaching itself, requires substantial reflection

- that collaboration among teachers is crucial for making teacher research meaningful, and for the improvement of teaching

- that teachers' knowledge of teaching has to be shared publicly, especially when gained systematically through action research

To see how these features look in practice, look at several examples of action research studies.

Example #1: Focusing on motivating students

A number of years ago, Patricia Clifford and Sharon Friesen published an account of their effort to develop a classroom program based on students' out-of-school interests and experiences (1993). Clifford and Friesen were co-teachers in a double-sized classroom which deliberately included children from first, second and third grades. Their interest in students' out-of-school experiences grew out of three more basic questions about teaching, which they phrased like this:

- How can curriculum remain open to children's unique experiences and connect with the world they know outside the school? Too often, the official school curriculum lacked meaning for children because it seemed cut off from the rest of the world. The result was unmotivated students and poor learning.

- Why is imaginative experience the best starting place for planning? The teachers felt that imaginative experiences—make-believe play, stories, poems—provided access to children's lives outside school—their make-believe play, or their stories or poems. Perhaps somehow these could be connected to the goals of the official curriculum.

- What happens when teachers break down the barriers between school knowledge and real knowledge? In drawing on children's outside experiences, would children actually become more motivated or not? Would they take over the program, and fail to learn the official curriculum goals?

To answer these questions, the teachers kept extensive diaries or journals for one entire school year. These became the "data" for the research. In the journals, they described and reflected on their daily teaching experiences. The teachers also talked with each other extensively about classroom events and their significance, and the results of the conversations often entered the journals eventually during the research. In their journal, for example, the teachers recorded an experience with students about ways of telling time. In preliminary discussions the students became interested in how a sundial worked. So the teachers and students went outside, where they created a human sundial, using the students themselves. The teachers' journal kept a chronicle of these events, and noted the comments and questions which students developed as a result:

- If you stood in the same place for a whole day you would see your shadow change places because the earth changes position.

- Why is my shadow longer than I am in the evening, but shorter at noon?

- Clouds can block the sun's rays so sundials won't work on rainy days.

- How did people start to tell time?

As the year evolved and observations accumulated and were recorded, the teachers gradually began to answer their own three questions. They found, for example, that connecting the curriculum with children's interests and motives was most effective when they could establish a personal bond with a child. They also found that imaginative expression helped certain children to feel safe to explore ideas. They found that blending school-based and personal knowledge caused children to learn much more than before—although much of the additional knowledge was not part of an official curriculum. With these conclusions in mind, and with numerous examples to support them, Clifford and Friesen published their study so that others could share what they had learned about teaching, learning, and students.

The study by Clifford and Friesen is interesting in its own right, but for our purposes think for a moment about their work as an example of action research. One of its features is that it formed part of the normal course of teaching: the authors were simply more systematic about how they observed the students and recorded information about classroom events. Another feature is that the research required conscious reflection over an extended time: their journals and conversations contained not only descriptions of events, but also interpretations of the events. A third feature is that the study involved collaboration: it was not just one teacher studying the major questions, but two. Th fourth feature is that the teachers not only developed their results and conclusions for themselves, but also shared them with others. These four qualities make the study by Clifford and Friesen a clear example of teacher research. Note, though, that sometimes studies conducted by teachers may not show all of these features so clearly; instead they may show some of the key features, but not all of them, as in the next two examples.

Example #2: Focusing on development

Since 1981, Vivian Paley has published a series of short books documenting and interpreting her observations of young children in classrooms (1981, 1986, 1991, 1998, 2000, 2005). Paley was interested in how young children develop or change over the long term, and in particular how the development looks from the point of view of a classroom teacher. In one of these books, for example, she observed one child in particular, Mollie, from the time she entered nursery school just after her third birthday until after the child turned four years old (Paley, 1986). Her interest was not focused on curriculum, as Clifford and Friesen's had done, but on Mollie as a growing human being; "the subject which I most wished to learn," she wrote, "is children" (p. xiv). Paley therefore wrote extended narrative (or story-like) observations about the whole range of activities of this one child, and wove in periodic brief reflections on the observations. Because the observations took story-like form, her books read a bit like novels: themes are sometimes simply suggested by the story line, rather than stated explicitly. Using this approach, Paley demonstrated (but occasionally also stated) several important developmental changes. In *Mollie at Three* (1988), for example, she describes examples of Mollie's language development. At three years, the language was often disconnected from Mollie's actions—she would talk about one thing, but do another. By four, she was much more likely to tie language to her current activities, and in this sense she more often "said what she meant". A result of the change was that Mollie also began understanding and following classroom rules as the year went on, because the language of rules became more connected in her mind to the actions to which they referred.

Vivian Paley's book had some of the characteristics of action research—but with differences from Clifford and Friesen's. Like their research, Paley's "data" was based on her own teaching, while her teaching was influenced in turn by her systematic observations. Like Clifford and Friesen's, Paley's research involved numerous reflections on teaching, and it led to a public sharing of the reflections—in this case in the form of several small books. Unlike Clifford and Friesen, though, Paley worked independently, without collaboration. Unlike Clifford and Friesen, she deliberately integrated observation and interpretation as they might be integrated in a piece of fiction, so that the resulting "story" often implied or showed its message without stating it in so may words. In this regard her work had qualities of what some educators call arts-based research, which are studies that take advantage of an artistic medium (in this case, narrative or story-like writing) to heighten readers' understanding and response to research findings (Barone and Eisner, 2006). If you are studying the use of space in the classroom, for example, then aesthetically organized visual depictions (photos, drawings) of the room may be more helpful and create more understanding than verbal descriptions. If you are studying children's musical knowledge, on the other hand, recordings of performances by the children may be more helpful and informative than discussions of performances.

Example #3: Focusing on collaboration

In 1996, an example of action research was published that was intended simultaneously for classroom teachers and for university researchers, and which focused on the challenges of collaboration among educators (Ulichny & Schoener, 1996). A teacher (Wendy Schoener) and a university researcher (Polly Ulichny) explored how, or even whether, teachers and university researchers could participate as equals in the study of teaching. Wendy (the two used first names throughout when they published their experiences) was a teacher of adults learning English as a Second Language (ESL); Polly was a specialist in multicultural education and wanted to observe a teacher who was successful at reaching the ethnically diverse students who normally study ESL. Polly therefore asked Wendy for permission to study her teaching for an extended period of time—to visit her class, videotape it, interview her about it, and the like.

What followed is best described as an extended negotiation between teacher and professor for access to Wendy's class, on the one hand, and for mutual respect for each other's work, on the other. In the published article, the negotiations are described separately by each participant, in order to honor the differences in their concerns and perspectives. Before, during, and after the observations, it was necessary for Polly and Wendy each to adjust expectations of what the other person could do and was willing to do. As the authors put it, some things were "easy to hear" from the other and some things were "hard to hear". Wendy, as a teacher, found it easier to hear criticisms of her teaching if they came from herself, rather than from the higher-status university professor, Polly. Polly, for her part, found it easier to hear Wendy's comments if she matched Wendy's self-criticisms and evaluations with some of her own experiences. Polly therefore made sure to tell Wendy about dilemmas and problems she experienced in her own (university) teaching. Because they needed to adjust to hearing and talking with each other, the two educators eventually focused less on Polly's original purpose—studying multicultural teaching—and more on the problem of how teachers and university researchers might collaborate effectively.

Overall, this study qualifies as a piece of action research, though it is not fully focused on classroom teaching. For example, the teachers did collaborate and reflect on their experiences, but not all of the reflection was about teaching in classrooms. The rest was about the relationship between Wendy and Polly. While the problem selected was originally about classroom teaching—Wendy's—it did not originate with the classroom teacher (Wendy) or concerns she had about her own classroom; instead it was chosen by the university researcher (Polly) and her desire to study multicultural teaching. The researchers did share what they learned by publishing their observations and ideas, but their published report speaks only partly to classroom teachers as such; in addition it speaks to academic researchers and educators of future teachers.

By pointing out differences among these examples of action research, we do not mean to imply that one is "better" than another. The point is simply to show how diverse studies by teachers can be and to appreciate their differences. Whatever their specific features, classroom studies by teachers hold in common the commitment to giving a voice to teachers as they reflect on problems and challenges intrinsic to classroom life. This goal can be accomplished in more than one way: through journals and other record-keeping methods, through oral discussions with colleagues, and through written reflections created either for themselves or for others concerned about teaching and learning. Diversity among topics and methods in action research studies should not surprise us, in fact, since classrooms are themselves so diverse.

The challenges of action research

Well and good, you may say. Action research offers teachers a way to hear each other, to learn from their own and other's experience. But there are also a few cautions to keep in mind, both ethical and practical. Look briefly at each of these areas.

Ethical cautions about action research

One caution is the possibility of conflict of interest between the roles of teaching and conducting action research (Hammack, 1997). A teacher's first priorities should be the welfare of his or her students: first and foremost, you want students to learn, to be motivated, to feel accepted by their peers, and the like. A researcher's first priorities, however, are to the field or topic being studied. The two kinds of priorities may often overlap and support each other. Vivian Paley's observations of children in her classes, described earlier, not only supported her children's learning, but also her studies of the children.

But situations can also occur in which action research and teaching are less compatible, and can create ethical dilemmas. The problems usually relate to one of three issues: privacy, informed consent, or freedom to participate. Each of these becomes an issue only if the results of a research project are made public, either in a journal or book, as with the examples we have given in this chapter, or simply by being described or shared outside the classroom. (Sharing, you may recall, is one of the defining features of action research.) Look briefly at each of the issues.

Insuring privacy of the student

Teachers often learn information about students that the students or their families may not want publicized. Suppose, for example, you have a student with an intellectual disability in your class, and you wish to study how the student learns. Observing the student work on (and possibly struggle with) academic activities may be quite consistent with a teacher's responsibilities; after all, teachers normally should pay attention to their students' academic efforts. But the student or his family may not want such observations publicized or even shared informally with other parents or teachers. They may feel that doing so would risk stigmatizing the student publicly.

To respect the student's privacy and still study his learning behavior, the teacher (alias the "action researcher") therefore needs to disguise the student's identity whenever the research results are made public. In any written or oral report, or even in any hallway conversation about the project, the teacher/researcher would use a pseudonym for the student, and change other identifying information such as the physical description of the student or even the student's gender. There are limits, however, to how much can be disguised without changing essential information. The teacher could not, for example, hide the fact of the intellectual disability without compromising the point of the study; yet the intellectual disability might be unusual enough that it would effectively identify the student being studied.

Gaining informed consent

Students may not understand what is being studied about them, or even realize that they are being studied at all, unless the teacher/researcher makes an explicit effort to inform them about the action research and how she will use the results from it. The same is true for the students' parents; unless the teacher-researcher makes an effort to contact parents, they simply will not know that their child's activities are being observed or may eventually be made public. Students' ignorance is especially likely if the students are very young (kindergarten) or have intellectual or reading difficulties, as in the example we described above. As an action researcher, therefore, a teacher is obliged to explain the nature of a research project clearly, either in a letter written in simple language or in a face-to-face conversation, or both. Parents and students need to give clear indications that they actually understand what class activities or materials will constitute data that could be made public. In most cases, indicating informed consent means asking students' parents signing a letter giving permission for the study. Sometimes, in addition, it is a good idea to recheck with students or parents periodically as the project unfolds, to make sure that they still support participation.

Insuring freedom to participate

When a student fails to participate in an ordinary class activity, most teachers consider it legitimate to insist on the student's participation—either by persuading, demanding, or (perhaps) tricking the student to join. Doing so is ethical for teachers in their roles as teachers, because teachers are primarily responsible for insuring that students learn, and students' participation presumably facilitates learning. If a teacher designates an activity as part of an action research project, however, and later shares the results with them, the teacher then also becomes partly responsible for how *other* teachers use knowledge of the research study. (Remember: sharing results is intrinsically part of the research process.) The resulting dual commitment means that "forcing" a student to participate in an action research activity can no longer be justified solely as being for the student's own educational good.

Much of the time, a simultaneous commitment to both teachers and students presents no real dilemma: what is good for the action research project may also be good for the students. But not always. Suppose, for example, that a teacher wants to do research about students' beliefs about war and global conflict, and doing so requires that students participate in numerous extended group discussions on this topic. Even though the group discussions might resemble a social studies lesson and in this sense be generally acceptable as a class activity, some parents (or students) may object because they take too much class time away from the normal curriculum topics. Yet the research project necessitates giving it lots of discussion time in class. To respond ethically to this dilemma, therefore, the teacher may need to allow students to opt out of the discussions if they or their parents choose. She may therefore need to find ways for them to cover an alternate set of activities from the curriculum. (One way to do this, for example, is to hold the special group discussions outside regular class times—though this obviously also increases the amount of work for both the teacher and students.)

Practical issues about action research

Is action research practical? From one perspective the answer has to be "Of course not!" Action research is not practical because it may take teachers' time and effort which they could sometimes use in other ways. Keep in mind, though, that a major part of the effort needed for action research involves the same sort of work—observing, recording information, reflecting—that is needed for any teaching that is done well. A better way to assess practicality may therefore be to recognize that teaching students always takes a lot of work, and to ask whether the additional thoughtfulness brought on by action research will make the teaching more successful.

Looked at in this way, action research is indeed practical, though probably not equally so on every occasion. If you choose to learn about the quality of conversational exchanges between yourself and students, for example, you will need some way to record these dialogues, or at least to keep accurate, detailed notes on them. Recording the dialogues may be practical and beneficial—or not, depending on your circumstances. On the other hand, if you choose to study how and why certain students remain on the margins of your class socially, this problem too may be practical as action research. Or it may not, depending on whether you can find a way to observe and reflect on students' social interactions, or lack thereof. Much depends on your circumstances—on the attention you can afford to give to your research problem while teaching, in relation to the benefits that solutions to the problems will bring students later. In general any action research project may require certain choices about how to teach, though it should not interfere with basic instructional goals or prevent coverage of an important curriculum. The main point to remember is that action research is more than passive observation of students and classrooms; it also includes educational interventions, efforts to stimulate students to new thinking and new responses. Those are features of regular teaching; the difference is primarily in how systematically and reflectively you do them.

Benefiting from all kinds of research

Although we authors both feel a degree of sympathy for the nature and purposes of action research, we are not trying to advocate for it at the expense of other forms of educational research or at the expense of simply reading and understanding professional publications in general. The challenge for you, as a classroom teacher, is to find the value in all forms of professional development, whether it be participation in a professional association, reading general articles about research, or engaging in your own action research. To the extent that you draw on them all, your ways of learning about teaching will be enriched. You will acquire more ways to understand classroom life, while at the same time acquiring perspective on that life. You will learn ways to grasp the individuality of particular students, but also to see what they need in common. You will have more ways to interpret your own experiences as a professional teacher, but also be able to learn from the professional experience of others. Realizing these benefits fully is a challenge, because the very diversity of classrooms renders problems about teaching and learning complex and diverse as well. But you will also gain good, professional company in searching for better understanding of your work—company that includes both educational researchers, other professional teachers, and of course your students.

Chapter summary

The complexities of teaching require teachers to continue learning throughout their teaching careers. To become a lifelong reflective practitioner, teachers can rely on colleagues as a resource, on professional associations and their activities, and on professional publications related to educational issues and needs. Understanding the latter, in turn, requires understanding the purposes of the published material—whether it is offering a general framework, recommending desirable teaching practices, or advocating for a particular educational policy or need. Interpreting published material also requires understanding the assumptions that authors make about readers' prior knowledge and beliefs.

An important additional strategy for becoming a reflective practitioner is action research—studies of teaching and learning designed and carried out by teachers in order to improve their own practice. By nature, action research studies are highly relevant to classroom practice, but there are also cautions about it to keep in mind, both ethically and practically.

Key terms

action research	insuring freedom to participate
assumptions about readers' prior knowledge	professional associations
informed consent	purposes of educational research
insuring privacy of students	reflective practitioner

reliability   validity

On the Internet

<**http://www.aera.net**> This is the official website of the American Educational Research Association (or AERA), a major "umbrella" professional association supporting educational research of all kinds. The home page has links to over two dozen special interest groups (called "SIGs"), each specializing in some form of educational research or practice. There is, among others, a special interest group called "teacher as researcher", intended primarily for educators involved in action research.

<**http://www.nea.org**> This is the website of the National Education Association (or NEA), another major professional association of educators. The difference between this association and the American Educational Research Association, however, is that the NEA focuses less on presenting research as such, and more on issues of teaching practice. Like the AERA website, it includes articles on numerous topics that can be downloaded or read online.

<**http://www.ed.gov/offices/OERI**> This is the website of the United States Office of Educational Research and Improvement. It summarizes current research initiatives about education that are sponsored by the United States Federal government, and includes links for finding information about the individual initiatives which it lists.

<**www.scra27.org**>, <**coe.westga.edu/arsig**> These two websites belong to professional organizations dedicated to action research. The first belongs to the Society for Community Research and Action, a division of the American Psychological Association. It promotes and publishes action research in many professions, one of which is education. The second website belongs to the Action Research Special Interest Group of the American Educational Research Association; as you might suspect from its name, it focuses exclusively on action research by educators.

References

Ackerman, R. & MacKenzie, S. (Eds.). (2007). *Uncovering teacher leadership: Voices from the field.* Thousand Oaks, CA: Corwin Press.

Barone, T. & Eisner, E. (2006). Arts-based research in education. In J. Green, g. Camilli, & P. Elmore (Eds.), *Handbook of complementary methods in education research.* Mahwah, NJ: Erlbaum.

Bissex, G. (1980). *GNYS AT WRK.* Cambridge, MA: Harvard University Press.

Brydon-Miller, M., Greenwood, D., Maguire, D. (2003). Why action research? *Action Research, 1*(1), 3-28.

Clifford, P. & Friesen, S. (1993). A curious plan: Managing on the twelfth. *Harvard Educational Review, 63*(3), 339-358.

Fenstermacher, G. (1994). The knower and the known: The nature of knowledge in research on teaching. In L. Darling-Hammond (Ed.), *Review of research in education, Volume 20,* pp. 3-56. Washington, D.C.: American Educational Research Association.

Hayes, D. (2006). Telling stories: Sustaining improvement in schools operating under adverse conditions. *Improving Schools, 9*(3), 203-213.

Hittleman, D. & Simon, A. (2005). *Interpreting educational research, 4th edition.* Englewood Cliffs, NJ: Prentice-Hall.

Jimenez, R., Garcia, G., & Pearson, D. (1995). Three children, two languages and strategic reading: Case studies in bilingual/monolingual reading. *American Educational Research Journal, 32*(1), 67-98.

Johnson, M. (2004). *A philosophy of second language acquisition.* New Haven, CT: Yale University Press.

Lortie, D. (1975). *Schoolteacher.* Chicago: University of Chicago Press.

Loughran, J., Hamilton, M., LaBoskey, V., & Russell, T. (Eds.). (2004). *International handbook of self-study of teaching and teacher education practices.* Dordrecht, The Netherlands: Kluwer.

McDermott, R., Goldman, S., & Varenne, H. (2006). The cultural work of learning disabilities. *Educational Researcher, 35*(6), 12-17.

Mills, G. (2006). *Action research: A guide for the teacher researcher, 3rd edition.* New York: Prentice Hall.

Paley, V. (1981). *Wally's stories.* Chicago: University of Chicago Press.

Paley, V. (1988). *Mollie is three.* Chicago: University of Chicago Press.

Paley, V. (1991). *The boy who would be a helicopter.* Cambridge, MA: Harvard University Press.

Paley, V. (1998). *Kwanzaa and me.* Cambridge, MA: Harvard University Press.

Paley, V. (2000). *The kindness of children.* Cambridge, MA: Harvard University Press.

Paley, V. (2006). *A child's work: The importance of fantasy play.* Chicago: University of Chicago Press.

Ragland, B. (2007). Positioning the practitioner-researcher: Five ways of looking at practice. *Action Research, 4*(2), 165-182.

Richardson, V. (1994). Conducting research in practice. *Educational Researcher, 23*(5), 5-10.

Russell, T. & Loughran, J. (2005). Self-study as a context for productive learning. *Studying Teacher Education, 1*(2), 103-106.

Samaras, A. & Freese, A. (Eds.). (2006). *Self-study of teaching practices.* New York: Peter Lang.

Schmuck, R. (2006). *Practical action research for change.* Thousand Oaks, CA: Sage Publications.

Schön, D. (1983). *The reflective practitioner.* New York: Basic Books.

Schön, D. (1987, April). *Educating the reflective practitioner.* Paper presented at the Annual Meeting of the American Educational Research Association, Washington, D.C.

Saltzstein, H., Millery, M., Eisenberg, Z., Dias, M., & O'Brien, D. (1997). Moral heteronomy in context: Interviewer influence in New York City and Recife, Brazil. In H. Saltzstein (Ed.), *New directions in child development: Culture as a context for moral development,* pp. 37-50. San Francisco: Jossey-Bass.

Seifert, Kelvin. (1981). Have we oversold mainstreaming? *Journal of the Canadian Association for Young Children, 4*(2), 6-9.

St. Clair, R. (2005). Similarity and superunknowns: An essay on the challenges of educational research. *Harvard Educational Review, 75*(4), 435-453.

Stenhouse, L. (1985). *Research as a basis for teaching.* London, UK: Heinemann.

Stringer, E. (2007). *Action research, 3rd edition.* Thousand Oaks, CA: Corwin Publications.

Tidwell, D. & Fitzgerald, L. (Eds.). (2006). *Self-study and diversity.* Rotterdam, The Netherlands: Sense Publishers.

Ulichny, P. & Schoener, W. (1996). Teacher-researcher collaboration from two perspectives. *Harvard Educational Review, 66*(3), 496-524.

Zeichner, K. (2007). Accumulating knowledge across self-studies in teacher education. *Journal of Teacher Education, 58*(1), 36-46.

CPSIA information can be obtained
at www.ICGtesting.com
Printed in the USA
BVHW052145180220
572740BV00009B/129

9 781616 101541